Charlotte

KATHRYN SHEVELOW

BLOOMSBURY

First published in Great Britain 2005

Copyright © 2005 by Kathryn Shevelow

First published in the US by Henry Holt and Company, LLC 2005

The moral right of the author has been asserted

Bloomsbury Publishing Plc, 38 Soho Square, London W1D 3HB

A CIP catalogue record for this book is available from the British Library

ISBN 0 7475 7494 4
ISBN-13 9780747574941

10 9 8 7 6 5 4 3 2 1

Printed in the United States of America by Quebecor World Fairfield

All papers used by Bloomsbury Publishing are natural, recyclable
products made from wood grown in well-managed forests. The manufacturing
processes conform to the environmental regulations of the country of origin.

www.bloomsbury.com/kathrynshevelow

To Ed, partner and collaborator

And to the memory of Liza Nelligan

Charlotte

CONTENTS

ILLUSTRATIONS

CHARLOTTE

PROLOGUE

The handsome actor glided across the makeshift stage, uttering his lines with the air of a man so confident of his attractiveness that he scarcely required language at all. Gazing up at him, the young lady in the audience hung upon his every word and gesture. Charles Brown seemed so much more refined than the men she knew, even the local gentry: his movements were more elegant, his voice gentler. And there was something else about him that intrigued her, although she was not sure what it was.

Onstage, Mr. Brown cut a dashing figure as a fashionable rake, his boyish face charmingly framed by the side curls of his periwig. His stylish clothes, however, would not bear close scrutiny: the embroidery of his waistcoat was beginning to unravel and his breeches shone with wear. Brown was the leading man in "Jockey" Adams's itinerant theatre troupe, a spirited if threadbare group of London players who were testing their luck in the provinces. The year was 1741.

The young lady in the audience was seventeen, an orphan heiress whose family had amassed their wealth from overseas trade and West Indies plantations. Her name has vanished from history, but let us call her Mary Harlowe. Having spent her entire life in the country, Mary had never before seen anyone quite like Mr. Brown. Though her town lay only four miles from London, she lived a world away from the clamour of the burgeoning capital.

Outside the theatre, as well as on the stage, Charles Brown conducted himself as a gentleman. Yet, for all his London-bred politeness, he retained a hint of mystery. His easy manners, his educated speech, and even his occasional lapses into melancholy suggested one accustomed to better company. Perhaps he had rebelled against his parents, or perhaps he was simply stage-struck, cherishing fantasies of London's Theatre Royal, Drury Lane, Britain's most venerable playhouse.

In eight months Mary would come of age and, unusually for a well-bred young virgin, her large fortune of £60,000 would be at her own disposal, as would be her hand in marriage. She had never before met a man she could marry, but now Charles Brown had captured her heart. Marriage to someone like Mary—accomplished, naïve, and rich—was an opportunity that most men would leap at, and word of his luck soon reached Charles. So when Mary cast propriety to the winds and invited him to tea, using the excuse that some other young ladies of her acquaintance wanted to hear him sing—he had a pleasant, light voice—the player accepted.

But Charles seemed uncharacteristically ill at ease as Miss Harlowe's servant conducted him to the drawing room door. He warily entered the elegant room, whose tall windows looked across an expanse of lawn, and bowed his greeting. When Mary, eyes downcast, invited him in a faint voice to take a seat, one of the other ladies sprang up and propelled him into the chair next to their hostess.

Charles sat frozen as Mary, blushing, spoke a few broken sentences, her trembling voice trickling off into a murmur. Enjoying their discomfiture, the bold lady suddenly burst into laughter and, abruptly rising, took the other guest by the sleeve and pulled her from the room, leaving Charles and Mary alone.

Charles fidgeted awkwardly as several minutes of excruciating tension passed. Then Mary, overcome, broke into tears. When Charles moved to comfort her, she gazed tenderly at him. He took her hand in his, looked into her eyes, and spoke.

Mary, he declared, was a charming woman, and he *wished* to offer her his hand. But alas, he could not. For, he regretted to tell her, he was not the person she conceived him to be. Surely Mary had heard of Colley Cibber, the famous Drury Lane actor and the reigning poet laureate of

England? Well, Mr. Cibber was his father—and he, explained Charles Brown, was Mr. Cibber's youngest ... daughter. His real name was Charlotte Charke.[1]

Charlotte Cibber Charke (1713–60) lived the rebellious, tragicomic life of a picaresque hero, opening a window onto a world that we usually meet only in fiction and satire—through Defoe's intrepid heroine Moll Flanders, for instance, and the harlots, rakes, drunkards, and thieves who crowd the dangerous streets in Hogarth's engravings. Charlotte was the contemporary of these fictional beings, and she knew firsthand the neighbourhoods in which their creators placed them. Hers, like theirs, is a story of eighteenth-century England seen from its margins. But unlike the heroines of novels, she was real, and her tale is the kind of account rarely preserved in the annals of history, all the more exceptional for being a woman's story.

Even as a child Charlotte scorned conventionality, and as an adult she scandalized proper society whenever possible. Inveterately theatrical both offstage and on, she was a truly original artist who became an occasionally acclaimed (but rarely ignored) actress and the most notorious cross-dresser of her day. Giddily indifferent to her society's strict notions about a woman's proper behaviour, Charlotte followed her own inclinations despite her family's rejection, suffering vicissitudes of fortune but responding to her setbacks with courage, high spirits, imagination, and humour. As an actress, she performed in all types of venues, and later she thrust herself further into the public eye by writing what she called an "Account of my Unaccountable Life," in which she characterized herself as one of the "greatest Curiosities that ever were the Incentives to the most profound Astonishment." Charlotte's sensational narrative was popular in the eighteenth century; it is known today as one of the earliest secular autobiographies written by a woman, and the first to be written by an English actress.

Charlotte's life encompassed the theatre world from its heights to its lower extremities. She inhabited a demimonde of players both famous and infamous, celebrated and obscure; of jealousies, quarrels, riots, and violent death; of candle-lit playhouses ranging from Covent Garden's sumptuous royal theatres to the playbooths of Bartholomew Fair and the provincial barns where ragged strolling players struggled to survive.

Charlotte began her career as a talented, up-and-coming comic actress, and soon became known for playing "breeches parts"—roles in which female characters don men's clothes. She achieved greater fame and notoriety, however, as an actress specializing in outright male impersonation, and was particularly celebrated for her caricatures of her famous father, whom she both idolized and rebelled against. Colley Cibber was the age's most renowned comic actor, one of its most important playwrights, and a manager of London's greatest theatre, the Theatre Royal, Drury Lane. In 1730, King George II named him England's poet laureate. Cibber was also one of the most divisive figures of his day, a political controversialist, a supporter of the corrupt government of Sir Robert Walpole, a butt of satirists, and a vain but cheerful bon vivant.

Charlotte's parents gave her a degree of freedom unusual for a girl and provided an education she later described as more suitable for a boy: she was more interested in geography and Latin than sewing, and handled her needle, she commented wryly, as clumsily as a monkey holds a kitten. When she left school as a young adolescent, she went to live with her invalid mother in the country, where she developed a taste for guns and horses, at one point shooting at a neighbour's chimneys and at another careening around the countryside in a runaway carriage. After she was allowed to accompany a doctor on his rounds, she set up her own practice, making medicines from mashed-up snails.

When she was seventeen, Charlotte fell in love with and impetuously married a libertine young musician named Richard Charke. Quickly, she became the mother of an infant daughter and found herself chasing her husband through the brothels of Covent Garden. More promisingly, Charlotte also began her theatre career at Drury Lane. There she displayed talent, and acted with some of the most famous stage personalities of her day: besides her father and her dissolute but undeniably talented brother, Theophilus Cibber, she worked with the great comic actress Anne Oldfield, who with a toss of her head could drive spectators mad with desire; Mary Porter, a formidable tragedienne who, when accosted on a dark road (offstage) by a highwayman, held him at bay with her pistol; and Kitty Clive, the pert comic actress known as a fierce backstage infighter. Charlotte also performed with her sister-in-law (and

Kitty's major rival), Susannah Cibber, who was celebrated for her pathos-laden heroines and notorious for her sordid marriage to Theophilus, who essentially sold her to another man. Charlotte held her own against the male players whose egos dominated life at Drury Lane—notably arrogant, imposing James Quin and hot-tempered Charles Macklin, who was once tried for murdering a fellow player in the green room, but whose performances revolutionized the stage.

When she was still quite young and inexperienced, Charlotte became one of the first women ever to manage a theatre company on her own, and she would manage several more during her life. Becoming embroiled in quarrels with the incompetent manager of Drury Lane (her father having retired), she was fired; she retaliated by satirizing the manager as a blockhead in a play she wrote and staged. Reinstated at Drury Lane after her father intervened, she almost immediately quit again, this time to become the leading player in an upstart theatre troupe run by Henry Fielding. This was the most significant career relationship of Charlotte's life, both for better and for worse. Fielding became best known as a novelist, the author of *Tom Jones,* but when Charlotte first knew him he was a young man, London's leading avant-garde playwright, and Colley Cibber's bitter enemy.

Charlotte enjoyed her greatest success as an actress with Fielding's company, playing hilarious roles designed to satirize, and mortify, her father. When Colley ordered her to leave Fielding, she refused, provoking her father to disown her. Not long after that, Parliament, irked by Fielding's antigovernment satire, passed a stage licensing act that shut down his troupe and limited production to the two major theatres, effectively banishing Charlotte from the legitimate stage.

During a swirl of adventures and incarnations—her life was itself a nonstop series of performances—she became the mistress of an elegant puppet show specializing in Shakespeare, and later a strolling player, forming an intimacy with another actress in what was probably the most important emotional and erotic relationship of her life. She and her friend were together for many years, and much of that time they travelleded throughout southern England and Wales calling themselves Mr. and Mrs. Brown. Charlotte never openly acknowledged a sexual attraction to women, but it might explain many people's disapproval of her, and it provides a partial context for her cross-dressing.

Charlotte's city was London, where the stylish artifice of gilded drawing rooms and royal playhouses clashed with the sordid parallel world
of filthy hovels and blood-spattered cockpits. Perfumed gentlefolk rode
in carriages through stinking streets crowded with beggars, prostitutes,
and thieves. But, for all its rawness and misery, all its vivid contrasts,
London was also a theatre writ large. Spectacle was everywhere, not
just within the playhouses' walls, but also flourishing in the city's
streets and alleys, its ballrooms and boudoirs. Crowds munched gingerbread at Tyburn Tree as they waited to watch criminals hang, and at
the docks, bodies of pirates dangled in iron cages, rotting. Mrs. Mapp,
the celebrated bone-setter, realigned a butcher's kneecaps in front of
a gasping audience. At balls and assemblies, bejewelled society ladies
flourished their fans as they traded witticisms with gentlemen in gold-
embroidered waistcoats, their gestures as finely choreographed as a
minuet.

The theatres themselves supplemented their repertoires of classical
and modern plays with crowd-pleasing entertainments of pantomimes,
jugglers, and rope dancers. Groups of actors set up performance
booths at public festivals such as Bartholomew Fair. On every street
corner, it seemed, puppet shows and monster displays, musicians, contortionists, tumblers, and dancing dogs competed with booksellers,
balladeers, and bawds for the attention of passersby.

Roving through the streets in her man's breeches, wig, and laced hat,
Charlotte relished her city's spectacle and contributed to it herself. Life
in London was a continual performance, from the mannered speech
and ritualized bows of the courtiers at St. James's Palace to the ringing,
age-old cries of the sausage sellers and milkmaids who plied their wares
on the streets. It was a society characterized by rigid distinctions of
rank and gender, but also one in which artifice reigned and appearance
often determined who people were. "Sodomites" slipped into Molly
houses to spend an evening luxuriating in corsets and petticoats, while
women donned soldier's uniforms and marched off to war. At masquerades, tradesmen costumed as kings rubbed shoulders with noble
lords disguised as shepherds. A beau's fancy dress might belie his empty
purse, and bigamists moved from one side of town to another to start
a new family and life. It was possible to play many different roles in

this big, anonymous city, if you could muster the appropriate clothes, mannerisms, and speech—as Charlotte could.

For all her wildness, Charlotte was passionately devoted to her craft as an actress. Throughout the vicissitudes of her life, she never stopped performing, onstage or off. Performance was an inextricable part of her being: it was in her genes, as it were, certainly in her upbringing. For her, the boundary between performing in the theatre and performing out of it was a thin and permeable one. In this, too, she was a woman of her day and of her city. Her career made her well known, her father's prominence made her newsworthy, and her reputation for wildness and penchant for men's clothing made her notorious. Always an exhibitionist, Charlotte knew that she was considered strange and outrageous—even "mad"—by most of eighteenth-century society, and she embraced that image, flaunting her status as a self-described "Nonpareil of the Age."

To us today, Charlotte appears particularly modern as an individual who rejected a fixed definition of her sexuality and her gender, testing the permeability of the cultural line that supposedly separates women from men. We also see her as an early example of an independent woman, one who paid a high price for her independence but struggled to preserve it. Charlotte saw herself both as the heroine of a tragicomedy and as a spectacle. "If Oddity can plead any Right to Surprize and Astonishment," she said, with her characteristic mixture of self-deprecating humour and pride, "I may positively claim a Title to be shewn among the Wonders of Ages past, and those to come." In Charlotte's day, a "wonder" might be viewed with admiration or with shock. For her, either response was preferable to indifference—a reaction that, admittedly, she encountered quite rarely.

DRESS REHEARSAL

Covent Garden, London
Late March, 1736

Charlotte Charke, appearing the very model of a fashionable young gentleman, stepped from the doorway of the Shakespear's Head Tavern, cinching her heavy greatcoat tightly around her waist. The coat, with its modish, elbow-high cuffs, was a good one, even if she had purchased it secondhand at a tally-shop. Her breeches were new, and her powdered periwig was gathered at the back into a tail tied with a large bow. The lace of her tricorn hat fluttered in the raw March wind.

Whiffs of John Twigg's delicious cooking—his turtle soup was particularly renowned—wafted from the tavern, its aromas mingled with tobacco fumes, wood smoke, and the pungent odour of damp, densely packed bodies. The diners lingering inside, calling for more bottles of wine, had settled into a round of after-dinner drinking before dispersing into Covent Garden's gaming houses and brothels. That evening, many of them would drop into one of the royal patent theatres nearby: either the Theatre Royal, Covent Garden, next door to the Shakespear's Head, or the Theatre Royal, Drury Lane, a few blocks away. Chances were high that the playhouse would be performing one of the thirty-year-old warhorses that dominated their repertories.

Less staid was the bill at a small theatre in the Haymarket, where an upstart young company was staging a farce called *Pasquin*. Its author, Henry Fielding, was not yet twenty-nine years old, but his troupe had earned a reputation for hilarious satire directed at many of England's leading figures, especially the prime minister, Sir Robert Walpole, and his supporters. Every night, large numbers of spectators were turned away from the packed playhouse.

Charlotte herself was due at the Haymarket for the performance that began promptly at six. At twenty-three, she was the principal player in Fielding's company, having recently broken her contract at the venerable Drury Lane Theatre to join him. Suddenly, she was on the cutting edge, a leading figure in the avant-garde of the London stage.[1]

Just outside the door of the Shakespear's Head lounged several prostitutes. Hundreds of these "Votaries of Venus" habitually patrolled Covent Garden in their signature topknots and cloaks. Lubricated by several bottles, a man might be enticed into the shadows, or taken to a bagnio or one of the coffeehouses whose signs pictured a woman's hand pouring coffee, the code for a bawdyhouse that offered rooms by the night or by the hour.[2]

As she strode along the piazza's arcade, Charlotte would have passed the quarters of the auctioneer Christopher Cock, whose reputation for "accidentally" double-billing his wealthy customers had not lessened his popularity. Covent Garden Piazza, bordering the square to the north and east, had once been graced by rows of aristocratic townhouses, but now the buildings contained a variety of businesses and lodgings interspersed among the private houses. Though Lord Archer at the far corner of the square still held his ground, most of the titled residents had fled the increasingly disreputable district.

In the elegant houses that remained, liveried servants, visible through the windows, would have been clearing away the remnants of their employers' multicourse dinners. By this point in the afternoon, the ladies would have left the table for the drawing room, while the gentlemen settled back in their chairs, calling for port, pipes, and chamber pots. Shopkeepers were heading back to their shops from their homes or local eating houses. Artisans and tradesmen, who had begun work that morning just as the drunken carousers were staggering back home, had long since finished their dinners of cheese, bread, and strong beer.

Along the streets where Charlotte passed, lurking pickpockets and ragged children shouted as they raced among the loggia's columns. Groups of itinerant musicians clustered on corners with horns, drums, and pipes, playing cacophonies while nearby running patterers chanted at the top of their lungs the news of the latest daylight robberies in Marylebone Fields.

To enter the open space of Covent Garden square itself, Charlotte would have had to cross the muddy carriageway into the square, skirting the street-raker. Near the centre, several women sold steaming bowls of barley broth and rice porridge, and beyond them, on the south side of the square, huddled the dishevelled market stalls, some open late to sell produce and pots of gin—the cheap, potent, and often lethal drink of the poor. Around the square, a few ill-clad bodies, men's and women's alike, slouched in a drunken stupor, oblivious to the city's clamour, while others crouched to warm themselves around an open fire.

Uninitiated visitors found London deafening. Along with street musicians, ballad singers, patterers, and proprietors of monster shows inviting all to come see, children wailed, dogs barked, asses brayed, and drunks shouted curses. Above this hubbub rose the famous "cries" of the sellers. The produce dealers hawked fruits, vegetables, and flowers from their stalls, while tinkers wandered, seeking pots to repair. Itinerant vendors lugged trays of goods: gingerbread, scissors, fish, coal, and medicines laced with opium. Their cries, half-syllables and snatches of song, filled the air: "What d'ye lack, what d'ye lack?" "Hot baked wardens!" "Ripe speragras!" "Buy a fine singing bird!"

Charlotte would have had to step carefully lest the heaps of rotting produce strewn about the cobblestones sully her white silk stockings. Around her were the kind of scenes William Hogarth, who lived nearby in Leicester Fields, was making his reputation painting: libertines fondling whores, a gentleman drunkenly swishing his sword in the air, thieves casing goods on display, an urchin tying a bone to a dog's tail. Through it all strolled occasional figures of respectability. Wealthy women hobbled atop the iron and leather overshoes called pattens that elevated their feet above the ground, affording their skirts and shoes some protection from the muck. Their hoop petticoats radiated like silken bells.

Across the open square, a small group gathered to watch an acrobat dance on a slack rope. Ragged boys lingered nearby, alert for anyone who might pay a halfpence to have a message delivered, shoes cleaned, a horse held, or a pot of strong beer carried to a private room. On the south side of the square squatted the all-night tavern run by Tom and Moll King. Tom had attended Eton, but he made his living running one of Covent Garden's most disreputable—and popular—alehouses. Little more than a shack, the tavern was mobbed from midnight to morning: market gardeners, chimney sweeps, bawds, and flower girls rubbed shoulders with wealthy merchants and noblemen. King George himself had been said to visit Tom King's, in disguise.

Evenings still came early in late March, and as the temperature dropped, the drizzle mixed with clouds of thick coal smoke, becoming a wet blanket of noxious fog. In dry weather, this smoke coated everything in grit, and in the rain, it smeared buildings and people alike with streaks of black, dripping off hats onto shoulders in inky rivulets. Charlotte walked west on King Street, clogged by market wagons and

Looking north through the neighbourhood that, during Charlotte's London career, so much of her world comprised. The Shakespear's Head was in the north-east corner of the piazza. (John Maurer, A Perspective View of Covent Garden, *1753. Courtesy of the Guildhall Library, Corporation of London.)*

coaches. Mud and reeking water fouled London's streets, whose open gutters contained all sorts of vile things, from manure and offal to dead rats and cats and human waste. Visitors and residents often complained about the filthy town, the streets like cesspools: Lord Tyrconnel, in an ineffectual speech to Parliament, once exclaimed that "the streets of London, a city famous for wealth, commerce and plenty, and for every other kind of civility and politeness, . . . [abound] with such heaps of filth as a savage would look on with amazement."[3]

Charlotte would have stayed as close to the walls of the houses as she could, lest the wide wheels of a lumbering wagon splash her with the foul water. To get to the Haymarket, she followed King Street as it angled north to become New Street, at the end of which she turned left into the wide expanse of St. Martin's Lane. Like most of the pedestrians, she would have hugged the walls, since at any time a servant in one of the houses, required to carry the master's brimming chamber pot down several flights of stairs, might have decided to shorten the stinking trip by tossing the pot's contents out the window instead.

Pedestrians kept themselves inside the row of posts that separated the footpath from the street, except when a jutting shop front forced them out into the muck and traffic. Even the footpaths were not entirely safe, for the single-person sedan chairs that had been ubiquitous on the London streets for the past twenty-five years used the walkways, too, and their burly carriers were known to run down pedestrians.

Passing the parish church of St. Martin-in-the-Fields, Charlotte would have continued through a cityscape of houses, hovels, derelict buildings, gambling dens, and gin shops. Churches and chapels adjoined brothels and decayed lodging houses where streetwalkers lived and took their clients. Gaudily painted wood and iron shop signs jutted out overhead, advertising trades with images of anchors, sugar loaves, stars, and pigeons.

On James Street, she would have passed the old tennis court with its shabby upstairs theatre, where puppet shows and performances by minor troupes were sometimes held. At Paulet's Ordinary at the end of the street, another group of prostitutes waited for the upper-class customers inside to drink themselves into recklessness. These women's numbers would increase as evening came, for the Haymarket, like Covent Garden, was notorious.

A wide thoroughfare running between Piccadilly and Pall Mall, the Haymarket took its name from the market for straw and hay held there on Tuesdays, Thursdays, and Saturdays. Mondays and Wednesdays belonged to the sellers of flesh. Country drovers arrived before dawn, driving their flocks and herds down the street in a cacophony of shouts, bleats, and bellows that resounded through much of the West End. By now, though, sellers and buyers alike were drinking tankards of strong beer in the taverns—the Bell, the George, the Cock, and the Black Horse—that lined the west side of the Haymarket.

The street was a reeking swamp of mud and manure, garbage and decaying straw, churned by thousands of hooves. Wagons, carts, and hackney coaches fought for right of way, their drivers filling the air with curses and shouts: "Make way!" "Make Room there!" "Stand up there, you blind Dog!"[4] As Charlotte approached the bottom of the street, she would have seen the looming bulk of the opera house.

The King's Theatre, built by the late John Vanbrugh, a playwright and the architect of Blenheim Palace, was a huge structure with barnlike acoustics, housing one of London's two Italian opera companies, the Opera of the Nobility. Though Italian opera enjoyed the royal family's patronage, many people despised it as both un-English and unnatural, with its foreign tongue, its feuding divas, and its castrated male singers. The playbill posted in front of the theatre advertised the upcoming benefit performance for the company's highly paid celebrity singer, the castrato Carlo Broschi, known as Farinelli.

Across the street from King's, wedged into a row of businesses and fronted by Fribourg's snuff and tobacco shop, sat the New Theatre in the Haymarket, Charlotte's destination. From the street, little more could be seen of the Little Haymarket, as it was also known, than an unremarkable door opening upon a passageway that led to the humble playhouse in the back. But the Little Haymarket housed London's most talked-about troupe, the Great Mogul's Company of Comedians, and the playbill posted beside the door announced that the company that night would perform their hit play, *Pasquin*. Capital letters in the bill called attention, by name, to the newest member of the cast, the only player to be distinguished in this way: "The Part of Lord Place is to be perform'd by Mrs. Charke, from Drury-Lane, who will also speak the Comedy Prologue."[5]

Charlotte paused at the door to read her name on the bill, as she always did, while the boot boy who sat there scraped the worst of the sludge from her shoes. Tossing him a penny, she made her way back along the narrow corridor to the theatre.

Two hours later, the warmth of the damp, steaming bodies packed tight on the theatre's backless benches had finally lessened the chill of the unheated playhouse. Hundreds of candles blazing in their candelabra and sconces cast a uniform light over all, actors and audience alike. The orchestra was approaching the conclusion of the third music—the last of the three musical pieces customarily performed before the opening of a play—and the house was already full. Still, people continued to trickle in, cramming themselves onto the benches and loudly greeting friends.*

Wealthier patrons took the places saved for them by their footmen, who then had to shove their way out of the boxes and pit to squeeze among the other servants and apprentices in the theatre's single gallery. The beaux in the side boxes, resplendent in embroidered silk and lace, leered at the ladies, but occasionally turned from this sport to fondle the orange-wenches working their way among them with baskets of fruit.

The law students from the Temple, and other self-appointed critics in the pit, readied themselves for the performance, during which they might feel moved to call out criticisms of the play or to supply the players with better lines. They would not be able to trump the wit supplied that night, however.

Suddenly the buzz from the audience increased in volume, the usual sign that a member of the royal family or a celebrity had entered. All around, heads turned in the direction of one of the boxes. There, replacing his servant in a seat at the front, was a rather corpulent, well-dressed man wearing an expensive, if old-fashioned, full-bodied wig. He was in his mid-sixties, but he moved as spryly as a much younger man.

---

* Silence was not a virtue for eighteenth-century playhouse audiences, even when the performance was under way.

Smiling, he scanned the house with his small, clever eyes, surveying the surroundings with amused contempt and nodding genially to those around him with the ease of a man who was used to being looked at. Nearly everyone recognized him as poet laureate, Colley Cibber. He had been retired from the theatre for three years, but excitement still surrounded him.

The spectators whispered delightedly to each other, since most knew that the laureate was one of the most prominent targets of this farce. Once Cibber, a loyal supporter of Walpole, and Fielding, one of the prime minister's most scathing critics, had worked together (under truce, if not with actual amiability), but now they were avowed enemies. Cibber, famous for his unflappability, was at the Little Haymarket to demonstrate his open-mindedness and indifference. He would require all of his reserves of poise that night.

The office of poet laureate was essentially a political appointment for which the ability actually to write poetry was not one of the more important qualifications (although the laureate was required to churn out commemorative odes for special occasions, notably the King's birthday and the New Year). Cibber, a highly accomplished playwright but no poet, dutifully produced terrible odes, earning the laureate's traditional stipend of £100 per year and a butt of sack (white wine). He was aware of his poems' quality—wags parodied them mercilessly, and *The Grub-Street Journal* annually subjected his New Year's odes to scathing reviews—but he was known to work hard on them and, despite his notoriously thick skin, to be sensitive about their reception.

The third music ended, the play began, and it was not long before Charlotte made her entrance costumed as the aristocratic fop Lord Place. The audience laughed appreciatively as she minced on, smirking and preening, in gaudily embroidered breeches and waistcoat, overly bedecked with lace. With her face nearly obscured by the curls of her enormous, heavily powdered wig, she spoke in a high-pitched voice, slurring her words superciliously. Clearly her Lord Place was a parody of Cibber himself. Charlotte, whom Fielding had recruited precisely to play this role, was able to mimic her father's speech and mannerisms with hilarious accuracy. She had been doing so since she was four years old. That she was a woman—and a woman becoming notorious for dressing in men's clothes not only onstage but off—added the provocative element of travesty to her performance.

Pasquin is a satire on political corruption, among other things, and Lord Place is a candidate running for election, enthusiastically engaged in bribing potential voters with money and promises of preferment (the patronage system by which Walpole maintained power). Having ingratiatingly promised one voter a position (or "place") at court in return for his vote, Charlotte was accosted by a second voter.

> "My Lord," said the Second Voter, "I should like a place at court too; I don't much care what it is, provided I wear fine clothes and have something to do in the kitchen or the cellar; I own I should like the cellar, for I am a devilish lover of sack."
>
> "Sack, say you?" replied Charlotte, airily. "Odso, you shall be poet-laureat."
>
> "Poet! no, my Lord, I am no poet, I can't make verses," protested the Second Voter.
>
> "No matter for that," said Charlotte. "—you'll be able to make odes."
>
> "Odes, my Lord!" said the Voter, puzzled: "what are those?"
>
> "Faith, sir," drawled Charlotte, "I can't tell well what they are; but I know you may be qualified for the place without being a poet." (II, i)

The audience roared with laughter at this dig and turned as if with one mind to gauge the laureate's reaction. They saw Colley Cibber laughing and applauding heartily. There was really nothing else he could do.[6]

Charlotte's fraught relationship with her father was a dominating theme of her life, as she both embraced and resisted his influence. Colley Cibber was an important, distinguished man who made major contributions to the English theatre and served the King as poet laureate for twenty-seven years, but he also achieved a dubious immortality courtesy of eloquent enemies, principally Henry Fielding and Alexander Pope, eighteenth-century England's greatest poet. (Dr. Johnson had some derogatory things to say about him, too.) Pope's long poem *The Dunciad* memorably enthrones Cibber as the "King of the Dunces," a corrupt, vain laureate reigning over a sleazy kingdom of political opportunism and bad writing.

Thanks to Fielding and Pope, the name Colley Cibber has long evoked the image of an incompetent writer, a political toady, and an impertinent fool: in short, a "coxcomb," his enemies' favourite epithet. While not unmotivated, this highly subjective picture of Cibber as a plagiarizing mediocrity and the epitome of "Dullness" has nearly blotted out the man's achievements, obstructing a more measured assessment of his career.[7] For all his genuine vanity, opportunism, and bad verse, Cibber was a brilliant comic actor, an innovative playwright, and a canny manager who made very real contributions to the British stage, which he served devotedly for most of his life.

Cibber's character and vanities did make him a ripe target for the satirists' attacks. He could be egotistical, buffoonish, and sycophantic. Married and the father of five living children, he frequented the notorious brothels and gambling dens of Covent Garden in the company of his rakish friends. He made lasting enemies (as well as staunch allies) by, on occasion, turning his playwriting into a vehicle of partisan politics. He attached himself to the courts of George I and George II and their controversial prime minister, Walpole. He wrote some mediocre plays, especially when he turned his hand to tragedy, and he openly raided earlier playwrights for ideas and plots (a common practice at the time). Most embarrassingly, he insisted upon casting himself on occasion in roles that his delivery and mannerisms rendered ludicrous. The contemporary critic Aaron Hill compared his performance as Richard III to "the distorted heavings of an unjoined caterpillar."[8]

On the other hand, Charlotte's father was perhaps the greatest comic actor of the eighteenth century, whose performances defined the characterization of the "fop" for years to come. Hill also observed that "Nature . . . meant Mr. Cibber for a comedian . . . he had an air and a mind which complete the risible talent, insomuch that, when he represented a ridiculous humour, he had a mouth in every nerve and became eloquent without speaking."

Cibber was also one of the most important playwrights of his day and, arguably, the most important member of the famous "triumvirate" of actor-managers who ensured Drury Lane Theatre's distinction and stability for nearly twenty-five years. As Henry Fielding's biographer Martin Battestin observes, to the aspiring young playwright encountering Drury Lane's managers for the first time, "Cibber, especially, would be an awesome figure . . . as dramatist, comedian, and manager, the most talented and powerful personality of the London stage—a 'star,' as we would say today, of the first magnitude."[9]

Charlotte's father worked very hard, pursued his pleasures with gusto, and came to enjoy the patronage and friendship of some of the country's most powerful men. He also cultivated a cheerful insouciance—his best biographer, Helene Koon, calls it his foppish mask—that enabled him to disarm enemies by confessing openly to his shortcomings. Beginning his autobiography in his characteristic tone of lighthearted narcissism, he pledged to give his readers "as true a Picture of myself as natural Vanity will permit me to draw. For, to promise you that I shall never be vain, were a Promise that, like a Looking-glass too large, might break itself in the making." After all, he observed with charming equanimity, "if Vanity be one of my natural Features, the Portrait wou'd not be like me without it."[10] It was precisely this sort of thing that made his enemies gnash their teeth.

In March 1736, when she abruptly left Drury Lane to join Fielding's company, Charlotte had not spoken to her father for nearly a year. They had quarrelled about her behaviour. But Colley had hinted that reconciliation might be possible, if only Charlotte would make the appropriate avowals of daughterly obedience.

Charlotte, flush with her new fame, was not interested. She could not know that in a little more than a year, her situation would change dramatically. But before we can proceed with Charlotte's future, we must turn to her past: to her family, her father, and the first twenty-three years of her extraordinary life.

PART

ONE

CIBBERS

(1660–1712)

Of all the spectacles in London, one of the most popular was Bethlem Royal Hospital, the madhouse. "Bedlam" drew crowds of the curious, eager to pay admission to stare with horror at the inmates, howling in frenzy or slumped in silent dejection. In 1676, Bethlem Hospital had relocated to Moorfields, just outside the City's northern wall. The stately design of its new building and gardens, said to resemble the Tuileries, contrasted starkly with the brutal treatment of the miserable "lunaticks" inside, who often were bound in chains and manacles, and routinely whipped and bled.

Bedlam's entrance gate itself produced an unsettling thrill, for on either side loomed the recumbent statue of a near-naked madman. One, *Melancholy,* reclined on his side in passive imbecility, gazing open-mouthed into space. The other, *Raving,* thrashed against his chains, his countenance twisted and angry. A little larger than life, these sculpted madmen were reputed to represent actual inmates once incarcerated inside Bedlam. But visitors familiar with Rome might have recognized the influence of Michelangelo's tomb statuary and Bernini's fountain sculptures in the Piazza Navona.

Bedlam's disturbing figures had been carved of Portland stone at the end of the seventeenth century by Caius Gabriel Cibber, and were widely acknowledged as his masterpieces.* To Caius Gabriel's son Colley, the Bedlam statues held more equivocal significance.

A common metaphor (then as now) equated artistic productions with children. A playwright might declare a play to be "a brat of my brain"; poets spoke of their poetical "offspring." Colley, the child of the creator of these lunatics, could thus be said to bear a kinship with them: all were "sons" of his father. This metaphorical affiliation provided an irresistible lure to Alexander Pope, who used it to strike a neat blow in *The Dunciad.* Pope imagined a "Cave" of hack writing, located near Bethlem Hospital, "Where o'er the gates, by his fam'd father's hand, / Great Cibber's brazen brainless brothers stand" (I: 29–32). Pope may not have been the first of Colley's contemporaries to think of this gibe, but he was the one who immortalized it.

The Bethlem statues evoke the contradictory legacy that Caius Gabriel Cibber bequeathed to his elder son, Colley, and that he in turn bestowed upon his family, especially his only son, Theophilus, and his

Charlotte's grandfather created the famous statues at the gates of Bedlam, London's most notorious madhouse. (Caius Gabriel Cibber, Melancholy *[or Imbecility]. Courtesy of the Guildhall Library, Corporation of London.)*

---

* C. G. Cibber's statues *Melancholy* (more accurately, *Imbecility*) and *Raving* are displayed today in the museum at Bethlem Hospital in Eden Park, Kent. Despite lamentable erosion, they remain evocative and unsettling.

Another of Caius Cibber's creations for Bedlam. (Caius Gabriel Cibber, Raving. *Courtesy of the Guildhall Library, Corporation of London.)*

youngest daughter, Charlotte. Each generation of Cibbers put its particular twist on that legacy, but the general outline remained constant. Virtually from its emergence into the public eye, the name of Cibber implied the idea of professional prominence marred by arrogance, recklessness, or misjudgment. For three generations (the name died out in the fourth), members of the Cibber family cultivated their inheritance of achievement and ignominy, acclaim and censure.

Colley Cibber was the ambitious son of an ambitious father. Like his son and granddaughter after him, Caius Gabriel Cibber, an émigré sculptor born in Flensburg, Holstein, sought and gained a place in the British public eye. He also invented the family name that he and his descendants would make notorious. When young Caius Gabriel (his original full name) immigrated to England from Copenhagen, where his father had moved the family, he added the new surname "Cibber" to his own. Caius Gabriel had studied in Italy, and the name was possibly an Anglicized form of Cibò, an Italian aristocratic patron of the arts, whose coat of arms he adopted.* Like his son after him, Caius Gabriel relished his associations with aristocracy.[1]

---

* Unlike the Italian pronunciation, the name Cibber in English was pronounced with a sibilant C—not a hard C, as many believe—evidenced by its frequent misspellings such as "Sibber," "Sybars," and "Zibber."

Caius Gabriel Cibber immigrated to London in the late 1650s, settling west of the old City walls in Covent Garden, where many of his descendants would also live. He arrived on the cusp of three great events that would shake the country and its capital: the Restoration of Charles II in 1660 after the collapse of the Commonwealth established by the Puritan victors of the Civil War; the return in 1665 of the Black Death (bubonic plague), which killed nearly 100,000 people; and the Great Fire of 1666, which destroyed most of the City of London and left as many as 200,000 people homeless.

After 1666, having survived both plague and fire, Caius was well positioned to profit from the latter. The burned-out City had to be rebuilt immediately, so the guilds that controlled London's trades relaxed their traditional restrictions against foreign builders, creating ripe opportunities for the young immigrant sculptor. Caius embarked upon a career that would leave a lasting imprint upon his adopted city.

Decades later, Charlotte Charke and her father would frequently have encountered vivid reminders of their family legacy. Charlotte, seeking employment or adventure within the old City walls, might have passed the massive columnar Monument to the Great Fire (it still stands today, on Fish Street Hill) and paused to scrutinize its vigorous bas-relief. If she had reason to enter the south door of St. Paul's Cathedral, she would have passed under the carved phoenix that symbolized London rising from its ashes.

If, after his parents' death, Colley ever visited the graceful Danish church in Wellclose Square (now destroyed) where they were buried, he could have admired the four vivid sculptures of burnished wood—Saints Peter and Paul, John the Baptist, and Moses (now displayed in the Danish Church in Regent's Park). In the West End, Charlotte and her father would have walked often through Soho Square, where a statue of Charles II stood (and where it stands again today, though much eroded).[2] All of these sculptures, and the design of the Wellclose Square church itself, were the legacy of Caius Gabriel. His work was rewarded in 1693 with his appointment as sculptor in ordinary to William III, a position in the King's household dedicated to the conservation and repair of the statuary at the royal palaces.[3]

In 1670, as his London career was beginning to flourish, Caius, a recent widower, achieved another kind of success by taking as his second wife, Jane Colley, daughter of an old Rutlandshire gentry family whose forebears had played prominent parts in local and national politics. (Colley Cibber later boasted that his maternal ancestors were recorded "as Sheriffs and Members of Parliament from the Reign of *Henry* VII.")[4] Though the Colley family had lost their land and most of their wealth, they retained vestiges of their former gentility.

Jane, who had control of her own considerable income of £6,000, must have found the young sculptor an appealing matrimonial prospect, since Caius's profession, though once ranked among the manual trades, had risen considerably in status. (Charles II, when creating the office of "Master Sculptor," had issued a statement declaring sculpture and carving in wood an "Art of more excellent skill and dexterity" than arts such as carpentry, masonry, and furniture-making.)[5] Caius was also a handsome man: in a surviving portrait his dark eyes focus intensely and his stylish moustache gives him a dashing air. A year after their marriage, on November 6, 1671, Jane gave birth to their first child, Colley, christened on November 29 at the church of St. Giles-in-the-Fields. But whatever prospects of marital happiness Jane may have envisioned were soon dampened if not completely blighted. For all of his public success, Caius left a private legacy of disappointment that would sour his family life and ultimately shape his descendants' history.

Caius Gabriel Cibber, observed his younger contemporary, the engraver George Vertue, was a "gentleman-like man and a man of good sense." However, Vertue added, "he died poor." His story was common enough: a wealthier gentleman who lodged in his house supposedly introduced him to gambling, creating an addiction Caius could ill afford.[6] Despite Jane's handsome dowry, he ran into debt within a year of their marriage. Bills mounted as he borrowed money from creditors and then defaulted. Finally, when Colley was a little more than a year old, the bailiffs arrested Caius and clapped him into Marshalsea, one of the debtor's prisons in Southwark, the rough district south of the river. Caius would become all too familiar with the Marshalsea and King's Bench prisons during the next five years.

The threat of debtor's prison hovered over the Cibber family during

Colley's early childhood. Caius would be released from one incarceration only to be arrested again for other debts. Fortunately, this did not entirely impede his career: he sculpted the Monument to the Great Fire during one of his periods of imprisonment, when a magistrate granted him day leave to do the work provided he return to Marshalsea every night. And after the early 1670s, Caius was never again incarcerated, though the bailiffs always loomed since he remained perpetually in debt and was periodically hauled into court by his creditors.[7]

The Cibbers' financial difficulties placed a particular strain upon Jane, who had three more children after Colley, though only one, Lewis, survived infancy. While the family never suffered the privations of the genuinely poor, their straitened circumstances interfered with their aspiration to gentility. As his reputation grew, Caius was often able to escape the stresses of London for months on end, executing commissions at aristocratic country houses such as Chatsworth, the magnificent estate of the Duke of Devonshire. Jane, on the other hand, seems to have remained in town to face the burdens of an insufficient income. She had been raised to expect better. Some years later, an enemy of Colley's described Jane Cibber as nagging and tightfisted, "a very carking, sparing Housewifely Woman."[8]

Among the children, the impact of a strained household atmosphere fell most acutely on Colley, and many components of his infamous personality might have resulted from his efforts as a child to cope with the stresses of family life. The adult Colley was notorious for his thick skin, insensitivity, and egotism, traits that a child might develop in an attempt to protect himself from the shame of his father's failings. And the stubborn, wilful streak that emerged in the adolescent Colley, who grew up to rebel against his parents, would have been intensified by his resentment of their shortcomings. He knew from an early age that his father's improvidence would force him to make his own way in life, with only a tiny inheritance from his mother's family. Ultimately, Caius's failure to provide for his son strengthened Colley's ability to defy him.

When Colley was ten, his parents enrolled him at Grantham Free School in Lincolnshire; his tenure there comprised the entirety of his

*Charlotte's paternal grand-father, a sculptor, invented the family name. (*Caius Gabriel Cibber, *engraving by A. Bannerman. Courtesy of the Henry E. Huntington Library.)*

formal education.[9] At Grantham, Colley established the checkered reputation that he would ever after maintain. He was, he later acknowledged, an "inconsistent Creature" at school, "always in full spirits, in some small Capacity to do right, but in a more frequent Alacrity to do wrong."[10] His "giddy Negligence" won him reproof as often as praise from his masters. And, he admitted, "my unskillful openness, or in plain Terms, the Indiscretion I have always acted with from my Youth" gained him the enmity of his schoolmates.

Colley's behaviour may be explained as defensiveness, but no one liked him better for it, and his cutting wit exacerbated his unpopularity. On one occasion, Colley recklessly struck a classmate for insulting him, and his much larger antagonist began to pummel him mercilessly. As other boys ran to see the fight, Colley heard one of his closest friends cry to his rival, "Beat him, beat him soundly!" Later, this boy explained that he wanted to see Colley beaten "because you are always jeering, and making a Jest of me to every Boy in the School." Reflecting back on this "first remarkable Error of my Life," Colley mused, "Thus I deserved his Enmity, by my not having Sense enough to know

I *had* hurt him; and he hated me, because he had not Sense enough to know, that I never *intended* to hurt him."

Colley never entirely absorbed the lesson of the gap between his intentions and the effects of his behaviour. During his six years at Grantham, he was several times the butt of his schoolmates' resentment, since his abilities often allowed him to show up the others and his vanity kept him from underplaying his achievements. Rather than learning lessons of modesty and diffidence, Colley instead learned to weather the consequences of his success and self-promotion.

As Colley entered his teens, his ambitious father planned his eldest son's future, fixing upon the church, to which plan Colley, grandiosely imagining himself in bishop's robes, acquiesced. Ordination in the Church of England required a university education, so Caius arranged for the sixteen-year-old to compete for admission to the prestigious Winchester College, which would then position him to enter New College, Oxford. Winchester and New College had been linked since the days of their founding by the priest William of Wykeham, who was an ancestor of Colley's mother.

Caius naïvely assumed that the family connection would assure his son's admission. As Colley later remarked, in the tone of exasperation he adopted when discussing his father, "Had he tacked a direction to my back and sent me by the carrier to the mayor of the town to be chosen Member of Parliament there, I might have had just as much chance to have succeeded in the one as the other." Arriving with no other sponsorship but his pedigree, he was rejected.*

Undeterred, Caius plotted to use his connections to get his son admitted to Trinity College, Cambridge, for which he had completed a sculpture commission. But the Revolution of 1688–89, which deposed King James II, intervened, and Colley's education had to wait. Instead of matriculating at university, he served briefly in lieu of his father in the regiment commanded by Caius's patron, the Earl of Devonshire. He saw no action, but the detour proved fateful. When the political future of Britain was temporarily settled the following year, with

---

* Colley's brother would receive the education their father envisioned for Colley. Lewis went to Winchester and New College, Oxford, took orders, became an Oxford Fellow, and quickly acquired a reputation as an improvident debauchee. He was said to have told a visiting clergyman "that he did not know any sin he had not been guilty of but one, which was avarice; and if the doctor would give him a guinea, he would do his utmost to be guilty of that too" (Spence: 217). Unsurprisingly, Lewis died young, around the age of thirty, in 1711.

William and Mary established on the throne, Caius abandoned his dream of an ecclesiastical career for his son. Devonshire had been made a duke; Caius sent Colley to London to wait upon him, in order to secure some government position. Caius was particularly anxious to fix his son in a respectable occupation, for Colley had begun to show disturbing signs of fascination with the theatre.

When Colley discovered that he was not to be admitted to Winchester College, he happily hastened home to London to spend his leftover travelling money on a theatre ticket. The Theatre Royal, Drury Lane was at that time home to London's single licensed troupe. (The two original Restoration royal patent companies had united in 1682.) We may imagine Colley fidgeting on one of the hard, backless benches waiting for the play to begin, drinking in the heady atmosphere of the playhouse—the raffish audience, the bitter smell of burning tapers and orange peel, the blaze of the giant candelabra, the shouts and laughter, the lively music. Then, the ponderous curtain slowly opens, and the players make their entrances. The stage-struck boy gazes transfixed at the reigning royalty of late-seventeenth-century English theatre, longing to be among them.

They were a dazzling lot, the luminaries of the Drury Lane company. Chief among them was Thomas Betterton, widely considered the greatest actor ever to tread the stage. Betterton was not handsome: the term "bearlike" might have been coined for him. He had a large head, a broad, pockmarked face, a stocky torso, fat legs, and short, thick arms. His voice was low and growling. He possessed a masterful economy of movement, great emotional intensity, and a subtle, nuanced power of speech that he could "tune," said the actor Tony Aston, to an "artful climax."[11] (When he began to speak, contemporary observers said, he made everyone forget his appearance.)

No other player could keep the normally rowdy playhouse audience as "hushed and quiet" as Betterton. Colley would recall that when Betterton played Hamlet confronting his father's ghost, he conveyed such a profound sense of solemnity, amazement, and fear that he made the ghost as terrifying to the spectators as it was to Hamlet.[12] Some satirists made fun of Betterton's egotism and arrogance, but no one questioned his complete domination of the stage.

Betterton's female counterpart was Elizabeth Barry, a tragedienne and the greatest actress of her day, who was known as the "famous Mrs. Barry, both at Court and City."[13] Her voice was "full, clear, and strong, so that no Violence of Passion could be too much for her," Colley said; she also possessed "an unsurpassed power in the Art of exciting Pity."[14] Very attractive to men, Mrs. Barry had been the mistress of the libertine Earl of Rochester—it was said that he had taught her how to act—and, after him, of several other high-born men, including the playwright Sir George Etherege and the Earl of Dorset.

Mrs. Barry was proud, popular with audiences, and very highly paid— a wealthy, assertive woman who wielded great power in the company. She could be formidable, even aggressive: in a choreographed fight onstage with the actress Elizabeth Bowtrell, with whom she had quarrelled over a veil, Mrs. Barry wielded her dagger "so fiercely that she pierced the other woman's flesh." She was routinely the target of misogynist satires that represented her as a mercenary whore (a powerful woman being so much more offensive to the satirists than her male counterpart). "Should you ley [*sic*] with her all Night," sneered Tom Brown, "She would not know you the next Morning, unless you had another five Pound at her Service."[15]

Counterbalancing Mrs. Barry at Drury Lane was Anne Bracegirdle, who matched her in popularity but projected a very different public image. Anne was not beautiful but she was utterly captivating: Colley said that at any given time half the audience was in love with her.[16] She affectingly played a range of leading parts, from heroic queens to charmingly manipulative coquettes (William Congreve wrote the role of Millamant in *The Way of the World* for her). Mrs. Bracegirdle was besieged ceaselessly in the green room by would-be lovers, titled admirers among them. (Many upper-class men assumed the right of free access backstage, not only to the green room but often to actresses' dressing rooms as well.) But Anne rejected them all, acquiring a reputation for chastity so unusual for an actress that it made her a phenomenon. Though satirists speculated that she must have lovers (Congreve was a particular suspect), her discretion remained absolute.

There were other stars in the Drury Lane company, such as the beautiful Edward Kynaston, who prior to the introduction of women on the English stage in 1660 had played female roles, and continued to play them until a coterie of actresses was trained. (Once, when King

Charles II had asked why a tragedy was not starting on time, he was
told that "the Queen had not shaved yet.") Samuel Pepys observed that
Kynaston was both the "prettiest woman in the whole house" and "the
handsomest man in the house."[17] In 1690, he was fifty years old but
remained a handsome figure: remarkably, he still had all his teeth.

With these figures, and others almost as alluring before him, Colley
was thoroughly smitten. As he cooled his heels in London waiting for
the duke to remember him, he went night after night to the playhouse.
Devonshire delayed, the theatre beckoned ever more seductively, and
finally, in defiance of Jane and Caius's protests, the youth heeded its
call. He could see "no Joy in any other Life than that of an Actor": only
the stage, he declared to his horrified parents, would make him
happy.[18] Ignoring his parents' remonstrances, Colley plunged into the
theatre world. He began assiduously to cultivate contacts at Drury Lane,
becoming friends with the rakish young actor John Verbruggen—"that
rough Diamond," Tony Aston said, who "shone more bright than all
the artful, polish'd Brillants [*sic*] that ever sparked on our Stage"—and,
more usefully, gaining the interest of the theatre's prompter, John
Downes.[19] In 1690, Downes recommended nineteen-year-old "Master
Colley" for a position as an unpaid apprentice actor.

Colley now considered himself "the happiest of Mortals," but Caius
and Jane were distressed. Though they struggled financially, her genteel
birth and his professional success allowed them to claim respectability;
acting was a step down on the ladder.

Actors were difficult to categorize socially. The salaries of the leading players of a major company placed them in the upper ranks of the
"middle station," and some of them moved in aristocratic circles. But
their profession was suspect, at best, and most actors never joined a
leading company, achieved well-paid leading roles, or had enough
money to ride out a poor season. For the most part, theatre folk, along
with musicians and other entertainers, belonged to their own demimonde, distinct from both the middling and the upper classes.[20] With
its risqué plays, its audiences that included rakes and prostitutes, its air
of sexual licence, its glamour, and its violence, the theatre was profoundly stigmatized.

Fellows in ignominy, players often banded together, forming friendships and alliances among themselves (when they were not engaged in rivalries and quarrels). So it was not surprising that Colley, having joined the theatrical world, found a wife within it too. Caius and Jane must have been particularly dismayed when Colley fell in love with a musician (though perhaps they consoled themselves—prematurely— that at least she was not an actress).

Twenty-four-year-old Katherine Shore, "a very beautiful and amiable young woman, whom [Henry] Purcell taught to sing and play on the harpsichord," was said to have one of the finest voices of her day. Katherine belonged to a family of professional musicians. Her father, Matthias Shore, held a court position as Sergeant of the Trumpeters, Drummers, and Fifes in Ordinary to Kings James II and William III. Her brother William, a trumpet player, also held a court appointment.

Her other brother, John, another trumpeter, eventually succeeded Matthias as Sergeant-Trumpeter: John is credited with inventing the tuning fork and, it was said, could produce from his instrument "a tone as sweet as that of a hautboy." A "man of humour and pleasantry," he also played in the orchestra of the Drury Lane Theatre, where he struck up an acquaintance with Colley.[21] One day after rehearsal, Colley accompanied his friend to the Shore family home where, as the young men entered, they heard a woman singing in an adjacent room. The singer was Katherine.

In his own distinctly unmusical, reedy voice, Colley complimented her upon her singing, telling her that he prided himself on his good ear and admired her musicianship. Now his eyes told him that she had a lovely person as well. He, on the other hand, was a short, skinny, bandy-legged, sandy-haired twenty-year-old, already acquiring a reputation for cockiness and dissipation. He had just enjoyed the professional break-through of promotion from *un*paid to *poorly* paid apprentice actor, but his acquisition of a salary was amusingly backhanded. In his first appearance on the stage, he was cast in a small part requiring him to carry a message to Thomas Betterton, and made his entrance gripped with such obvious terror that he discomposed everyone. Afterward, Betterton indignantly demanded from Downes the name of the youngster who had botched the scene. "Master Colley," replied the prompter. "Master Colley! Then forfeit him," Betterton thundered. "Why sir," said Downes, "he has no salary." "No?" retorted Betterton. "Why then put him down for ten shillings a week and forfeit him five."[22]

Colley understandably might have refrained from giving Katherine these details, but he did charm her with his sassy wit and self-confidence. After some months of courtship, Colley proposed. He had to offer only his pittance of a salary, his tiny inheritance of £20 a year, and his unbounded ambition. Some accounts suggest that Matthias Shore actively opposed the marriage, seeing little potential in Master Colley's prospects and perhaps alerted to the young man's growing reputation for rakishness. If so, however, he later reconciled with his daughter, leaving her an inheritance, though he specified that it go to her rather than to Colley. (Matthias also built a houseboat, known as Shore's Folly, where entertainments of music—and less respectable pleasures, for it doubled as a bawdyhouse—could be enjoyed. The German visitor Uffenbach encountered there "one female who, for a small fee, did all kinds of dance figures with a bare sword.")[23]

Regardless of her father's opinion, Katherine saw something promising in her cocky young suitor, and accepted his offer. The "happiest young Couple, that ever took a Leap in the Dark," as Colley remembered them, were married on May 6, 1693, at St. James's, Duke's Place, Aldgate, London.[24] Colley's parents must have been even more dismayed than Matthias. Marriage to a dowryless musician was one more step away from the life of prosperous gentility the Cibbers had envisioned for their elder son.

The newlyweds set up housekeeping on a meagre income. Katherine went onto the stage, acting in occasional roles but more often performing entr'acte songs written by leading composers, including the Purcell brothers and John Eccles. Colley's biographers have assumed that Katherine became a professional performer entirely because Colley's salary was inadequate to support them both. But we cannot discount the possibility that, however necessary her salary, she also welcomed the opportunity. Several Drury Lane actresses were married, often to other actors, and even a few of those whose marriages moved them upward on the social ladder continued to act. The stage may not have been respectable, but it represented one of the very few professional opportunities available to women.

For his part, Colley laboured to prove himself. The popular actor William Mountfort kindly took him under his wing, giving him his first small speaking part, a servant, in Thomas Southerne's comedy *Sir Anthony Love*. (The character of Sir Anthony Love is a woman who passes as a man for almost the entire play.) But Mountfort's patronage of Colley was cut short the next year. A seventeen-year-old army officer, Captain Richard Hill, who mistakenly thought that Mountfort was having an affair with Anne Bracegirdle, trailed the thirty-three-year-old actor home from the playhouse and stabbed him on his own doorstep. William staggered through the door and died at the feet of his wife, Susanna, who was pregnant with their second child.[25]

Shocked and saddened, Colley persevered, yet all the best parts were claimed by the older, established actors, who jealously guarded their privileges against potential rivals. An opportunity presented itself in the season of 1694–95, when long-simmering disputes erupted between many of the company's principal actors and the theatre's patentee, Christopher Rich. Colley said Rich was "as sly a Tyrant, as ever was at the Head of a Theatre; for he gave the Actors more Liberty, and fewer Days Pay, than any of his Predecessors: he could laugh with them over a Bottle, and bite them, in their Bargains: he kept them poor, that they might not be able to rebel; and sometimes merry, that they might not think of it."[26]

Betterton, Barry, and Bracegirdle were not poor, however, and they did, finally, rebel. They, along with many other veteran players, seceded from Drury Lane and obtained a licence from the lord chamberlain to start a second, competing company under their own management at a theatre in Lincoln's Inn Fields. Colley, however, saw that his own interests were best served by remaining with the unscrupulous Rich at Drury Lane, for the suddenly decimated company would have to promote younger actors to fill the vacated roles.

But Colley now found his progress blocked by another obstacle—George Powell, the most powerful player remaining, who had pegged Master Colley as an upstart. Powell, an excellent actor, was also an envious, quarrelsome alcoholic: he would go on stage so aggressively heated with drink, according to John Vanbrugh, that his romantic scenes with his leading lady resembled assault more than courtship.[27] Powell was often in a position to deny Colley roles. Continually frustrated, the ambitious youth finally realized that in order to act in good parts he would have to create them himself.

So, over the summer of 1695, Colley wrote a comic play entitled *Love's Last Shift; or, The Fool in Fashion*. The playwright Thomas Southerne read it and recommended that it be staged. The comedy premiered in January 1696, with a strong cast that pointedly did not include George Powell: Colley cast John Verbruggen (now married to the former Susanna Mountfort) instead.

The play's plot centres around the plight of Amanda, a virtuous wife, played by Mrs. Rogers, who was neither. (It was said that she considered herself virtuous because she played chaste characters.) Amanda's libertine husband, Loveless (Verbruggen, cast much more according to type) abandoned her shortly after their marriage, but for ten years Amanda has remained faithful to him, as he has impoverished himself through debauchery in Europe. The play begins with the destitute Loveless returning to England because he has heard that his wife has died from smallpox. Amanda, whose illness has not killed her but has altered her appearance, hides her identity and lures him into bed for a night of rapture. Only in the morning does she reveal that their supposedly illicit love was licit all along. Loveless, guilt-struck but also impressed by the pleasures of the previous night, vows to redeem himself within the bonds of faithful marriage (and, presumably, good sex). The play ends with Loveless's proclamation that true happiness can be found only in "the chaste Rapture of a virtuous Love."

Love's Last Shift became an instant hit, striking a note that would define Colley Cibber's career, namely, a plot that allowed the audience both the pleasures of sexual intrigue and the satisfaction of a sentimental ending. As Cibber's epilogue reminds the audience with a verbal wink, the rake may reform at the end of the play, but "he's lewd for above four acts" first. Having enjoyed the play's licentious situations and sexy banter, the audience could conclude with tears of moralistic pleasure.

Colley wrote for himself the role of Sir Novelty Fashion, the first of his many upper-class fops who would mince across the stage overdressed in parodies of the latest Parisian fashions. Sir Novelty's entrance brought down the house: his wig was an extravagant confection of curls and ties, the lace on his sleeves reached his knuckles, and the buttons on his coat were, he pointed out with false modesty, "not above three Inches diameter." Colley's high-pitched voice and flattened vowels—he pronounced his "o's" as "a's"—gave Sir Novelty an affected drawl, which he punctuated with the exclamation "Stap my Vitals!" His vacuous expression and unprepossessing, bandy-legged figure made the fop's preening narcissism all the more incongruous.

At age twenty-five, Colley had found his calling and his character, vindicating his choice of career. Basking in the acclaim that greeted *Love's Last Shift,* Colley laughed off the insistence of some critics that he must have plagiarized the play because it was too good for him to have written. Suddenly he was acknowledged as a promising playwright and actor, and he began to gain influence with Rich. His parents did not live to see him famous—Jane would die in 1697 and Caius in 1700—but they were both alive to hear of the triumph of *Love's Last Shift.* Perhaps they even went to see it.

Ironically enough, given its embrace of virtue and marital fidelity, *Love's Last Shift* also made Colley his first high-born rakish friend, Colonel Henry Brett, who marched backstage after a performance, bent upon acquiring Sir Novelty's wonderful wig. Though Colley refused to surrender the wig, the two men became immediate friends. Brett, who at the time was seeking to repair his ruined fortune by marrying a rich woman, would eventually provide the model for Colley's most famous libertine character. And his friendship opened the door to the society of upper-class rakes, whose example stimulated Colley's developing taste for the pleasures of gambling and whoring in high company—additional fruits of his success.

During the next decade, Colley exerted increasing influence over Rich, and continued to perfect his craft as a comic actor.[28] As a playwright, however, he experienced flops as well as successes. He also began to adapt other plays, a routine practice that nonetheless opened him to charges of plagiarism from his critics. The already thin company was hit by a series of blows, too. Hildebrand Horden, a promising young actor positioned to take Mountfort's place, was killed in a brawl at the disreputable Rose Tavern adjacent to the theatre. In 1703, Susanna Verbruggen, a sparkling comic actress, died in childbirth at age thirty-seven. And the theatre's treasurer, Ralph Davenant, was stabbed to death on his way home one night. Christopher Rich, opportunistic and often incompetent, paid his actors irregularly while skimming off the profits for himself, driving the company into debt as it struggled to hold its own against Betterton's troupe. Talk of an actors' mutiny was again in the air, despite one promising development: Rich's importation of the dashing Irish actor Robert Wilks. This, however, created tensions with George Powell, who presciently feared that the short-tempered but highly disciplined Wilks would eventually supplant him.

The theatre generally was facing increasingly vociferous criticism as a sink of immorality and a threat to public decency. Reform was in the air. The reign of William and Mary, neither of whom was fond of plays, both coincided with and encouraged a backlash against Restoration excesses. In 1692, the Society for the Reformation of Manners was founded and began to execute its mission of rounding up prostitutes, prosecuting people for swearing in public, and threatening the playhouses and players. Jeremy Collier's diatribe, *A Short View of the Immorality and Profaneness of the English Stage*, spoke for many when it was published in 1698, castigating the most popular plays for their indecent plots, characters, and language. The accession in 1702 of Queen Anne, another monarch who did not care for the stage, intensified the reformist mood. A shock of alarm ran throughout the theatre world.[29]

This was the climate in which the comedy considered Colley's masterpiece, *The Careless Husband*, premiered in December 1704. He had begun writing it some years before for Susanna Verbruggen, for whom he intended the principal role of Lady Betty Modish, a narcissistic society coquette. Colley had sorrowfully laid aside the play when Mrs. Verbruggen died, intending never to complete it. Susanna's old parts had been taken by a young actress who had been in the company for a year without distinguishing herself.

Anne Oldfield seemed to Colley a poor substitute for Susanna; he found her manner diffident and her delivery flat. When she was cast in Susanna's part in *Sir Courtly Nice*, Colley, who played Sir Courtly, only grudgingly agreed to rehearse with her. Understandably, the rehearsal went badly, but on the night they first took the stage together, everything changed. Mrs. Oldfield turned in a performance whose brilliance amazed Colley—all the more so because "it proceeded from her own Understanding, untaught and unassisted by any more experience'd Actor" (to wit, himself).

Openly admitting his mistake, Colley became Oldfield's ardent supporter and admirer, speaking of her as "the foremost Ornament of our Theatre."[30] He paid Anne his greatest compliment when he returned to writing *The Careless Husband* and shaped for her the role he had begun for Susanna. Mrs. Oldfield inhabited the role of Lady Betty so definitively for the next twenty-five years as to blur the distinction between the actress and the character.

A great beauty, with a figure "tall, genteel and well-shaped" and large expressive eyes, Mrs. Oldfield had an irresistible manner of tossing back her head and half-closing her eyes as she delivered a clever, cutting line.[31] Anne herself was of humble origins, literate but not well educated; her father, probably the son of a tavern-keeper, had been a trooper in the Horse Guards who lived extravagantly and died young, leaving his family impoverished.[32] But despite her low birth, Anne could play the coquettish society lady as perfectly if she had been bred to it.

The sentimental part of *The Careless Husband*'s plot features Lady Easy, whose libertine husband, Sir Charles, has recently seduced her maid. In her sensible and forbearing way, she has refused to sour her marriage by complaining. One afternoon, however, Lady Easy discovers her husband and her maid asleep in adjoining chairs in obvious postcoital slumber. She does not awaken them, but lays her scarf over his head for him to find when he awakens: an act of wifely solicitude lest he catch cold, but also an eloquent statement of her awareness of his adultery, and her forbearance.

Cibber was said to have modelled Sir Charles Easy after Henry Brett, who was reputed to have been discovered by his wife, the former Countess of Macclesfield, in a similarly compromising position. In keeping with his own dramatic principles, however, Colley gave his play an ending apparently absent in the real-life domestic comedy enacted by Colonel and Mrs. Brett. When Sir Charles awakens to find the scarf, he realizes that he has been a fool. In his wife, he has long possessed a valuable jewel whose very familiarity has caused him to overlook its beauty and its worth. At the end of the play, as in *Love's Last Shift*, the libertine repents, vowing to become the faithful husband such a virtuous wife deserves. This play was one of Colley's greatest successes: it would be performed more than two hundred times during his lifetime.[33] Even Alexander Pope praised it.

The Careless Husband featured a series of comic scenes centering around Lord Foppington, the Sir Novelty Fashion character who has bought himself a peerage—Colley's most famous role.* By now, Colley had definitively laid claim to the fop, and to his stature as a comic actor. However much those who disliked him might carp about his unwise persistence in trying to play tragic roles, Colley's brilliance as a comedian was evident. As the stuffy Aaron Hill backhandedly acknowledged, "It is not possible to look at him without acknowledging this remarkable talent and confessing he was *born* to be *laughed* at." Hill went on to describe Colley's stage manners: "In his face was a contracted kind of passive yet protruded sharpness, like a pig half roasted; and a voice not unlike his own might have been borrowed from the same suffering animal while in a condition a little less desperate."[34]

In the *Tatler* (no. 182), Richard Steele wrote:

> The First of the present Stage are Wilks and Cibber, perfect Actors in their different Kinds. Wilks has a singular Talent in representing the Graces of Nature, Cibber the Deformity in the Affectation of them. . . . Cibber in another Light hits exquisitely the flat Civility of an affected Gentleman-Usher, and Wilks the easy Frankness of a Gentleman. . . . To beseech gracefully, to approach respectfully, to pity, to mourn, to love, are the Places wherein Wilks may be made to shine with the utmost Beauty: to rally pleasantly, to scorn artfully, to flatter, to ridicule, and to neglect, are what Cibber would perform with no less Excellence.

The Careless Husband, Steele continued, was "a Play that is acted to Perfection, both by them and all concerned in it, as being born within the Walls of the Theatre, and written with an exact Knowledge of the Abilities of the Performers."

---

* Sir Novelty was first elevated to the peerage in *The Relapse,* John Vanbrugh's sequel to *Love's Last Shift,* which is critical of the sentimentality of Cibber's play. It is characteristic of Colley's appreciation of a good role—and, we might say, demonstrates his lack of investment in his own play's moral professions—that he not only played Lord Foppington in *The Relapse* but also maintained the character in his own masterpiece.

Colley Cibber, Charlotte's father, was one of the greatest comic actors in the history of the London stage. (J. H. Robinson, Colley Cibber as Lord Foppington. Engraved from the portrait by J. Grisoni. Courtesy of the Henry E. Huntington Library.)

Colley responded to political pressures and changes in audience taste by writing plays that created emotionally charged scenes illustrating the value of family life and the raptures of faithful married love. Colley's own behaviour, however, was not modelled upon this ideal. Twice he was arrested on charges of sexual misconduct. In October 1697, four years after he and Katherine were married, he was briefly imprisoned on charges of indecent assault upon Jane Lucas, an actress and dancer. The charges were apparently dropped. (After several more years of continuing to act and dance in small roles—she played the maid in *The Careless Husband*—Jane Lucas vanished from the theatre's records.)

In June 1712, Colley was arrested for siring a child with an unmarried woman named Mary Osbourne. This time Colonel Brett paid his bail, and the case was settled out of court before it could come to trial. The fate of Mary Osbourne and her illegitimate child, not likely a happy one, remains obscure.[35]

These accusations may have been completely false or exaggerated. But they gained at least some credibility because of Colley's reputation.

His biographer, Helene Koon, argues that while Colley self-protectively wore a mask of rakishness and foppery in public, his real sexual behaviour was in fact exemplary. But there survives much innuendo about Colley's conduct outside of his marriage. He himself referred to his familiarity with brothels, and his acknowledged predilection for drinking and gambling in rakish company shows that he embraced a libertine milieu.*

In fact, Colley Cibber never pretended that he himself was a model, despite the fact that he created examples of morality for the edification of others. "I am for the church, though I don't go to church," he would say. The actress Mary Porter once asked him, "How can you draw such admirable portraits of goodness and live as if you were a stranger to it?" To which he replied, coolly, "The one, madam, is absolutely necessary, the other is not."[36]

---

* Koon: 34. Koon's biography provides an invaluable service by countering the biased image of "Colley Cibber the coxcomb" bequeathed to later generations by his enemies and all too often accepted uncritically by modern readers. Koon's argument that Colley wore a mask of foppishness offstage as a means of guarding his privacy and protecting himself from hurt is astute, but its truth is not dependent upon construing him as a paragon of marital virtue. It seems much more likely that, in this respect, Colley was very much a man of his time. In company with a great many of his contemporaries, both male and female, Colley took it for granted that a man would consort with prostitutes or keep mistresses. Such behaviour did not necessarily imply that his marriage was unhappy or that he did not love his wife.

The Impertinent Intruder

(1712–13)

When, sometime during the summer of 1712, Katherine Cibber realized that she was with child, she must have been shocked, for at forty-five she would have expected that her childbearing days were over. It was her twelfth pregnancy.

Katherine had been married to Colley for nearly twenty years, and she had long ceased to practise her profession. She was last listed as a member of the Drury Lane company in 1698–99, when she may have sung in one concert that season, but her final recorded performance was in late summer 1697.[1] Colley was earning a larger, more secure salary by that time, but this is not necessarily an adequate explanation for the end of Katherine's theatrical career.

Katherine suffered from chronic asthma, and she lived in the worst city in England for an asthmatic. Dirty at the best of times and hot and grimy in the summer, London was downright toxic in the winter, when coal fires burned by the thousands. The newspapers were filled with apothecaries' notices advertising remedies for asthma and other respiratory ailments, and many residents complained that they had trouble breathing. Katherine was particularly vulnerable, and her strength had probably been further sapped by the physical and emotional strains of constant pregnancy.

Within the first fourteen years of her marriage, Katherine had given birth eleven times. Six of those infants died, usually within hours or days. (She may have had unrecorded miscarriages, too, and one son who was still living in 1712—he had been born blind—would subsequently die in childhood.) Her eleventh child, the second son to be named Colley, had died in infancy as the first namesake had done. Then nearly five years had passed with no more pregnancies—until the summer of 1712.

It was not unusual in the eighteenth century for a prosperous, relatively well-nourished woman to undergo childbirth often, nor was it unusual for infants to die at an early age. Queen Anne herself had conceived at least eighteen children, all but one of whom were either born dead or died very young. (And the sole child to survive infancy, Prince William, died when he was eleven.)[2] Multiple pregnancies took their toll even among the upper classes, often permanently damaging the health of an otherwise healthy woman—and the asthmatic Katherine, like the sickly Queen, was not an otherwise healthy woman.

If Katherine had wished to limit the number of her pregnancies, she would have had few options. Birth control was primitive in the eighteenth century. Besides abstinence, the usual method was coitus interruptus, which required greater self-control than many men were willing or able to exert. Unwieldy (and unreliable) condoms of sheep gut or brine-soaked linen were available in London, but most men used them to protect against venereal disease from a prostitute rather than to prevent conception in a wife. Abortionists most frequently served unmarried women, forced by desperation to risk their lives. Married women were known to try other methods to induce a miscarriage— such as ingesting strong herbs, taking hot baths, galloping on horses, and jumping off tables—with varying degrees of success.[3] Given the state of Katherine's health, these methods might have proved as risky as childbirth itself.

Even for young, vigorous gentlewomen, childbirth was an anxiety-provoking event. Women frequently died during the agonies of labour or succumbed to fever soon afterward. There were no effective anesthetics, no antibiotics—just the real possibility of a protracted, painful struggle that might culminate in death of the mother, the child, or both. Many women faced their lying-in—that elaborate ritual of seclusion and confinement to bed that characterized childbirth among the wealthier classes—with great trepidation. They put their financial affairs in order, wrote letters to their families, and often took care to leave words of maternal love and counsel for the newborn who might survive never to know its mother. And then they prepared themselves emotionally and spiritually for death. Katherine could have assuaged her own fears somewhat by considering that she had survived labour many times, just as she had survived those terrifying asthma attacks. But she was older now and her health more precarious. She already had seen six infants to the grave, and she must have considered the possibility that this time, she might join them.

For his part, Colley probably preserved the cheerful detachment not uncommon among men of his time and temperament. Later in life, when he looked back upon his marriage and career, he described them complacently as an outpouring of complementary forms of creative production: "my Muse, and my Spouse, were equally prolifick . . . the one was seldom the Mother of a Child, but in the same Year, the other made me Father of a Play. I think we had about a Dozen of each sort between us; of both which Kinds, some dy'd in their Infancy, and near an equal number of each were alive, when I quitted the Theatre."[4]

On January 13, 1713, Charlotte made her debut on the stage of life, receiving mixed reviews. She was born at the Cibbers' house in Spring Garden, located just above Whitehall in the shadow of Charing Cross, and her birth seems to have been uneventful: both mother and child survived in reasonable health, and this twelfth lying-in proved Katherine's last. The Cibbers christened their new daughter on February 8 at the parish church of St. Martin-in-the-Fields. When Charlotte was about a year old, Colley moved his family into more spacious quarters in Southampton Street West, a wide street running south from Covent Garden square.[5]

Katherine responded warmly to this daughter of her middle age, and we can imagine Colley smiling benignly if distractedly upon her. But the Cibbers' other children were a different matter. According to Charlotte, she arrived as "not only an unexpected, but an unwelcome Guest into the Family, (exclusive of my Parents)." The other children, she said, dismayed by her unexpected arrival, greeted her more as an "impertinent Intruder, than one who had a natural Right to make up the circular Number of my Father's Fire-Side."[6]

Charlotte's disconnection from her siblings would have been exacerbated by the difference in their ages. The eldest, her sister Catherine, was more than seventeen years her senior, and her other two sisters, Anne and Elizabeth, were fourteen and twelve, respectively, when she was born. Closest to Charlotte in age was six-year-old James, who was blind; but he seems to have died within a year or two of her birth.[7] Theophilus, her only brother to reach adulthood, had just turned ten, but he was away at school during most of her childhood. The resentment Charlotte felt seems principally to have come from her sisters, especially Catherine and Anne.

We do not know whether Colley and Katherine followed the established custom in wealthier families of putting their newborn "out to nurse"—that is, sending Charlotte to a wet nurse in the country for her first year or two. Depending upon the state of Katherine's health, she may have nursed Charlotte herself or, as a compromise, brought a wet nurse into the house instead of sending the infant out of it. (At some point, Charlotte seems to have had a French nurse or nanny, for she later commented that she understood the alphabet in French before she was able to speak English. It is unlikely that this woman was a wet nurse.)

The family's domestic circumstances could have given the older children additional grounds for ill will towards the interloper. Charlotte was born to advantages that had been unavailable to them, particularly to Catherine. She, the couple's first child, would have had an early life characterized by uncertainty and stress, as Colley struggled to establish his career, Katherine was almost always pregnant, and the family's straitened finances limited their prospects. By the time Charlotte was born, however, Colley's professional success had elevated the family to relative wealth. They lived in a handsome London house, spent each summer in a fashionable country resort, kept a staff of servants, and had a coach. As Charlotte innocently luxuriated in the privileges of the youngest-born—including, perhaps, that French nurse—her older siblings might well have eyed her with jealousy and resentment.

Charlotte's belief that her sisters saw her as an intruder must have helped to shape her singular personality as an adult. It is always possible, of course, that her memory of their resentment was faulty or even fictional, more a product of her later estrangement from her family than an accurate recollection of her childhood experiences. (She was forty-two and burdened by grievances when she described, in her autobiography, her siblings' conduct towards her.) Consciously or not, she might have applied retrospectively to her earliest life the alienation that she later felt.

But Charlotte's character itself gives credibility to her claim that she was singled out from infancy as an object of resentment within her family, for her rebelliousness manifested itself early. According to one analyst of the effects of birth order, youngest children are "born to rebel" (a pattern that apparently has persisted through the ages).[8] But hostility from her much older siblings could also have contributed to Charlotte's defiant eccentricity. In her autobiography, she repeatedly described herself, comically but also with conviction, as an "oddity" and a "nonpareil," and during the course of her life she displayed an abiding sense of singularity. Feeling ostracized from infancy may well lead a child to develop the notion that she is, in some fundamental way, different. If this was Charlotte's case, rather than prompting a retreat into shy self-consciousness, anger, or self-pity, it produced in her a self-affirming (if also self-protective) sense of uniqueness.

During Charlotte's infancy, Great Britain was undergoing its own version of a family drama. When Queen Anne died without an heir in August 1714, the Stuart monarchy ended. The search for a successor brought a new political dispensation to the throne, in the form of the Protestant house of Hanover, Germany—the "Hanoverian succession"—and in the person of George Ludwig, the Elector of Hanover, the great-grandson of James I. (At George I's public entry into the city, Charlotte's uncle John Shore paraded in his Sergeant-Trumpeter's uniform, holding his mace.)[9]

The new king was a military hero, though physically unprepossessing, short and fat, with bulging eyes. He was also taciturn and unsociable. The foreign entourage he arrived with included his Hanoverian courtiers, his two Turkish body servants, Mehemet and Mustapha, his German mistress (tall, thin Melusine von Schulenburg, afterward Duchess of Kendal, was known in England as the Maypole), and his half-sister (Charlotte Sophia Kielmansegg, afterward Countess of Darlington, often called the Elephant), inaccurately rumoured to be his mistress. Both women were said to exert enormous influence on the King. The opposition writer (and misogynist) Nathaniel Mist complained: "We are ruined by trulls, nay, what is more vexatious, by old ugly trulls, such as could not find entertainment in the most hospitable hundreds [meaning the brothels] of old Drury."[10]

George had divorced his wife, Princess Sophia Dorothea, for adultery, though he himself had already established Melusine as his mistress when still married. His wife's lover had been murdered, probably by his courtiers. (He kept Sophia Dorothea a prisoner in Germany from 1694 until her death in 1726. During those thirty-two years of strict confinement to her house, she was forbidden access to her children, who included the Prince of Wales, later George II, and she died without ever seeing them again. The prince never forgave his father.) Though many in England considered Melusine, with whom George had three daughters, in effect to be his wife—Robert Walpole commented that she was as much "Queen of England as anyone ever was"—George never remarried.[11]

George I spent as much time back in Hanover as he could, to hunt, take the waters at Pyrmont, and visit his family. During his reign of thirteen years, he went to Hanover five times.[12] He had little affection for his new British subjects, many of whom reciprocated the sentiment. Substantial numbers of the English held allegiance to James Edward Stuart, the son of the exiled King James II, seeing him, despite his Catholicism, as the divinely ordained ruler of Britain. The Old Pretender, as he was called, resided in France and was known among Jacobites (Stuart loyalists) as James III, "the King across the Water." A Jacobite rebellion in 1715–16 collapsed, but the threat of invasion from abroad, and treason from within, remained real.

Colley Cibber was a staunch supporter of the new monarchy and of those Whig politicians who supported George I and now began to dominate the government. Though he has been accused of political opportunism, his politics, while certainly self-interested, were also consistent. During the revolution of 1688–89, his own father had aligned himself with his patron Devonshire against James II, and Colley, it may be remembered, had been one of Devonshire's troops. Colley consistently supported Hanoverians and the court Whigs, most particularly Walpole and his allies, who would dominate English political life during the reigns of George I and II.

By the time of Charlotte's birth, Colley had become "the most powerful man in the English theatre."[13] The scrawny, striving youngster had

rounded into portly, well-dressed middle age. He had established a reputation as a gifted comic actor and prolific playwright, and had become
a highly visible public figure, both celebrated and reviled, nearly as
famous for his flashy behaviour off stage as for his hilarious performances on. Furthermore, since 1710, Cibber had been one of the three
actor-managers of the Drury Lane Theatre.[14] Through a complicated
series of events and machinations, he and his allies had succeeded in
breaking Christopher Rich's hold, bypassing his royal patent and
acquiring a licence that, though less valuable than a patent, authorized
them to perform at Drury Lane.

Drury Lane now had a new management intimately familiar with,
and deeply invested in, every aspect of the profession. Colley, Wilks,
and a third actor, initially Thomas Doggett and later Barton Booth,
constituted the famous "triumvirate" that would run the theatre
admirably for more than twenty years. Wilks directed the rehearsals,
but Colley selected the plays.

In 1714, the triumvirate was joined by Richard Steele—playwright,
essayist, and newly elected, soon to be knighted, Whig member of
Parliament—whose influence with the King secured the group a new
royal patent in Steele's name. Once again the actors at Drury Lane
came under the sponsorship of the crown as "Gentlemen of the Great
Chamber." Despite periodic financial problems produced by competition from Lincoln's Inn Fields Theatre, now under the management of
John Rich (who had inherited his patent from his father, Christopher),
Drury Lane achieved a stability it had not had for many years.

Colley's rise to wealth and power, and his association with Walpole,
a brilliant and unscrupulous politician, underlay the controversies that
surrounded him throughout Charlotte's life. They made him a reviled
figure among the opposition, motivating the attacks on him by Pope,
Fielding, Mist, and a host of lesser figures and thus contributing to his
sullied place in history. But at the same time, these associations benefited him enormously, gaining him fame, money, royal patronage, and,
eventually, appointment as poet laureate.

Colley's political connections played a dramatic role in Charlotte's
life, too. As a child, she certainly benefited from her family's prosperity.
But the very alliances that helped to secure Colley's wealth and position
would one day have quite a different effect upon the fortunes of his
youngest daughter.

A Passionate Fondness
for a Periwig

(1717–20)

One morning in the summer of 1717, four-year-old Charlotte arose from her bed unusually early. Slipping on a coat over her nightdress, she took up her shoes and stockings and crept cautiously from her chamber. Though the Twickenham lodging house was full of people—her brother, her sisters, her parents, and other tenants—it stood silent as they slept on. The servants had risen, but they had not yet begun to go about their duties.

Stealing undetected into the servants' hall, Charlotte located a broom and pulled it towards the coat rack. All was going according to plan: there on the pegs hung her brother's waistcoat, her father's silver-headed sword on its wide, heavy belt, his large beaver hat bedecked with lace, and, most gloriously, his full-bottomed wig. Even at four years old, Charlotte said, she harboured a "passionate Fondness for a Perriwig." Long and bulky in the style of the day, Colley's headpiece boasted cascades of curls and bunches of tied hair. Elabourate wigs were his trademark, and his foppish characters wore particularly outlandish ones. When, as the pompous Lord Foppington, he called for his periwig, two burly men would carry it onstage in a sedan chair, straining with the effort.

Moving carefully, Charlotte hoisted the broomstick to lift the garments from their pegs. Wrapping her coat around her waist in lieu of a pair of breeches, she donned the waistcoat, strapped on the sword, settled the wig carefully on her head, and crowned it with the hat. The giant wig enveloped Charlotte's infant frame like a cloak, flapping at her heels as she walked. Waistcoat skimming the ground, sword dragging awkwardly behind her, and cumbersome hat weighing down her head, Charlotte lurked unnoticed near the door as she waited for the gardener to leave the house and slipped out behind him. Her costume was as complete as she could make it. Now she needed a stage—and an audience.

Outside the house, the community was beginning to stir. In the early eighteenth century, Twickenham was a leafy village west of London on the River Thames, a country resort whose genteel residents built stately houses where they could indulge the new craze for picturesque gardening, vying for the services of landscape architects who filled their patrons' estates with bowers, wildernesses, grottoes, and exotic plants. A good address year round, Twickenham burgeoned in the summer as London's elite fled the sweltering city.

For several summers in a row, Charlotte's family had rented part of the fashionable lodging house on the Richmond road, conveniently located between London and Richmond Palace. (This house, enlarged and greatly redecorated, would become famous later in the century as Horace Walpole's Gothic fantasia, Strawberry Hill, which stands today; the outlines of the building Charlotte knew can still be discerned.) During most of the year in town, Colley was too caught up in his demanding professional schedule and his enthusiastic pursuit of rakish pleasures to take much notice of his youngest daughter. But here in the country, Charlotte plotted to capture his attention.

As she stepped into the fresh summer morning, she would have seen farm labourers trudging along the roads towards the outlying fields, while laundresses and milkmaids headed towards the wealthier houses. Servants dashed about on errands as early risers among the gentlefolk emerged from their doors for a pre-breakfast stroll. Scrutinizing her potential audience, Charlotte realized that first she must remove the one remaining obstacle to her transformation. She still wore her little girl's stockings and shoes. She quickly hit upon a solution: the deep, dry ditch running along the road in front of the house would hide her feet from the sight of passersby. Charlotte rolled herself in and began her performance as Colley Cibber, parading up and down the length of the ditch, bowing gravely to all who came near with his familiar condescension, glowing, she said, with "the happy Thought of being taken for the 'Squire.'" This outlandish spectacle soon attracted a boisterous crowd of onlookers. Charlotte savoured their attention, basking in their laughter, as the principal actor in a play of her own devising.

At four years old, Charlotte could already feel the heady allure of celebrity, the gratification of attracting an audience and making them laugh. Performing was in her blood: she had already acquired from her father his flair for self-dramatization. For Colley, attention of any kind was far preferable to neglect, and in her own performance, Charlotte imitated her father's example. Despite her tender age, however, her infantile homage already contained an element of parody.

While Charlotte paraded and bowed, the other members of the household arose and, missing her, began to search. Eventually, Mrs. Heron, mother of a young Drury Lane actress, was drawn by the commotion outdoors. Spotting Charlotte amid her spectators, she called the others to witness the scene. Charlotte was delighted to attract the attention of her entire household, especially since the crowd included her father. For their part, Colley and Katherine were relieved to find their youngest child, and even rather amused at the spectacle she had staged, though it embarrassed them, too. Charlotte found herself abruptly swept up and borne off into the house on the shoulders of a footman. There, to her great mortification, she was stripped of her purloined wig and breeches, and forced back into her petticoat.

While his family summered in Twickenham that year, Colley worked on his latest play, an adaptation of Molière's *Tartuffe,* which he called *The Non-Juror.* It was a blatantly partisan play that attacked Tories, nonjurors (Jacobite clergymen who had refused to swear loyalty to William and Mary and their successors), and Catholics in what many felt to be an opportunistic and scurrilous way. Others, particularly the members of the ruling Whig party, found it to be a brave and accurate political statement, especially in the years immediately after the Jacobite rebellion of 1715, when political emotions ran high.

Upon its debut at Drury Lane in December 1717, *The Non-Juror* became a smashing success, running for sixteen consecutive nights and fanning the flames of partisan sentiment. Colley took the role of the villain, Dr. Wolf, who presents himself as a nonjuring Anglican clergyman,

From her early years, Charlotte exhibited the unmistakable symptoms of a highly theatrical sensibility. (F. Garden, Mrs. Charke walking in the Ditch at four Years of Age, *1755. Courtesy of the Department of Prints and Drawings, British Museum. Copyright British Museum 1851-2-8-180.)*

but at the end of the play is unmasked as an even greater monster: a Roman Catholic priest. When Colley later published the play, his dedication to the King proclaimed it the fruit of his patriotic duty to undermine the forces of repression—the "lurking Enemies of our Constitution"—that threatened English liberty. *The Non-Juror* earned Colley over £1,000, the patronage of King George, the gratitude of the Whigs, and the undying enmity of many Tories and the small, embattled population of British Roman Catholics (Alexander Pope among them). In an era of intensely divided party politics, Colley Cibber and Drury Lane Theatre were firmly identified with the Whig government.

The opposition, roiled into a frenzy of vituperation, struck back in newspapers and in pamphlets. One writer of doggerel charged him with sycophancy: "Fled is the Poet's *Rage,* and in its Place, / Stands smiling *Flatt'ry,* with her Harlot's Face."[1] Often accused of consorting with whores, Colley was now accused of being one.

His endurance of such poisonous attacks did not go unrewarded. As one of the first signs of his favour, King George ordered a series of command performances by the Drury Lane company at Hampton Court, to commence in September 1718. Command performances at court were a great honour but a mixed blessing, for the gratification of playing for a crowded house of courtiers was greatly lessened by their painful decorousness, which was exacerbated by the royal presence. Court etiquette dictated that those in the company of the king must preserve solemnity, so the atmosphere was particularly deadly to comedy. The courtly audience could do little more than crack a smile, a far cry from the laughter (or tears) and vociferous applause dear to the hearts of actors. The King himself, though he was willing to patronize the theatre, could do little to set an example of appreciation for a playwright's worthy sentiment or an actor's witty ad-lib, since he did not know English.

But the area around Hampton Court was a delicious summertime retreat. Its riverside setting, its lakes, fountains, and canal, its ample hunting grounds, and its extensive gardens had made it a favoured resort of successions of royal families. The Cibbers could claim their own familial connection to the place, for Caius Gabriel Cibber had executed statuary there. Like his father, Colley had reached the height of professional success signified by a royal commission.

The Cibbers took up residence in nearby Hampton Town early in the summer, enabling Colley to supervise the preparations for the upcoming performances. That summer their immediate family circle was lessened by one, for seventeen-year-old Elizabeth Cibber had married Dawson Brett the previous spring.[2]

When members of the royal family were in residence—the King arrived in the middle of August, and was often joined of an evening by the Princess of Wales—they brought with them flocks of courtiers and court ladies (and scores of servants and tradespeople to supply their needs).[3] Charlotte was five; this courtly presence must have sparked her imagination. Hearing strains of music in the distance, she would run to watch the banner-bedecked barges float by, carrying parties of lords and ladies. She would gaze enraptured as handsome carriages festooned with footmen in colourful livery rumbled by on the country roads, offering glimpses of elegant passengers venturing forth to take the air.

On occasion her parents must have taken her to Hampton Court itself, where members of the royal household strolled in the shaded walks of the great gardens that ran down to the water's edge. There Colley could proudly have pointed out the exquisite marble urns, standing on their stone pedestals, that her grandfather had sculpted. Charlotte might have even glimpsed the reclusive King himself, surrounded by his attendants.

In the spirit of imitation and self-exhibition that had motivated her the previous summer, Charlotte found inspiration in her new setting. Following standard medical advice of the time, Katherine was building her strength against asthma by drinking ass's milk, considered to be a particularly nourishing and effective way to eliminate faulty humours. The lactating ass, a kind of equine wet-nurse, had one foal "about the Height of a sizeable Greyhound." As Charlotte eyed the baby ass, remembering the stylish ladies she had admired, "I immediately formed a Resolution of following the Fashion of taking the Air early next Morning." Like royalty, Charlotte wanted to appear with a retinue: she would script a performance for an entire company.

Charlotte readily recruited "a small Troop of young Gentlemen and Ladies, whose low Births and adverse States rendered it entirely convenient for them to come into any Scheme, *Miss Charlotte Cibber* could possibly propose." The children enthusiastically threw themselves into their assigned roles as stablehands and attendants. Off they all ran to the field where the asses were grazing. Charlotte wished to use her mother's saddle, but the other children pointed out that the tiny foal would scarcely be able to carry it. And when they tried to fasten her mother's bridle to the little animal, "the Head of the Fole [*sic*] being so very small, the Trappings fell off as fast as they strove to put them on." One of the children ingeniously hit upon the solution of using their garters as reins. Charlotte was able to mount the little ass in style.

Here was a scene to rival anything the court could produce. "I rode triumphantly into Town astride, with a numerous Retinue, whose Huzzas were drown'd by the dreadful Braying of the tender Dam, who pursued us with agonizing Sounds of Sorrow, for her oppress'd young one." Another child added to the cacophony by sawing at a twelve-penny fiddle Charlotte had been inspired to provide "to add to the Dignity and Grandeur of this extraordinary Enterprize."

Inside the house, Charlotte's father was distracted from his writing by the clamour outside. Stepping to the window, Colley gazed upon the spectacle as Charlotte and her entourage paraded before him. Proudly, but anxiously, too, she scrutinized her father to gauge her effect: "I perfectly remember, young as I was then, the strong Mixture of Surprise, Pleasure, Pain, and Shame in his Countenance, on his viewing me seated on my infantical *Rosinante*." The actor in Colley was highly entertained; the father in him was appalled. They were, after all, in the vicinity of the Court. However mortified, Colley Cibber was never at a loss for an oath or a witticism. "Gad demme!" he exclaimed. "An Ass upon an Ass!"

Once again, Charlotte had succeeded in focusing all eyes upon herself; once again, those eyes included her father's. And once again, as Colley must have recognized, his daughter's performance verged on parody of himself. Even at age five, Charlotte, with her comically grandiose display, succeeded in capturing something fundamental about her father's foppish persona. Perhaps Colley's ambivalent response revealed his discomfort at seeing his daughter so skilfully imitate him.

As always when dealing with Charlotte's childhood antics, Colley left the actual discipline to Katherine, who acted with unusual force, pulling Charlotte from the foal and whipping her with a birch in front of the other children. Then she marched her daughter into the house and leashed her by a string to a table leg. Charlotte was outraged. "'Tis not to be conceived, the violent Indignation and Contempt my Disgrace rais'd in my Infant-Breast; nor did I forgive my Mother, in my Heart, for six Months after, tho' I was oblig'd to ask Pardon in a few Moments of her, who, at that Time, I conceiv'd to be most in Fault."

Drury Lane's 1718–19 season proved almost as much of a headache for Colley as the year before, as he continued to endure abuse generated by

The Non-Juror, even though Drury Lane only performed it once that season. Denunciations fastened upon whatever weakness his enemies could detect (or invent); they ranged from attacks on his acting and literary abilities to charges of dissipation and selfish treatment of his family. Cibber's penchant for gambling in the company of his rich friends particularly opened him to accusations of negligence and hypocrisy. In 1707, he had premiered a comedy, *The Lady's Last Stake,* which, he later wrote in the preface, was intended to expose the dangers of gambling. But, once again, Colley had used his play to preach what he did not practise, and his warning focused on the dangers of gambling to *women,* whose debts might lead them to compromise their honour. Like his visits to brothels, the play provided his enemies with ammunition they did not hesitate to use.

An anonymous letter published in Mist's *Weekly Journal* accused Colley of negligence and greed in gambling away his income at the expense of his young daughter—Charlotte, now six years old—whom he shamefully forced to dress in rags. Furthermore, the writer claimed, when members of the Drury Lane company came to her relief with a benefit performance, Colley appropriated the proceeds: "the other Masters of the Play-House, seeing his Daughter very bare in Cloaths, kindly offered him a private Benefit for her; and I am credibly informed, that it amounted to fourscore Pounds, which this unhuman Father, rather than let his Child have Necessaries, made away with also."[4]

The actor and theatre historian Tom Davies said that when Colley lost money at gambling, he would exclaim, "Now I must go home and eat a child!"[5] But there is no more evidence that Charlotte was forced to dress in rags as a girl than that she was served up for supper. On the contrary, she repeatedly referred to her childhood as secure and indulged. Colley loved gaming, but his family did not suffer privations on account of it.

In June 1719, having weathered another year of political vituperation, Colley must have been relieved to escape London for the summer. This year, the Cibbers chose Richmond as their resort. Just across the river from their former haunts in Twickenham, Richmond—with its ruins of the medieval royal palace; its wild, vast deer park with its manor house; and its handsome village green, around which stately houses were being constructed—offered the necessary enticements of trees, river, and mineral wells. This location also satisfied Colley's social aspirations, for it was another popular resort of royalty, the summer court of the Prince and Princess of Wales. Other members of the social elite (known in that revealing eighteenth-century shorthand as "the Quality") also kept houses there. In the summers, observed Daniel Defoe, Richmond attracted "a great deal of the best company in England," a company "shining and sometimes even illustriously bright."[6]

The prince and princess were more lively and sociable, more engaged in English cultural life, than the dour King. George I and his heir enjoyed a relationship of mutual antipathy, the King viewing the prince as a predator awaiting his death in order to pounce upon the throne, and the prince resenting his father's imprisonment of his mother, Sophia Dorothea. As a result, the two royal households constituted rival courts, where scandal and intrigue flourished. But unlike the King, who patronized the theatre more for the sake of political expediency and out of a sense of duty than from real interest, the prince and princess were genuine patrons who attended Drury Lane and the other theatres frequently.

There was a sizeable theatrical presence in Richmond during the summer. The previous year, a member of the Drury Lane troupe, the whimsical Will "Pinky" Penkethman, famed for his low comic roles and his ungovernable tendency to ad-lib on stage, had begun his own summer company at the theatre he had converted from a stable for asses. Penkethman had originated the role of Snap the randy servant in Colley's first play, *Love's Last Shift*. He brought with him to Richmond several of the Drury Lane troupe, and on opening night, in honour of his new venue, he spoke the prologue sitting on an ass.[7] Although Colley was not formally connected with the Richmond company—his salary was large enough to allow him to spend the summers writing rather than acting—certainly the society of his Drury Lane associates was another part of the town's appeal as a summer resort.

Charlotte's public whipping in Hampton the year before had done little to diminish her spirit or arrest her precocity. Now, at six years old, she possessed an active imagination and an indomitable will. Summertime acted as a spur to her imagination. The safety of the country community allowed the indulged little girl to run outdoors with relatively little supervision. Free to exercise her talents for mischief, Charlotte could concoct her schemes and, with the assistance of the inevitable troupe of local children, put them into action.

Charlotte's upbringing was lax by eighteenth-century standards for a girl of her class. Her father's absence from the house and her mother's frequent illnesses and mild temperament left the girl without consistent supervision except for the limited authority of servants. Most likely she encountered little interference with her games. As Charlotte grew older, the consequences of her licence began to manifest themselves in what she later called "strange, mad pranks" less benign than her odd but essentially harmless earlier performances. That summer in Richmond, Charlotte would demonstrate a new, more complex dimension of her talents.

One day, while off on her own as usual, Charlotte encountered a "cross old woman" to whom she apparently did or said something—she never revealed what—that provoked the woman to "beat" her. Later, Charlotte implied that the woman, who seemed "old" to a six-year-old, was ill-tempered by nature, poorly prepared to tolerate a saucy youngster. Of course, it may well have been Charlotte's egregious behaviour that made this woman cross. Whatever the incitement, the pampered child was unused to such punishment. The beating was not serious enough to do any damage, but it did raise Charlotte's ire. Not easily cowed, she vowed to avenge this insult to her dignity.

She assembled a group of the neighbourhood children and gave them their instructions: they were to steal the old woman's caps and linens that were hanging out to dry, then send them floating down a nearby stream that emptied into the Thames. Though childish, this was not a negligible revenge: the loss of such an expensive commodity as linen could have been a severe blow. Though Charlotte was motivated by petulance rather than by viciousness, this was one time in which her youthful disregard of consequences may have injured someone other than herself. The adult Charlotte called this episode the "only piece of malice" that she perpetrated as a child. But regrets came later. At the time, while her cohorts carried out their mission, innocent-faced Charlotte strolled in the family's parlour, "secretly pleased with the thoughts of my revenge." Her retribution was no less satisfying for being secret.

The 1719–20 theatre season brought new controversy to Drury Lane. Political conflicts between Drury Lane's patentee (still Sir Richard Steele) and the lord chamberlain (the Duke of Newcastle) escalated. At one point, the duke struck at the company by forbidding Colley to act and serve as manager, then had him imprisoned briefly, and then shut the playhouse down altogether. Finally, Newcastle offered Colley, Wilks, and Booth a licence to perform in their own names, excluding Steele (who still held the patent); they agreed reluctantly and took the loyalty oath he required, though under protest.

This crisis produced its inevitable pamphlet war. The powerful critic John Dennis, who bore a personal grudge against Colley for having bungled, he thought, the staging of an unsuccessful play Dennis had written, accused him anonymously of rather wild depredations: "It is credibly reported, that he spit on the Face of our Saviour's picture at the Bath [the resort town], with words too execrable and too horrible to be repeated."

Dennis also repeated the accusation that Colley neglected his family. Cibber, he ranted, "has neither Tenderness for his Wife, or natural Affection for his Children, nor any sympathizing regard for the rest of Men. He has, in the Compass of two Years, squander'd away Six Thousand Pounds at the *Groom Porter's* [a gambling club], without making the least Provision for either his Wife or his Children."[8] Colley, guessing who was responsible, felt stung enough to make the rhetorical gesture of offering a £10 reward for the slanderer's identity.

Again, there is no credible evidence that Colley failed to provide for his family, while all the evidence we have indicates that his penchant for gambling never compromised his care of them.[9] He seems to have taken to heart the lesson of his father's example.

Late in the summer of 1720 (or early in 1721), Colley moved his family to a new and better house.[10] Geographically, they did not move far, though seven-year-old Charlotte must have experienced leaving the home of her infancy as a disruption, albeit an exciting one. Number 3 Charles Street (now Upper Wellington Street) was also in Covent Garden, two blocks east of their former residence in Southampton Street West. Drury Lane Theatre was just one block farther east.

Colley would live in this house for the next twenty years, years that would encompass the marriages of his children, his elevation to the laureateship, his retirement from the theatre, and Katherine's death. Though Charlotte would spend more of her later childhood at school or in the country than in this house, 3 Charles Street was to develop a particular significance in her story. It was her London family home. From this house she would leave when she married, and to this house she would return in the years following to visit, show off her infant daughter, complain about her husband, mourn her mother, and beg money and favours from her family.

And from this house, fifteen years after the family moved there, her father would banish her.

∗ 4 ∗

EDUCATING CHARLOTTE

(1720–27)

Charlotte's Covent Garden was a far cry from the exclusive enclave originally envisioned by the fourth Earl of Bedford, who developed the district in the mid-seventeenth century, and his architect, Inigo Jones. Even at the height of the district's fashionableness, elite residents shared their neighbourhood with actors, artists, dressmakers, tailors, carriage makers, and stoneworkers (including Charlotte's grandfather Caius Gabriel) tucked away in the adjoining side streets and courts. The district's coffeehouses were known as places where men could, at least nominally, shed distinctions of rank, where aristocrats and gentlemen took their places on the rough benches beside silversmiths and mercers to engage in conversation and political debate.

Wealthy householders also shared their public space with the vendors of the fruit and vegetable market, who supplied their tables but also crowded the square with wagons, sheds, and piles of rotting produce. The Drury Lane Theatre brought to the neighbourhood raffish actors and musicians and their audiences, who often stayed on after the performances to seek out food, drink, and revelry. The presence of the playhouse fostered other forms of entertainment, too, ranging from the relatively respectable to the illicit. Taverns, bathhouses, brothels, and gambling dens dotted the surrounding streets, and prostitutes plied their trade even in the square itself, lingering in the shadows of the arcades fronting the wealthy houses. (One satirist dubbed Covent Garden the "Grand Seraglio to the Nation.")[1] These activities became particularly concentrated as one approached the district's easternmost boundary, Drury Lane.

By the time Charlotte moved with her family to Charles Street, Covent Garden had lost much of its cachet among the Quality in favour of the new, more exclusive developments in Bloomsbury, Soho, and St. James's. Some genteel residents did retain a foothold in the neighbourhood, and the area still contained substantial middle-class and artisan populations, but other pockets—and much of St. Giles to the north—were squalid slums. In the eighteenth century, according to one modern historian, "Covent Garden and its surroundings . . . contained then some of the worst social conditions London has ever known."[2] Covent Garden had already acquired the notoriety that would make it a byword for poverty, drunkenness, violence, gambling, and prostitution for the next two hundred years.

One of the Cibbers' immediate neighbours included Elizabeth Hay-

Charlotte's London was a metropolis where high spirits overflowed. (Anon., A Drunken Riot in Covent Garden, 1735. Courtesy of the Guildhall Library, Corporation of London.)

ward, the former proprietor of the King's Head tavern on adjoining Russell Street, a notorious brothel and gaming house. In March 1721, Mother Hayward and her husband, Richard, were sentenced to serve a prison term and stand in the stocks for "evil activities." Upon their release, they promptly opened a bagnio on Charles Street, probably right across from the Cibber residence, and carried on their trade. It was a prosperous enterprise, with a well-heeled clientele: at her death in 1743, Mother Hayward was said to have amassed a fortune of £10,000.[3]

Venturing outside for an airing or perhaps accompanying a servant to the market, driving in a coach to and from school, travelling to the Cibbers' country house, or walking over to Drury Lane, Charlotte would have glimpsed elegantly dressed ladies and gentlemen, even the Prince and Princess of Wales, descending from their coaches to enter the Theatre Royal; and she would have seen famous wits, writers, and politicians emerging from the coffeehouse doors, still engaged in animated debate. She would have passed silversmiths and coach makers at work in their shops, while servants went about their domestic errands and ladies shopped for kid gloves. Charlotte also would have seen prostitutes soliciting their customers, drunks staggering out of a tavern, angry men erupting into blows, boisterous playgoers leaving the theatre with orange-women in tow, and packs of dangerous young rowdies cruising the streets.

Charlotte's formal education, such as it was, began when she was about eight years old. Sometime in the early 1720s, most likely in autumn, 1721, her parents enrolled Charlotte in a boarding school run by a Mrs. Draper in Park Street, Westminster.

Why her parents decided to send Charlotte to board at a school not far from the family house is unclear; Katherine's health may have had something to do with it. We have no indication whether Charlotte's sisters had also gone away to school, but it is unlikely that the Cibbers would have been able to afford the fees when Catherine and Anne were young. Charlotte's older brother, Theophilus (unlike his father), had been able to benefit from the family connection to Winchester College, but he was privileged as the only son. Whatever the reason, her education at Mrs. Draper's school would only reinforce the distinction between Charlotte and her sisters.

Charlotte left no account of her feelings upon this first separation from her family, but she could have seen her mother regularly. She also said nothing about the other students, about how she was accepted, whether she became a ringleader or a wallflower. (With her energy and charisma, the former is more likely.) If she was mocked or shunned for her theatre connections, she never mentioned it. Possibly, as was often the case in boarding schools of the time, the girls were encouraged to stage amateur theatricals. If so, Charlotte would have been in her element.

No information seems to survive about Mrs. Draper's school in particular, but John Strype's description of such educational establishments would certainly apply: "There be also in and about the City, Schools for the Education of young Gentlewomen in good and graceful Carriage, Dancing, Singing, playing on Instruments of Musick; in Reading, Writing, speaking *French,* raising Paste [that is, making bread or pastry dough], &c. which render Women, that have these commendable Qualifications, so much beyond others in their Behaviour, Conversation, and good Housewifery."[4] For most of its pupils, Mrs. Draper's academy must have resembled that "real, honest, old-fashioned Boarding-school" run by Mrs. Godard in Jane Austen's *Emma,* "where a reasonable quantity of accomplishments were sold at a reasonable price, and where girls might be sent to be out of the way and scramble themselves into a little education, without any danger of coming back prodigies."

Contemporary critics belittled girls' schools; the *Spectator* (no. 36) ran a mock advertisement promising to teach "all Sorts of Birds of the loquacious Kind"—parrots, starlings, and magpies—to utter "all the fashionable Phrases and Compliments now in use either at Tea Tables or visiting Days." The parody had a point: these schools focused more on the body and on polite accomplishments than on the mind. Their model of female excellence was a woman who could move gracefully, dance well, and engage in light conversation without awkward silences or, even worse, opinions. Such a woman could entertain the company with a song in English, French, or Italian, accompanying herself at the keyboard. She painted a little in watercolours, wrote a legible hand, and might have a taste for poetry, certainly for novels. She knew how to make preserves and embroider cushion covers. In her two years with Mrs. Draper, Charlotte picked up a few of these accomplishments: she learned to dance, sing, and write a good hand. At housewifery, however, she failed abysmally. She handled her needle, she said, "with the same clumsy awkwardness a monkey does a kitten."

Despite—or because of—her domestic ineptitude, Charlotte *was* in danger of coming back a prodigy, for Mrs. Draper, whom Charlotte found to be "a Woman of great Sense and Abilities," allowed her an education that "might have been sufficient for a Son instead of a Daughter." Her language tutor, M. Flahaut, finding his pupil already adept in French, received her mother's permission to teach Charlotte not only Italian but also Latin—a boy's subject.

In general, it was considered inappropriate to give girls the classical education deemed essential for their brothers. Latin was the preserve of elite boys' schools and the universities, a marker of gender and class privilege; knowledge of it rendered women indelicate. Charlotte's father and brother had studied Latin as a matter of course. Now, just as she had once appropriated Theo's waistcoat and Colley's wig, Charlotte took up their masculine education.

Enjoying his star pupil's intelligence (as well as the extra income he earned from these lessons), the intrepid M. Flauhaut next requested permission to teach Charlotte geography. While less exclusively masculine than classical languages, geography was nonetheless another subject unusual in girls' education. As an adult, Charlotte said of geography, a little ruefully, "I cannot think it was altogether necessary for a Female," but as a schoolgirl she embraced it wholeheartedly, "delighted at being thought a learned Person." The learned persons of her day, of course, were almost all men. To make herself one of them, Charlotte flung herself into the study of geography with a total absorption bordering upon obsession: "The vast Application to my Study almost distracted me [drove her insane], from a violent Desire I had to make myself perfect Mistress of it." Charlotte pored over her geography books and two globes, celestial and terrestrial, borrowed from her uncle John Shore.

The image of study producing an obsession that bordered on madness was a stereotypical characterization of learned women. Female brains being too weak to sustain rigorous intellectual effort, it was popularly held, women who attempted it either became impossibly affected and conceited or they went mad—or both. Gossip, literature, and advice books abounded with cautionary examples of insane or ludicrous learned women, such as the notorious "Mad Madge" (Margaret

Cavendish, the Duchess of Newcastle, an eccentric but brilliant and original thinker). A variation on this theme was seen at Drury Lane's premiere, in 1721, of *The Refusal,* a play by Colley Cibber.[5]

Colley had lost a considerable sum in one of the biggest financial scandals of the eighteenth century, the stock market crash centering around the South Sea Company. The inflated stock and reports of huge returns on investments of this trading company had driven a mania of speculation during the second decade of the century; the bubble burst in 1720, ruining thousands of investors. Colley wrote *The Refusal* to help recoup his losses and to satirize the speculation mania and greed that produced the debacle. (The play was disrupted by Colley's enemies and ran only five nights.) Its domestic plot features a Latin-spouting mother and daughter, whose intellectual airs disguise their shared inter-est in the romantic hero, Frankley. Frankley, however, is in love with the younger daughter, who, unlike her mother and sister, remains unspoiled by intellectual pretensions. Ironically enough, the younger daughter's name is Charlotte. (Her mother and sister plot to marry her off to an egregious fop she hates—Witling, played by Colley—but she foils their attempts.) *The Refusal* echoes conventional notions that learning in a woman—as indicated by her ability to quote Latin—makes her silly, though the play stops short of claiming that it makes her mad.

In practice, a girl permitted to explore subjects such as Latin and geography might find herself frustrated by her introduction to a realm that she would most likely never be allowed to enter. As M. Flauhaut's zealous pupil, Charlotte discovered the life of the mind as privileged boys did, who might choose to devote themselves to a scholarly career. In her study of geography, her imagination was cast wide, out into the world where boys, as naval officers, might venture to other lands or, as merchants, engage in foreign trade. Though she was ultimately too rest-less to become a scholar, thus escaping the stigma of the *femme savante,* Charlotte was destined to become a wanderer. The precocious girl imag-inatively circumnavigating the globe anticipated the outcast woman who would roam southern England and Wales. Charlotte felt that her education gave her "a different Turn of Mind than what I might have had, if my Time had been employ'd in ornamenting a Piece of Canvas with Beasts, Birds, and the Alphabet." That different turn of mind pro-vided, for better and for worse, the impetus of her extraordinary career.

In the spring of 1723, Charlotte returned to Charles Street, where she finished her schooling with the aid of masters. She continued her language study (though apparently not her geography) with her admirable M. Flauhaut. Her music education was originally monitored by the elderly Dr. King, former Composer in Ordinary to William and Mary, then by Anthony Young, the organist of St. Clement Danes church. The "celebrated Mr. Gasconet" was her dancing master.

Charlotte received this unusual education because her affectionate parents indulged their youngest child, omitting nothing, she said, "that could improve any natural Talents Heaven had been pleased to endow me with." But they may have had a more pragmatic consideration in mind, too. Charlotte's instruction in the pronunciation of foreign languages, singing, and dancing was comparable to that of many well-to-do girls whose marriage prospects depended upon their mastery of polite accomplishments. But these were also necessary skills for an actress: Charlotte was given an education that could help prepare her for a stage career.

Charlotte's return to the Charles Street house must have been a thrilling improvement upon the claustrophobia of boarding school. Besides affording opportunities to venture over to the theatre, the house itself would have seen constant activity as Colley, his well-born friends, and members of the Drury Lane company came and went. Charlotte would have been surrounded by some of the biggest names in the theatre world. Colley's co-managers, Robert Wilks and Barton Booth, must have been frequent visitors. Hot-tempered and driven, Wilks was temperamentally at odds with Colley, who often felt the brunt of his fellow manager's temper yet managed to work well with him for over twenty years. To Charlotte, the tall, handsome Irishman would have been a charismatic figure comparable to the romantic heroes he played on the stage.

The well-born, graceful Booth, who lived just next door, had been intended for the clergy but had run off to Ireland to be an actor; he was best known for playing tragic heroes. Mrs. Booth, formerly Hester Santlow, a fine actress and a splendid dancer once notorious for promiscuity but now happily married to Barton, would also have been familiar to Charlotte. So would Mary Porter, a spirited, kind-hearted woman celebrated as a tragedienne, as well as Anne Oldfield, Drury Lane's captivating female star.

All of these people must have been both glamorous and familiar figures in Charlotte's eyes; she must have had opportunity to see them
onstage, too, in rehearsals if not in actual performances. They must
have provided rich material for her role-playing, particularly Wilks and
Booth.

At Charles Street, Charlotte also had more opportunities to see her
brother than ever before. Theophilus was now a member of the Drury
Lane company. Too slight of build and too pockmarked of face to play
romantic or tragic roles convincingly, he was developing as a skilful
comic actor; like his father he was talented enough to make a virtue out
of necessity (though, also like his father, he would grab these unsuitable
roles whenever he could). Rakish, arrogant, and intemperate, rapidly
earning a reputation for debauchery, Theo was nonetheless a serious
actor, dedicated to his profession. Perhaps this is the point at which
Charlotte began to identify with her brother, attracted to both his professionalism and his wildness.

Charlotte's exposure to the exciting milieu in Charles Street was
short-lived, however. Katherine, increasingly plagued by illness, could
no longer bear to live in the city. Colley had taken a long-term lease on
a summer house in the country village of Hillingdon, outside Uxbridge,
northwest of London. At the end of the summer of 1723, Katherine did
not accompany her husband back to London.

She had few maternal duties to call her back to town: most of her
children had already left the house. The previous February, Catherine
had married, very well indeed. Her husband, Lieutenant Colonel James
Brown, was the son of a wealthy businessman; Catherine's new
brother-in-law, Robert Brown, had made a fortune as a merchant
banker in Venice, and later served as Sir Robert Walpole's money manager and received a knighthood; his wife was a member of the illustrious Cecil family and a notable patron of the arts.[6] Elizabeth, who now
had a daughter, had rather surprisingly begun a stage career in 1721;
her husband's financial troubles may have been a precipitating factor,
since Elizabeth had shown no earlier inclination for acting. Theophilus
was becoming professionally well established. Anne, who alone of the
other children probably continued to reside in the Charles Street house,
had established an independent career for herself selling tea and gro-
ceries in a London shop.

It would have been possible for Colley to move to Hillingdon with his ailing wife, but it would not have been practicable, for it would have entailed a long commute on isolated rural roads where highwaymen lurked. So, while he probably made brief visits, Colley lived principally in the Charles Street house, where he was close to Drury Lane and had the social life he craved. Probably with Anne as her nominal guardian, Charlotte returned to Covent Garden that autumn to finish her lessons. Sharing a house with her father must have delighted her, but she had little time to concoct new schemes to force his attention. The following winter, when she was eleven, her formal education of less than three years ended, and Colley sent her to live with her mother in Hillingdon.

The country in the winter was not nearly as appealing to a restless girl as it was in the summer. Buried in the provinces, Charlotte would have been keenly aware that London's winter social season was in full swing. However, isolation in the company of her loving mother, who was often confined to bed, had the advantage of offering freedom to roam and play imaginary parts. With no other candidates in the offing, Charlotte could cast herself as man of the house, and continue, self-directed, her unconventional education. Now, in the place of Latin and geography, Charlotte took up a new set of enthusiasms: horses and guns.

In the autumn, the woods around Hillingdon rang with gunshots as shooting parties took their sport. In her father's absence, Charlotte could play the country squire. She acquired a carbine and schooled herself in this new role with the same determination she had earlier brought to the study of geography. She became a creditable shot, filled with pride at her ability as a marksman and at bringing home game. Her mother, perhaps too ill to notice, or perhaps pleased that her daughter had found a diverting occupation with useful consequences for the dinner table, did nothing to stop her.

Illness, however, did. Sometime during her first winter in Hillingdon, perhaps as a consequence of tramping around the sodden fields with her gun, Charlotte contracted a "fever." (In an age without antibiotics or other effective drugs, these were often fatal.) Katherine, who had had so much experience with the deaths of children, feared for her daughter's life. Charlotte survived, but her illness seems to have forced Katherine to confront her inability to impose discipline, alarming her about her daughter's indifference to feminine domestic interests. So when Charlotte was no longer in danger, Katherine sent her to her relatives in eastern Hertfordshire, about fifty miles away. This, she hoped, not only would restore the girl's health, but also teach her to become "a good housewife—in which needful accomplishment," Charlotte said, "my mind was entirely uncultivated."

Katherine's relative Dr. William Hales, son of an Essex clergyman, lived with his wife, Elizabeth, at Twyford House in the village of Thorley, located just outside of Bishops Stortford in the rolling hills of east Hertfordshire, close to the Essex border.[7] Dr. Hales, as a physician, could monitor Charlotte's health, and his wife and two sweet-natured daughters, well versed in feminine domestic accomplishments, would become her new teachers.

Sending a child off to live, temporarily or even permanently, with others, often relatives, was not unusual. (Charlotte's sister Elizabeth had spent several of her childhood years living with her childless uncle and aunt, William and Rose Shore, who became very attached to her and left her a substantial inheritance, which Colley appropriated for the use of his entire family.) But Charlotte must have suffered: any visits home would have required one or two days' travel over England's tortuous, unpaved provincial roads, and it is quite possible that she did not see her family at all during her stay there. The Haleses offered Charlotte a consistency of companionship unlikely to be available from her invalid mother, however. They welcomed her kindly and set about her education. It could not have taken them long to realize the magnitude of their task.

Models of domestic middle-class feminine industry, the Hales women spent their time in embroidery, upholstery, the making of preserves, and conversation. Charlotte found in them everything she did *not* want to be. These women could not curry a horse, much less race one. They spent their days "ornamenting a well-dispos'd, elegant Table" and "poring over a Piece of Embroidery, or a well-wrought Chair." Charlotte pitied their boring lives, and indulged a feeling of "inward Contempt" that these insipid occupations contented them.

Spurning all domestic employment, Charlotte spent her days ensconced in the stable. "Many and vain Attempts were used, to bring me into their [the women's] Working-Community," but she remained impervious to their appeals and arguments. "If all the Fine-Works in the Family had been in the Fire," she said, "I should not have forsook the Curry-comb, to have endeavoured to save 'em from the utmost Destruction." To their credit, the Haleses, failing to persuade her to leave the stables, did not resort to force. In fact, they gave her a little horse for her own use.

Charlotte did find a member of the Hales family worth emulating, however—Dr. Hales, who seems to have welcomed her as an apprentice of sorts, sending her to visit his patients (most likely the poorer ones) to check upon their progress. This gave her, she said, "a most pleasing opportunity of fancying myself a physician." Affecting the "solemnity and gravity" of Dr. Hales, Charlotte succeeded in convincing some of his more impressionable patients that she was a worthy surrogate of the doctor. She also convinced herself.

Charlotte's residence with the Hales family lasted for two years until 1726, when Mrs. Hales died. Whatever grief Charlotte felt for the loss of this kind, generous woman, it was accompanied by a sense of gain, for she was sent back to Hillingdon and her mother.

If Katherine had cherished any illusions about her kinsfolk's success in domesticating Charlotte, they were shattered by her daughter's return. Charlotte remained indifferent to the arts and responsibilities of conventional feminine life. But she was a bolder horsewoman than ever before, and she could curry a horse as well as the most experienced groom. She also fancied herself a doctor. During the next two years, Charlotte threw herself into a remarkable set of self-scripted performances. Once again, all the roles she undertook were male.

Persuading her mother to allow her the use of a small room in an unused part of the house for her "Dispensary," Charlotte spread the news among "all the old women in the parish" that she was setting up a medical practice. With a few phrases of Latin remembered from her schooling, a small collection of medical books culled from the family library, and a stock of remedies secured from an apothecary's widow in Uxbridge, Charlotte presented herself to her rustic patients as a convincing simulacrum of a doctor.

The apothecary's widow, assuming that Charlotte's orders were sanctioned by her parents, extended her credit. Returning home with a "cargo of combustibles, which were sufficient to have set up a montebank for a twelvemonth," Charlotte found her stock rapidly depleted as her practice grew. The locals quickly realized that "Dr. Charlotte" was dispensing medicines for free, and accordingly "began to fancy themselves ill because they knew they could have physic for nothing, such as it was." Since her formula medicines were probably laced with opium, the demand is understandable. Laudanum, a tincture of opium dissolved in alcohol, was a "very popular prescription, very much the aspirin of the period." A concoction such as "Dr. Sydenham's laudanum" (widely marketed a little later in the century), consisted of "2 oz. Strained opium, 1 oz. saffron, 1 drachma each of cinnamon and cloves in a pint of canary wine."[8] It was undoubtedly efficacious.

Charlotte's practice received a setback when the apothecary's widow sent her father a bill. Colley, who had been unaware that he had a doctor in the family, paid and immediately shut down Charlotte's line of credit. But he underestimated his daughter's resourcefulness.

When an elderly woman came to her with rheumatism and a stomachache, Charlotte ground up a quantity of snails with some brown sugar and distilled them into a syrup, prescribing one spoonful every two hours. She mashed together more snails, green herbs, and mutton fat as an ointment. She packaged these concoctions in vials bearing her own labels— Charlotte had an eye for the telling detail—and handed them over, along with bottles of sal volatile and hartshorn stolen from her mother.

Charlotte's remedies were less peculiar than they sound to modern ears: many recipes using snails could be found in the medical and cookery books of the time. A formula for "Dr. M——'s Snail Water" (Dr. Richard Mead was one of London's most eminent physicians) instructed: "Take Garden-Snails cleansed and bruised 6 Gallons, Earth-worms washed and bruised 3 Gallons, of common Wormwood, Ground-Ivy, and Carduus, each one Pound and half, Penniroyal, Juniper-Berries, Fennel-seeds, Aniseeds, each half a Pound, Cloves and Cubebs bruised, each 3 Ounces, Spirit of Wine, and Spring-water, of each 8 Gallons; digest them together for the Space of 24 Hours, and then draw it off in a common Alembick." The result was "as good a Snail-water as can be made."[9]

It was not unusual for a woman to develop a far-reaching reputation for her cures—there was, for instance, the celebrated (and wonderfully named) Mrs. Plunkett Edgcumbe, who advertised her success at curing cancer. More locally, a parish lady or gentleman might routinely treat family, servants, and the surrounding communities: "Gentry, ladies bountiful and clergymen commonly laid claims to pharmaceutical knowledge and kept a medicine chest open to the parish poor."[10] However, at age fourteen, Charlotte—who later described herself at this period as a Lady Bountiful (a character in George Farquhar's comedy *The Beaux' Stratagem*; Charlotte's allusions were invariably theatrical)—was a bit young for the position.

When her snail supply dried up (and her memory of Dr. Hales waned), Charlotte found inspiration for role-playing elsewhere. To her old interests in guns and horses she now added gardening. At some point, presumably during the summer, Colley travelled to France. During his absence, the servant who combined the duties of gardener and groom got drunk and verbally abused the other servants, then insulted Katherine when she intervened. Katherine fired him and advertised for a new groom-gardener. Charlotte promptly seized her opportunity, and stood guard at the gate in order to turn away applicants, telling them that her father had already hired someone in Paris. Then she assumed the positions herself.

Charlotte's new duties represented actual occupations less than they did characters: "I thought it always proper," she explained, "to imitate the Actions of those Persons, whose Characters I chose to represent; and, indeed, was as changeable as Proteus." Though these roles included duties that required genuine labour, Charlotte worked even harder at making her interpretation of the role convincing. After a morning's work in the garden, "a broiled Rasher of Bacon upon a Luncheon of Bread in one Hand, and a Pruning-Knife in the other," she made "Seeds and Plants the general Subject of my Discourse." After a few hours spent in the stable, she would stomp into the house, heave a halter and a horse blanket onto a chair, and, with "a Shrug of the Shoulders and a Scratch of the Head, with a hasty Demand for Small-Beer," she would exclaim: "God bless you make haste, I have not a single Horse dressed or watered, and here 'tis almost Eight o-Clock, the poor Cattle will think I've forgot 'em; and Tomorrow they go a Journey, I'm sure I'd need take Care of 'em."

Charlotte's performances of these roles negotiated between her mother and her absent father. While she strove to impress her mother, to "convince her of the Utility of so industrious a Child," she strove to *replace* her father, and more generally to compensate for the lack of a masculine presence in the house. (Not only was there no paterfamilias, there seems not even to have been a male servant once the drunken groom-gardener was dismissed.) Charlotte conflated all these male roles, filling in, taking charge.

But her performances were not free of danger. When someone thought she spied the fired groom-gardener lurking around the house, Charlotte gathered the plate and all the family's firearms in her bedroom and stood guard at the window overnight. Upon hearing a dog bark, she "fir'd out of the Window Piece after Piece, re-charging as fast as possible, 'till I had consumed about a Pound of Powder, and a proportionable Quantity of Shot and Balls," terrifying her mother. (The supposed prowler was discovered the next morning to have left for London long before.)

Unsurprisingly, a "strait-lac'd, old-fashion'd" neighbour complained that having Charlotte shooting at everything that moved was both unsettling and downright improper, "as she really thought it inconsistent with the Character of a young Gentlewoman to follow such Diversions." Forced to respond, Katherine stripped Charlotte of her carbine. Outraged, Charlotte stole the muscatoon that hung over the kitchen fireplace, marched to the neighbouring property, and tried to shoot down the complainer's chimneys. Fortunately, chimneys and neighbour survived unscathed.

Charlotte's role-playing soon resulted in a close brush with disaster, however. One day when Katherine was particularly ill in bed, Charlotte took it upon herself to test a horse that was offered for sale in Uxbridge, having heard her father say, before leaving for France, that he intended to buy a new chaise horse. Since she was often seen driving her father's horses, the owner allowed her to drive this one, despite the fact that it was unbroken. Setting out in the chaise upon Uxbridge Common, the horse took the bit and, Charlotte said, "dragg'd me and the Chaise over Hills and Dales, with such Vehemence, I despaired of ever seeing *Hillingdon* again." The animal finally bolted for home, but as Charlotte careered down the road, she ran over a three-year-old boy who was playing there. The child had been lying in the rut and somehow escaped serious injury, but a potentially ugly scene followed, as the parents, accompanied by a mob, brought him to the place where Charlotte had stopped. If his injuries had been more serious or bloody, Charlotte might have found herself in danger, but when a surgeon pronounced the boy unharmed and Charlotte placated the parents with a shilling and the promise of a shoulder of mutton, the crowd dispersed.

In the meantime, however, someone had rushed to tell Katherine that her daughter had murdered a child, which gave her such a shock that she suffered a severe asthma attack.

For a time, the consequences of her actions threw Charlotte into "a Kind of Melancholly." Her chastened spirits did not lead her into self-reflection, however: "For I don't remember any Impression left on my Mind by this Accident after my Mother's Recovery, and the Assurance I had of the Boy's being living and well."

⁓ 5 ⁓

LAUREATE

(1720–30)

On December 3, 1730, Colley Cibber, elegantly attired, entered the royal drawing room at St. James's Palace, where courtiers and ladies milled about, resplendent in court finery. Moving through the glittering assembly, Colley bowed occasionally to men who, like himself, wore suits of silk or velvet, intricately embroidered waistcoats shot with threads of silver or gold, and fine lace framing their wrists and necks. Their snowy silk stockings complemented the diamond buckles of their shoes. Their white or gray wigs (the most expensive colours) were powdered and worn full to the shoulders, as was Colley's preference, or pulled back into a queue caught in a black silk bag and tied with a bow.

With graceful gallantry, Colley acknowledged the ladies of the court, whose embroidered robes were trained in back and open in front to reveal quilted petticoats of silk or satin. Beneath these, a fine ankle encased in white silk might occasionally be glimpsed, rising above a delicate high-heeled shoe. Their hair pinned up, interwoven with ribbons and jewels, the ladies ornamented their white-powdered faces with touches of red paint and black velvet patches. Each carried a fan that she flourished expressively, opened to hide her face at one moment or collapsed to tap a man's shoulder.[1]

As a kind of theatre, with its own highly formalized ceremonies of costume, speech, and gesture, the court must have felt familiar to a veteran actor. Colley was accustomed to the company of peers and courtiers, whom he had long encountered backstage at Drury Lane and more recently in friendly banter at White's, the exclusive gambling club where he had had the honour of being the first actor admitted to membership. He stepped with confidence as he was ushered through the crowded room into the royal presence. Kneeling before the King, Colley kissed his hand. His Majesty, reported the *Daily Post* the next day, "graciously receiv'd" his new poet laureate. Colley had only to take the Anglican sacrament, which he did the following week, and the title, along with the annual stipend of £100 and a butt of sack (approximately 120 gallons of Canary Islands white wine), was his for life. He would serve the King as poet laureate for nearly twenty-seven years.

When Colley's predecessor as laureate, the clergyman Lawrence Eusden, died at the end of September 1730, speculation had immediately erupted about who would replace him; people placed wagers on their favourite candidates. The obvious choice, if the position were meant to recognize England's greatest *poet*, would have been Alexander Pope. But Pope's Tory sympathies would have barred him from the laurel even if his Roman Catholicism had not automatically disqualified him. The laureateship really had little to do with actual merit as a poet, anyway, and the term was more broadly applied than it is now, encompassing various categories of writers, including playwrights.

The laureateship was a frankly political position: the appointee not only had to be a member of the Church of England (the one formal requirement) but also had to be acceptable to the Whigs, Walpole, and the lord chamberlain, who was directly responsible for the appointment. Though he would have to produce poems for significant occasions, he would not necessarily have to be much of a poet: the last laureate of real poetic stature had been John Dryden, who reigned from 1668 to 1688, and his appointment was based upon his court connections as well as his literary abilities. The recently deceased Lawrence Eusden, whose sobriquet was "the drunken parson," had done little to elevate the office's artistic standards or its dignity.

The names of several candidates besides Colley were bandied about in the intervening months; two were considered particularly serious contenders. One was the attorney Lewis Theobald, whose valid criticisms of Pope's edition of Shakespeare had already earned him the title of King of the Dunces in the first version of *The Dunciad*. The other candidate was Stephen Duck, the "thresher poet," a former agricultural labourer from Wiltshire whose poetry had gained him the Queen's patronage; Duck's wife had died in childbirth that autumn, so he was the object of considerable sympathy and some gave him the edge in the competition. Pope, who watched the ongoing contest with understandable bitterness, wrote mockingly of the contenders Cibber, Theobald, and Duck, urging King George to keep his money and drink the wine himself:

> Shall royal praise be rhym'd by such a ribald,
> As fopling C——R, or Attorney T———D?
> Let's rather wait one year for better luck;
> One year may make a singing Swan of *Duck*.
> Great G——! such servants since thou well can'st lack,
> Oh! save the Salary, and drink the Sack![2]

The choice of Colley Cibber as poet laureate actually was not the cynical move many have assumed, and artistic merit had not been completely overlooked. Colley certainly was not very good at writing poetry, especially the requisite written-to-order panegyrics that would be published in the newspapers. His own verse principally took the form of dramatic prologues and epilogues, written to be performed by actors in the context of the playhouse. (The odes he would write as poet laureate would be set to music and sung, however, so their unimpressive appearance on the printed page does not capture the circumstances of their performance at court, which ameliorated their shortcomings.)

Colley's real claim to the title lay in his long career as an actor, playwright, and manager, genuine artistic contributions denied only by his enemies and those congenitally contemptuous of the theatre. He had produced a significant body of important, stage-worthy work that remained in the repertory throughout the century and was seen in his day as instrumental to the reformation of an immoral stage. He certainly merited the position more than any of his predecessors had since Dryden.

Of course, Colley had all of the necessary political connections, too, first of all with the lord chamberlain, the Duke of Grafton, but also with noblemen such as the Earl of Chesterfield and the Duke of Devonshire, heir of his father's patron. Colley had earned the political sponsorship of such men, and the gratitude of Walpole and the King, by long and consistently serving the Whig and Hanoverian causes.

As Charlotte grew into adolescence practising her performances in Hillingdon and Hertfordshire, her father had fought an unending series of battles. The 1720s had in many respects been a particularly difficult period for Colley and the Drury Lane Theatre. Though Colley expanded his circle of aristocratic friends, who found him delightful, lively company, the number and vehemence of his enemies also increased. His role as the manager empowered to select the plays Drury Lane produced inevitably made him resented by unsuccessful playwrights; his arrogant and tactless behaviour sometimes turned that resentment to hatred. His reputed delight in "choaking singing birds" (discouraging the aspirations of fledgling playwrights) was widely reported, as was his manner of rejecting a play with a peremptory "Sir, it will not do." Though respected by his actors, he was not popular with them; he did not socialize in the green room.

In Colley's case the personal was compounded with the political—indeed, it was often impossible to separate the two in the eighteenth century. *The Non-Juror* was neither forgiven nor forgotten by those whom it had offended, and Colley became the Whig the opposition loved to hate, second only to Walpole himself; it became a common device to attack the prime minister through Colley, a safer target. Both Colley and Walpole exemplified the self-made man's rise to prominence, "examples of the bourgeois success story of the rise from humble beginnings, a story of Christian advancing through conversion to self-understanding [a reference to *The Pilgrim's Progress*] or, seen from a different perspective, of a toadstool rising from a dunghill."[3]

Throughout the 1720s, Colley endured attacks from those who viewed him as a particularly obtrusive toadstool: he was castigated in poems, pamphlets, plays, and newspapers; his stage appearances were sometimes jeered; his plays were hooted down. During most of this period, none of Colley's new plays or adaptations had a successful run, since his enemies routinely appeared at performances in order to hiss, catcall, and throw rotten fruit. This is partially because he persisted in writing tragedies, which were not his forte as a playwright; but even a comedy such as *The Refusal,* not his best play but - certainly a stage-worthy one, was condemned by his enemies in the audience.

During this decade of political turmoil, Drury Lane's management structure remained solid and its actors superior. The theatre was, relatively speaking, orderly and well governed, but it was often less successful than the playhouse in Lincoln's Inn Fields at satisfying audience tastes. Seeing itself as the guardian of the classical British dramatic tradition, the Drury Lane company long resisted the audience desire for spectacle that the stage extravaganzas of Italian opera provided for the elite, and that programmes of music and dance, or tumbling and rope-dancing, provided for other spectators. But even "ancient Drury" had to succumb to popular tastes.

By the 1720s, a typical theatre evening had evolved into a kind of variety show, in which the play was supplemented by additional entertainments. The evening would include the mainpiece, a full-length play, and one or two shorter afterpieces in the form of short plays, masques, and/or pantomimes. From the "first, second and third music"—the three musical pieces that preceded the mainpiece—to the end of the afterpieces, these programmes inserted music and dancing everywhere: between the plays, between the acts of an individual play, and, eventually, within the acts as well. These musical numbers might have little or no relevance to the play that surrounded them. Costumes, sets, and stage machinery had become more elabourate, and were often advertised as attractions themselves. The installation of several sliding layers of scenery facilitated multiple scene changes. And stage machinery became ever more ambitious, with wires allowing chariots to ascend into the clouds, enthroned deities to descend from above, and dragons to soar across the stage.

Drury Lane under Cibber, Wilks, and Booth did resist the bear garden taste for prizefighters, rope dancers, and contortionists on their stage, but the company bowed to pressure for more music, dance, and spectacle. In fact, Drury Lane was responsible for introducing a type of entertainment, the British harlequinade or pantomime, that would become its particular nemesis in the hands of its rivals at Lincoln's Inn Fields. Responding to troupes of French players who for years had been coming to England to perform such popular entertainments featuring the commedia dell'arte figures Harlequin, Pierrot, and Scaramouche, the

London companies had staged European pantomimes in earlier years, but the piece considered the first true *English* pantomime was the *Harlequin Doctor Faustus,* produced in 1723 by Drury Lane. With its music, extravagant sets, dancing devils, flying fire-breathing dragon, and "Grand Masque of the Heathen Deities," the *Harlequin Doctor Faustus* was an enormous hit.

Lincoln's Inn Fields immediately rushed into production a close imitation, *The Necromancer; or, Harlequin Doctor Faustus.* The two pantomimes were such "triumphs" that "almost overnight they revolutionized the whole economy of the London theatres."[4] But it was Lincoln's Inn Fields, rather than Drury Lane, that gained the upper hand in the war of the harlequins. The pantomimes performed there became wildly popular, and its patentee John Rich became famous as London's best-known Harlequin, a role he played under the stage name Lun.

Drury Lane's revenues suffered from this competition, which compounded the financial stresses created by the political disruptions the company experienced. But towards the end of the decade, Drury Lane rebounded with two huge successes. Imitating the great pomp and ceremony of George II's coronation in Westminster Abbey the previous June, it added a pantomime "Coronation" to a production of *Henry VIII* in the autumn of 1727. Representing the coronation of Anne Boleyn, the scene was almost as lavish as the real thing: "Choir boys and privy councilors, aldermen and knights of the garter, earls, dukes, and bishops followed one another over the stage, and finally in regal robes the Queen herself appeared under a canopy supported by the four barons of the Cinque Ports."[5] The managers pleased the crowds with this spectacle, while cleverly declaring their allegiance to the Hanoverian monarchy.

Drury Lane achieved another welcome success in January 1728, with Cibber and Vanbrugh's *The Provok'd Husband,* which temporarily ended Colley's string of failures. This comedy was based upon a manuscript of a play entitled *Journey to London* that Sir John Vanbrugh had left uncompleted at his death. Colley finished it, making some substantial changes but preserving other parts intact, and gave Robert Wilks and Anne Oldfield two of their greatest roles.

Colley took particular pains to coach Mrs. Oldfield in the part of Lady Townly, a spoiled woman of fashion whose penchant for gambling threatens her marriage; the actress responded with a performance that was widely considered to be her greatest: "She slided so gracefully into the foibles, and displayed so humorously the excesses of a fine woman, too sensible of her charms, too confident of her power, and led away by her passion for pleasure," said Tom Davies, that no actress who later succeeded her in the role could match her. According to the actor Charles Macklin, Oldfield played Lady Townly with "all the *rage* of fashion and vivacity," fully conscious of the power of her youth and beauty.[6] Wilks, as Lord Townly, rose to her level, playing such a perfect gentleman that, when he had to reproach his wife for her misbehaviour, "in his warmest anger he mixed such tenderness as was softened into tears."[7]

Yet as had become usual with Colley's plays, a hostile crowd gathered on opening night in order to disrupt the performance. Its authorship confronted them with a dilemma, however, for Vanbrugh was popular (and dead). Confused, the hecklers vigorously applauded the refined and high-minded scenes they thought to be Vanbrugh's, while they disrupted some scenes of coarse "low" humour that they assumed were Cibber's. The hisses and catcalls were sometimes so virulent that the actors had to stop speaking and wait for the clamour to die down. The actors persisted bravely—though they were in some danger from flying fruit—and completed the performance. They, like Colley, must have been secretly gratified by the irony that the hecklers had gotten the authorship wrong: they "had applauded those Scenes wrote by Cibber, and mal-treated those written by Sir John."[8]

Anne Oldfield did Colley and the company one other service on opening night when she came forward at the end to speak Colley's epilogue. She had scarcely uttered the first line when a hiss from the pit interrupted her. Drawing herself up in all her majesty, Mrs. Oldfield fixed the culprit with her brilliant eye, paused, and with perfect timing, "spoke the words *poor creature!* loud enough to be heard by the audience, with such a look of mingled scorn, pity, and contempt, that the most uncommon applause justified her conduct in this particular, and the poor reptile sunk down with fear and trembling."[9] Anne's performance as Lady Townly was such a tour de force, Colley wrote in the preface to *The Provok'd Husband,* that she "outdid her usual outdoing." The hoots of derision that greeted this infelicitous turn of phrase forced Colley to rewrite it in later editions—though it would dog him

Anne Oldfield was Colley Cibber's favourite leading lady and a legend of the London stage. (Anne Oldfield. Courtesy of the Henry E. Huntington Library.)

for the rest of his life—but the admiration and gratitude he meant to express remained undiminished.

Despite these triumphs, misfortunes and mistakes continued to haunt the company. In the middle of the 1727–28 season, the co-manager and admired actor Barton Booth, who was increasingly plagued with poor health, quitted the stage. Known for his tragic roles of Cato, Lear, and Othello, he was equally famous for his indolence (except, reputedly, in the part of Lear), despite his capacity to rise to the occasion in the middle of the play if he discovered that an important critic was in the house. Yet Booth was capable of nuanced, meticulous performances: playing the Ghost in *Hamlet,* he wore "cloth shoes, (soles and all,) that the sound of his step should not be heard on the Stage."[10]

Praised for his understanding, learning, eloquence, and good nature, Booth was a heavy drinker until he fell in love with and married the dancer and actress Hester Santlow. Hester, notorious for her affairs, had been much satirized as a whore in bawdy verse, but marriage reformed both of them. (Apparently sentimental endings sometimes did occur in real life.) Hester became a devoted wife, and Booth, realizing that "Home, and her Company, were his chief Happiness," gave up the bottle. He did not, however, give up heavy eating. "His Appetite for Food had no Abatement," said Drury Lane's prompter, William Rufus Chetwood. "I have often known Mrs. Booth, out of extreme Tenderness to him, order the Table to be remov'd, for fear of over-charging his Stomach."[11]

The combination of his former love of drink and his constant love of food, it was widely thought, damaged Booth's health. He intended his retirement from the stage to be temporary, but in fact he was in the throes of a long decline from which he would not recover. Booth never acted again. Although he continued to appear at the playhouse and retained a voice in managerial decisions until his death several years later, Wilks and Cibber assumed more of the daily responsibility for running the theatre. Drury Lane's stability was beginning to weaken.

If Booth's retirement were not enough of a blow, Drury Lane's triumph with *The Provok'd Husband* was cast into the shadows by the premiere, at Lincoln's Inn Fields, of an odd, unprecedented play called *The Beggar's Opera*. Its author, John Gay, dubbed his strange hybrid a "ballad opera," for it used words and music in a new way that parodied the Italian operas that Handel, the court composer, was producing at the King's Theatre.

Unlike Italian opera, however, which proceeded through a combination of aria and recitative, *The Beggar's Opera* featured sections of spoken dialogue interspersed with songs—rather like a modern musical—in which new lyrics were set to preexisting, mainly traditional British, tunes. In writing it, Gay provided a satiric alternative for those ideologically opposed or personally hostile to Italian opera and the sectors of society with which it was associated: the Hanoverian court (Handel's principal sponsor) and its aristocratic supporters. These critics castigated Italian opera as an enervated foreign import that sapped the vigour of the robust English stage; they were disgusted by its castrated male singers and its temperamental Mediterranean divas.

A rivalry between the two sopranos Francesca Cuzzoni and Faustina Bordoni, each possessing her army of devotees, had recently escalated to the point of riot. On June 6, 1727, the two sopranos sang together in a performance of Buonconcini's *Astyanax* at King's, where their rival factions in the audience erupted into hissing, clapping, and catcalling; even the presence of the Princess of Wales in the audience did nothing to restrain them. When the divas themselves became so caught up in the excitement that they exchanged blows onstage, the performance was cancelled. Much of the Town continued to be split into warring Cuzzoni and Faustina factions. Lord Hervey wrote to his lover, Stephen

Fox: "As to Opera feuds, they are hotter than ever. . . . In short, the whole world is gone mad upon this dispute. No Cuzzonist will go to a tavern with a Faustinian; and the ladies of one part have scratched those of the other out of their list of visits."[12] This did nothing to endear Italian opera to those already disposed to dislike it.

In contrast, *The Beggar's Opera* proclaimed itself loyal to native English forms, satirizing Italian operatic conventions and the arrogance of opera stars. Whereas Italian opera used settings drawn from mythology or ancient history, populated by gods or legendary heroes and heroines, *The Beggar's Opera* evoked a world-turned-upside-down version of contemporary London, where the heroes and heroines were thieves, pimps, and whores. In the play's rivalry between Polly Peachum, daughter of a fence, and Lucy Lockit, daughter of a jailer, for the affections of the highwayman Captain Macheath, Gay brilliantly mocked the feuding divas.

Opera was not John Gay's only target in *The Beggar's Opera*. He also worked sly variations on popular British songs in order to satirize the English ruling class and, most specifically, the Whig political establishment. Gay took the Walpole administration as a particular target. The play did not endear itself to the government, but the audiences loved it.

From its first performance at Lincoln's Inn Fields Theatre, in January 1728, *The Beggar's Opera* became a theatrical phenomenon. Its initial run lasted for an unprecedented sixty-two consecutive performances, and it would become the most frequently staged play of the eighteenth century. Most of London's actors and actresses performed in it at some point during their careers (including Charlotte herself, who played several different parts; her role of choice, unsurprisingly, was the hero, Captain Macheath).

Colley must have watched spectators pack themselves into Lincoln's Inn Fields Theatre with considerable irritation, for Gay had offered *The Beggar's Opera* first to Drury Lane, and Colley had turned it down. His reasons were justifiable: the costs of staging new plays were high, and this one seemed too bizarre to succeed. There were political reasons, too; the work did not appeal to the staunch Whigs of Drury Lane. But the tide of subsequent events has obliterated the defensibility of his decision. Colley has gone down in history as the manager who held in his hands the greatest theatrical phenomenon of the eighteenth century, and rejected it. As for his rival John Rich and the play's author, John Gay, the oft-repeated witticism sums it up: *The Beggar's Opera* made Gay rich and Rich gay.

The play also brought fame and fortune to another of its participants, seventeen-year-old Lavinia Fenton, an actress said to be the bastard daughter of a Navy lieutenant, who created the lead role of Polly Peachum. The third Duke of Bolton attended a performance in early April, and was smitten. He attended again and again, even bringing his wife to one performance. Then on June 22, Lavinia Fenton disappeared from the playbills: the duke had swept her from the stage to make her his well-subsidized mistress. Gay wrote to Jonathan Swift: "the D of Bolton I hear hath run away with Polly Peachum, having settled 400£ a year upon her during pleasure, & upon disagreement 200£ a year."[13] Lavinia remained the duke's mistress for twenty-three years until, upon the death of his long-suffering wife, he married her, making her the new Duchess of Bolton.[14]

When the 1728–29 season began, Colley, never one to ignore a theatrical phenomenon, optimistically wrote his own ballad opera, called *Love in a Riddle*. His version was intended both to capitalize upon the success of *The Beggar's Opera* and to correct its "faults" by recommending, instead of cynical immorality, "Virtue and Innocence." But when the play opened, on January 7, 1729, Colley's enemies, aroused by the false rumour that he had been responsible for the lord chamberlain banning John Gay's *Polly* (his politically provocative follow-up to *The Beggar's Opera*), came to Drury Lane prepared to damn him. Though *Love in a Riddle* really was riddled with flaws, the audience did not hear enough of it to make a judgment based upon the play itself rather than on the playwright. Instead, from the opening scene, such a clamour resounded from the pit that the actors, hardened though they were to audience disruptions, were stunned by the near pandemonium.[15] When, in one scene, the tragedienne Sarah Thurmond held a spear to Colley's breast, the audience roared, "Kill him! Kill him!" This reception would have quashed the play immediately, except that the Prince of Wales had ordered a command performance for the next night. The play had to go ahead one more time.

Even the presence of royalty did not deter the pit from disrupting the second night. Spectators created such a din that not long into the play Colley suspended the action, strode to the front of the stage, and addressed the audience. If, he told them, they would respect the prince's wishes by permitting the play to go forward, he would promise that it would never be performed again. The disruptors, smug in their victory, ceased their whistles and catcalls, the play continued to its conclusion, and Colley pulled it from the repertoire. Later he fashioned the play's subplot into an afterpiece called *Damon and Phillida* that would hold the stage for many years, but he never ventured to write another full-length play. At the age of fifty-seven, Colley had seen the end of his career as a playwright.

Another problem for Drury Lane during this troubled time was the increased competition for London's limited number of theatregoers. Rich's Lincoln's Inn Fields continued to pose a challenge; the Royal Opera House and various fringe theatres, most particularly the Little Haymarket—which sometimes housed a troupe that produced a successful run—also drew audiences away. In the autumn of 1729, a new theatre opened in a converted workshop in the unfashionable City neighbourhood of Goodman's Fields, after a fierce struggle with the local businessmen, who cited its bad influence on their young apprentices and clerks. (The City was an area strong in middle-class Nonconformists and Puritans who took a dim view of the theatre.) Despite some initial setbacks, Goodman's Fields developed into a solid, well-run company that widened London playgoers' choices, gave its playwrights another possible venue, and posed a challenge to Drury Lane, even though it tended to attract spectators who had not often ventured into the West End.

The season of 1729–30 also saw the emergence of Henry Fielding as a force in the theatre—yet another unwelcome development. Colley had accepted Fielding's first play, entitled *Love in Several Masques,* for production at Drury Lane in 1727–28. The play should have been a success, but its timing was unfortunate, for it opened immediately after *The Provok'd Husband*'s great run (literally, a hard act to follow), and it ran opposite *The Beggar's Opera,* impossible competition for any first play. It closed after four nights.

So in the autumn of 1729, when Fielding approached Drury Lane with his next play, *The Temple Beau,* Colley rejected it, probably brusquely. Fielding succeeded in having his play produced with moderate success at Goodman's Fields, but the young playwright and satirist now had a score to settle with Colley Cibber.

In spring and summer 1730, Fielding assembled a company at the Little Theatre in the Haymarket to stage three plays he had written. Unsurprisingly enough, one of them included an attack on Colley, Fielding's first offensive in a satiric war that would, except for a temporary truce, occupy the rest of his literary career. *The Author's Farce,* whose plot pointedly centres on the unsuccessful attempts of the young playwright Harry Luckless to have his play produced, satirizes mercenary booksellers, Italian opera singers, female amatory novelists, the contemporary audience's degraded taste for mindless sensation, and the powerful theatre managers who pander to them. It energetically parodies Colley Cibber in three separate guises.

A more personal and profound misfortune struck Colley and Drury Lane—and indeed, all of theatregoing London—in 1730, when Anne Oldfield ended her acting career in April. She had been suffering with increasing severity the symptoms of a painful illness that eventually would be diagnosed, in the words of a female friend, as "a Malady known by every body to be incident to our Sex although we were Vestals"—that is, a nonvenereal disease specific to women, probably cancer of the reproductive system.[16] Six months later, "the celebrated Mrs. Oldfield" was dead.

For many years Anne had fascinated the Town, which thrived on "stories about her luxurious style of life and socially prominent friends, gossip about her lovers, and rumours about the extent of her wealth."[17] Anne never married, preferring, apparently, to retain her economic self-sufficiency. She was an independent woman and a dedicated professional who, unlike Lavinia Fenton, for instance, had chosen her career over the opportunity to become the mistress of a nobleman: many years earlier, it was reported, she had turned down a settlement of £600 per year offered her by the Duke of Bedford.[18] But during her life she accepted as lovers two distinguished and devoted men who did not demand that she abandon her profession. The first was Arthur Maynwaring, a gentleman from an ancient Shropshire family who, though not wealthy, moved in elite Whig circles, held a government position, and became a member of Parliament; Davies described him as "one of the most accomplished men of his age."[19] Anne and Maynwaring lived together openly from 1703 until his death in 1712, and had a son. After Maynwaring's death, Anne began a relationship with Colonel Charles Churchill, the illegitimate nephew of the Duke of Marlborough and a man of fashion who also moved in Whig circles. She lived with him until she died, associating with his aristocratic friends and bearing him a son who, like her first, lived into adulthood.

Drury Lane Theatre closed its doors on October 23, the day of Anne's death, and was dark again on the twenty-seventh, the day of her burial. She was interred in Westminster Abbey, an honour unusual for an actress. Her pall was borne by "courtiers and gentlemen" rather than her actor colleagues, the sign that despite the stigma of her career, she moved in elevated society. Churchill paid a fine in order to bypass the protectionist law requiring the dead to be buried in clothes made of English wool rather than imported fabrics. Mrs. Oldfield was interred, as she had lived, attired in silk and lace. Alexander Pope, no friend to Anne or actresses, satirized her as "Narcissa," who approaches the grave as a misogynist's image of women's shallowness and vanity:

"Odious! in woolen! 'twould a Saint provoke,
(Were the last words that poor Narcissa spoke)
"No, let a charming Chintz, and Brussels lace
Wrap my cold limbs, and shade my lifeless face:
One would not, sure, be frightful when one's dead—
And—Betty—give this Cheek a little Red."[20]

Mrs. Oldfield was buried near the tomb of William Congreve, who had died the year before. But Charles Churchill's request to erect a monument to her in Westminster Abbey was denied. Her burial there was itself an uncommon honour, but there were limits: however much she had been revered for her art and accepted by at least some members of high society, Anne had died unmarried, the mother of two illegitimate children, and an actress.

PART

TWO

6

The Provoked Wife

(1729–30)

On June 10, 1729, the *Daily Post* published a favourable account of a production of Charles Coffey's ballad opera *The Beggar's Wedding*, then being performed by a fringe troupe at the Little Theatre in the Haymarket. The play, said the reviewer, "is very entertaining; but the Part of Hunter, in particular, is perform'd by a Person, who, altho his Voice is but indifferent, sings, in the Opinion of all Judges, with a Manner almost as agreeable as Senesino."[1] The role of Harry Hunter was played by a new arrival to the London stage, a young singer, dancer, violinist, and aspiring composer named Richard Charke.

The paper's notice may have been a genuine review or simply a puff, but in either case, the *Daily Post* was paying the novice Charke a high compliment.[2] Senesino, the stage name of the Sienese castrato Francesco Bernardi, had been for the past several seasons the reigning star of London opera, greatly admired, Colley Cibber wrote, for his "strong, clear, Sweetness of Tone."[3] Senesino had been brought to England by Handel, who, although his relations with the Italian singer grew strained, wrote more parts for him than for any other castrato. Though there were certainly many in the eighteenth century who viewed the castrati as monsters, many others thought of them as celestial beings, whose "angelic" voices fell somewhere in between masculine and feminine.[4] In a culture that prized illusion and artifice, Senesino and the other castrati were great luminaries, objects of admiration and desire.

So the comparison of Richard Charke to a lionized castrato was not only a tribute to the young man's pleasing manner of singing, but also an implicit comment upon his ability to stir feminine hearts. Many society women sought out the company and (so it was said) the beds of these celebrities. Henry Carey's song, "The Ladies Lamentation for the Loss of Senesino," mourned the singer's departure for Italy as a bereavement suffered particularly by women. Bawdy poems celebrated the superiority of the castrati as lovers, depicting them as sexually less crude and violent than other men, and as giving pleasure without the threat of pregnancy. (The method of castration used on these singers removed a boy's testicles but not his penis, so castrati were capable of erections and ejaculation, but did not produce sperm.) In a risqué poem addressed to Farinelli, Teresa Constantia Philips wrote:

[Ladies] know, that safe with thee they may remain;
Enjoy Love's Pleasures, yet avoid the Pain:
Each, blest in thee, continue still a Maid;
Nor of a Tell-tale Bantling be afraid . . .

The *Daily Post*'s words helped make Charke so celebrated that new songs were added to *The Beggar's Wedding* for him to sing. His popularity was no doubt enhanced because, unlike Senesino, he sang in English, in ballad operas imitative of *The Beggar's Opera* (the obvious progenitor of *The Beggar's Wedding*).

The company in which Charke performed *The Beggar's Wedding* at the Little Haymarket in the summer of 1729 presented unwelcome competition for the Theatre Royal, Drury Lane, which was mounting a summer season for the first time since 1723. It was managed by Theophilus Cibber. Summer performances gave opportunities to younger actors: after the regular season ended in late May or early June, and the better-paid veteran actors departed for their residences in Richmond, Twickenham, and Hillingdon, the younger company members staged their season into August, supplementing their modest salaries and gaining experience with jealously guarded leading roles.

The summer season was not a particularly lucrative one. Audiences were often thin, and temperatures in the playhouses could rise beyond endurance. Ladies' fans did little to combat the heat, and—standards of personal hygiene being low in the eighteenth century—a hot, sweaty audience also stank, adding another powerful odour to the stench rising from the theatre's hundreds of tallow candles and oil lamps. Theatregoers might well find an outdoor pleasure garden more appealing than a stuffy playhouse.

The fringe company playing at the Little Haymarket that year, a large, shifting group of actors managed by Richard Reynolds, had already shaken up the established theatres' complacency during the winter season, when it scored a big hit with the fantastic *Hurlothrumbo; or, The Supernatural,* written by Samuel Johnson of Cheshire, a dancing master (to be distinguished from Samuel Johnson of Lichfield, the formidable Dr. Johnson).[5] This strange play, whose author was reputed to be "half mad," ran for more than thirty consecutive nights. With successes such as this, the Little Haymarket, according to theatre historians, posed "the first significant challenge to the domination which Drury Lane and Lincoln's Inn Fields had exercised in the presentation of English plays."[6] And when they continued to perform into the summer season, this troupe posed a new challenge, especially with the introduction of their attractive new singer Mr. Charke. Their ads also promised any vacillators that the theatre was "extraordinary cool."

But Drury Lane was not without muscle, and Theophilus moved to cripple the opposition by poaching its newest star. He lured Charke to Drury Lane in midsummer, where he first appeared on July 18 as Rako in another ballad opera, Essex Hawker's "Tragi-Comi-Pastoral-Farcical" *The Country Wedding.*

Carrying his appeal to the cooler and more elegant Drury Lane, Richard secured his reputation by taking other leading roles, such as that of the rake Rovewell in Henry Carey's *The Contrivances.* For August 7, Drury Lane advertised a performance of *The Contrivances,* "Intermix'd with several new Songs in the Character of Rovewell and Arethusa."[7] Arethusa was played by a young singer and budding comic actress named Catherine (Kitty) Raftor, whose "facetious Turn of Humour, and infinite Spirits" charmed audiences, who wildly applauded her droll, comical songs.[8] Two nights later, at the season finale, "There was a very handsome Audience, and the young Actors were dismiss'd with general Applause."[9]

The summer's end brought the big festivals of Bartholomew Fair and Southwark Fair, where small groups of actors maintained theatre booths, performing for the crowds throughout the day. Early in August, the

Richard Charke's singing voice captivated the public. His marriage to Charlotte was brief but rarely boring. ("The Batchelor's Wife Sung by Mr. Charke set for the German Flute." Courtesy of the Department of Special Collections, University of California, Davis.)

papers announced that Charke would perform in the *Beggar's Wedding* at Bartholomew Fair in the booth run by Timothy Fielding, an actor from Drury Lane. With this, Richard Reynolds's unhappiness at Richard's defection earlier in the summer flared into public controversy.

On August 6, Reynolds inserted a letter in the *Daily Post* complaining that he had previously engaged Charke to perform with him. Richard defended himself in another letter, prompting a long, indignant reply from Reynolds recounting his dealings with Charke. Reynolds claimed that he had hired the young singer "as a dancing master" the previous winter, gave him opportunities, and felt badly treated by him now that he was in demand.[10]

Richard was now even more of a sensation. Praised by the reviewers, compared with an operatic superstar, stolen away by London's most august theatre, fought over by theatre managers in the papers, he was a figure of some controversy and glamour—young, handsome, lively, and talented. If his treatment of Reynolds raised some doubts that might be relevant to his conduct in other walks of life, they were overshadowed by his sex appeal.

It is not surprising that, when she met him at the age of sixteen, Charlotte dropped her guns and currycombs and threw herself into love.

Charlotte met Richard sometime that summer, presumably through her brother's auspices and probably sometime after July 18, when Richard joined Drury Lane. She was attracted by Richard's musical talent, his good looks, and his spirited, if coarse, sense of humour. The music historian Dr. Charles Burney called him "a facetious fellow, gifted with a turn for b. g. [bear garden, that is, crude] humour," who was known for his "tricks and stories."[11] That he had a vulgar streak was not a deterrent to Charlotte. Both of the men in her family did, too.

Richard wasted no time in beginning a courtship: Charlotte recounted in sober hindsight that he "was pleased to say soft Things, and to flatter me into a Belief of his being an humble Admirer." She, dazzled by his attentions, "indulged myself in a passionate Fondness for my Lover." No doubt she genuinely loved him, "as foolish young Girls are apt to be too credulous." But how she must have relished playing the part of the leading lady—"Charlotte in love"—in her own romantic drama, even if it was, for the first time in her role-playing career, a stock female part.

But what were Richard's feelings and motivations? Was he, initially at least, in love with Charlotte or was he, as Charlotte later asserted, playing a cynical role? Historians have generally followed Charlotte's own disillusioned lead in assuming that Richard pursued her only for the professional advantages her father could give him. But such marital calculations were commonplace at that time. Charlotte's disenchanted account of her husband's motivations probably has much truth in it, but she also does herself a disservice.

Why should Richard *not* have found her appealing in her own right as well as in her family connections? Even if he had first considered her purely for mercenary motives, he might well have found himself drawn to her spirit and intelligence, and amused by her clever theatricality. Perhaps he warmed to her undisguised enthusiasm for him: as Jane Austen would remark shrewdly in *Northanger Abbey*, a man's knowledge of a woman's partiality for him was a common inducement to love in the real world. But whatever impelled his actions, Richard moved quickly to win Charlotte, and Charlotte ardently allowed herself to be won. With characteristic impetuosity, she pressed her father for permission to marry her lover, and Colley consented.

At the time, Charlotte was effusively grateful for her father's indulgence in permitting her to marry at so young an age, but later she blamed him for not putting a stop to her immature passion. The newlyweds "were both so young and indiscreet," she said, "we ought rather to have been sent to School than to Church, in Regard to any Qualifications on either Side, towards rendering the Marriage-State comfortable to one another." Charlotte later felt that Colley should have separated her from Richard by sending her on a tour of the country or taking some other steps to break the attachment. (She never mentioned her mother's attitude towards the marriage. But Katherine had long become resigned to nonintervention in Charlotte's schemes, and would have been unlikely to interfere.)

Colley probably gave his permission as the course of least resistance, knowing that Charlotte would not let him rest otherwise; he always tried to distance himself from conflict and unpleasantness within his family. Perhaps he also suspected that Charlotte might elope were he to withhold his consent. Richard's desire not to alienate his potentially useful father-in-law might have made him cautious in such circumstances, but Charlotte would certainly have been capable of scheming to run off to get married in Scotland. And she would have been equally capable of imagining a tearful scene in which she and Richard, repentant but irrevocably married, threw themselves at her father's feet and were forgiven.

It is difficult to escape the suspicion that Colley was relieved to have his troublesome youngest daughter taken off his hands; but he did not abdicate responsibility for her, as has sometimes been suggested. Colley and Katherine probably hoped that marriage would tame Charlotte and mature her. At seventeen, she was young to be married, but not remarkably so. Though her sisters Catherine and Anne were in their later twenties when they wed, Elizabeth, the first Cibber child to marry, had been seventeen when she took her first husband. And Colley had reason to judge that Charlotte's match with Richard was not a bad one.

Though he might have expected his daughter to marry someone more economically substantial, Colley would also have recognized that Charlotte was far from an ordinary marital prospect: it would need a certain type of man to take her on. Such a man was most likely to be found in the theatre, where Charlotte would soon begin her own career and where Colley's position would serve as an inducement. True, Richard was penniless, with only talent and ambition to recommend him. But Colley had once been such a young man himself, and his experienced eye saw that Richard Charke had potential.

After a few months on the London stage, Richard had already made a name as a singer and actor and had quickly found a place during the regular season at Drury Lane. He soon became even more celebrated as a violinist: people came to the theatre just to hear him play.[12] He aspired to compose.

Colley was well positioned to give Richard valuable advice and to help advance his career. As Charlotte said, "My father was greatly inclined to be his Friend, and to promote his Interest extreamly amongst People of Quality and Fashion." Colley could patronize Richard within the theatre world and recommend him among the upper-class people he counted as friends. Musicians often supplemented their performance incomes by giving private lessons and concerts for wealthy families, as well as playing in the summer pleasure gardens and fairs, and Charke was qualified as a dancing master as well. That Richard ultimately did not benefit more from his position as Colley Cibber's son-in-law reveals his own shortcomings rather than Colley's dereliction; in Charlotte's words, Richard was not "skilful enough to manage his Cards [with her father] rightly."

On Wednesday, February 4, 1730, six months after they met, Charlotte and Richard were married with the full blessing of her father at the parish church of St. Martin-in-the-Fields.[13] She had just turned seventeen and he was probably about to turn twenty-seven.[14] *The Daily Courant,* mistaking Richard's surname, reported, "Last Wednesday, Mr. Clark of the Theatre Royal in Drury-Lane, was married to Miss Charlotte Cibber, Daughter to Mr. Cibber, one of the Managers of the said Theatre." The newlyweds seem to have been graced with good weather for their wedding. On that day, the paper said, "their Majesties with the three eldest Princesses, attended by a great Number of the Nobility, walked for a considerable time in St. James's Park."[15] Perhaps Charlotte and her new husband walked there, too.

Charlotte, predisposed to view her own life through analogies drawn from plays, might have indulged a vision of marital bliss equivalent to the romantic promise offered by Hunter to his bride, Phebe, at the end of *The Beggar's Wedding.* Richard, who continued to play Hunter at Drury Lane, presumably continued to stir feminine hearts as he sang: "At last Love triumphant ill Fortune controuls. / Thus happy ten thousand new Joys we'll explore, / And with mutual Constancy solace our Soles [*sic*]. / No more shall false Pleasure enervate my Mind / . . . For Phebe's the Joy of my Life."

If she had been so inclined, however, Charlotte easily could have found more sobering views of matrimony in the "marriage-problem plays" staged so often at Drury Lane. Stage lovers might have sung of marital delights, but stage husbands and wives—at least those married to each other—presented a darker picture. Richard's first play at Drury Lane, for instance, contained a striking scene whose portrayal of the married state might have given any courting couple pause.

Advertisements for *The Country Wedding* promised spectators a "hudibrastick Skimmington" inserted into the ballad opera. "Hudibrastic" signifies a type of satiric or mock-heroic doggerel verse, and a "skimmington" was a rough popular custom designed to punish marital transgressions by parading figures of the offending couple through a community. (Thomas Hardy depicted a disastrous skimmington a century and a half later, in *The Mayor of Casterbridge*.)

At a certain point in *The Country Wedding*, the progress of the ballad opera plot was interrupted by a band of unruly women who marched onto the stage carrying aloft a shift and petticoat.[16] The skimmington travesty of marriage followed, with a "husband" and a "wife" mounted back to back on an ass. As tradition dictated, the husband faced the animal's rump and held a distaff (the sign of woman's place), while the wife twisted around to beat him with a ladle. The women leading the parade sang a satiric song urging wives to "follow this Example":

> This man-like buxom Dame,
>   The Breeches long has worn;
> Henceforth no more be tame,
>   But valiant in your Turn.

It is striking—sometimes almost uncanny—how often the fictional worlds created on the eighteenth-century stage, the plays that Charlotte herself saw, and often those in which she performed, seemed to predict, echo, or comment upon the circumstances of her life. It is easy to understand why she so often turned to the drama of her day for analogies to her own situation. In light of the course her life and career would follow in less than a decade's time, for instance, the satiric portrayal of the "woman on top" who is metaphorically "wearing the breeches" could seem prescient. And simply as an enactment of the pains of marriage, this scene, contained in the play that introduced Richard as a member of the Drury Lane company, might have boded ill indeed.

Initially, however, Charlotte delighted at hearing herself addressed as "Mrs. Charke" instead of the maidenly "Miss Charlotte," and Richard congratulated himself upon becoming Colley Cibber's son-in-law. The couple took up residence in London, possibly taking inexpensive lodgings located on one of the streets running from the Strand not far from the playhouse. Settling into life with her new husband, Charlotte believed "that the Measure of my Happiness was full, and of an ever-during Nature," echoing Phebe, Hunter, and their mutually constant joy. "But alas!" she continued, "I soon found myself deceived in that fond Conceit."

The new Mrs. Charke had been married for only two months when she received the opportunity to realize her other, more enduring passion: performing on the stage. Charlotte was offered a role in John Vanbrugh's comedy *The Provok'd Wife,* the contemporary stage's most vivid comic—yet not entirely funny—portrayal of a bad marriage. Once again the playhouse seemed to offer timely commentary upon Charlotte's reality. Though she was cast in the part of the maid rather than in the title role, she was already beginning to rehearse the part of the "provoked wife" in private life.

Charlotte had understood that she would make her acting debut the following year, in the 1730–31 season. But in the spring of 1730, the veteran actress Sarah Thurmond requested that Charlotte be permitted to make her first stage appearance on Mrs. Thurmond's benefit night that April. She would play the French maid, Madamoiselle (a role that Charlotte's sister Elizabeth had briefly played more than two years before). At seventeen, Charlotte was not particularly young for her debut—actresses might begin their careers at fifteen, or even as children. But the part of Madamoiselle was not a negligible role for a neophyte, since it was one of the most fully realized comic characterizations of the play, calling for the actress to be onstage in seven different scenes, speaking in a contrived accent a series of very funny lines.

Ecstatic, Charlotte eagerly awaited the printing of the playbill for the performance. But when the bill appeared, Charlotte's "Joy was somewhat dash'd," she said, to see herself billed anonymously as "a young Gentlewoman, who has never appear'd on any Stage before." Colley cautiously wanted her name kept secret until he could be sure that his daughter could handle the role; perhaps he was also concerned that if her name were known, his enemies might show up to hiss and catcall her because she was his daughter. Filled with "melancholy Disappointment" at this development, Charlotte promptly set about to subvert her father's prudent safeguard, running up "an unavoidable Expence in Coach-hire" as she raced around town "to inform all my Acquaintance, that I was the Person so set down in Mrs. Thurmond's Benefit-Bills."

The kindness of Sarah Thurmond's offer was not negated by the fact that it bore an element of calculation. Benefit nights were the yearly (in some cases twice-yearly) occasions when a player or another member of a theatre company would reap the proceeds of that night's ticket sales, usually, though not always, minus the theatre's costs. The greater the box office receipts, therefore, the larger the proceeds: a good bene-fit might nearly double a player's yearly income. (The player receiving the benefit usually took a block of tickets to sell personally, making them available at her house, as Mrs. Thurmond did, or even, as did lesser players, selling the tickets door to door.) Mrs. Thurmond was well liked by audiences—despite her reputation for heavy drinking—but she was not one of the company's biggest names.[17] She chose as the mainpiece a play that featured almost all of Drury Lane's principal players. (She herself played in the afterpiece, *The Lovers Opera*.) And she cleverly added another element of interest by casting Charlotte.

As Mrs. Thurmond was well aware, audiences loved a debut, espe-cially when the new player was a "young Gentlewoman." Charlotte's anonymous billing added the alluring element of mystery. Sarah's own supporters would be joined by other spectators drawn by the opportunity to scrutinize and encourage (or sometimes discourage) the new player.

It is hard to imagine a more enticing opportunity for Charlotte's debut. Since its first performance in 1697, *The Provok'd Wife* was a perennial audience favourite—if also a perennial object of attack from moralists for its risqué language and its cynical view of marriage. Vanbrugh made up for his sketchy plotting with his flair for witty but naturalistic comic dialogue.

For her Drury Lane debut, Charlotte joined a cast comprising many of London's best-known actors: the players that night included Robert Wilks, who, "tall and erect in his Person . . . with an Address so ele-gantly easy," was the ideal gentlemanly romantic hero.[18] Playing oppo-site him for one of the last times before her retirement and death was Anne Oldfield as Lady Brute. In the cast also were the beloved low-comic actors, the rotund John Harper, famous for his performances of Falstaff and his "drunken man dance," and Henry "Jubilee Dicky" Norris, with his "singular, squeaking Tone of Voice."[19] The beautiful Christiana Horton played the female fop, Lady Fancifull, the employer of Charlotte's Madamoiselle. Most significantly of all for Charlotte, the production featured her father in one of his best roles as Sir John Brute, the provoking husband; his performances in this role characteristically received "great and deserved applause; his skill was so masterly."[20]

A Cibber theatrical dynasty was much in evidence on the night of Charlotte's debut. She and Colley played in the mainpiece, while the afterpiece, written by Drury Lane's prompter, William Rufus Chetwood (who later married into the Cibber family), featured three other members of Charlotte's family: Richard, Theophilus, and Theophilus's wife, Jane. Theatrical families were not unusual but the Cibbers were a particularly large presence. With the inclusion of Charlotte's sister Elizabeth Brett and her daughter, Ann, who belonged to the company as dancers and occasional actresses, they encompassed three generations.

On Wednesday, April 8, 1730, in Act I, scene ii of *The Provok'd Wife*, Charlotte stepped onto the stage of London's most venerable theatre and uttered her first professional line. Addressed to her employer, Lady Fancifull, as she sits at her dressing table, it is a sentence of calculating dishonesty, spoken in broken, French-inflected English: "My opinion pe, matam, dat your ladyship never look so well in your life." This was the moment for which Charlotte had been preparing since childhood, and it is appealing to imagine the well-disposed audience greeting her high-pitched, mock-Gallic delivery with a rumble of encouraging laughter.

As Madamoiselle's employer, the handsome, vain Lady Fancifull, a female fop who thinks that all mankind swoons with desire in her presence, Christiana Horton was perfectly cast. Considered one of the most beautiful women who ever trod the stage, she had been married when very young to a musician who, it was said, abused her. Now in her mid-thirties, she was known for her coquettish roles onstage and her coquettish behaviour off it: "Her sole passion was to be admired."[21]

In Charlotte's first scene, Lady Fancifull gazes lovingly into her looking glass—"I'm almost afraid it flatters me, it makes me look so very engaging"—while Madamoiselle, knowing that no degree of flattery is too great, feeds her mistress's vanity in the hopes of being rewarded with presents of clothes:

MADAMOISELLE: Inteed, matam, your face pe handsomer den all de looking glass in te world, *croyez moi!*
LADY FANCIFULL: But is it possible my eyes can be so languishing, and so very full of fire?
MADAMOISELLE: Matam, if de glass was burning glass, I believe your eyes set de fire in de house.

The part of Madamoiselle was a challenge for a young actress's debut, but Charlotte was both too elated and too naïve to be nervous. She had been prepared for her part either by Wilks or by her father, for the task of rehearsing the players fell to the manager who was the principal performer in it.[22] In any event, she must have received individual instruction from her father and she probably got advice from Mrs. Thurmond as well.

Charlotte threw herself into her scenes, speaking in the high-pitched voice conventional for this type of comic character, emphasizing the French inflection of her English lines as she slyly manipulated her employer. The facility in languages that had won her praise at school served her well in the many lines written for Madamoiselle in French.

At the end of the play, Charlotte played a comic love scene with Madamoiselle's lover, the manservant Razor, in which she tells him that she has spied on Lady Brute when, in disguise, she met with her lover Constant. As Madamoiselle recounts the scene, she and Razor act out the amorous encounter of Lady Brute and Constant:

MADAMOISELLE: De lover say soft ting.
  De lady look upon de ground.
  He take her by the hand.
  She turn her head, the oder way.
  Den he squeeze very hard.
  Den she pull—very softly.
  Den he take her in his arm.
  Den she give him leetel pat.
  Den he kiss her tetons [breasts].
  Den she say, pish, nay, see.
  Den he tremble.
  Den she—sigh.
  Den he pull her into de arbor.
  Den she pinch him.
RAZOR: Aye, but not so hard, you baggage you.

The sympathetic audience, wishing to encourage this seventeen-year-old actress who was showing such spirit on her first appearance, applauded warmly. And equally gratifying, her performance earned praise from Mrs. Oldfield and her father, whose approbation, Charlotte commented, gave her "no trifling Addition to my conceit."

Charlotte repeated her triumph twenty days later, when it was Richard's turn for a benefit, which he shared with Kitty Raftor, and they chose a repeat performance of *The Provok'd Wife*. Richard performed a violin solo in addition to his role in the afterpiece.

If the anonymous billing of a young gentlewoman's first appearance had enticed audiences into the theatre, her success in her debut made her second performance in the role almost as interesting. Whether Charlotte performed as an unpaid apprentice or received compensation for her work is unknown, but her name, which now appeared on the playbill in its own right, would have brought in additional spectators to swell the benefit proceeds.

This time there was no need for the cover of anonymity, and the playbills declared that Madamoiselle would be played by "MRS. CHARKE, being the second Time of her Appearance upon the Stage."[23] (The same playbills that listed her name for the first time listed Mrs. Oldfield's for the last.) Seeing her name in the capital letters of an established player filled Charlotte with such giddy delight that she dashed "from one End of the Town to the other for the first Week" just to gaze upon the bills wherever they were posted: "Nor do I believe it cost me less, in Shoes and Coaches, then [*sic*] two or three Guineas, to gratify the extravagant Delight I had, not only in reading the Bills, but sometimes hearing myself spoken of, which luckily was to my Advantage." In her tizzy of "conceited Transport," she said, she probably would have fallen into pitched battle with anyone so unwise as to criticize her in her hearing.

On the evening of her second performance, Charlotte's "conceited Transport" incited her to behaviour that, though rather comical, was profoundly serious to her at the time. The object of her wrath was, of all people, her sweet, mild sister-in-law Jane Cibber, Theophilus's wife. The cast of *The Provok'd Wife* that night remained the same as before, with the exception of Mrs. Horton, who was ill. The part of Lady Fancifull was assigned at the last minute to Jane, who knew the role but had not performed it for two years.[24]

The repertory system common to eighteenth-century theatres required actors, as their careers developed, to memorize a daunting number of roles, and it was not unusual that a player would be required to perform a part on short notice. Jane was already an accomplished actress in a variety of roles, one of Drury Lane's brightest young stars. But she was nonetheless anxious at reprising this part with no opportunity to rehearse it.

That evening, as the sisters-in-law awaited their call in the green room, Charlotte noticed that Jane remained silent, her countenance solemn and pale. Charlotte, bubbling with excitement and not the least bit nervous, was incredulous and rather irritated at these signs of stage fright in the more experienced actress. "Like a strange Gawky as I was," Charlotte said, she berated Jane, saying that she was "surprised at her being frightened, who had so often appeared; when I, who had never played but once, had no Concern at all." Jane replied that Charlotte's nonchalance was a result of her inexperience. "When you have stood as many Shocks as others have done, and are more acquainted with your Business," she said gravely, "you'll possibly be more susceptible of Fear."

This mild caution was only a pinprick, but Jane's words, and her serious manner of speaking—a product of her own anxiety rather than any affront she intended to her sister-in-law—were enough to deflate the bubble of Charlotte's self-congratulation. She was outraged: "I turned short on my Heel and broke off our Conversation, nor could I bring myself, but on the Stage, to speak to her the whole Evening."

Since Charlotte played all but one of her scenes opposite Jane, indulging her indignation throughout the course of the play's five acts required her to engage in lively repartee with Jane onstage and freeze her with silence the minute they exited it. Feuding actors forced to play scenes with each other were hardly news in a theatre company, notorious for resentments, jealousies, and large, fragile egos. Very few players, however, were likely to allow themselves such indignation as early in their careers as their second performance. But Charlotte, for whom the Drury Lane company was in some sense an extended family, reacted to the common sense of her older sister-in-law in much the same way that, as a child, she had resented attempts by her family to restrain her. Her indignation, in adulthood as in childhood a product of her impulsive temper, was short-lived. Later, when she had gained enough experience to understand the truth of Jane's observation, the two actresses laughed about her display of naïve arrogance.

Charlotte's delight in her newfound success on the stage that spring was soured only by the growing discord at home. Whatever rapport had existed between the lovers quickly evaporated as the husband and wife faced the realities of marriage. Financial strains must have arisen quite soon. Presumably Charlotte brought some sort of dowry, but neither she nor Richard was able, or inclined, to manage money. That Charlotte spent a small fortune in coach hire to dash about town inspecting her name on the playbills wherever they were posted reveals her attitude towards domestic economy, and Richard was similarly reckless in pursuing his own pleasures. The couple, as they were beginning to discover, agreed on very little, but they were of one mind in spending freely until Charlotte's dowry was exhausted.

The consequence, most likely, was that within the first few months of marriage the Charkes were reduced to relatively pinched circumstances, quite different from the style Charlotte was accustomed to enjoying in her father's houses. They would have been unable to afford more than one or two irregularly paid servants at the most; possibly they kept none at all. Charlotte would not have been much of a housekeeper: having grown up with nothing but contempt for domesticity, she did not change her attitude as she grew older. Financial problems in themselves might have been bearable, especially since Colley was willing to give the couple money on occasion. But the marriage was still in its early days when Charlotte learned two unsettling facts. One was that she was pregnant. The other was that she had married an incorrigible rake.

Charlotte became pregnant within two months of her marriage. She probably did not realize her condition until sometime in the summer, but in fact she was already with child when she made her first appearance on the stage. She had begun to discover the truth about her husband's character earlier. Richard's friendship with Theophilus, who had already acquired a reputation for dissolute behaviour, might have given her a clue (though, living so much in the country, she probably had not seen enough of her brother to know this then). But Charlotte soon learned that she had more in common with Jane than a shared stage. Whether or not Richard had been a thoroughgoing libertine before their marriage, he certainly lived a debauched life afterward. He and Theo haunted the taverns, gambling dens, brothels, and bagnios of Covent Garden and the Strand. However dismayed she must have been by his drinking and gambling, it was Richard's philandering that most distressed and angered Charlotte.

Handsome Richard's musical gifts and sex appeal made him subject to the attentions of "those Sort of Ladies, who, regardless of their Reputations, make 'em the unhappy Sacrifices to every pleasing Object." Charlotte's new husband, she discovered, was quite receptive to the sacrifice of reputations, and fond of the company of prostitutes, too. Within the first year of their marriage, Charlotte, seventeen years old and pregnant, found herself scouring Covent Garden's seedier pockets in search of her wayward husband. She, so recently arrived in London from the country, became acquainted with parts of her old neighbourhood she had never before seen as she ventured, in a distressed state of mind, into its squalid alleys. She described herself as a "married Miss," possessed of a husband in name only, "industriously employed in the Pursuit of fresh Sorrow, by tracing her Spouse from Morn to Eve through the Hundreds of Drury."

If Richard expected—like many eighteenth-century men, including Charlotte's father and brother—that his wife would accept her subordinate status and his libertinism, he must have been unpleasantly surprised. All the evidence he had had of her personality, even upon their short acquaintance, should have warned him that Charlotte would have even less inclination for wifely deference than she had for domestic duties. If Richard had left a record of *his* side of their story, perhaps he would have faulted his wife for her aversion to conventional feminine roles, or even suggested that they were sexually incompatible. It is possible that Charlotte, so entranced by the romantic idea of marriage, recoiled from its sexual realities. Always prone to identify with male rather than female models, she may have found herself repelled by Richard's sexual demands.

But Richard did not write his autobiography (and none of his letters, if he wrote them, have survived), so we do not know if he rushed into the arms of prostitutes out of his own frustration and disappointment in his marriage, or simply because he was a congenital libertine. Judging by Charlotte's account, Richard resembled the debauched rake hero of the first four acts of a Colley Cibber comedy. But if Richard was a Loveless, Charlotte was no Amanda: there was none of the long-suffering wife in her. She did not hesitate to express her feelings of neglect and anger.

The Charkes' married life degenerated into a constant tension and bickering, undoubtedly conducted at the highest histrionic pitch. In this respect, at least, they were well-matched. Dr. Burney painted an illuminating picture of this ill-assorted couple: "Charke was a dancing-master, an actor, a man of humour, and an excellent performer on the violin. He was married to Colley Cibber's daughter, who had likewise acute parts [sharp intelligence], and merit, as an actress; but there was nothing in which this ingenious pair exercised their talents more successfully, than in mutually plaguing each other."[25]

7

Chambermaids and Pretty Men

(1731–32)

Swaggering onto the stage in male disguise, Charlotte confided to the audience: "I think I'm a pretty man whate're I am for a woman: and this beardless boy may have as good success with the fair Sex, as if I had been a Page in a particular Family, and Destin'd from my childhood for a comfort to my Lady's old age." It was November 12, 1731, and she was playing Mrs. Raison, the spendthrift wife of a grocer, in the final act of *Greenwich Park*, a comedy written by William Mountfort a few years before his murder.[1] Even in petticoats, Mrs. Raison is no submissive female; her husband complains that he cannot control her: "you took an Oath, too, Wife, to Love, Honour, and Obey me; but you have taken your own Measure for all that; you have a Spirit that the Devil cannot Conquer" (I, i).

In Act V, Mrs. Raison disguises herself as a man in order to catch her lover, Young Reveller (played by Colley), in the act of courting another woman, Florella (played by Hester Booth), at a masquerade. She intends to seduce Florella and prove her unfaithful to Young Reveller, unaware that Florella has hatched the same plot against her. Some funny moments ensue as the two cross-dressed women try to outdo each other in macho bluster, vying to court a disguised character named Dorinda (played by Mrs. Horton), whom each believes to be the other. When, at the conclusion of the play, Mr. Raison is told that "this Lady in Breeches" is really his wife, he responds: "Nay, 'tis no great wonder, for she always wore 'em since I had her."

In the light of the course her life and career would take, Charlotte's performance that evening was a memorable occasion, for it was her first appearance on the stage in men's clothes. (She would play Mrs. Raison twice more that season.) At the beginning of her second full year as an actress, eighteen-year-old Charlotte was already embarked upon the path that would eventually make her both celebrated and notorious. How she must have relished this part! It was only a few years earlier that she had worried her mother and scandalized the neighbours as she stomped around Hillingdon with a gun slung over her arm. Now she could play the man with impunity—and people paid to see her. Colley, the manager who would have borne responsibility for this production (since he starred in it), must have cast her in this part, so he clearly thought that she looked convincing (and attractive) in breeches. Did he recollect that morning in Twickenham fourteen years earlier, when he discovered his four-year-old daughter parading in a ditch, wearing his wig and hat?

Charlotte's own daughter, Catherine Maria Charke, whom everyone called Kitty, had been born at the end of November 1730, and christened on December 6, at the parish church of St. Clement Danes. The location of her christening indicates that Charlotte and Richard lived in that parish at the time, perhaps in one of the small alleys that ran eastward from Drury Lane. Large numbers of prostitutes roamed by day as well as night there, and footpads lurked in shadowy doorways. Both groups found rich pickings among the patrons of the theatre and the denizens of the brothels and taverns—such as the notorious Rose, which abutted the playhouse—where outbursts of drunken rage periodically led to violence, even murder. For Charlotte and Richard, though, the location had its advantages of proximity to the theatre, and cheap rents.

Charlotte initially had hoped that Kitty's birth would improve her marriage, that affection for his daughter might encourage Richard to exercise some degree of responsibility, perhaps even to embrace family life. But Kitty failed to inspire that sentimental reformation: Richard proved as bad a father as he was a husband.

Soon after Kitty was born, Charlotte had returned to acting: she must have wished not to suspend her new career longer than necessary, but she also understood that she could not rely upon Richard to support her and their child. She bore most of the weight of maintaining her household, yet as her husband, Richard was entitled to control her earnings as well as his own. Since he exhausted his own income and poached hers, Charlotte could not have lived on her salary of twenty shillings a week without periodic contributions from her father (who must by now have realized the extent of his son-in-law's negligence), although Richard wheedled a portion of Colley's monetary gifts from Charlotte, too.

It is unclear how Charlotte managed to care for her infant daughter under these circumstances, since she does not seem to have sent Kitty out of London to nurse. Perhaps she employed a nurse in town. Or, when Kitty was older, Charlotte may have taken her to Colley's house on nearby Charles Street to be looked after by one of the servants. Her mother would probably have been unable to help: Katherine's health remained fragile and she continued to live outside of town, having taken up lodgings in Kensington. Whatever Charlotte's arrangements, Kitty seems to have flourished. She was, apparently, a robust little girl—as she would have to be, to survive the childhood that awaited her.

Charlotte may have returned to the stage as early as December 19, 1730, to play Madamoiselle; in any event, she did play that role on the following January 11, and repeated it twice more before the end of the 1730–31 season. But if she had hoped that this successful performance would quickly lead to other roles equally important or better, she was disappointed. Like most other new members of the company, Charlotte had to wait for parts to become available, usually through the deaths or retirements of veteran company members or the staging of a new play that might offer her a part unclaimed by a senior actress. Meanwhile, she had to content herself with small roles in mainpieces and larger roles in afterpieces.

On February 15, 1731, Charlotte took over from Mary Heron the role of Aurora in an afterpiece entitled *Cephalus and Procris*, her only role besides Madamoiselle that season. This piece, with its mythological content, songs, and interspersed series of "pantomime interludes" (called "Harlequin Grand Volgi"), was characteristic of the imaginative

Charlotte as a young woman. (Anon., Mrs. Chark, daughter of C. Cibber. Brown wash drawing. Courtesy of the Garrick Club [ET Archive]. The authenticity of this portrait is not definitively established, but seems likely: see Folkenflick, "Images," 149–50.)

spectacles that were so popular on the eighteenth-century stage but were decried by traditionalists, who accused these "irrational" entertainments of pandering to the vulgar desire for dances, ambitious sets, extravagant costumes, and complicated stage machinery.

Cephalus and Procris followed the customary model of a two-part pantomime, in which a comic harlequinade was interwoven between the acts of a serious story derived from classical antiquity. In this case, the Greek myth of Cephalus and Procris progressed through dialogue and song, while the harlequin story proceeded through silent pantomime. In her role of Aurora, Charlotte would have been clad in the glittery splendour that befitted the goddess of the dawn (possibly sporting a pair of wings), as she sang of her unrequited love for the shepherd Cephalus, and set into motion the events that would result in his beloved Procris' death. As this tragic story unfolded, it was periodically interrupted by completely unrelated scenes in which Harlequin and Columbine romped through an antic series of comic misadventures.

Charlotte played the role of Aurora often during the 1730–31 season: the masque had at least fifteen more performances before June. Though she was never billed as a singer—unlike Kitty Raftor, for instance, who was brought upon the stage first as a singer and then gained fame as a comic actress—Charlotte must have possessed a singing voice pleasant and strong enough to carry this role and the ballad opera parts she later assumed. On April 24, she and Richard shared a benefit night, for which they chose to repeat *Cephalus and Procris* as an afterpiece to John Fletcher's early-seventeenth-century comedy *Rule a Wife and Have a Wife*.

Richard and Charlotte probably selected *Rule a Wife and Have a Wife* because of its perennial popularity and particularly good roles for Drury Lane's stars (since neither of them acted in it). *Rule a Wife and Have a Wife*, as its title indicates, is a marriage comedy whose main plot tells a "taming of the shrew" story, in which a husband brings his assertive wife to heel. But the play includes a mirroring subplot in which these roles are reversed: a blustering husband is mastered by his wife.

Charlotte and Richard must have recognized the applicability of this play to the power struggles in their own marriage, and perhaps they were still able to share a moment of amused, if strained, self-recognition. Most of the proceeds from their benefit must have gone directly into

Richard's purse, however, and from there to publicans and prostitutes, where it would have done little to promote domestic harmony.

Attending the Charkes' benefit performance was "Adomo, Oronoco Tomo Caboshirre of the Great Country of Dawhomay, under the Mighty Trudo Audato Povesaw Danjer Enjow Suveveto, Emperor of Pawpaw in Africa, who lately conquer'd the great Kingdoms of Ardah and Whidah."[2] Like other West African coastal kingdoms, Dahomey was a crucial link in the British and European slave trading chain, receiving guns and other goods in exchange for slaves who were shipped across the Atlantic to the sugar and tobacco colonies of the West Indies and the Americas. The horrors of the Middle Passage and the extreme brutality of slavery on the West Indies plantations killed large numbers of the slaves, creating a constant need for new ones; good relations with Britain's West African trading partners, therefore, were critical to preserving this profitable system. An ambassador from such a partner would be treated with careful hospitality, and a trip to the theatre was de rigueur for visiting dignitaries.

The presence of an African prince would have been welcome on a benefit night, for it probably increased the house receipts: some spectators would have considered Adomo—especially if he wore his tribal robes—a spectacle as much worth the price of admission as the show itself. (The emissary was all the more interesting because his kingdom was famed for its army regiment of women warriors, a select group who dressed as soldiers and guarded the emperor. Europeans referred to them as Amazons.)

When the season ended that June, Charlotte and Richard joined other young players in Drury Lane's summer company, once again under Theophilus's management. They both played a number of small roles, and Charlotte was given the distinction of reciting the epilogue to one play.[3] What is much more important, though, that summer Charlotte made a contribution to theatre history by creating a character in the premiere of a new, groundbreaking play, George Lillo's *The London Merchant*.

Often dubbed the first "bourgeois tragedy," *The London Merchant* tells the unhappy story of George Barnwell, an innocent apprentice whose tragic fall begins when he is seduced by a malicious, mercenary older woman, Millwood. Millwood manipulates Barnwell's erotic obsession with her to corrupt him into robbing his honest employer, and then robbing and murdering his beloved uncle. Theophilus played Barnwell. Charlotte's role was Lucy, Millwood's maidservant, one of this didactic play's more complex characters.

The London Merchant was a surprise hit, enticing some unfamiliar faces into the theatre. The second author's benefit, on the sixth night of its run, was performed, "with great Applause, to a crowded Audience, there being present most of the eminent Merchants of the City of London."[4] The eminent merchants were not the only ones to show an interest: the Queen, then at Hampton Court, sent a messenger for a copy of the play, presumably with the idea of ordering a command performance.[5] (This apparently did not materialize, but the King and Queen did see it in London that October.)

Lillo's tragedy ran for seventeen performances that summer, and—greatest triumph of all—the managers brought it into the repertory in the autumn, staging it twelve times during the 1731–32 season, and retained its original cast. Not yet nineteen years old, Charlotte had already created her first role, played in front of illustrious audiences, and enjoyed her first sustained run in a celebrated mainpiece during the regular season. (She appeared as Lucy in a total of twenty-nine performances over the course of the year.) The managers raised her salary to thirty shillings per week, and also gave her the breeches part of Mrs. Raison.

The summer of 1731 brought bad news as well as good to Drury Lane, however, when the veteran actress Mary Porter suffered a very serious accident. Mrs. Porter, despite her physical unattractiveness and tremulous voice, was greatly admired as London's leading tragedienne. Chetwood explained that although "Nature had been niggard in Voice and Face," Mrs. Porter was so powerful an actress that "her just Action, Eloquence of Look and Gesture, mov'd Astonishment!" She possessed, echoed the theatre manager and historian Benjamin Victor, an "elevated Dignity in her Mien, and threw out a spirited Propriety in all Characters of Rage; but when Grief and Tenderness possessed her, she subsided into the most affecting Softness."[6]

Though she kept a house in Covent Garden, Mrs. Porter also had a home near Hendon, on the outskirts of London, where she was accustomed to drive alone in her chaise, carrying a brace of pistols for protection against the highwaymen who haunted lonely country roads to rob, and sometimes wound or murder, travellers. Some "gentlemen of the road," such as Dick Turpin—and his fictional equivalent Captain Macheath—became folk heroes for their daring exploits and escapes from the law, but highwaymen represented real dangers, as the continual newspaper accounts of armed robberies and assaults testified. "The Northern Roads have been lately, and continue so still, infested with Highwaymen, that the People in those Parts are fearful of coming to town on their Business, they making it a constant Practice to rob at Noon-Day," reported *The Daily Advertiser* on August 10.

Nonetheless, independent Mary Porter braved the dangers of the road, and in the summers, when she did not perform, she enjoyed driving out to take the air. One night in early August, a highwayman burst from the shadows as she passed, grabbed the reins of her horse, and jerked her chaise to a stop. He must have thought that this lone woman was an easy target, until he found himself staring into the barrel of her pistol. Pleading for his life, the highwayman told her that he had taken up banditry only out of desperation, because his large family was starving. Mary, deeply moved by his account, gave him all the money in her purse, about ten guineas (a considerable sum), took his name, and let him go.

When the man left, she applied her whip to the horse to continue on her way, but the animal started, throwing the chaise out of the track and overturning it. Mary was dashed violently onto the ground, dislocating her thigh.[7] Grave as this injury was, she was in fact lucky: the papers that summer reported several similar chaise accidents in which the passengers had been killed. But her injury incapacitated her for two years, and left her unable to walk normally ever again.* Despite the highwayman's partial responsibility for her painful injury, soon after her accident Mary caused his claims to be investigated, and, when she found that he had told her the truth, she took up a collection for him, raising nearly £60.[8]

Mrs. Porter was obviously both a formidable and a kind-hearted woman. Many at Drury Lane must have been sincerely dismayed by her accident and missed her presence in the green room during her long con-

---

* Mrs. Porter returned to the stage in 1733, limping and using her cane as an expressive prop. Playing Queen Elizabeth deciding to execute Mary, Queen of Scots, she slammed her cane down with such force that the audience jumped.

valescence. But in the way of the theatre world, her misfortune made others' fortunes. Most of Mrs. Porter's important roles were claimed by other veterans, especially Mrs. Horton, Mrs. Thurmond, and Jane Cibber. They in turn vacated roles for younger players. Charlotte herself would eventually benefit from Mrs. Porter's accident when, two years later, she was given her role of Alicia in *Jane Shore*.

During the 1731–32 season, Charlotte reprised her roles of the year before, and acquired a new one, Trusty, maidservant to Mary Heron's Lady Townly, in *The Provok'd Husband*. Once again, Charlotte played a maid to a narcissistic woman. Trusty was a less meaty part than Madamoiselle or Lucy, but she did have some of the requisite pert, lively scenes. In the best one, Trusty rescues her mistress, who has gambled away all her money, by snatching back a sum that Lady Townly had previously given her steward to pay her debt to a tradesman:

> TRUSTY: There they are Madam—[*Pours the money out of the Bag.*] The pretty Things—were so near falling into a nasty Tradesman's hand, I protest it made me tremble for them—I fancy your Ladyship had as good give me that bad Guinea, for luck's sake—thank you Madam. [*Takes a Guinea.*]
>
> LADY TOWNLY: Why, I did not bid you take it.
>
> TRUSTY: No, but your Ladyship look'd as if you were just going to bid me, and so I was willing to save you the trouble of speaking, Madam.

Charlotte was beginning to develop a line in chambermaid roles. Her casting in these parts, though not exclusive, was consistent enough in her early years at Drury Lane to reveal something about how Colley, Wilks, and Booth perceived her strengths at this early point in her career. Her youth had something to do with it, since these usually were not starring roles (though they could be important ones), and ladies' maids were expected to be young or at least to look it. Yet there must have been other reasons for casting Charlotte in these parts than her mere youth, for she was not the only young actress in the company.

The convention of the chambermaid role, as it was inherited from Restoration comedy, required the actress to enact a particular set of character traits. An actress playing a chambermaid, said John Hill in

The Actor, a 1750 treatise on the art of acting, "must never be without an extreme volubility of tongue." The chambermaid has to *talk*—to chatter, to engage in quick, witty repartee. Furthermore, Hill stipulated, the actress must be able to assume "an arch and cunning look, with a world of discernment, and occasional secrecy in it."[9] The maid is often a confidante and collabourator with her mistress, in innocent or less innocent matters—affairs, seduction, extortion. She is often a go-between in an intrigue, and a fixer when the intrigue threatens to go awry. She enjoys a freedom of expression that comes from her constant proximity to her employer, but she is also a working-class woman operating in an upper-class context. She is worldly, sexually aware, even capable of blackmail. Chambermaid roles suited Charlotte's assertive, voluble personality.

In January 1732, Charlotte turned nineteen. That winter, she met Henry Fielding. It seems astonishing that, after his vigorous satire of Cibber (and Wilks as well) in *The Author's Farce,* Fielding would once again be writing for Drury Lane, but so it was.[10] With that play and his popular burlesque, *Tom Thumb: A Tragedy,* at the Little Haymarket, Fielding had made himself the hottest playwright in London. But one of his afterpieces at the Little Haymarket the previous spring, called *The Fall of Mortimer,* had gotten the company into big trouble with the authorities by attacking Walpole. *The Fall of Mortimer* played fifteen times, but aroused such controversy and threats from the government that some of the troupe became afraid to continue. In July the piece was included in a grand jury warrant against libellous and seditious literature, and later in the month the high constable and his men appeared at the theatre with a warrant for the arrest of the performers, though they all managed to escape.[11] But on August 23, *The Daily Advertiser* reported that "we hear that the Players who acted *The Fall of Mortimer,* have thereby render'd themselves so obnoxious to the Government that several of them are taken up, and that Warrants are out against the rest."

Though the precise history of the government's persecution of Fielding's Little Haymarket company at this time is confused, Fielding's company was effectively suppressed that summer, and London's most successful playwright found himself without a theatre.[12] The Drury

Lane managers were not so protective of their dignity that they would pass up the opportunity to bring his kind of success into their fold, for they badly needed new plays. Past insults were forgiven.

For Fielding's part, whatever the depth of his animosity to Cibber and Wilks, the opportunity to have his plays staged by Britain's best theatre company was irresistible, and there was the fact of Drury Lane's larger audience and profits. In any event, he did not have much choice. Fielding associated himself with the company, for which he would write seven new plays in the next season and a half.

When Charlotte met him that year, Henry Fielding was a magnetic man of twenty-four whose oversized personality complemented his tall, robust frame. He was not handsome, with his long chin and exceedingly aquiline nose, but he had penetrating, lively eyes and a ready laugh. The son of a high-ranking army officer, Fielding was born to aristocratic family connections but no money; as he once remarked to his second cousin Lady Mary Wortley Montagu, in his need to earn his bread he would have to become either "a Hackney Writer or a Hackney Coachman."[13]

High-spirited, passionate, and witty, Fielding was a great conversationalist, a graceful dancer, and a libertine, equally at home in upper-class drawing rooms and Covent Garden brothels. Classically educated at Eton College and the University of Leyden in Holland, he was learned and intellectually vigorous. He was hot-tempered, with a tendency to get into fights; more than once he was hauled before a magistrate for brawling. Owing to his robust appetites for food, drink, and women, his love of gambling, and his general improvidence, he was perennially strapped, even when the success of his plays brought him considerable sums in author's benefits. Yet he was also a moralist whose zany farces and burlesques served as the vehicle for serious social and political commentary.

Fielding gave Charlotte her second opportunity to create a role, this time during the regular season. In *The Modern Husband,* a satiric drama that his biographer describes as "the work that may fairly be considered the masterpiece of his career as a [conventional] dramatist," Charlotte played Lately, another in her line of chambermaids.[14] Opening on February 14, 1732, *The Modern Husband* featured Colley in a particularly powerful role as the vicious, debauched Lord Richly, and had parts for Theo and Jane as well. The play is a dark one, evoking a vicious world in which corruption and self-interest dominate all levels of society, from wealthy lords to chambermaids.

Mr. Modern, the "modern husband," is both a cuckold and a pimp: he essentially prostitutes his wife to wealthy men and lives off the monetary presents they give her. Mrs. Modern is grimly conscious that she has become a whore. She clings to her reputation, and when Mr. Modern points out that it is strange she should treasure the shadow of virtue when she has so easily sacrificed the substance, she replies " 'Tis the Shadow only that is valuable—Reputation is the Soul of Vertue."

The plot revolves around Mr. Modern's refinement of his prostitution scheme, in which he plans to set up a trap to "discover" Mrs. Modern with one of her lovers and sue the lover for damages under the law against "criminal conversation." (Crim con, as it was called, was an eighteenth-century law by which a man's sexual intercourse with a woman married to another man was considered to violate her husband's property rights in her body.)

The part of Lately owed a lot to Madamoiselle—Charlotte uttered virtually the same sycophantic lie to Mrs. Modern (played by Mary Heron) as she did to Lady Fancifull, in a comparable looking-glass scene: "In my Opinion your Ladyship never looked better." This is a harsher world than Vanbrugh's, though: Lately emphasizes the calculating, manipulative aspect of the chambermaid. Mrs. Modern, acutely aware that her beauty is fading and with it her livelihood, indulges a desperate maliciousness upon which Lately skilfully plays.

> MRS. MODERN: I never could see any want of Sense in you, Lately. . . . What think you of Mrs. Charmer?
>
> LATELY: Think of her! that were I a Man, she should be the last Woman I attacked. I think her an ugly, ungenteel, squinting, flirting, impudent, odious, dirty Puss.
>
> MRS. MODERN: Upon my Word, Lately, you have a vast deal of Wit too. . . . (*Exit*)
>
> LATELY: I know not whether my Talent of Praise, or of Slander, is of more Service to me; whether I get more by flattering my Lady, or abusing all her Acquaintance. (IV, iv)

The Modern Husband was a solid success that ran thirteen consecutive nights (its thirteenth performance was a benefit for Mrs. Porter in her convalescence). Fielding was now entrenched as Drury Lane's most important playwright.

In early May, Charlotte joined most of the company's principal players— her father, Jane, Mrs. Horton, Wilks, and Mrs. Heron—in Colley's comedy *The Double Gallant,* her second opportunity to act in one of his plays, and her second breeches part. Colley cast her in Mrs. Thurmond's old role as Clarinda, the self-assertive young heroine who dons men's clothes, torments Clerimont, the man who faithfully loves her (and whom she really loves), and vies with another woman, Silvia (played by Jane), for the attentions of the rakish Atall (played by Colley), who has made love to each of them under different false names. The scenes in which Atall becomes caught between Silvia and Clarinda must have projected an additional perverse amusement as a family drama: no matter how caught up they were in the play's fiction, the audience still would have known that the romantic triangle of these characters consisted of Colley, his daughter-in-law, and his daughter.

In another fifth-act transformation, Charlotte strode onstage in a white wig and breeches, pretending to be a man seeking Clarinda's hand, boasting that "he" has lain with Clarinda many times, swaggering, blustering, and threatening swordplay. With this role, Charlotte was now on her way to developing a second line in breeches parts. Tall and lithe, she clearly had the figure for these roles, and she had long possessed an inclination for them as well.

8

SHOW, SHOW, SHOW, SHOW!

(1732)

A strong scent of singed hide and roasting flesh drifted from the direction of Pye Corner, where the carcasses of pigs dangled in cookshop windows. Up near the sheep pens of West Smithfield, performers danced in gaudy costumes, sang the latest playhouse ballads, played oboe concerts, juggled swords, and walked the slack rope, balancing glasses full of liquor on the backs of their hands. Throughout the adjacent streets, rubber-boned contortionists tied themselves into knots, conjurers pulled trees from hats, tumblers cartwheeled and somersaulted, wrestlers (both men and women) grunted as they grappled, and fire-eaters swallowed flaming torches.

The Great Hog, temporarily spared the fate of his roasted brothers, slumbered and snuffled as spectators gaped in awe at his bulk. Conjoined twins, hermaphrodites, bearded women, dwarfs, and giants displayed themselves in tents before the "scientifically" curious. Wax likenesses of the royal family stood stiff and proud in gorgeous clothing. Punch and Joan fought their perennial domestic battles, while flesh-and-blood actors in brightly coloured costumes performed farces on the balconies of their wooden booths, inviting people to buy tickets for the "droll" inside.

Taverns offered ale and song, street vendors sold peaches, pears, apples, and nuts, and quacks hawked patent medicines. Gamblers cajoled passersby into rigged games of chance, pickpockets slipped handkerchiefs from pockets, cutpurses silently severed the cords binding purses and canes to their owners, and preachers railed against the evils of it all. Behind the rows of booths and tents, children whirled around in flying swings and merry-go-rounds, whose proprietors kept up a continual cry of "Come, who rides?"

Charlotte would have been no stranger to Bartholomew Fair, but now for the first time she was part of the spectacle as a performer. She must have felt a thrill of anticipation when on August 23, 1732, the Lord Mayor of London made his stately progress to West Smithfield to proclaim the beginning of the fair, pausing at Newgate prison, where "Mr. Nichols in the Absence of the Keeper of that Gaol, drank to his Lordship out of a Cool tankard, and his Lordship was pleased to pledge him according to Custom."[1] Everyone was delighted by the pomp and ceremony of the fair's beginning, with the likely exception of the hundred wretched inmates jailed in that pestilent prison, awaiting trial at September's sessions.

Whereas London's playhouses were largely the provinces of the more privileged classes, who could afford admissions ranging from one to five shillings, the fairs of London belonged to the people. From labourers to lords, paupers to princesses, the crowds packing themselves into the streets and fields of Smithfield at the end of August represented a riotous cross section of London society. The fairs were originally markets—the ancestor of Bartholomew Fair was the annual cloth market—but by the eighteenth century, the mercantile purpose of the London fairs had been long engulfed by entertainment. Despite many attempts over the years by ecclesiastical and civil authorities to suppress them as disorderly gatherings and affronts to public decency, the London fairs—Mayfair, Tottenham Court Fair, Southwark Fair, and others—flourished. Bartholomew Fair was the largest and oldest of all, held for fourteen days beginning August 23 (the twenty-fourth was St. Bartholomew's Day), with the exception of September 2, a fast day in commemoration of the Great Fire, when it was suspended. The fair had long ago overflowed its original grounds at the ancient St. Bartholomew priory, expanding around the medieval church and hospital of St. Bartholomew into the open area of West Smithfield and its adjoining streets.

Ned Ward, writing as the London Spy in 1699, reported a

misanthrope's nightmare of the "innumerable throng, whose impatient desires of seeing merry-andrew's grimaces had led them ankle deep into filth and crowded as close as a barrel of figs."[2] Describing Bartholomew Fair a century later, William Wordsworth exclaimed, "What a shock / For eyes and ears! What anarchy and din!" To the poet of wild nature, the utterly urban fair was grotesque, a "Parliament of Monsters, Tents and Booths."[3]

Plays had long been performed at Bartholomew Fair by strolling troupes, but in the late seventeenth century, actors from the established playhouses began to join together to offer programmes of short pieces in the small wooden theatres called playbooths. The booths were wooden buildings fronted by a "gallery," a balcony set before a show-cloth that pictorially advertised the show within. Costumed actors would play a short entertainment on the gallery—Ward described the "kings, queens, heroes, harlots, buffoons, mimics, priests, profligates, and devils in the balcony"—to lure the crowd to pay their money for the programme inside.

Performances ran continually all day, starting in the late morning or early afternoon, punctuated by half-hour intervals: the programme might consist of abridged versions of standard plays or the traditional "drolls"—farcical short plays, puppet shows, or pantomimes—that enacted traditional tales such as the story of Dick Whittington, the poor boy who became lord mayor of London, and his cat. As they sat in the booths waiting for the performances to begin, the audience fidgeted and chatted restlessly, passed around baskets of fruit and nuts, and periodically broke out into the impatient bear garden chant, "Show, show, show, show!"[4]

Though fair booths charged only a penny, the volume of spectators and the duration of performances made this venue extremely lucrative for actors: if they could endure the taxing schedule, players could earn in one day what they earned in a week at the playhouse. Competition was fierce amidst the sea of spectacles. Several groups of actors operated rival playbooths, and other sorts of booths offered all sorts of ingenious entertainments.

That summer, Charlotte's troupe not only had to face the competition of other actors, but also to vie with shows such as those offered by Richard Yeates, whose entertainments included "The celebrated Story of Fryar Bacon, Fryar Bungy, the Brazen Head and Miles their Man: in which these characters attempt to make a Brazen Head speak with human Voice." Also on display was a "curious Musical Clock, with three hundred Moving Figures. The Scenes entirely new." If these exhibits were not enough, Yeates Junior could demonstrate his "incomparable Dexterity of Hand, his Showers of Gold and Silver; he sticks a Pack of Cards to the Ceiling, and calls 'em down one by one." The booth topped off this menu of sights with "the Little German boy and French Girl who perform a variety of Sword-Dancing and Tumbling, and were never shewn in England before."[5]

Part of a troupe managed by two fellow actors at Drury Lane along with a member of the Lincoln's Inn Fields company, Charlotte performed in the Great Booth opposite the gate of St. Bartholomew's Hospital. The programme was *The History of King Henry the VIIIth and Anna Bullen:* "Containing, Her Marriage, Coronation and Tragical Fall, by the Artful Insinuations of Cardinal Wolsey; the Intercession of the young Princess Elizabeth; and several other Historical Passages. Intermix'd with a Comic Opera set to Old Ballad Tunes and Country Dances. With the diverting humours of Squire Nump-Skull and his Man Lack-Brains." Preceding the play, "there was rope dancing by Mlle de Reverant and two children and tumbling by Miss Derrum, a child of nine years." The play was followed by dancing, "particularly a *Highlander* by a Gentleman for his Diversion."[6]

Charlotte played "Lucy the Chambermaid" in the comic opera. Among their audience may have been the Prince of Wales, who brought the three princesses royal to the fair, accompanied by the Dukes of Grafton and Newcastle, the Earl of Tankerville, and "several other Persons of Quality," a newspaper reported. "After having view'd the several Performances there, they return'd to Kensington very much pleased with their Diversions."[7]

Bartholomew Fair ended a summer that for Charlotte had been exhilarating and exhausting, both physically and emotionally. When the regular season had ended the previous June, she and Richard had remained in London. Once again, Theophilus managed Drury Lane's summer company, and that summer he cast Charlotte as the leading lady in two of the most important tragedies of the eighteenth-century stage. On June 9, Charlotte played Andromache in *The Distrest Mother,* one of the tragic roles in which Mrs. Oldfield, though principally a comedienne, had achieved great fame. And at the end of the summer, on August 15, she assumed Mrs. Porter's role of Alicia in *Jane Shore*.[8] With the exception of the idiosyncratic *London Merchant*, these were Charlotte's first performances in tragedy. Theophilus, for all his rakish ways, was a thoroughly professional manager who would not have assigned Charlotte the roles if he had not believed she could handle them. But he seems to have assumed some responsibility for encouraging his sister, doing what he could to broaden her acting experience in the training ground of summer theatre.

In later years, Charlotte retained a vivid, humorous memory of her feelings as she played these characters, following in the footsteps of the country's greatest actresses. Now she reconsidered her sister-in-law Jane's admonition that anxiety was the price of experience, and rued her former arrogance: "By this Time I began to FEEL I FEARED; and the Want of it [that is, her lack of fear in her first performances] was sufficiently paid home to me, in the Tremor of Spirits I suffered in such daring Attempts; However, Fortune was my Friend, and I escaped with Life; for I solemnly declare, that I expected to make an odd Figure in the Bills of Mortality——DIED ONE, OF CAPITAL CHARACTERS." Even accounting for the licence allowed the young performers in the summer company, Andromache and Alicia were intimidating challenges for any actress, especially a nineteen-year-old with two years of experience in mostly lesser comic roles. No wonder Charlotte felt that these characters might kill her.

Andromache and Alicia are tragic characters whose emotions are writ large: Andromache suffers deeply and stoically; Alicia is propelled by jealousy into violent passion and madness. The performance of these two different models of tragic heroines demanded that Charlotte master the highly stylized tragic acting techniques of the eighteenth century. Tragedy, to a greater extent than comedy, was dominated by a body of theory that governed rather strictly the expression of character and emotion.

Styles or schools of tragic acting were always developing and shifting, and famous actors were associated with one or another approach over the decades: the restraint of Thomas Betterton, the elegance of Barton Booth, the emotionality of James Quin (then a leading player at

Lincoln's Inn Fields), the cadence and tonality of Colley Cibber, the later "naturalism" of Charles Macklin and David Garrick. Every generation declared that its preferred style was closer to "Nature" than those that preceded it. But to our modern eyes, all acting styles of the eighteenth century would seem highly artificial, even camp, including that of Garrick, the mid-century actor-manager most celebrated for reforming acting in the direction of naturalism.

Tragic acting traced its theory back to classical and Renaissance oratory, painting, and sculpture, actors shaping their delivery and arranging their stance and gestures in a manner beholden to classical models: the well-educated Barton Booth was said to study history painting and statuary in order to devise the much-praised "attitudes" that he struck on the stage. Distinct qualities of recitation, expression, and gesture were considered to belong to each different emotional state. High emotion was conveyed in the form of the "rant."

In the early 1730s, in particular, "violence" of speech and gesture was the preferred mode. Actors delivered speeches in an oratorical or declamatory mode, planting themselves on the stage and expecting the audience to respond to the beauty and power of their voices: this prevailing style of delivery may be compared illustratively to the aria in opera. Actors "toned"—intoned—their lines, obeying the requirement of attention to cadence and sonority; the volume and musicality of an actor's voice were all-important. A weak actor (or a great actor having a bad night) could reduce a speech intended to convey powerful feelings (and to arouse them in the audience) to "whining monotony."[9]

Charlotte's two roles exemplified the tragic extremes of her day. Younger actors usually attempted to imitate the performance style of the players who had immediately preceded them, so Mrs. Oldfield and Mrs. Porter would have been much in her mind. Andromache, the "distrest mother," is the widow of Hector in the aftermath of the Trojan War; the role is permeated from the beginning with the emotions of grief and loss. Mourning her husband's death and the desecration of his corpse at the hands of Achilles, Andromache is given the opportunity of saving the life of her young son, Astyanax, by marrying one of the conquering Greeks, Achilles' son Pyrrhus. Though she experiences this as a violation of love and sacred duty, Andromache agrees to the marriage, planning thus to secure her son's safety and then kill herself.

When Charlotte recited the words Andromache speaks to her maid near the end of the play, as she goes to what she thinks will be her death, she would have tried to convey the pathos of heroic suffering that, if well performed, would cause the audience to weep:

> Oh, my Cephisa! my swoll'n heart is full!
> I have a thousand farewells to my son:
> But tears break in!—Grief interrupts my speech—
> My soul o'erflows in fondness—Let him know
> I dy'd to save him:—"And would die again."
> Season his mind with early hints of glory;
> Make him acquainted with his ancestors;
> Trace out their shining story in his thoughts;
> Dwell on th' exploits of his immortal father,
> And sometimes let him hear his mother's name.

In Nicholas Rowe's *Jane Shore,* a "she-tragedy" (as Rowe called his plays that revolved around the sufferings of women), Jane Shore herself is a pathetic tragic heroine of the Andromache mold. Charlotte's character, Alicia, is her opposite counterpart: whereas Jane confronts her reversal of fortune passively, Alicia is consumed by raging emotion. Once Alicia loved Jane, but now she loathes her because Alicia's lover Hastings, alienated by her temper and wild jealousy, has deserted her and turned his attentions to Jane. In an attempt to exact revenge on Jane, Alicia sets in motion events that cause Hastings to be executed. Guilt, jealousy, and loss propel her into frenzy and, finally, into madness.

To play Alicia's scenes, Charlotte had to rise to a fever pitch of emotion, requiring all of Mrs. Porter's celebrated vehemence. When, after Hastings's death, Alicia is distraught with guilt and horror, Charlotte had to throw herself into raving madness, hallucinating Hastings's figure before her:

> Hark! Something cracks above! —It shakes, it totters!
> And see, the nodding ruin falls to crush me!
> 'Tis fallen, 'tis here! I feel it on my brain!
>
> A waving flood of bluish fire swells o'er me;
> And now 'tis out, and I am drowned in blood.

—Ha! What are thou, thou horrid headless trunk?
It is my Hastings! —See, he wafts me on!
—Away! I go! I fly! I follow thee. (V, i)

Charlotte played three other roles at Drury Lane that summer, including Mrs. Slammerkin (meaning "slut") in *The Beggar's Opera,* one of the prostitutes and thieves who drink with Captain Macheath in a tavern near Newgate prison. More significantly, she played Roderigo in Shakespeare's *Othello.* Roderigo, the "gulled gentleman" whose foolishness and love for Desdemona allow him to be dominated by Iago, is an important secondary character who is on stage fairly often until Iago murders him near the end of the play.

Othello was not only Charlotte's first attempt at Shakespeare, it was also her first opportunity to play a man. Roles in which actresses played male characters are often called "travesty parts" to distinguish them from "breeches parts," in which an actress played a female character who cross-dresses within the play. In the latter the audience understood the character to be a woman in breeches, and the play exploited the discrepancy between the masculinity projected by the clothing and the female body underneath it. Greater ambiguity attended a travesty role, because the audience theoretically could have been unaware that underneath the male dress was a female body. Even when the spectators were conscious of the player's identity (the playbills customarily made clear that an actress would be playing a male role), the illusion was not broken in the course of the play, and the male character was never revealed to be a woman in disguise. (Travesty roles ran the gamut from "straight" impersonation, as when Charlotte played Roderigo, to the sorts of parody or burlesque roles she would play later, in which the gender reversal was emphasized as part of the joke.) In a breeches part, Charlotte needed to signal (to the audience if not to the other characters) her character's femaleness underneath the male clothes, and in a travesty role, she needed either to pass as a man, or to parody one. Women pretending to be men, and men themselves, were starting to become her signature roles.

One role Charlotte did not play onstage was the sentimental, self-sacrificing wife waiting patiently for the fifth act when her husband will realize his errors—and she was not inclined to play this part at home, either. Richard persisted in running after the "common Wenches that were to be had for Half-a-Crown," and Charlotte had beseeched and protested, railed and stormed long enough. So, rather than following her father's characteristic plotline, in which the wife forgives her repentant husband, Charlotte and Richard enacted a scene from a more overtly cynical kind of comedy. "Finding that we were in the same Circumstances, in regard to each other, that Mr. Sullen and his Wife were," Charlotte said, "we agreed to part." Her allusion to the divorce scene in George Farquhar's *The Beaux' Stratagem* conjures up a vivid picture of the state of Charlotte and Richard's marriage.

> MRS. SULLEN: Have we not been a perpetual offence to each other—
> a gnawing vulture at the heart?
> SULLEN: A frightful goblin to the sight?
> MRS. SULLEN: A porcupine to the feelings?
> SULLEN: A perpetual wormwood to the taste?
> MRS. SULLEN: Is there on earth a thing we could agree in?
> SULLEN: Yes: to part.
> MRS. SULLEN: With all my heart.

But legal divorce with the right to remarry was unobtainable in eighteenth-century England for all but those who could afford to solicit the requisite act of Parliament, and who also felt able to withstand having intimate details of their married lives bandied about in newspaper reports and chanted on the streets by ballad singers, as often happened. With divorce out of the question, Charlotte and Richard chose not to pursue other types of formal separation, such as the kind granted by the ecclesiastical courts or the quasi-legal private deed of separation. (The former, "separation by bed and board," did not allow the members of the couple to remarry, while the latter usually did, though such arrangements were by mutual consent and not enforceable in a court of law.)

Both types of separations did provide financial settlements and protection from debts and claims upon income.[10] But separations, too, were costly and time-consuming, and were more often granted for the wife's adultery than the husband's. So Charlotte and Richard simply moved into separate lodgings. Charlotte took Kitty, the only one of

Richard's contributions to her life that she considered valuable: "I thought myself more than amply made Amends for his Follies, in the Possession of her."

It is impossible to say for certain when Charlotte and Richard actually separated. Charlotte is vague in her autobiography, saying only that it happened sometime after Kitty's birth. Because their separation was informal, it generated no court records. Circumstantial evidence points to some time between April 1732, when Charlotte and Richard shared a benefit, and May 1733, when Charlotte was given a benefit of her own: this may suggest she was no longer perceived at Drury Lane as connected to Richard. However, the more senior players did not share benefits, so it is also possible that Charlotte's solo benefit simply indicated that she had risen to a certain stature in the company. And Richard (who is not recorded as having a benefit that year himself) played a violin concerto on that occasion. This may signify little more than professionalism and self-interest, though: the informality of their separation meant that Charlotte and Richard remained legally married. In consequence, Richard retained the legal right to all of Charlotte's earnings (and remained legally responsible for any debts she might contract).

Koon speculates that after the separation, Charlotte and Kitty moved temporarily into Colley's house on Charles Street. There is no evidence for this, but it is certainly possible. With Katherine in Kensington and all the other children out of the house—with the possible exception of Anne, who ran a shop nearby and may not have yet married John Boultby—there would have been ample room. And at this point, Charlotte was still on good terms with her father.

Charlotte and Richard continued to work together and they remained cordial. Charlotte treated Richard, on his occasional visits, "with the same good Nature and Civility I might an old, decay'd Acquaintance, that I was certain came to ask me a Favour." The "favours" Richard sought were actually demands for money that, he reminded her, was legally his. He did not turn to the law to enforce his rights, but it was still in Charlotte's interest, thinking not only of herself but also of Kitty, to keep relations with him as amicable as possible. When Richard's debauchery exhausted his funds, he did not scruple to press Charlotte, and she complied: "I as constantly supplied his Wants; and have got from my Father many an auxiliary Guinea, I am certain, to purchase myself a new Pair of Horns." The image is a curious one: it was a wronged husband, not a wronged wife, to whose forehead a cuckold's horns were affixed. Thus Charlotte described herself as an unfortunate man, figuratively emasculated by his wife's adultery. It is as if Richard's "effeminate" financial dependence upon her bestowed upon her a kind of masculinity that his infidelities then undermined.

Charlotte's father had also had an eventful summer, though it was not until September that he completely understood its significance. In June, Colley had taken Katherine off to the northern seaside resort of Scarborough, having particular reason to relax and celebrate. Three years earlier, Sir Richard Steele had died, still holding the patent under which Drury Lane operated (although he had long ceased to involve himself in the playhouse), and the patent was due to expire three years after his death. So the triumvirate had to negotiate a new patent for themselves, a long, uncertain, politically delicate business; in the meantime, they could not feel entirely secure in their governance of the theatre. That May, the hearings were finally completed, and the King granted the patent to "Robert Wilks, Colley Cibber, Barton Booth . . . their Heirs, Executors, Administrators, and Assigns" for a period of twenty-one years.[11]

Colley must have enjoyed the sea bathing and gambling at Scarborough with a feeling of relief that it had all been settled. His satisfaction was short-lived, however, for on July 13 Barton Booth sold half of his share for £2,500 to a wealthy young man named John Highmore. The consequences would be profound, drawn-out, and for some, ruinous.

The era of the triumvirate of actor-managers, who had for more than twenty years brought stability, renown, and financial success to Drury Lane Theatre, abruptly ended. Drury Lane, wrote Victor in 1761, had been the "best conducted, and, consequently, the most flourishing Theatre, in this, or the last Century," managed by "the best Actors of the Age in which they lived."[12] They were stage veterans; Highmore, on the other hand, was only stage-struck. The theatre world fascinated him, but he had no credentials, nor had he much promise of acquiring them. Though he had enjoyed a brief, unpaid (and unsuccessful) flirtation with acting, Highmore's principal relationship to the playhouse was as a member of the audience.

Highmore bargained for the full share of Booth's managerial power, however.[13] He was to become the worst kind of manager: not only had he no professional experience but also, as time would reveal, he had no managerial skills either. And his unmerited self-importance was unbearable. Colley could have reasoned initially that Highmore was an irritant but not much of an obstruction, since he and Wilks together could simply override him. But Colley could not anticipate the next, much more devastating blow.

On September 4, *The Daily Advertiser* contained a correction that might in other circumstances have been grimly humorous: "The Death of Mr. Wilks, the celebrated Comedian, and Master of the Drury-Lane Play-House, as was inserted in one of the Daily Papers, and one of the Evening Posts of Saturday last, is without Foundation, that Gentleman who was a Day or two somewhat indispos'd, being entirely recover'd of the same." Colley's own death had once been erroneously (and in his case, maliciously) reported after he had suffered a brief illness; such mistakes were not uncommon in the papers. But this time *The Daily Advertiser* followed up this notice three days later with another, more alarming one: "Mr. Wilks lies dangerously ill at his house in Bow-street, Covent Garden."

Though Wilks was now in his late sixties, his youthful vigour had always belied his age. His illness fell suddenly and unexpectedly. When the season began in early September, Colley and Booth scrambled to prepare plays that did not include Wilks as a member of the cast, and to find replacements for him in plays that did. As the days went by with no improvement in Wilks's condition, his friends began to fear the worst. On September 14, *The Daily Advertiser* reported that "Mr. Wilks, the celebrated Comedian, continues still so dangerously ill, that there is but little Hope of his Recovery."

On Wednesday, September 27, "about Nine of the Clock, after a long and tedious Indisposition with a Stoppage of Urine, &c., died Mr. Wilks at his House in Bow Street, Covent Garden."[14] The *Daily Post* reported his death with the comment that "the reputation the English

Robert Wilks was a dashing leading man and one of Colley Cibber's partners at the Drury Lane. (Robert Wilks, Esq. in the Character of Harry Wildair. *Courtesy of the Henry E. Huntington Library.)*

theatre has had, was very much owing to his indefatigable care, and regular conducting of the whole." And *The Post-Boy* lamented, "It may be truly said, that his death is the greatest loss the English Stage has ever sustained."

Drury Lane was dark that night as the company mourned the loss of their popular actor and manager. The theatre was dark again on October 4, when at midnight Wilks's body was carried from his house to be interred in the church of St. Paul Covent Garden. "The funeral was very private, according to his own desire."[15] Colley and Theophilus were among the pallbearers.

Charlotte must have joined the rest of the company in mourning deeply the death of an admired actor whom she had known since childhood. For her father, the loss was immeasurable. Wilks's death, he felt, was the last of a series of "unavoidable Accidents" that had begun with Booth's retirement and the death of Mrs. Oldfield. It changed everything.

Colley, now sixty-two years old and as shrewd as ever, saw himself growing increasingly isolated. As the new season got under way, "Old Cibber," as he was now called to distinguish him from his up-and-coming son, Theophilus, foresaw that he would find little pleasure and much frustration working with Highmore. When Wilks's widow, Mary, designated the painter John Ellys, another man completely unfamiliar with the theatre, to manage her share of the patent, he could bear it no longer. To escape "the Importance of One and the Ignorance of the Other," Colley decided, he would appoint his own deputy.[16] He turned to his son, who had long aspired to inherit his father's role. Hiring himself as an actor at an appropriately large salary, Colley leased to Theophilus "his Title, full Power and Management of the Theatre as a Patentee," and began the process of withdrawing, physically and emotionally, from Drury Lane.[17]

9

STORMY WEATHER

(1732–33)

Theophilus Cibber was born in a tempest. The winds were rising from the Channel when Theo arrived on November 25, 1703; at midnight on the twenty-sixth they escalated to hurricane force. Savage gales raged across the south of England, ripping trees from the ground, splintering walls and collapsing roofs, crushing scores of people; at sea, more than fifteen hundred sailors died as their ships foundered in the violent waves. The Great Storm of 1703 still figures in the record books as perhaps the worst in British history. Theo liked to inform people that this tempest had heralded his birth, for he saw the Great Storm as an emblem of his own mind—his passionate temper, his oversized ambitions, and his readiness to court controversy. One wonders if his reading of Shakespeare ever suggested to him that a tempest might also be interpreted as an omen of doom. Comparison with Julius Caesar or Macbeth would probably have gratified Theophilus; he could not have suspected how true the omen would prove.

In the autumn of 1732, when he assumed Colley's place as an actor-manager of the Theatre Royal, Theophilus had been a member of the Drury Lane company for twelve years and had risen rapidly in its hierarchy. Physically he seems to have resembled his father as a youth; he appears to have been similarly short, wiry, and bandy-legged. Offstage he liked to clad his unprepossessing body in showy clothing, so that he resembled one of his father's fops. He was less attractive than Colley, with a pockmarked visage that onstage he often twisted into a "grimace." From an early point in his career, Theophilus accumulated enemies, many inherited from his father, others of his own making. But even many who did not like him had to acknowledge the truth of Chetwood's statement that young Cibber had a "strong Genius for the Theatre."[1]

By 1732, Theophilus had developed into an accomplished, hardworking actor who, as his oversight of the summer company demonstrated, possessed a gift for innovative management. In his third year at Drury Lane, Theo had begun to play an unusually large number of good roles for a young player, and he maintained a heavy schedule of performances thereafter.[2] He was popular with audiences and tireless in his ambition to develop new characters in both comedy and tragedy. He also demonstrated a great flair for pantomime: his vigorous dancing and energetic physical comedy made him one of Drury Lane's leading harlequins. The gusto with which he threw himself into these roles had its consequences, however. In 1726, "as young Mr Cibber was performing the Part of Harlequin in Apollo and Daphne [a pantomime he had created], his Foot slipp'd, and he fell down the Stage and broke his Nose."[3] (This would have done little to improve poor Theo's appearance.)

In 1723, when he was only nineteen, Theo was put in charge of the summer company and managed it successfully; he assumed its direction again for three seasons beginning in 1730.[4] By 1727, he also had begun to assist Wilks in his capacity as manager of acting. Theophilus spared no effort in learning every aspect of the profession he considered himself born to, seeing himself, with justification, as his father's professional heir. Theophilus surely owed his early access to so many good roles, and his position as Wilks's assistant, to Colley's influence. Yet he also owed his success to his own hard work and dedication.

Like his sister Charlotte, Theophilus inherited from their father a flair for the dramatic too large to be confined to the stage, and also like Charlotte he ultimately would display his theatricality in ways that Colley disapproved of. Well before 1732, Theo had manifested on numerous occasions an eagerness to push himself into the public eye, thus earning the censure of those already predisposed to dislike all Cibbers. He was only twenty-five when Pope bestowed upon him the dubious honour of a quartet of unflattering lines in the 1728 *Dunciad*:

> Mark first the youth who takes the foremost place,
> And thrusts his person full into your face.
> With all thy Father's virtues blest, be born!
> And a new Cibber shall the Stage adorn. (III: 131–34)

Like Colley, Theo did his best stage work in comic roles, though he also seems to have inherited his father's unfortunate attraction to heroic characters for which his figure and voice unsuited him.

A letter from "Philo-Dramaticus" published in *The Grub-Street Journal*—a relentless Tory paper delighted to have a second Cibber to attack—complained that in a production of *Macbeth,* Theo, "in every particular less than man," was woefully miscast in the character of "the tall, manly Macduff." Macduff had been Wilks's role, and Theophilus first assumed the part on the night immediately following Wilks's death; it is unlikely that any actor would have been able to please the audience under the circumstances. But the terms in which Theo was attacked were particular to him. His "remarkable little strut," huffed Philo-Dramaticus, "put me in mind of the fly in the fable, who sitting upon the spoke of a chariot-wheel, said to herself, *What a dust do I raise!*" This characterization of Theo as indiscriminately smirking and posturing remained so common throughout his career that it must have had a basis in fact, however much exaggerated by his enemies. Philo-Dramaticus did concede, however, that despite his cocky egotism, young Cibber possessed "a genius well adapted to the stage" as long as he stuck to comic parts.[5]

By 1732, Theophilus had already developed his signature stage role of a strutting, bantam mock-hero. This role, like his father's fops, coloured the public perception of his offstage personality, which admittedly did often resemble these characters he enacted. As Colley's defining stage persona was Lord Foppington, Theo's became Ancient Pistol in Shakespeare's *Henry IV, Part 2,* performed in Thomas Betterton's late-seventeenth-century adaptation. For the rest of his life, Theophilus owned this role. "No actor, however well instructed and judicious, has gained great applause in the representation of the burlesque and boisterous humour of Pistol since it was played by Theophilus Cibber," said Tom Davies. "He assumed a peculiar kind of false spirit, and uncommon blustering, with such turgid action, and long unmeasurable strides, that it was impossible not to laugh at so extravagant a figure, with such loud and grotesque vociferation."[6] Illustrations of the time often pictured Theo as Pistol, usually in order to satirize his offstage arrogance, hot-headedness, and self-aggrandizement.

Young Theophilus had not long been a member of the Drury Lane company when he also began to acquire a reputation as a dissipated spendthrift. Even in his early days at Drury Lane, Theophilus, though he was paid unusually well for a young actor, lived beyond his means, running up large debts in support of expensive clothes, an elegant carriage, and fine dinners. He imitated his father's life without his father's income. Like Colley he developed a passion for gambling, although unlike his father he could not afford his losses.

Theo's reputation as a rake far outdid Colley's. Young Cibber threw himself headlong into a wild life of gambling, drinking, and whoring— pastimes in which he would later be joined, to Charlotte's disgust, by Richard Charke. In 1725, Theo had fallen passionately in love with and married his fellow actress Jane Johnson. But rather than prompting

Theophilus Cibber, Charlotte's brother, was one of her most loyal supporters, despite his own reputation for conduct not always becoming a gentleman.
(Theophilus Cibber as Pistol, *engraving, after John Laguerre,* The Stage Mutiny. *Courtesy of the Henry E. Huntington Library.)*

him to reform, marriage if anything increased his expenditures, since it gave him the excuse that he wished to support his wife in the style she deserved. Marriage did not put an end to his gambling, drinking, and whoring, either, despite his genuine love for Jane and his emotional and financial dependence upon her.

Jane Johnson had been stage-struck from an early age. Once, when she and her best friend, Kitty Raftor, were girls, they caught sight of glamorous Robert Wilks in the streets and adoringly trailed him to the theatre door. The girls must have swooned with joy when each was accepted into Wilks's company at the Theatre Royal. At Drury Lane, seventeen-year-old Jane met twenty-year-old Theophilus, whom she married two years later. Even as she agreed to be his wife, though, Jane must have known the nature of the man she was marrying. Unlike Charlotte, Jane had not the excuse of naïveté to explain her choice. Though sweet and mild-mannered, she was not unsophisticated: she had grown up in London, she had already begun an independent career as an actress, and she had known Theo for two years when she married him. In addition, up until her marriage, Jane, an orphan, was the ward of the poet and notorious debauchee Richard Savage.

This might help explain why she did not look askance at Theophilus's debauchery. Savage's behaviour was quite different from the genteel manliness so seductively represented onstage by Robert Wilks. It is hard to imagine a less reliable guardian for a young girl than this dissipated, impoverished—but eloquent and charismatic—rakehell, who in 1727 was convicted of murdering a man in a tavern brawl and was saved from the gallows only by the intervention of powerful friends who secured him a royal pardon. Savage is known to posterity as the author of highly accomplished poems, but he is remembered even more as the feckless, embittered compatriot of the young Samuel Johnson, with whom he would later roam the London streets all night when neither of them had money for a bed. After Savage's death in debtor's prison at the age of forty-five, Johnson immortalized his friend in the first of his *Lives of the Poets*.

Throughout his life, in private speech and public writings, Savage insisted that he was the illegitimate son of the Countess of Macclesfield by her lover Lord Rivers, and that all his problems stemmed from his

mother's cold-blooded refusal to acknowledge him. In 1725, the former countess had long been married to her second husband, Colley's
great friend Colonel Henry Brett. Savage must have felt the irony that
his ward would marry into a family closely aligned with the mother
who, he believed, had so cruelly forsaken him. Whatever the strain on
his relations with Colley, however, he and Theophilus were on good
terms at the time. As manager of the summer company in 1723, Theo
staged Savage's tragedy *Sir Thomas Overbury,* a play whose story bore
similarities to Savage's own family romance. Savage forced the point
home by performing the title role himself.

In the years immediately following her marriage, Jane achieved considerable success as an actress. She was liked and respected by the audience, managers, and fellow actors for her sweetness, her appealing
stage presence, and her versatility as a performer. An admirer compared her favourably with Mrs. Oldfield and Mrs. Porter and, from an
earlier generation of great actresses, Mrs. Barry and Mrs. Bracegirdle.
("She enters so justly into her Character, and feels so sensibly the Passions at parting from her Mother, that that tender Scene is really
heighten'd by her manner of performing it.")[7] As a wife, Jane was an
invaluable professional aid to Theophilus, helping to moderate others'
reactions to him. So well liked herself, she could soften the effect of his
contentious personality upon other members of the company. She also
showed herself capable of buffering a hostile audience's propensity to
damn him as a Cibber, on one occasion rescuing Theophilus's fledgling
career as a playwright.

Theo's ambition to follow in his father's footsteps extended to his
writing of plays. He had already written two, which had been performed to mixed success, when, in 1730, he aspired to enter his father's
métier by writing a full-length comedy, entitled *The Lover.* The satiric
pseudo-autobiography, *An Apology for the Life of Mr. T—— C——,
Comedian,* contains a funny scene in which "Theophilus" announces
to his father his decision to become a playwright. Gathering together his
tools—a pen, ink, and a volume of plays to plagiarize—Theo sketches
out his characters and plot. Then he approaches Colley and tells him
that he is writing a comedy: "He heard me with an indolent Air, and
gave me no Answer, but lolling back in his great Chair, took a Pinch of
Snuff, and fell asleep."[8]

In truth, Colley would not have discouraged his son's ambition to write a comic play on its own merits, though he may have feared that the fate that had met his own late efforts would also meet Theo's. If so, opening night proved his fears justified. For the first performance of *The Lover,* a large group of Colley's enemies showed up to damn it, convinced that Cibber Senior was the real author and was hiding behind his son's name. The rowdy audience booed and catcalled throughout the performance so vehemently that Jane, who played one of the leads, was visibly terrified. Seeing this, some of the spectators took pity on her and ceased their jeering, at least while she was onstage.

Jane appeared again to recite the play's epilogue in tandem with Theophilus. Unlike the play proper, the epilogue was Colley's work. Because he had anticipated trouble, he had cleverly cast it as an ingratiating, bantering dialogue between the young wife and husband. Jane, in a mock-scolding tone, reminded Theo that she had warned him "you were your Father's Son," predicting that his surname alone would provoke the audience to damn his play. "Who wears the wiser Head?" she demanded, "your Wife or You?" Theo replied that it was in her power to save her husband if she would only wheedle the audience on his behalf, and promised her "All the clear Profits of my Third-Day House"—that is, his third-night author's proceeds. Jane then turned to beseech the spectators directly: "Gallants, I hope, in this He has touch'd your Hearts; / Let me not suffer for his weak Deserts: / Do not, to last Extreams, your Censure drive; / Give us, at least, an Honest Chance to live. / Our Fate is in your Hands." The audience was charmed.

The Lover ran for a gratifying nine performances, giving Theophilus three author's benefits. When he published the play, he dedicated it to Jane, who alone had saved it: "Your Behaviour in the Epilogue reach'd even the Hearts of Enemies, and made them my involuntary Friends for Your Sake." And he ended by declaring—with perhaps real, if momentary, sincerity—that she had now convinced him "of what vast Use to any Actor, is a Good Character in Private Life."

By the autumn of 1732, Jane and Theo might have seemed, from an outsider's perspective, to be a model of a young theatre couple happily coming into their own. Theo had established himself as a promising actor, playwright, and manager; both he and Jane routinely played full schedules of good roles. They had convenient if not elegant lodgings in Playhouse Passage, the narrow alleyway that connected Drury Lane to the theatre. Both young Cibbers were poised to assume the mantles of the principal players when the older generation of actors retired or died, and Charlotte, with their assistance and encouragement, was following in their footsteps. As Theo took the helm of the company from his father that year, confidently expecting soon to take permanent possession of Colley's share of the patent, the professional futures of all three of these young members of the Cibber family looked bright.

But their personal lives were a shambles. Charlotte's wretched marriage had collapsed, while the sheen had long since worn off Jane and Theo's union. The marital tensions banteringly enacted in Colley's epilogue to *The Lover* put a comic face on genuine unhappiness. Theophilus's compulsive dissipation eroded Jane's affection for him, while his gambling losses and reckless expenditures plunged them into financial distress. Charlotte, knowing the pain of marriage to a wastrel husband, must occasionally have suspended her loyalty to her brother to commiserate with her sister-in-law, whose situation was even more desperate than her own. Creditors continually hounded the Cibbers. It exhausted both of their salaries just to keep Theo out of debtor's prison, a constantly looming threat. As Jane's husband, of course, Theo had full title to her earnings, and he seems to have had fewer scruples than even Richard did about appropriating his wife's income.

As stories circulated of her poor treatment by her husband, Jane also battled ill health. She was not a robust woman in the best of circumstances. Acting was a strenuous, even physically abusive profession, requiring strong lungs to project the voice and a strong constitution to endure the seasonal heat and cold of the playhouse and the stress of performing frequent scenes, sometimes in two separate plays the same evening. "A good constitution is a material point," explained the French actress Hippolyte Clarion: "there is no profession more fatiguing."[9]

Acting was even more taxing if you were pregnant, as Jane's mother-in-law, Katherine, had learned many years before. During the first four years of her marriage, Jane carried children to term three times. This was not an unusual rate of childbirth by contemporary standards, but it was exhausting, especially since Jane usually continued to perform until her pregnancies were well advanced. Two of Jane and Theo's three children had died in infancy, but their daughter Jane, born in July 1729, survived. The necessity of caring for the infant Jane, whom they called Jenny further strained the young Cibbers' desperate finances. And in the autumn of 1732, Jane was pregnant once again.

Unlike her unfortunate sister-in-law, Charlotte could face the new season with some optimism, for she was beginning to emerge from the mess of her marriage. Kitty, now a toddler nearly two years old, was a serious responsibility, but also a source of love and delight as she took her first faltering steps and began to utter words. And within the Drury Lane company, Charlotte's situation looked promising.

The new dispensation at the playhouse initially appeared to suit Charlotte. Despite his domestic difficulties and his contentiousness, Theophilus boded well as a new-generation actor-manager, bringing to the company his flair for innovation and his concern for his fellow actors. However abrasive his personality to others, he had proved a good brother to Charlotte, deserving and reciprocating her affection. Theo probably recognized that he had much in common with his younger sister. He had made it his business to encourage and develop her career, casting her in challenging roles during the summers, expanding her repertoire. His inclination to stage new pieces could give Charlotte opportunities to create roles that would remain hers as long as she wanted to play them. So Charlotte had reasons to believe that, for her at least, 1732–33 would be a good year, bringing new professional opportunities and personal stability.

But the condition of the Drury Lane company that autumn told a different story. The company was in turmoil, a result of external pressures and internal conflict. First, there was the competition. Lincoln's Inn Fields and the King's Opera House were running seasons, as customary, and new companies seemed to be springing up at an alarming rate.

The capable manager Henry Giffard had just opened an ornate new theatre in Goodman's Fields: its ceiling was lavishly decorated with mythological and literary figures and it featured, "on a large Oval over the Pit," a fresco of King George II, "attended by Peace, Liberty, and Justice, trampling Tyranny and Oppression under his Feet."[10] And everyone at Drury Lane eyed uneasily the growing edifice of the large theatre John Rich was building very close by, in Covent Garden Piazza. Rich had announced his intentions to open later that autumn.

Furthermore, at the Little Haymarket, Signora Violante's newly arrived troupe from Dublin was advertising an exciting menu of entertainments. The Signora herself danced on the slack rope in a series of increasingly impressive feats, which began with a minuet, followed by a dance with a ten-foot board, after which she danced "with two Boys fasten'd to her feet; which Occasions great Mirth," and then trumped that by dancing with "two heavy Men ty'd to her Feet." Her advertisements promised that "After that surprising Performance," she would "Dance a Louvre in Boys Cloaths."

Chetwood thought that Signora Violante's "strength of limbs" was "shockingly indecent" and even worse, "masculinely indelicate . . . of a piece with the Features of her Face."[11] Perhaps the public thought so, too, since her company played at the Little Haymarket for only a month. But during that time she directly competed with Drury Lane by performing plays as well, including a production of *The Beggar's Opera*, "after the Irish Manner," that starred, as Captain Macheath, a fetching young actress from Dublin named Peg Woffington.[12]

Not only did Drury Lane face the pressures of increased competition but also conflict among the company's managers arose as soon as the season began. John Highmore proved unwilling to leave the running of the theatre to the professionals, demanding full consultation on all decisions. His concern for profits—for his was a financial investment in the theatre as a revenue-generating business—made him stingy and overcautious. Unfortunately, John Ellys, acting in place of Mary Wilks, allied himself with Highmore when he joined the management at the end of October. (Wilks had said on his deathbed that he wished Colley to represent Mary's share after his death, but either she ignored his request or Colley was unwilling to undertake the responsibility.) Now the management was heavy with those whose interest in the theatre was principally financial and who sought to protect their investment by reducing costs and eliminating risk. Theophilus found himself enmeshed with partners whose strongest instincts were to clip his wings. Conflict was inevitable.

At first, Theophilus held serious discord at bay by moving quickly in October to exert his authority. With Booth's support, he overruled Highmore's protests and made expensive, but justifiable, changes. He pleased several actors by increasing their salaries, gave Kitty Raftor a present after a particularly good performance, spent money on new sets and costumes, and made plans to stage new productions. His self-assertion, energy, and expertise as an actor-manager gave him the upper hand, and he had the confidence of Booth and his father, who must have continued to exercise influence.

But Ellys and Highmore agreed in their desire to move cautiously lest they lose money. And they also shared a growing aversion to Theophilus, who made no secret of his contempt for them. They did not like him personally, nor did they did like his claim to represent the interests of the theatre personnel, particularly the actors. They thwarted him whenever possible, most commonly opposing his desires to spend money on sets, costumes, and salaries. And they preferred to stage popular older plays rather than take a chance on new material for which they would have to pay author's benefits during the first run.

Inevitably, the tensions mounting among the managers permeated the company. Green room gossip ran rampant as the actors complained, argued, and took sides, most of them allying themselves with Theo. Quarrels erupted, management meetings degenerated into rancor, and personal relationships became poisonous. Charlotte was caught up in the escalating conflict. She supported her brother and added her voice—undoubtedly with characteristic tactlessness—to those criticizing the ignorant pretensions of Highmore and Ellys. She may have been dissatisfied with her relatively light performance schedule (she performed four times in October and November), and blamed it on them.

But whatever Charlotte's dissatisfaction, it might have been somewhat assuaged by the fact that two of these appearances were command performances for the King and his family: Charlotte was becoming accustomed to regal audiences. And December loomed promisingly, for she was given the chance to create another character in an interesting new tragedy Theo had persevered in staging.

In late November, Charlotte celebrated Kitty's second birthday and worked hard at the rehearsals for her part in that play, Charles Johnson's *Caelia; or, The Perjur'd Lover.* The tragedy opened on December 11, with Jane—at the end of her eighth month of pregnancy—in the title role of the naïve heroine who has become pregnant out of wedlock and whose faithless lover, Wronglove, has dumped her in a brothel under the pretence that it is a midwife's house. Jane's obvious condition was perfectly suited to the heroine's, hence Theophilus's timing of the play, though his wife's health at this point would have been better served if she had ceased performing altogether.

Charlotte's character was a predatory, drunken bawd, Mother Lupine, who runs the brothel. Charlotte must have been well supplied with models for the part from her searches for Richard through the dives of Covent Garden. Mother Lupine, whose scenes are set in her bawdy-house surrounded by her prostitutes, wants to add Caelia to their number, and sizes her up in graphic, insinuating language:

LUPINE: Why, upon my Soul, she's a fine Creature—There is Hair, a glossy bright brown; there are Teeth; there's a Hip!—a Chest, and an Air!—there are a Pair of living Brilliants. [*Attempting to sing.*] *Those Eyes are made so killing*—Upon my Soul, Madam, your great Belly becomes you, infinitely well, it becomes you. How does the Boy in the Basket—Um! She tans at the mention of it—Fresh and lovely—Her colour good, she treads firm, a little too much spread in the Fillets, but——If she were but half—Ay, just a half a handful higher—

WRONGLOVE: Why, you praise her as a Horse-courser does a Filly.

CAELIA: [Aside] This is a very strange Woman; she talks, and looks as if she were crazy.

LUPINE: What, melancholy, my Rose-bud? Um! It is to be separated half a Mile from its Dearee—Poor thing—Why, my pretty one, thou would breed thy little one a Saint, or an Idiot, if thou feed'st him with nothing but Sighs and Tears—Oh, when you come to my House you shall leave all your Vapours at the Threshold. There we are all Laughers, no Thinkers—What—you—Mr. Slyboots—have you not a Dram? (I)

As dealers in female flesh, bawds were often portrayed as having an "unnatural" sexual interest in their wares, looking at their whores with the desirous eyes of a man. Caelia later says to Mother Lupine: "You wear a Female Habit, but your Behaviour, your Looks, your Actions, and your Morals, declare you monstrous." Charlotte seems to have played this scene very convincingly—too convincingly for the audience: Charlotte was not onstage long before exclamations of outrage and disgust began to follow her lines; soon her voice was drowned by a rising tide of boos and hisses directed at her and the actresses playing the prostitutes. The playwright wrote in the play's preface that, sitting in the theatre, he "had the Mortification . . . to hear the Character of Mother Lupine and her Women disapprov'd by several of the

Audience, who, as if they thought themselves in bad Company, were very severe."

Representations of brothels and prostitutes ran the risk of offending the audience, as Theo well knew: just that previous June, the summer company's production of Fielding's *The Covent-Garden Tragedy,* also set in a brothel, had provoked audience outrage and had to be withdrawn after one night. Perhaps Theophilus judged that setting a she-tragedy (rather than a farce) in a brothel would defuse such objections, since in Johnson's play there was little funny about the vicious bawd and her prostitutes. But apparently any representation at Drury Lane Theatre of what could readily be seen on Drury Lane itself was unacceptable. The audience's anger so intimidated the actors that they refused to perform the tragedy again, and the managers cancelled the next night's performance.

Charlotte was damned for the part she played, and for playing it too well. At nineteen, she had her first experience of a hostile audience, whose hostility moreover was directed specifically at her. Her self-confidence must have faltered as she felt herself engulfed by hisses. We can surmise that Jane tried to comfort her, and that her father and brother told her a Cibber had to expect these things. In any event, Charlotte's spirits and confidence survived, and her skin must have thickened a bit.

But the debacle of *Caelia* appeared to justify the caution of Theophilus's fellow managers. The tragedy's failure was all the more painful because Drury Lane was now facing its stiffest competition in recent history. After a series of delays, on December 7, John Rich inaugurated to great acclaim his new Covent Garden Theatre (the forerunner of the current Covent Garden Opera House, which stands on the same site in the northeast corner of the Piazza). Spectators flocked to the beautiful new playhouse, with its excellent acoustics, to see the opening-night performance of Congreve's *The Way of the World:* the play was old, but the sets, scenes, and costumes were sparkling new. For much of December and January, Drury Lane attempted to undermine its rival by mounting competing productions of the same plays—a *Beggar's Opera* war was waged during the middle of December—but although Drury Lane was a superior company, the advantage of novelty belonged to Rich. To make matters worse, he poached some of Drury Lane's actors, luring them to Covent Garden with the promise of larger salaries and more opportunities to perform. And there were more disasters in store for Drury Lane, and the Cibber family, that winter.

On November 15, King George and several members of the royal family rode into Richmond Park to hunt deer. Queen Caroline, however, stayed indoors. "Her majesty being slightly indisposed of a cold, did not go abroad," the papers reported.[13] On November 30, the Queen apparently felt well enough to join the King, the Prince of Wales, and the three eldest princesses at Drury Lane to see *The Provok'd Wife,* in which Charlotte performed as Madamoiselle, but on December 9 the newspapers reported again that her majesty was "indisposed." She was not the only person to fall ill. The Count of Albemarle, it was noted, had been ill for some time, and he "is not getting better." It was not long before the papers' domestic news columns were filled with notices that prominent people, including Robert Walpole, were "indisposed." The reports of illness were accompanied by unusually high numbers of deaths.[14]

Much of the country was falling ill of a disease that everyone described as a "cold," but that seems to have been an epidemic of influenza. "The whole world, high and low, rich and poor, are ill of this epidemical cold," wrote Lord Hervey to Henry Fox in January. People he knew were dying of it.[15]

The epidemic decimated the theatre companies, as both players and spectators fell ill. By mid-December, the Drury Lane company was reduced to a skeleton. The shows went on, but the audiences were scanty, as people became sick, left the city, or prudently stayed home. Throughout December and January, actors collapsed, and sometimes their replacements were just slightly less ill themselves. Theophilus and Jane both were struck hard. But Theo's high fever and inflamed lungs did not save him from being summoned by Highmore and Ellys to the playhouse at seven o'clock one night—an hour after the mainpiece had begun—to substitute for an even sicker actor in the afterpiece. Theo gamely performed a strenuous pantomime role, then dragged himself home, more ill than ever. In late December or early January, a newspaper noted, "We hear Mr Cibber Junr of the Theatre Royal in Drury Lane is gone out of Town for the recovery of his health, having had a

violent cold, attended with a fever & an inflammation in his stomach."
(Perhaps he went to stay with his mother in Kensington.) The same
paper reported that "Mrs Cibber lies dangerously ill of a fever."[16]

Jane's rehearsal and performance schedule that month, as the troupe
prepared for the debut of *Caelia,* had severely taxed her waning strength.
Tragedy was particularly hard on an actress, as Madame Clarion
observed: "Irritable nerves, weak lungs, or delicate constitutions, cannot long sustain the weight of tragic characters."[17] At least Jane had to
sustain the weight of Caelia for only one night, though the uproar in
the playhouse must have upset her greatly. Three nights later she performed another major role. Then, quite alarmingly for a woman in the
advanced stages of pregnancy, she succumbed to the fever. During the
following few weeks, when she was conscious enough to worry, Jane
must have feared her upcoming ordeal, for her child was due very soon.

Throughout the Christmas season, both Jane and Theo lay ill. But in
January Jane's fever broke and she gained a little welcome strength as
her lying-in approached. On January 18 or 19, 1733, she gave birth to
a daughter they named Elizabeth, who, remarkably enough under the
circumstances, survived; she was baptized on January 24.[18] For almost
a week after Betty's birth, Jane rallied. But suddenly she was seized by
a raging fever, perhaps the return of the influenza or perhaps the onset
of puerperal fever. She felt forebodings of doom, telling her husband
that her work schedule had fatally impaired her health. She "found her
Spirits had made her venture to undertake more Fatigue in her Business
than her constitution was able to bear," Theo later said, "and she was
certain she could not recover it." On the morning of January 25, Jane
died. She was twenty-six.

In its notice of her death, *The Daily Advertiser* complimented Jane
Cibber as "a very just and amiable Actress." The *Daily Post* added,
"She is truly lamented by all who knew her, to whom her virtues in private Life render'd her very amiable. Young Mr. Cibber is very much
indisposed."[19] Theophilus, still weak from his illness, was overcome by
grief. His sorrow must have been made all the more acute by his feelings of guilt. For all that she—or he speaking for her—might have
ascribed her fatal overwork to her over-ambitious "Spirits," he knew
that it was on account of his debts that his wife had continued to perform when her fragile health made it unwise. She had feared that if she

did not perform, the other managers would withhold her salary—and that could have meant prison for her husband.

The day after Jane died, Theo may have stumbled next door to the playhouse to join the royal family and a full house gathered to celebrate Mrs. Porter's return to the stage. When Jane was interred on January 28 in St. Paul's Covent Garden, he wept inconsolably. Always a man to surrender to his passions, he tormented himself with guilt and sorrow (and sought, it was alleged, the company of prostitutes).[20] Slow to recover his health and slower to recover his spirits, he did not resume his full duties at the theatre until mid-February.

10

MUTINY

(1733)

An engraving that circulated in June 1733 depicts the neighbourhood outside the Theatre Royal, Drury Lane as if it were a curtain-draped stage. At the centre stands Theophilus in his attitude as Ancient Pistol—feet planted wide, hands on his waist, elbows thrust belligerently out. Behind him clusters a group of actors, many in ancient military costume, their spears thrust into the air. Rotund John Harper, dressed as Falstaff, looms at Theo's right shoulder, brandishing sword and shield; behind Theo is the actor William Mills, wearing a Roman soldier's plumed helmet. Close beside Theo stands the bold figure of an actress: some have identified her as Mary Heron, but more recently others have asserted that this is a representation of Charlotte. Her defiant stance and her position by Theo's side make this identification credible. She waves a banner that proclaims, "Liberty and Property."[1]

Opposite the crowd of actors huddle Drury Lane's patentees. Slender John Highmore gestures weakly to a paper he is holding, which reads, "It cost £6000." John Ellys, wearing a painter's smock and holding a prop sword, turns towards him in solidarity; behind Ellys a woman stands—perhaps John Wilks's daughter Mrs. Shaw, perhaps Hester Booth—raising a banner inscribed, "We'll starve 'em out." At Highmore's back hunches Mary Wilks in widow's weeds, weeping into a handkerchief. In the centre background a sign shaped like a large rose juts from the Rose Tavern, and atop the sign crouches a monkey holding a flag declaring, "I am a

Charlotte and Theo were at the centre of this well-documented dispute involving performers and theatre managers. (John Laguerre, The Stage Mutiny, *1733. Courtesy of the Harvard Theatre Collection, Houghton Library, Harvard University.)*

Gentleman." In front of the theatre curtain, well removed from the confrontation, sits Colley Cibber, wearing a laurel crown and cradling three bulging moneybags on his lap; more bags lie heaped at his feet. Colley points towards Highmore with a mocking smile. The title of the illustration, by John Laguerre, is *The Stage Mutiny.*

The events that culminated in the walkout by Theophilus, Charlotte, and most of Drury Lane's best actors in May 1733 tell a story of rivalry, arrogance, conflict, and betrayal. After his convalescence, Theophilus returned to the theatre in mid-February to find that Highmore and Ellys had closed ranks against him. That he had dragged himself from his sickbed to act when they needed him apparently counted for little. They had even contemplated withholding his salary while he was ill, Theo claimed, and only Booth's intervention had stopped them.[2]

Highmore and Ellys had further affronted Theophilus by pulling from production his new afterpiece, *The Harlot's Progress,* replacing it with a pantomime written by Ellys. Theo was able to reschedule his piece, but the episode deepened his disdain for his fellow managers. For their part, Highmore and Ellys found their partner unbearably pushy and arrogant; they resented the way he flaunted his superior knowledge of the theatre. They loathed him all the more because they knew that despite his obnoxious manner, most of the other actors respected his judgment while they held the other two managers in contempt.

The 1732–33 season was a troubled time when, as *The London Stage* puts it, "the best kind of leadership was necessary" at Drury Lane—but good leadership was largely unavailable from the warring managers, as Theophilus struggled to reassert his dominance and Highmore and Ellys attempted to thwart him.[3] Its ranks thinned by illness, retirement, and death, the company also found its audience depleted by new competitors. Not only were Goodman's Fields and Covent Garden proving to be serious rivals, but also at least three houses were staging operatic performances.

One recently established group calling itself the English Opera Company had taken over the theatre at Lincoln's Inn Fields. In March, it prepared to stage a new opera, *Rosamond,* written by the group's young proprietor, a relatively unknown, self-educated musician named Thomas Arne. Arne, who despite his youth and inexperience grandly titled himself "the Proprietor of English Opera," strengthened his claim to that appellation when *Rosamond* was a huge hit. Its popularity had much to do with the singer who performed the title role, a recent newcomer to the stage. Audiences were entranced by the shy, delicate young woman, who sang without much technique but with great expressiveness. She was Thomas Arne's nineteen-year-old sister, Susannah.

At Drury Lane, Theophilus threw himself into a full schedule of acting, but his own plays received a mixed reception. His afterpiece *The Mock-Officer,* written for his own benefit in March, was hooted off the stage.[4] (Charlotte was a member of its cast.) This new disaster strengthened the resolve of Highmore and Ellys to resist Theo's ambitions to stage new works, though it was too late for them to forestall *The Harlot's Progress,* which was finally in rehearsal. This time their obstructionism rebounded against them, for upon its premiere on March 31, *The Harlot's Progress; or, Ridotto al Fresco*—based upon William Hogarth's popular series of engravings narrating a prostitute's career—proved one of the big hits of the season, bringing, Victor observed, "a great deal of Money into the Theatre."[5] Everyone profited from its success, and Highmore and Ellys looked like fools for trying to quash the piece.

But Theophilus's victory was hollow, for even as he won this particular battle, he knew that he had already lost the war. His defeat came at the hands of his father.

By the winter of 1733, Theophilus believed, he had already made an oral agreement with Colley that he would continue to lease the share of the patent for a twelvemonth, beginning with the expiry of his current lease in June. No money had yet changed hands—the agreed-upon amount was £300, reflecting the patent's decline in value under the new management—but Theo had already consulted a lawyer to draw up the contract and planned to pay the fee before the season was out. He clearly envisioned that this rental arrangement would be continued year by year until he could purchase the share from his father or, even better (and more likely, given his debts), until he inherited it from him. Theo seemed to view Colley's share of the patent as property equivalent to a landed estate, handed down, by patriarchal tradition, from father to eldest son. As the only male among the Cibber children, Theo saw himself as the rightful heir, who had prepared himself all his adult life to take on these responsibilities. Recently, in anticipation of his possession of this "estate," he had invested in improvements, bearing one-third of the expenses of the new sets, costumes, and repairs.

In early March, illness forced Colley to excuse himself from a performance of *The Careless Husband*. Theo assumed the part of Lord Foppington, claiming his father's most famous role as a part of his birthright. He acted Foppington again a week later, this time in *The Relapse*, when he played opposite Charlotte as Hoyden, Foppington's tomboyish, provincial fiancée, eager to marry anyone who will take her to London. (Charlotte unfortunately left no comment about whether she found it more or less appealing to play opposite her brother rather than her father.) Theo was positioning himself to step, quite literally, into his father's shoes when Colley finally retired from the stage altogether. Colley must have encouraged Theo to take on these parts as well as his management duties, thus affirming, or so his son thought, their arrangement.

But Colley was growing weary of the troubled company and anxious about its future. Throughout the autumn and winter, he had watched the growing dissension among the managers and actors, keeping himself above the fray. Now that his time was not engulfed by management, he preferred to focus on his new role as the King's laureate and man about town, enjoying afternoons gambling at Tom's coffee-house in Russell Square and welcomed by night into the company of aristocrats at his exclusive gaming club, White's Chocolate House, on St. James's Street. He would dine sumptuously with the proprietor of White's and then make his entrance at the club, to boisterous acclamation from the elite bons vivants within: "O King Coll!" they would shout. "Come in, King Coll! Welcome, welcome, King Colley!"[6] This reception must have been as gratifying to the ageing laureate as the most thunderous applause.

Colley enjoyed an enviable detachment from the personality conflicts and confrontations that were roiling the company. But as a patentee, whose income depended upon the theatre's profitability, he was seriously concerned about his future. External competition and internal dissension were eroding the company's ability to attract an audience. His actor's salary was high, but he was growing tired of acting. Furthermore, Wilks's illness and death reminded him that, at sixty-one, he could not know how long he would remain physically able to perform.

This concern became all the more acute in March. Colley had remained untouched by the influenza the previous winter, but as the epidemic was beginning to wane in early spring, he fell victim to it: the newspaper reported on March 5 that "Colley Cibber . . . is so ill of a Cold he is not able to Act."[7] Colley's illness kept him from performing again until March 29. This reminder of his physical vulnerability, combined with his waning desire to act, must have made an impression.

Highmore, sensing his advantage, made his move, apparently judging that the best way to protect his investment was to acquire a greater share of the patent and the power that came with it. So he quietly offered Colley three thousand guineas for his full share of the patent, scenes, and costumes—a handsome sum, though proportionally less than he had paid Booth. Soberly considering the diminishing value of the patent under the new management and ignoring his verbal arrangement with Theo, Colley agreed. The two kept their plans secret as the documents were prepared and signed, and only then did Colley disclose the sale. At the same time, he announced that at the end of the season, he would retire from the stage.

Theophilus was devastated. Suddenly, he was transformed into a lame-duck manager, whose authority would end when his lease expired in June. With Colley's third share and the sixth he had purchased from

Booth, Highmore now controlled half of the patent. Theo's position at Drury Lane was utterly undermined, and it was his father who had robbed him of his birthright.

While he must have confronted Colley personally to express his hurt and anger, Theophilus in his public pronouncements blamed Highmore for, essentially, seducing his father. The patent, though heritable, was not an entailed estate, of course: Colley's share was his to dispose of as he saw fit. But to keep Theo uninformed about his intentions until the deal had been settled was underhanded. Theo would inevitably have accosted him, and perhaps would have thwarted the plan. Many people, even those who disliked Theo, did think that his father had treated him shabbily. A letter to the *St. James's Evening Post* found it necessary to defend Colley against the "various ill-natured reflections cast upon him, for selling his share of the patent for Drury-Lane house, and for not making it over to his son."

Yet Colley's actions were not indefensible, however selfish they seemed. He argued that to bestow the patent upon Theo would in effect disinherit his daughters, so "he chose to convert it into ready money, that he might make a proportionable division of what fortune he may happen to have among all his children."[8]

Charlotte must have had mixed feelings about her father's behaviour. His refusal to disinherit his daughters would seem to favour her, but his effective removal of Theo from the management, and his own retirement, had immediate consequences for her career. She lost her influential mentors at Drury Lane, and the troupe would now be governed by her brother's enemies. She had played with some regularity that winter—including a good new breeches role, Lucy Fainlove, in Steele's *The Tender Husband*—but she was still not performing regularly enough to satisfy her ambition, and it was unclear now how she would advance. She was staunchly loyal to her brother, and like the majority of the players she was convinced that he was the superior manager. Surely Highmore and Ellys must have identified her with him. Their dislike of Theo could well have coloured their relationship with his sister, even if she had behaved temperately to them—and this, given her contempt for Highmore and her ingrained resistance to authority, was highly unlikely. Her future at Drury Lane was suddenly uncertain.

As for Theophilus, though bitterly disappointed, he was not one to accept defeat. He swallowed his pride and wrote Highmore a letter of congratulation, in which he also proposed a plan that Highmore would have been well-advised to accept: that he deputize Theo to run the daily operations of the theatre, essentially as a stage manager. But Highmore refused, too caught up in savouring his adversary's defeat to see the advantages to himself and the company in Theo's proposal.

So Theo set about fomenting rebellion. He did not have to work very hard. Words like "oppression" and "tyranny" were already in the air, bandied about in taverns and coffeehouses where actors congregated, muttered in lowered voices in the green room. Players began to liken themselves to the slaves who worked the West Indies plantations—an enormous exaggeration, but a powerful analogy nonetheless. Their discontent intensified in mid-May when the lord chamberlain, probably at the behest of the patentees, reissued an order that prohibited the managers at each of the two patent theatres from hiring "any Actor, Actress, Singer or Dancer" from the other theatre without permission from his office.

Actors had no formal contracts; their names were just written down in the company roster each year. The lord chamberlain's order, reinforcing an agreement among the theatre managers known as the cartel, held down actors' salaries by preventing the patent houses from competing for players. The cartel was not new—the triumvirate had exploited it—but now it took on a new portentousness, subjecting the players to the mercy of these novice managers prone to view them as expenses rather than assets. Actors began to question the basis and justice of the patentees' power over them, and to wonder aloud whether playhouses should be governed by incompetent gentlemen rather than knowledgeable professionals. Charlotte, quick to resent injustice and strongly identifying with her brother, must have vigorously added her voice to those complaining that working under such conditions for such men was an abrogation of the players' freedom.

The only figure who might have been able to moderate the ill will between Highmore and the actors that spring was Barton Booth, but illness now claimed him for the last time. In April he suffered another bout of fever and jaundice. Desperate for a cure, Booth placed himself into the care of one Thomas Dover, aka Dr. Quicksilver, who had just published a treatise in which he claimed to have effected miraculous cures with mercury. Over five days of treating the ailing actor, Dr. Quicksilver fed him almost two pounds of the toxic element. Soon

Booth was seized by a raging fever (nausea, fever, and pneumonia are symptoms of acute mercury poisoning), and the eminent physician Dr. Hans Sloane was quickly summoned to replace Dover. Sloane applied more orthodox medicine, dosing Booth with a regimen of "plasters, blooding, purges, and clysters" that, as Koon remarks dryly, "brought the end with merciful speed."[9] Barton Booth died on May 10.

Booth's death saddened the company, and must have made many of them despair more than ever of their current fate under Highmore and Ellys. His beloved wife Hester, the veteran actress and dancer, inherited the remaining half of his share, but her effect on the management was uncertain.

The actors prudently suspended their plotting during the benefit season. Charlotte, who had performed irregularly throughout the spring, chose for her benefit on May 7 a performance of *Henry IV, Part 2* with Colley as Justice Shallow and Theo as Pistol. Even in his anger and disappointment, Theophilus continued to try to help his sister, writing an afterpiece for the occasion called *Damon and Daphne,* in which Charlotte played the male part of Damon. She would have been grateful for the attempt to help, though not for the result: Theo's "rural tragedy" was poorly received. One critic called it a "moving" play: "it obliged the best part of the audience to move off, before it was half over."[10]

When the benefit season ended, the actors' rebellious talk flared into open defiance. Theophilus devised a bold and ingenious plan. The patent that assigned the patentees control over the material goods of the company—sets, costumes, etc.—omitted one crucial component: the playhouse itself. Theophilus's strategy was simple: he and the other actors would lease Drury Lane Theatre away from Highmore. Theo consulted the other players and approached the leaseholders with a good offer, which a large majority of them, happy to have the assurance of a lease, accepted. The actors planned to secure the playhouse, then offer to rent the patent and stock from the patentees for a reasonable sum—initially £900, later increased to £1,200. They would govern themselves as a cooperative—or "commonwealth," a politically loaded term—and set their own salaries. For the patentees, this would not have been a bad deal, as Robert Hume points out: "Highmore, for example, would have recovered his £6,000 in ten years, or just half the remaining time the patent had to run."[11]

But before the negotiations could be completed, word of the actors' plan was leaked to the patentees. Incensed at the players' insubordination, they counterattacked. On the afternoon of May 28, the players arrived at the theatre to find the doors locked and a group of armed men barricaded within. The *Daily Post* reported the next day: "We are assur'd that there will be no more Plays acted this Season at the Theatre-Royal in Drury-lane."

According to Theo, the patentees had entered the theatre, "and having barricado'd all the Doors and Avenues thereunto, placed a Set of Ruffians on the Inside with Fire-Arms, and a proper Provision of strong Liquors, &c. to keep their Bloods warm, and stupefy their Senses, lest a little common Morality should touch their Consciences to the obstruction of their performing any desperate act."[12] Since Theo's managerial contract had not yet expired, the lockout was illegal. He and his confederates immediately appealed to the lord chamberlain, the Duke of Grafton, but the duke refused to intervene. So the actors turned to the law, suing the patentees for "ejectment and possession." Their suit "disappeared into the courts," leaving "the managers without a company, and the players without a theatre."[13]

Thus began a summer of discontent that shook the London theatre world. As if to further stoke the fires of confrontation, unseasonably hot weather descended upon the city in early June, fraying nerves and straining tempers. Horse-drawn water carts trundled up and down the streets, spraying water in an effort to settle the dust. Windows and doors were flung open, and residents rich enough to escape the city fled. Crowds converged on St. James's Park and anyplace else there were trees; at night the outdoor pleasure gardens were mobbed. The Little Haymarket and Covent Garden theatres, which ran summer seasons, advertised seven o'clock curtains and promised that "Care will be taken to keep the House Cool," usually by keeping the buildings closed up until late afternoon. The heat overcame even these measures, however: in late June Thomas Arne's company at the Little Haymarket had to suspend performances "on account of the excessive heat of the Weather."[14] And all that summer, the Theatre Royal, Drury Lane remained dark, chained and bolted.

With the theatre under lock and key, Charlotte and the other younger members of the company who relied on summer acting to swell their income were left idle and poor. When she was not congregating with her fellow mutineers, Charlotte probably spent her time with Kitty, taking her to St. James's Park to look at the fallow and red deer that grazed there, going boating on the river, or visiting her mother in lovely Kensington, where cool breezes cleared the air.

Back in the turbulent Town, actors and spectators took sides in the Drury Lane dispute, newspapers published passionate commentary in support and condemnation of one side or the other, and a fiery letter war was waged in periodicals and pamphlets. Theophilus stood at the centre of the controversy as the players' ringleader, a mutinous Ancient Pistol mustering his army of rebels. Public debate raged over the mutual obligations of patentees and actors. On June 2 and 9, *The Craftsman,* a paper unfriendly to the Cibbers, viciously attacked the actors for insubordination.

The patentees presented their case to the public in a broadside that was reprinted in the *Daily Post* on June 4. The players, they maintained, had "threaten'd to desert the Service" of the patentees "without the least Pretence of Hardship or Injustice done them." Therefore, the actors were "in contempt and defiance" of the King's authority. The letter listed the ostensibly generous salaries of many of the principal actors, and claimed that even when illness prevented them from acting, players were paid. The document was signed by Highmore, Ellys, Mary Wilks, and Hester Booth.

On June 4, the patentees also sent a threatening message to the mutineers by firing Benjamin Griffin, a popular player. On June 11, Griffin fought back in a letter to the *Daily Post,* in which he charged that the patentees had misrepresented the conflict "in almost every article," and complained that Highmore and Ellys "have no Experience, no Knowledge, no Capacity, For Gathering together, Forming, Entertaining, Governing, Privileging, and Keeping a Company of Comedians."

Theophilus's own response was to publish a pamphlet "Letter to John Highmore," in which he asserted that the managers had nearly destroyed Drury Lane, and that those ostensibly generous salaries published by the patentees were lies. He accused the patentees of killing his beloved wife with overwork—at least, he exclaimed, she did not live to see "the Support of our Infants" dependent upon the caprice of such people, who would "render Actors the only Slaves in Great-Britain."

The patentees had often threatened to "starve us poor Devils the Players into a Compliance with their Wills," he thundered. "Excuse me, Sir, that can't be, We must and will eat."

During the height of the controversy, a dialogue took place on the stage of Covent Garden Theatre, which was performing Edward Phillips's farce, *The Stage Mutineers; or, A Play-House to be Lett*. Truncheon, an actor, encounters a mutinous actress, Mrs. Haughty. A fervent revolutionary, Mrs. Haughty waves a banner inscribed "Liberty and Freedom."

> TRUNCHEON: Enough, enough, my Amazonian, my Female Patriot, who
> wildly talk'st of Liberty and Freedom.
> HAUGHTY: Wildly I talk because I am a Woman
> But tho' a Woman I'm inspir'd with Liberty,
> And in her Cause have boldly plac'd my Standard,
> Under which Banner, Sir, I hope you'll [en]list." (19)

Mrs. Haughty is a fierce Amazon, a warlike woman who makes an issue of her gender. She is both feminine in her wildness—a stereotypical image of women as ungovernably swayed by emotion—and masculine in her political zeal. Like the banner-toting actress in the illustration *The Stage Mutiny* (upon which the play was based), Mrs. Haughty is a representation either of Mary Heron or of Charlotte. Mary was the more important actress, but the Amazonian imagery points to Charlotte, who would have stood beside her brother at the forefront of the rebellion. Her depiction as an Amazon was appropriate, since, as a direct result of the mutiny, Charlotte's image as a masculine woman would become firmly imprinted upon the public mind.

11

WEARING THE BREECHES

(1733–34)

William Hogarth famously caricatured the mutineers at Bartholomew Fair that year. His engraving, later misleadingly entitled *Southwark Fair*, depicts several playbooths in close vicinity.[1] A tightly packed crowd mills, flirts, and fights in front of the booths, a dancer performs on a slack wire, two men thrust their faces into the windows of a peep show, a dog struts on its hind legs sporting a hat, cape, sword, and cane, a gambler cheats at dice, and musicians and vendors work the crowd.

Overhead, the balcony of one of the playbooths is collapsing, sending props and actors flying. Above the collapsing balcony hangs a show-cloth depicting Laguerre's illustration of the mutiny, with an additional legend at its bottom: "Pistol alive." In the foreground of the picture, an actress beats a drum to advertise her troupe, who march behind her. A bailiff and his assistant grab by the throat a player wearing a Roman soldier's uniform, complete with plumed helmet. (Bailiffs haunted the fairs and playhouses.) Hogarth's unfortunate Roman has been identified as Charlotte—and indeed, she played at Bartholomew Fair that year. But she would not have been the only player on the run from creditors in the late summer of 1733.[2]

During the preceding months, as the summer had sweltered on with no resolution of the standoff between the managers and mutineers, a current of anxiety must have run below Charlotte's brave revolutionary rhetoric. How would she be able to maintain herself and Kitty while the

The work of William Hogarth captured the colour and vitality of Charlotte's London (William Hogarth, Southwark Fair. *Courtesy of the Henry E. Huntington Library.)*

mutineers' lawsuit slogged through the courts? Her debts mounted steadily, as did her estranged husband's. Richard had joined the mutiny, too, and in his own distressed circumstances he undoubtedly reminded Charlotte of his financial claims on her. Surely she had recourse to an unusual number of her father's "auxiliary guineas" that summer.

Highmore had been certain that time was on the patentees' side, that debt and hunger would wear the mutineers down, but he underestimated their resolve. Theophilus, acting for the cooperative, took the audacious step of renting the Little Haymarket Theatre for the upcoming season. Its owner, John Potter, was thrilled at the opportunity to house such a distinguished group of actors instead of the second-rate companies that typically performed there, and agreed to refurbish the scruffy playhouse according to Theo's instructions.

Startled to hear that his locked-out players had constituted themselves as a rival company, Highmore hastily conferred with the other patentees. In mid-July, they proposed that the dispute be set before an arbitrator, offering to raise the salaries of several of the rebels and to cancel the cartel, in return for the players' willingness to relinquish their claim to the lease on the Drury Lane Theatre and to sign multi-year contracts fixing their salaries. But this proposal, which probably would have been welcomed in early May, came too late: "Tempers were too high and the battle-lines too clearly drawn."[3]

At the end of August, desperate to replenish their empty purses before the autumn began, Theophilus and several other players operated a playbooth at Bartholomew Fair. Charlotte acted there, along with many of the mutineers; "A Company of Italian Rope-Dancers, Posture-Masters, Tumblers, &c." was on hand "to entertain the Audience till the Droll begins."[4] Charlotte played Haly in the droll, *The Tragedy of Tamerlane the Great, with the Fall of Bajazet, Emperor of the Turks.* (It was Bajazet's "fall" that Hogarth parodied with his collapsing balcony.) A eunuch, Haly was an interesting addition to her repertory of male roles.

Charlotte's company featured another provocative enticement in the person of the infamous prostitute Betty Careless, who joined them as an actress. Betty, famed for her wit and beauty, was a regular companion of the rowdy rakes at the Shakespear's Head and Tom King's, and the proprietor of a bagnio-brothel on Tavistock Row, not far from Colley's house on Charles Street. Lovely and deceptively innocent-looking, she was memorialized by Henry Fielding, who knew her well. His novel *Amelia*, written years later, contains a scene in which "the inimitable B——y C——s" is glimpsed in a theatre audience "in company with a young fellow of no very formal, or indeed sober appearance." Two respectable ladies sitting near the narrator are gulled into worrying that "so modest and so innocent" a girl might be endangered by her association with a libertine.

In the final plate of Hogarth's *The Rake's Progress,* a dejected madman incarcerated in Bedlam sits gloomily on a staircase, where he has scrawled the cause of his ruin—"Charming Betty Careless"—on the rail. So Betty contributed her own tarnished luster to the troupe at Bartholomew Fair that August, and there Charlotte got to know her. She would have reason to value Betty's friendship in the future.

Betty Careless, whose name revealed something of her character, rides to her bagnio in her sedan chair. One of her lovers, Captain Montague, rides on top. (L. P. Boitard, A Covent Garden Morning Frolick, 1747. Courtesy of the Guildhall Library, Corporation of London.)

On Friday night, September 7, Charlotte completed her last long day of performances at the fair. Perhaps she celebrated at a Smithfield tavern with Theo, Betty, and other players before heading home to Kitty. Two weeks of all-day performances would have left her weary and hoarse, with aching legs, but after a long summer of deprivation she once again had a bit of money jingling in her purse.

It would have been entirely in character for Charlotte, despite the debts she had accumulated that summer, to indulge in a hackney coach to carry her back to Covent Garden. We can imagine her in the coach as it rumbled westward along the broad, dark expanse of Holborn, fitfully illuminated by the lamps attached to the buildings. She may have shuddered slightly as the coach descended from Holborn Hill into the decaying, rat-infested rookeries of St. Giles, home to some of London's most wretched inhabitants, before it turned south down Drury Lane.

As her coach pitched and jolted over the cobblestones, Charlotte might have turned her thoughts to the season ahead. Rehearsals would be starting very soon at the Little Haymarket. No one could guess what would happen as the mutineers attempted to compete with the theatres at Drury Lane, Covent Garden, and Goodman's Fields. Certainly Highmore and the other patentees, still infuriated by their defiance and anxious to protect their own depleted company, would not falter in their attempts to bring them to heel. But over the summer the rebel players had achieved a strong sense of solidarity and even power. They knew that many in the Town sympathized with their mutiny and would turn out to support them, at least for a while. Now that the hot, turbulent summer had ended, spirits among the mutineers soared.

Though Charlotte was not cast in the rebel company's debut performance scheduled for September 26, in early October she was to play a new role in a play by her father; and she would also reprise Hoyden opposite Theo's Foppington in *The Relapse* and her breeches part as Lucy Fainlove in *The Tender Husband* soon thereafter. And there would be more parts, old and new, to come.

Weary as she was, Charlotte must have felt a thrill of anticipation. She had more than three years of acting experience, and her brother was firmly at the helm of the rebels' company. Since theirs was a smaller group—fifteen of the forty-five players had remained loyal to Highmore—more roles would be available, and Theo would steer some of them her way. Her weekly salary was now doubled from thirty shillings to three pounds, and she could feel confident that she was poised on the brink of a career breakthrough. Behind her lay the familiarity and security of her three years at Drury Lane, anchored by her father's presence; ahead lay a future that was uncertain, but filled with promise.

The mutineers began their season in late September, with a production of William Congreve's *Love for Love,* chosen for its symbolism: this was the first play that had been performed by the troupe of mutineers led by Thomas Betterton, Elizabeth Barry, and Anne Bracegirdle. In aligning himself with the legendary Betterton, Theo (as he undoubtedly knew) was departing from the precedent of his father. In 1695, Colley had advanced his own career by staying behind at Drury Lane to grab roles vacated by the mutineers and cultivate influence with Christopher Rich. Now his children were staking their own careers on the rebels.

It was a heady, if anxious, time. In the Little Haymarket's green room—less commodious than Drury Lane's, but redolent of the players' feeling of liberation—Charlotte was surrounded by most of the old Drury Lane company. Some big names were missing, particularly Kitty Raftor—who had recently married and was now appearing as Kitty Clive—the ageing but still beautiful Christiana Horton, and the lame but formidable tragedienne Mary Porter. Henry Fielding had also remained at Drury Lane, perhaps because he, who always displayed his own social status by signing his name as "Esq.," identified with Highmore as a gentleman, or perhaps because he wished to support his friend Jack Ellys. Perhaps he simply judged that the patentees would win and his career would be best served by remaining loyal.[5] If this was his thinking, Fielding had made a serious miscalculation.

At the Little Haymarket, the Company of Comedians of His Majesty's Revels (or so they called themselves on the dubious strength of an illegitimate licence granted them, for a fee, by the Master of the Revels) included Mary Heron, John Harper (the famous Falstaff and a perennial audience favourite), Elizabeth Butler, who specialized in tragic roles, and Ann Grace, a comic actress. They also picked up a new attraction, a young singer-actress named Hannah Pritchard, daughter of a Drury Lane staymaker and wife of an engraver, who had only begun to perform regularly at the fairs that summer, but was already the object of adulatory verses in the newspapers celebrating her beautiful voice and genteel person.[6] Charlotte and Theo's niece Ann Brett, a veteran dancer thirteen years old, followed her uncle and aunt to the Little Haymarket, as did Richard Charke. Charlotte may have wished that Richard, at least, had stayed behind, but his popularity as a musician was invaluable, and he could act when necessary.

Theo added two more players who had been inspired by the mutineers to desert from Covent Garden. And he took another step that turned out to be professionally acute and personally fateful. He invited into the troupe the musical family whose productions of English opera had aroused so much attention the year before: the composer Thomas Arne, his young brother, Henry Peter, and his shy but fetching sister, Susannah.

As the mutineers plunged into an ambitious schedule of performances that autumn, their primary goal was to hang on while their lawsuit worked its way through the courts: the Little Haymarket was too small to support such a troupe for very long. Everything rested upon their winning their suit, for then the patentees would have no choice but to negotiate with them on their own terms.[7] In the meantime, their show went on, with gusto.

The Comedians of His Majesty's Revels performed at the Little Haymarket from late September 1733 until early March 1734. In those five exhausting but exhilarating months—not much more than half the length of the usual season—Charlotte appeared onstage nearly twice as often as she had during the entire preceding season. During eight months at Drury Lane the year before, she had performed twenty-five times, for an average of a little more than three performances per month. In five months at the Little Haymarket, she performed forty-eight times, averaging nearly ten performances per month.

The previous year, she had played thirteen different roles, four in afterpieces and nine in mainpieces; this year she played seventeen different roles, only one in an afterpiece and sixteen in mainpieces. At Drury Lane, her mainpiece roles had varied in importance; at the Little Haymarket, nearly all of her roles were leading characters. During the entire season the year before, she had had to learn six new parts; now, in the half-season, she had to learn twelve—an average of two to three new parts per month—while she continued to act her previous roles.

With the mutineers, Charlotte became accustomed to important parts and established a professional reputation. Her signature roles at this time became female characters who exercised some kind of power, or blurred the lines of gender, or both. Though she appeared for one performance as Lucy in *The London Merchant,* in all her other roles Charlotte moved beyond chambermaids to play a group of more powerful, and often more disturbing, female characters. These women were eccentric, disreputable, and forceful, sometimes sinister and even violent— prone to behave as if they "wore the breeches" even when they did not actually cross-dress. There is no reason to believe that Charlotte was cast against her inclination: these were her roles of choice.

At the age of twenty, Charlotte was defining herself as an actress who specialized in gender ambiguity. She continued to play conventional breeches parts, in which an audacious heroine cross-dresses to pursue the man she desires, and she seems to have played these saucy, sexy heroines well. But many of Charlotte's performances during this season at the Little Haymarket were more disturbingly ambiguous, if not downright masculine.

Charlotte's new roles included Marcia in Addison's tragedy *Cato*— the hero's resolute Roman daughter, who is explicitly contrasted to her more conventionally feminine friend, Lucia. And for the first time, she played Louisa in Colley's *Love Makes a Man*. Louisa is a wealthy woman who defies feminine propriety, aggressively pursuing Carlos and making explicit her desire for him; when rebuffed in favour of the virtuous, feminine Angelina, she threatens to kill her rival. Louisa is finally restored to a sense of "proper femininity" by the example of Carlos and Angelina's virtuous love. But, to paraphrase Colley's flippant description of his first sentimental hero, Loveless, she is lewd (and aggressive) for above four acts first.

Charlotte also appeared as Tatlanthe, the Queen's favourite attendant, in Henry Carey's musical afterpiece, *Chronohotonthologos*. (One wonders if anyone ever actually pronounced this title.) Tatlanthe carries her flattery of the Queen to a near erotic level, presenting tea with the irresistible line, "The Water bubbled and the Tea Cups skip, / Through eager Hope to kiss your Royal Lip." At another point she declares, "Wou'd I were a Man" [for the Queen's sake].

Charlotte's most challenging opportunities came in the plays of Ben Jonson. Theo seemed to have particularly responded to the strong stuff of this Jacobean playwright's comedies, with their eccentric, even grotesque characters and wild, convoluted plots. He staged a trilogy of Jonson plays that season, casting Charlotte in three of her most assertive and striking—if misogynistically drawn—comic women. In *The Alchemist,* she played Dol Common, a voluble and conniving prostitute who in a moment of anger grabs her crony Subtle by the throat and threatens to strangle him; Subtle, pinned at the neck by Dol's powerful hand, makes it clear that he knows she could throttle him easily if she wanted, and submissively placates her. In *Volpone*—a play whose characters also include a eunuch and a hermaphrodite—Charlotte appeared as Lady Wouldbe, one of Jonson's absurdly assertive, garrulous women who aspire to the masculine preserve of learning. (Perhaps Charlotte called upon her boarding school aspirations with Latin and geography in this picture of female pretension and pretentiousness.)

Mrs. Otter in *The Silent Woman* (*Epicoene*) was Charlotte's most disturbingly ambiguous character of all. In this play, which turns on a man who marries another man disguised as a woman, Mrs. Otter's inverted relationship with her husband, Captain Otter, enacts another sexual displacement that is indicated by their name (otters were thought to be hermaphroditic). The drunkard Captain Otter, who loathes and fears his wife, has married her for her money, but in exchange has signed an agreement that essentially turns their marriage into a perpetual skimmington: his wife will "reign" as the "princess" in her own house and he will "be her subject and obey" her.

Mrs. Otter wields her sceptre with an iron fist, doling out her husband's allowance and beating him when he misbehaves. She figuratively "wears the trousers" in her marriage to such a degree that this role is virtually a travesty part without requiring Charlotte to don the literal breeches. Mrs. Otter foregrounds the disturbing ambiguities of masculine women, ambiguities often submerged in conventional breeches parts. Though she is comic, this "woman on top" is a termagant, even a monster. It was a forceful role for Charlotte, the most striking of her powerful, sexually ambiguous women, and reminiscent of her disturbing performance as Mother Lupine.

Amid this string of assertive, masculine-seeming female characters, Charlotte also established herself as the Little Haymarket company's leading performer of breeches parts. She reprised her former role as Clarinda in her father's *The Double Gallant,* and once again played the cross-dressed Lucy Fainlove in Steele's *The Tender Husband.* Fainlove, though identified to the audience as female from the play's beginning, appears only in men's clothes. Charlotte played seduction scenes with Ann Grace as Mrs. Clerimont. Though Steele attempted to defuse the potentially shocking nature of these scenes by having Fainlove recall her own seduction by Mr. Clerimont as the model for her technique—thus reminding the audience of her "real" heterosexuality—Mrs. Clerimont thinks that it is a man who is kissing her and responds accordingly, while the audience thrills with the knowledge that her seducer is a woman.

Charlotte's new breeches parts included Charlotte Welldon in Southerne's *Oroonoko,* who passes as a man until the fifth act. Welldon plots to secure a husband for herself by marrying the amorous widow Lackitt, successfully perpetuating her disguise even in the marriage bed by substituting her co-conspirator, Jack, under the covers each night. And in the era's most popular breeches part, Charlotte assumed Anne Oldfield's former role as Silvia in Farquhar's *The Recruiting Officer*. Silvia cross-dresses to pursue her inconstant lover, Captain Plume, but before she appears in men's clothes she establishes her masculine credentials by boasting of her physical vigour and complaining, "I think a petticoat a mighty simple thing, and I'm heartily tired of my sex." Her friend Melinda retorts, "O' my conscience, Silvia, hadst thou been a man, thou hadst been the greatest rake in Christendom."

If Charlotte, tall and slender, had not looked dashing in men's clothes, London's notoriously picky audiences would not have accepted her in so many breeches parts. Probably few, if any, actresses could wear breeches as convincingly, or move in them as confidently, as she. The pleasure audiences received from watching a lithe, attractive actress perform these roles was varied and complex. Some spectators inevitably disapproved on grounds of morality or propriety, but they were in the minority: breeches parts were popular. Scholars today usually explain this by positing that, despite their apparent gender-bending, breeches roles played into an entirely conventional sexual system. Appealing to the heterosexual fantasies of men in the audience, breeches emphasized the lower half of the actress's body, outlining her hips and legs.

This explanation has truth in it, but it is not the whole story. While the ability to leer at an actress's exposed legs undoubtedly aroused many, not everybody in the audience was male or what we now call heterosexual: surely, for instance, there were women who found that breeches-clad female figure arousing, and men who did not. And there must have been spectators of both sexes susceptible to the pleasures of sexual ambiguity, who responded to the contradictions embodied in a female body clad in men's clothes and engaged in masculine behaviours. The cross-dresser's status as simultaneously "both-and" and "neither-nor" must have delivered, for some, its own erotic charge.

Charlotte's ease in breeches probably made her resemble a man to a greater degree than most other cross-dressed actresses. And she herself must have taken increasing pleasure in her sanctioned donning of men's clothes; perhaps she began to feel irritated by the necessity of changing back into her cumbersome hoop and petticoats, and to regret the loss of her freedom of movement. Perhaps she also missed the sense of authority and entitlement that attached itself to men's clothes, even in a breeches part onstage.

~

At the end of November, Charlotte celebrated Kitty's third birthday. She continued to revel in her new importance, but she also had to face its consequences. During November, when she performed six times, and December, when she performed eleven, Charlotte acted nine new roles, including all three of the Jonson ones. The demands on her memory and her energy were enormous.

Charlotte must have felt as if she were constantly learning lines those days, and with memorization, rehearsing, performing, and caring for her toddler, she probably had little time to visit her mother, particularly as the autumn progressed and the roads to Kensington, notorious in the winter, became impassibly muddy. Katherine was now sixty-five, an advanced age by eighteenth-century standards, even for someone who was not a chronic invalid. Every year she was afflicted more severely as London's damp winter cold closed in. It is possible, though doubtful, that she came into town to see Charlotte, Theo, and her granddaughter Ann perform, or to visit Kitty. Perhaps Charlotte and Kitty braved the roads for a visit at Christmas, when her father and siblings may have joined her, but Charlotte was back in London the next day, for she performed on December 26, and four more times that week.

January began as hectically. It is possible that Charlotte had not seen her mother since Christmas, perhaps not even then, and she must have been shocked when, just a few days after she celebrated her twenty-first birthday, she was told that her mother had died. The cause of Katherine's death was not recorded but it could have been an asthma attack, or simply old age finally claiming a constitution long weakened by chronic illness. Katherine was interred at St. Martin-in-the-Fields on Sunday, January 20.[8] The entire Cibber clan must have been there.

Charlotte left no record of her feelings immediately after her mother's death, but they must have included deep, raw grief; perhaps there was guilt that she had been too busy to visit her at the end. Did she also feel a new sense of uneasiness about her place in her family? Despite Charlotte's greater proximity in recent years to her father and brother, it was her mother who had most uncritically accepted and doted upon her youngest daughter, often in pointed contrast to her elder sisters. With Katherine in the grave, Charlotte had lost the person who had been her staunchest ally and defender in the family. The loss was incalculable.

⁓

While the mutineers played to appreciative audiences in the autumn, Drury Lane was a shadow of its old self, with Kitty Clive and Mrs. Horton far outshining the inferior cohort Highmore had cobbled together. Only an Irish actor named Charles Macklin, culled from a troupe of strollers, showed much ability. With scant houses and large operating expenses, the theatre was falling into arrears by £50 to £60 each week, and Highmore, who was an honest man if a poor manager, made up the difference from his own pocket. Over a thirty-week season, expenses like these would ruin him.[9]

At the beginning of November, the mutineers' action against the patentees came to trial at the King's Bench, and a strong case it was. Knowing this, Highmore moved against the rebels on the morning of the day the verdict was expected—and he made a grave mistake. Seeking to apply a vagrancy act from the reign of Queen Anne that was occasionally used to persecute unlicensed troupes—most frequently strolling players without "fixed abodes"—as "rogues and vagabonds," Highmore had John Harper arrested and carried off to Bridewell Prison, hoping to shut down that evening's performance.

His move backfired spectacularly, for jolly John Harper was much loved. The public outcry was immediate, and that night at the theatre, Theo cleverly fanned the flames of outrage. With public opinion castigating Highmore, Harper was released from jail a few days later. Although a date was set for his trial, his admirers celebrated his release as a victory.[10] The feeling of triumph was all the more powerful because on the very day of his arrest, the mutineers had won their ejectment suit.

Highmore capitulated. In December, he sold his share to another ambitious, non-theatrical young gentleman named Charles Fleetwood—

who also bought Mary Wilks's share, at a bargain price—and turned his back on Drury Lane. The ex-patentee was beaten and bitter: burdened with debts, he had sold his shares for less than half of what he had paid for them, suffering a strong cure for his theatrical ambitions.

Fleetwood, a handsome, disarmingly genial man with great gifts of charm and sociability, was a very different personality from his predecessor. He was said to be much richer than Highmore, possessing a landed estate reputed to bring him £6,000 per year. Though it was not yet apparent, he was also much more devious. Fleetwood immediately opened negotiations with the rebels.[11]

The news of Highmore's sale came none too soon, for fissures had begun to open in the mutineers' solidarity. As the novelty wore off, audiences declined, and some of the troupe began to weary of Theophilus's command. The green room was often tense with exhaustion, tension, and anticipation. However aware they were of Theo's abilities, and although they acknowledged that he served their interests well, many of the actors simply did not like him. Always arrogant and abrasive, he became particularly obnoxious when exercising authority. If the players indeed had a commonwealth, he was its "first citizen," and there were no handsome profits to share that might have made his exercise of power tolerable.

Despite the rising tensions, Theophilus, always adroit, managed to meet with the new patentee alone and made himself the principal negotiator. Both he and Fleetwood played their cards well. Meanwhile, the actors at Drury Lane, both those who had refused to join the mutiny and those whom Highmore had hired as replacements, watched with trepidation, for most of them had much to lose if the rebels were restored to their old positions. And even for some of the mutineers themselves, including Charlotte, a return to Drury Lane would be a mixed blessing.

On March 12, that return took place.[12] Under the terms Theophilus negotiated with Fleetwood, not only the original mutineers, but also the additional actors and singers who had joined them at the Little Haymarket, were taken into the newly combined company. Theo became Fleetwood's deputy manager. The new arrangements pleased both the patentee and the leading players, at least for the moment: "The patentee had the senior actors and the theatre; the actors got large raises and improved benefit terms, guaranteed in writing."[13] But some players would find the new dispensation less than satisfying; Charlotte was among them.

Now there were essentially two troupes at Drury Lane, the mutineers and the loyalists, former enemies who now combined uneasily to form one large, fractious company. The most immediate casualties of the peace were the newer actors hired by Highmore, who were displaced in roles by the returning veterans. Many of them feared, with good reason, that when their contracts expired at the end of the season they would be fired.

Tensions rose immediately. As far as the victorious rebels were concerned, those who had not joined their walkout had been traitors to the players' cause. Kitty Clive, Mary Porter, and Christiana Horton preserved their leading lady status—Theophilus was no fool—but he and the other ex-mutineers remembered their betrayal. Other players among the loyalists were less well protected by their status; these found themselves cold-shouldered in the green room and their roles usurped. Several plays the loyalists had rehearsed and even performed earlier that year were now dropped from the schedule, replaced with the Revels Company's own repertoire, and benefits went to the rebels. Angry and dispirited, the loyalists seethed helplessly.

Theophilus was not greatly concerned for their feelings. He revelled in his new position: he had led a successful walkout, defied the arrogance of gentleman-managers, and returned triumphant to a higher salary, a better benefit, and a greater degree of job security—or so it seemed at the time. Owning a share of the patent himself would have been better, of course, but at the moment his ascendancy over Fleetwood seemed complete. The patentee could scarcely make a decision without asking Theo's opinion, and the deferential attention with which he listened to, and indeed acted upon, Theo's advice was most gratifying. Theophilus brimmed with self-consequence that spring, especially when he capped his triumphant restoration to power at Drury Lane with another great victory. On April 21, he led a new bride to the altar.

12

Mad Company

(1734–35)

Theophilus had fallen in love passionately and intemperately—as he was wont to do nearly everything—with Susannah Maria Arne. The demure singer had not at first welcomed the attentions of her flashy suitor, whom she found overbearing and physically repellent. His pockmarked visage, set off by his embroidered waistcoats and superabundance of lace, gave him the air of a backstage Lord Foppington, without the title. Susannah had heard the gossip about young Cibber's extravagance, his wildness, his dissipation, and his debts. And she had heard the mutterings that he had been a faithless husband who had overworked his poor wife Jane into the grave.

On the other hand, inexperienced Susannah knew that, despite their grumblings, the other players respected Theo's acting abilities and had benefited from his leadership. Now the de facto manager of Drury Lane, he lived in high style and kept a carriage—and her own family, with one notable exception, was delighted by Theophilus's attentions to her. Allied with the scion of the Cibbers, the new power at Drury Lane positioned to advance not only Susannah's career but also her two brothers', seemed handily to serve her family's interests. Her father did what he could to push his daughter into Theophilus's arms.

Thomas Arne, Sr., was an impecunious but ambitious upholsterer and undertaker who kept a shop at the sign of the Two Crowns and Cushions on King Street in Covent Garden. (Upholstery and undertaking were intertwined professions then, there being no great distance between stuffing an armchair or silk-lining a coach, and dressing a coffin or shrouding a corpse.) In more prosperous times, Arne had sent his elder son, Tom, to Eton to be trained in the law and had hired tutors to give Susannah a gentlewoman's education— French, drawing, music—that would prepare her to make a good marriage to a wealthy man. But his business began to decline, he went into debt, and his son defied his wishes by secretly pursuing a musical career. Ultimately, Arne himself encouraged Thomas in music and supported his idea that Susannah should sing the lead role in his Little Haymarket production of Lampe and Carey's English opera *Amelia*.

Susannah was not an obvious candidate for a career on the operatic stage. She had a lovely, if limited, contralto voice, but she was not a trained musician. Her tutors had given her the education of a gentle-woman, not a professional: they had not taught her to read music. Nor was she particularly beautiful or genteel. But she possessed a natural dignity and a plaintive air that played well on the stage. Her portrayal of Amelia created a great stir in London, and her subsequent perfor-mance in her brother's *Rosamond* confirmed her as a sensation. Then Handel, seeking a voice for his new oratorio *Deborah*, approached her to sing for him, despite the limitations of her training.

Now that Susannah's career was under way, her father calculated, marriage to Theophilus would be a strategic next step, and the girl, dif-fident, soft-spoken, and easily dominated by the strong masculine per-sonalities in her family, was not temperamentally equipped to defy her father. Marriages were usually arranged by fathers or male guardians; many a woman gave in to parental pressure. It is also possible that her lover's ardour had begun to soften Susannah's feelings towards him.

Susannah's mother was not won over, however: Anne Arne, a pro-fessional midwife, thought that this marriage was a potential disaster, given Theophilus's debts and extravagance. So Mrs. Arne took the only step she could, insisting that the marriage documents include an unusual article that placed Susannah's income into a trust for her "sole and separate use" after marriage. Susannah's modern biographer, Mary Nash, remarks that it was an indication of Theophilus's passion for her that he agreed to sign it. It was probably also an indication of his con-fidence that his demure young wife could never have interests separate from his own.[1]

If any member of Theophilus's family was present at the wedding, it would have been his loyal sister Charlotte. Elizabeth might have joined them, perhaps accompanied by her daughter, Ann, who as a dancer in the troupe was in constant contact with her uncle. But Theo's older sisters, Catherine and Anne, are unlikely to have attended, for they took their cue from the groom's father—whose absence was conspicuous. Colley opposed his son's choice "because," he later said, "she had no Fortune."[2] There may have been another reason for Colley's disapproval, as Koon suggests. Though Thomas Arne, Sr., was a member of the Church of England, Anne Arne was a Roman Catholic, and Susannah had been raised in her mother's faith. Colley, staunch Hanoverian and author of *The Non-Juror,* with its caricatured vicious Jesuit Dr. Wolf, was sincerely anti-Catholic.

Theophilus obviously did not share Colley's views, but many eighteenth-century British Protestants saw Catholicism as a tyrannical religion, imbued with superstition, corrupted by "priestcraft," and allied with absolutist political regimes such as France. Many British Catholics were loyal to the "King across the Water"—the Old Pretender, James Francis Edward Stuart, exiled son of James II—and they appeared to pose a real threat to British liberty. (There had already been one abortive Jacobite invasion in 1715, and a subsequent series of uprisings in Scotland.) For Colley, the sight of his son repeating wedding vows before a Roman Catholic priest would have been abhorrent—especially since the bride had no money to soften the blow.

Charlotte, who had no such prejudice, would have been pleased for her brother's prospects. But as she considered her own future that spring, she must have felt impatient and frustrated. She welcomed the increase in salary, certainly, and she was probably relieved in some ways to be back in the relative opulence and apparent security of Drury Lane, especially under Theo's direction. (Initially at least, she had little reason to chafe, since her opportunities to perform were fairly abundant that spring.) But as she looked ahead to the next year, when she would compete for new parts with several of the troupe's leading ladies, some of whom also had claims on roles she had played with the mutineers, her usual optimism must have wavered.

During the remaining three months of the regular season that year,

Charlotte played Dol Common, Hoyden, Fainlove, and Mrs. Otter, performing the last role, on one occasion, in a programme that included a "new Serenata" composed by Thomas Arne "on the present joyous Occasion of the Royal Nuptials"—the long delayed marriage of Princess Anne, the King's eldest daughter, to William, Prince of Orange. (It is an illustration of the bizarre conjunctions possible in eighteenth-century theatre that Ben Jonson's perverse comedy of grotesque marriages could ever be considered an appropriate companion to a piece celebrating a royal wedding.)

On May 3, Charlotte replaced Mrs. Heron for one night in the major role of Primrose in *The Mother-in-Law*—another of her pert chambermaids, but this conniving minx was one of the play's central and funniest characters. (At one point in the play, Charlotte dressed Theophilus's character in women's clothes and instructed him in walking and talking like a woman.) But besides this isolated performance, she assumed only three new roles, all small ones. It may have been Theo who asked her to resume her old part as Aurora in *Cephalus and Procris*, intending to make use of her experience. But to Charlotte, it must have seemed as if time had run backward, as if those heady, challenging months at the Little Haymarket had never occurred. She was not easily discouraged, however, and as the tempestuous season of 1733–34 approached its end, she took matters into her own hands.

On May 20, a new troupe of players burst onto the scene, clamouring for the Town's attention. *The Daily Advertiser* announced that "a mad Company of Comedians having lately taken the Hay-market Theatre, propose to convert it into a Mad-house, and humbly hope the Town will be as mad as themselves, and come frequently to see their mad Performances, which will be madly exhibited, two or three Times a week, during the Summer Season." Intrigued readers found a bit more light cast upon the identity of the "Mad Company" in the next day's *Daily Journal*: "We hear that the Mad Company at the Haymarket design to keep up that Character, by performing the Beggar's Opera in Roman Dress, and exhibiting Hurlothrumbo, in which Mrs. Charke attempts the Character of Lord Flame."

Hurlothrumbo, that bizarre play by an eccentric author who himself acted the original Lord Flame speaking in several registers and hopping around the stage on stilts, was an appropriate choice for a mad company. But Charlotte never got her chance to attempt Lord Flame with or without the stilts, since this production never materialized—not a good omen. However, the company's "mad" rendition of *The Beggar's Opera*—retitled *The Beggar's Opera Tragedized*—did make its debut on June 3 and, as promised, the entire cast was dressed as ancient Romans. We can only imagine the spectacle: Peachum and Lockit parading across the stage in togas, Polly, Lucy, and the prostitutes swathed in classical drapery, thieves baring their legs in tunics, outbursts of high-flown, "tragedized" rhetoric supplementing the songs. Perhaps this tragic *Beggar's Opera* actually sent its womanizing hero Captain Macheath to the gallows instead of saving him at the last minute, as the original did. If so, the gallant highwayman would have gone to his death clad in the breastplate and plumed helmet of a Roman soldier, facing his fate with dash and swagger. Charlotte, who played him, would have made sure of that.

Details are sketchy about the organization of the "Mad Company" that occupied the Little Haymarket in the summer of 1734, but one thing seems certain: this was Charlotte's troupe. The company's newspaper blurbs bore her zany, exhibitionistic stamp, and their advertisements for their performances prominently featured references to her. Throughout the summer, Charlotte had principal parts in nearly every play they performed. On the night of the Mad Company's debut, for instance, she played leading roles in both the mainpiece and the afterpiece. She also spoke a prologue (which she, as the troupe's leader, probably wrote) in which she introduced the company to the Town. (After the troupe's last performance that summer, she spoke an epilogue, which she probably wrote as well.) With only four years of stage experience behind her, Charlotte, like her father and brother before her, was making a foray into the art of management.

Charlotte had leaped to exploit a vacuum. Drury Lane was still in considerable disorder and Theophilus was uninterested in managing a summer season there. He and Susannah were living the first, by all accounts happy, months of their marriage in even more extravagant style than was Theo's wont, and he probably carried her out of town that summer to some leafy, expensive resort such as Richmond. With the exception of the King's Theatre in the Haymarket, where Handel staged a short season of opera that ended in early July, no other London playhouse offered summer performances in 1734.

There were more needy actors in London than ever. Joining Charlotte's troupe were the ranks of the discarded, disaffected, rebellious, and inexperienced. The Mad Company included two young members of Charlotte's own extended family, her fourteen-year-old niece, Ann Brett, and Theophilus's younger brother-in-law, Henry Peter Arne, also about fourteen. Making his first stage appearances with her troupe was young Robert Wilks, nephew to the late actor-manager.

With her Mad Company, Charlotte became one of the first women in English theatre history to become a manager of her own troupe. She may have been, in fact, the first woman on the London stage to assume the sole responsibility of management—to rent a playhouse, scenes, and costumes, and to perform a repertory of plays throughout a season, even a summer season. It was an unusual, masculine thing for any woman to do, since management was not considered women's work. And it was a gamble: Charlotte was twenty-one years old, and she had no practical experience in management—she had not all that much experience in *acting* yet—nor did she have in her troupe anyone who did. But her father and brother had been managers, and so would she. Besides, Charlotte was drawn to unconventionality and risk. Disregarding the uncertainties and hazards, she threw herself with all her energy into her new experiment.

"Madness," that summer, became Charlotte's signature, as she added to her repertory of powerful women and breeches parts an impressive number of male characters. For an actress to develop a line in travesty roles—playing men—was considered by many to be a risky and disreputable step. Speaking, he said, "in the Name of all sober, discreet, sensible, Spectators," Benjamin Victor warned actresses that if they assumed such roles and succeeded, "you may be condemned as a Woman," and if they did not succeed, "you are injured as an Actress." Comic breeches parts—"the wearing Breeches merely to pass for a Man"—were acceptable, but such cross-dressing "should not be in the least extended—when it is, you overstep the Modesty of Nature."[3] Such was the reputation for eccentricity and masculinity that Charlotte was beginning to establish.

The Mad Company, in its antic style, performed an exhausting schedule that summer. Between June 3 and August 22 they played twenty-nine times, usually twice a week, most performances featuring two plays as well as singing, dancing, and the occasional novelty piece. Charlotte played a lead role in virtually every play, and she even ventured to dance on occasion: she joined her niece Ann in dancing "The Black and White Joke," an Irish jig set to the tune of a traditional (and obscene) song.

Nearly all of the characters that Charlotte chose to play that summer were men. Her Captain Macheath was not the first transvestite performance of this part: Signora Violante had cast Peg Woffington, the young Irish actress destined for great fame on the London stage, in that role during their brief series of performances in 1732. But when Charlotte assumed the role two years later and played it most of the summer (relinquishing it to another actress, Mrs. Roberts, twice), she helped to establish what would become a theatrical tradition of gender-switching performances not only of that character, but of the play's entire cast. Charlotte would play Captain Macheath in many different venues during the rest of her life; as late as 1820, the famous breeches actress Madame Vestris—in some ways a theatrical descendant of Charlotte—played him, too.[4] Charlotte's zany decision to dress all her players as Romans also spawned a history of other "creative" productions of Gay's ballad opera.

As an afterpiece to *The Beggar's Opera*, the Mad Company performed a droll of *Henry IV* called *The Humours of Sir John Falstaff, Justice Shallow, and Ancient Pistol*. Unsurprisingly, Charlotte took the role of Pistol, and in so doing she also played, and parodied, her brother. Charlotte had been developing her talents as a mimic since childhood and now, for the first time (onstage, that is), she turned those skills upon a member of her family. She must have leered, grimaced, and strutted bow-legged around the stage in a burlesque of Theophilus likely to have been much appreciated by the audience. Their sibling relationship and the fact that she, his sister, was playing her brother as a travesty part, clad in an oversized tricorn hat and brandishing a large sword, made her performance particularly wicked. Theo was not very tolerant of mockery, but he took his sister's imitation of him without recorded complaint.

Charlotte probably considered her mimicry to be a form of flattery, not unlike what Theophilus himself did when he played their father's former roles, although her performance supplied the extra comical (and potentially insulting) dimension of travesty. As in her infantile imitation of her father, Charlotte also vied with a powerful male member of her family. And her imitations of her brother were not limited to Pistol. She also played the role of the Mock Doctor in Fielding's play of that title—another of Theophilus's most celebrated roles—and his part of Ramilie in Fielding's *The Miser.* In all these performances, her imitation of her brother's portrayal of these comic characters would inevitably have shaded into a burlesque of her brother himself, especially since the latter was likely to get the louder laughs.

In her father's *The Provok'd Husband,* Charlotte played Wilks's old title role of the husband, Lord Townly. In Cibber's *The Non-Juror,* she played Mr. Heartly, and in *The Devil to Pay,* she played Sir John. Charlotte played Lovemore in *The Lottery,* the libertine Lothario in *The Fair Penitent,* and Sir Charles in *The Beaux' Stratagem.* For her own benefit at the end of the season, she repeated *The London Merchant,* but this summer, instead of the maid Lucy, she played the tragic hero George Barnwell. She also played Harry in *The Humourous Election.* And in *The Contrivances,* she took on Richard's early role of the rake Rovewell. (She must have parodied her estranged husband with a particularly ironical glint in her eye.)

Charlotte played only four female roles that summer, and those included her breeches part of Charlotte Welldon, who dresses as a man through most of the play, in *Oroonoko.* In only three plays did she actually appear in petticoats, or their equivalent, throughout.

It sometimes has been suggested that Charlotte played so many male roles because her troupe was short of male actors. She did have more females than males in her company, but there were male actors who could have taken her roles, as well as Mrs. Roberts, who had experience playing breeches parts. Charlotte played men because she wanted to play them: this was her company, and she had the power to choose roles to suit herself. It seems clear that the heroes satisfied her better than did the heroines. Men's clothes suited her figure, and the masculine mannerisms and stride that went with the clothes came easily to her. The emotional satisfaction she derived from these roles can only be guessed at, but it obviously ran deep.

Possibly it was during this summer of 1734 that Charlotte's masculine role-playing onstage slid into her offstage life. Her own accounts of the circumstances under which she began to wear men's clothes outside of the theatre are vague and contradictory. But she probably became an offstage cross-dresser gradually, at first wearing men's clothes on occasion, and then more and more often until they became her customary garb. While playing at the Little Haymarket she would have acquired

Charlotte

KATHRYN SHEVELOW

Published in Hardback by Bloomsbury
29th August 2005, £18.99

A TRUE ACCOUNT OF AN ACTRESS'S FLAMBOYANT
ADVENTURES IN
EIGHTEENTH-CENTURY LONDON'S WILD AND
WICKED THEATRICAL WORLD

**She was a child of the theatre who scandalized proper society –
whenever possible. Meet Charlotte, an unforgettable heroine who
lived in London's most fascinating times, in a work of brilliant
popular history.**

Eighteenth-century London was a theatre writ large: Fielding's satires
mocked the Prime Minister, *The Beggar's Opera* drew raves, and riots
broke out over dueling divas of the stage. Spectacle abounded:
aristocratic ladies paraded past fire-eaters, prostitutes, and public
hangings. Mrs Mapp, the bone-setter, realigned butchers' kneecaps
for happy crowds. Yet Charlotte was rarely overlooked. Everyday
of her life was a grand performance.

Born into the famous, sometimes
scandalous, theatrical clan of Colley
Cibber, Charlotte was an actress
destined for greatness. But she would rebel,
and started dressing as a man. When her
father disowned her, her life became an
adventure extending from the pinnacles of
posh London to its dangerous depths.
Kathryn Shevelow captures Charlotte – an
artist, a survivor – in all her guises, from her
time among the leading lights of glamorous
Drury Lane Theatre to her trials as a strolling
player and puppeteer, to her comeback as author
of one of the first autobiographies written by a
woman.

"A remarkable
book which
admirably captures
this most elusive of
social rebels"
Amanda Foreman

A specialist in eighteenth-century British
literature and culture, Kathryn Shevelow has
been an award-winning professor at the University
of California in San Diego for twenty years. **Kathryn will be
in London for publication and available for interview.**

For further information, please contact:
Katie Bond, Tel: 020 7494 6012
Email: katie_bond@bloomsbury.com
www.bloomsbury.com/kathrynshevelow

Praise for *Charlotte*

"Precocious, gifted, charismatic, and eccentric, Charlotte Charke illuminated the eighteenth century with the fleeting brightness of a shooting star. Kathryn Shevelow has written a remarkable book which admirably captures this most elusive of social rebels."
Amanda Foreman, author of Georgiana, Duchess of Devonshire

"A fascinating account of this eccentric dynamo's adventures in eighteenth-century trade, theatre and love, Shevelow's book should win Charlotte Clarke the multitudes of admirers she deserves."
Emma Donoghue, author of Slammerkin and Life Mask

"Charlotte is a remarkably learned and even more remarkably entertaining history - not only of a truly fascinating and startlingly-original woman, but also of her times and culture. Kathryn Shevelow brings to life the madness, absurdity and baseness of 18th-century Britain, and the recreates for modern readers the fascinating peculiarities of its theater world. This is a brilliant piece of popular history."
David Liss, author of *A Conspiracy of Paper* and *The Coffee Trader*

her own suit of male clothing (if she had not done so already): the clothes would have been used, but of good quality—Charlotte was vain about her masculine appearance—perhaps purchased on credit from a tallyman who received them in pawn from a gentleman down on his luck or was fencing them for a footpad who had stripped his victim. Charlotte wore these clothes onstage almost constantly that summer, and there may have been times when she succumbed to a temptation not to change back into her petticoat afterward.

We can picture Charlotte, a tall, slim figure standing in the dressing room at ease in a pair of breeches and shirt, eyeing with resignation the unwieldy pile of lace and whalebone that were her hoop and stays. Gradually her resignation gives way to disgust, then defiance, and her face sets with resolve. She abruptly casts the hoop, stays, petticoat, and mantua into a heap in the corner, slings her coat over her shoulder, claps her tricorn firmly onto her periwigged head, and strides boldly into the summer night, grinning with satisfaction.

If Charlotte enjoyed such a personal victory of inclination over propriety that summer, her groundbreaking experiment in managing a theatre troupe was less successful. (Unfortunately for those who must eat, milestones in history are not always profitable.) Theatre management, Charlotte discovered, was a daunting task, especially when undertaken alone and on a very limited budget. The schedule of rehearsals and performances was exhausting, the hot theatre nerve-fraying, the demands of acting, directing, and doing business overwhelming. Charlotte was a whirlwind of activity, but whirlwinds are not the most disciplined of phenomena. She would have been responsible for nearly everything, even if she delegated some of the tasks to her least inexperienced colleagues: choosing the plays, coaching and rehearsing the actors, deflecting jealousies, soothing wounded egos, arranging the entr'acte entertainments, paying the accounts or (more likely) staving off creditors, counting the receipts, placing the advertisements, and ordering the playbills from the printer.

While at Drury Lane that spring, she had been lodging at the Golden Harp in Little Russell Street, a dodgy neighbourhood near the Strand.[5] If she still lodged there, the daily and nightly commutes between the far side of Covent Garden and the Haymarket would have been long and wearying, too. And there was little Kitty to consider, a toddler who had not yet reached her fourth birthday. Did Charlotte park her in the green room with an obliging actress or dresser as an attendant, entrust her to her landlady at the Golden Harp, or leave her under the eye of a servant at her father's house?

All these responsibilities, both professional and personal, came in addition to the challenge of learning, in a very short time, a large repertory of roles in both mainpieces and afterpieces—most of Charlotte's roles that summer were new to her—and then performing them, sometimes more than one in an evening. Charlotte acted, she sang, she danced, she recited prologues and epilogues. She worked ceaselessly. But audiences did not come. After a year of upheaval, London spectators may have been soured on the stage, or perhaps this troupe was simply not enough of a draw to entice customers away from the parks and pleasure gardens.

Charlotte probably had better success when on August 20 she took her troupe to Lincoln's Inn Fields, where she played Lord Townly at a benefit for Henry Peter Arne. They performed "at the Desire of" a group of visiting dignitaries, the American Indian chief Tomo-chichi of the Yamacraw branch of the Creek Indians, his wife, Benauki, and his nephew Tooanahowi and their compatriots. The Native Americans had come to England with their friend George Oglethorpe, founder of the Georgia colony (which was much in the news at the time). In London they presented eagle feathers to the King, had audiences with influential people, toured the town, and went to the theatre. As sights themselves, the Indians might have pulled some additional spectators into the playhouse. But American Indian chiefs did not visit the theatre every night.

Ten days before the Mad Company closed its season, Charlotte advertised a performance of *The Beggar's Opera,* that established crowd-pleaser, as a benefit for the theatre servants—quite possibly the only wages they would receive. Her ad closed with a wistful plea: "N.B. As the Summer Season has prov'd very unsuccessful, the Servants humbly hope that in Consideration of it the Town will favour them this Night."[6] Perhaps the Town took pity, for once.

Charlotte must have been exhausted. The frenetic acting schedule and the headaches of management had taken their toll on her health. Although she badly needed the income, she did not act at Bartholomew

Fair that year, probably because she did not have the strength or the voice to perform all day. After reciting, on the Mad Company's last night, an epilogue "address'd to the Town" (we can imagine what she wished to say to them), she must have dragged herself across Covent Garden, lacking the money to take a coach or even a sedan chair home. She trudged past the prostitutes and staggering drunks, dodging the chairmen who hurtled past carrying their more fortunate passengers, crossing momentarily the pools of light created by the link boys' blazing torches as they guided their often inebriated customers home (or, sometimes, into dark byways where their confederates waited to plunder).

As she plodded along she would have kept a wary eye out for the footpads who lurked in the dark doorways and alleys all along her route, particularly as she approached the squalid streets that abutted her own. If she still had on the clothes in which she had played George Barnwell that evening, perhaps now she fully appreciated that dressing as a man on the streets carried additional advantages beyond satisfying a personal inclination. The clothes gave her an extra degree of security. Her coat, hat, breeches, and long masculine stride protected her from potential rapists, and with her fine clothes now worn threadbare, the footpads would have ignored her.

Charlotte must have felt some relief when she returned to the newly painted, newly decorated Drury Lane Theatre in the autumn and her salary resumed. But the 1734–35 season would see new difficulties for the venerable playhouse. Despite its cosmetic improvements, Drury Lane struggled. Part of the problem was a general crisis in London theatre, brought about by changes in audience tastes and increased competition for a finite number of theatregoers. As Charlotte had learned the previous summer, crowds had begun to lose interest in serious British drama, both the old standards and new plays.

That autumn, the public could occupy itself with a variety of distractions. A visiting French troupe at the Little Haymarket was performing a series of foreign plays, and, for the second successive season, a rival Italian opera company was doing what it could to force Handel's group into bankruptcy. Some of Handel's players, including Senesino, had seceded to form "the Company of the Nobility," patronized by the Prince of Wales in rivalry with the King: just as the feuding father and son had two courts, so did they sponsor two opera companies. While Handel performed a limited season at Covent Garden (on which nights the house company used the theatre in Lincoln's Inn Fields), the Company of the Nobility ensconced themselves at King's, where they scored the greatest opera coup of the century by bringing to London the celebrated castrato Carlo Broschi, called Farinelli. Early that November, Lord Hervey reported that "this being the time of the Norfolk Congress [a Whig political meeting], the palace & town are both thin. No place is full but the Opera; and Farinelli is so universally liked, that the crowds there are immense." Calling Farinelli "universally liked" understates the sensation the handsome *musico* produced when he sang. Upon hearing him, a woman is reported to have cried, "One God, one Farinelli"— while other women in the audience fainted around her.

Over at Covent Garden and Lincoln's Inn Fields, John Rich was staging the crowd-pleasing, elabourate pantomimes and ever inventive spectacles with which the name of Rich had long been synonymous. (John's father, Christopher, had once planned to bring an elephant into his playhouse at Dorset Gardens, until his bricklayer advised him that the hole he would have to cut in the wall to accommodate the creature was likely to collapse the building.)[7] "Low" entertainment venues such as Sadler's Wells were attracting audiences with tumblers, contortionists, merry andrews, and rope dancers. Fleetwood moved to compete in kind, much to Theo's and Charlotte's disgust.

At Drury Lane that season, novelties and expensive spectacles claimed an expanding portion of the evening; the playbills often advertised "New Habits, Scenes, Machines and other Decorations." Pantomimes became more and more elabourate and novelty driven, as their descriptions indicated: Charlotte had a part in John Kelly's *The Plot*, subtitled "a New Tragi-Comi-Farcical Operatical Grotesque Pantomime." Mrs. Webb, "the Tall Woman from Leicestershire," made a series of appearances as "Signora Garagantula," while Richard Charke played his violin and Susannah Cibber sang before, during, and after plays. Dancing occupied an ever more prominent place, with dances such as "the Black Joke," "the English Maggot," "the Russian Sailor," and "the Drunken Peasant" taking up more of the space in the advertisements. New, foreign dancers, such as the French Mlle. Roland and M. Poitier and the Polish M. Denoyer, joined those already in the company. On one occasion when the popular Roland and Poitier did not perform as billed, the audience became "incens'd," and a small riot ensued.[8]

Beset by competition from without, and unsettled by fickle audiences, the large, fractious company suffered internecine problems as well. The playhouse became a hotbed of rivalries, intrigues, and jealousies. One new source of conflict joined the company that autumn, when Fleetwood added to the troupe, at great expense, a considerable new talent—and an equally considerable ego—in the person of the famous actor James Quin. Large and imposing, brilliant and arrogant, Quin had been the leading tragedian at Covent Garden; an unusually versatile actor, he was accomplished in certain comic roles as well. Many a drunken argument had been waged in Covent Garden taverns over who was a better Falstaff, Quin or Harper; the general opinion had it that the former was more "judicious," though the latter was funnier.[9]

When Fleetwood offered Quin the breathtaking salary of £500 per annum to act at Drury Lane, the actor offered to stay at Covent Garden for a somewhat smaller sum. John Rich, whose passions were more invested in pantomimes than in plays, and more in costumes, sets, and stage machinery than in players, replied brusquely that in his estimation, no actor was worth more than £300. So Quin moved to Drury Lane, displacing Harper as Falstaff, establishing himself as the leading tragic actor, and immediately, inevitably, coming to loggerheads with Theophilus. Quin made it clear from the outset that he considered the younger Cibber "a vain, impertinent coxcomb" and had no intention of bowing to his authority. Theo, for his part, "thought him a proud, imperious blockhead," frustratingly impervious to Theo's attempts to provoke him.[10] On one occasion, Quin responded to Theo's "smart cutting Repartees on him" by exclaiming, with a laugh, "Quarrelling with such a Fellow, is like shitting on a Turd." Then he walked off, "as cool as a Cucumber."[11]

Theophilus Cibber's position at Drury Lane was becoming increasingly difficult, and not only because of his quarrels with Quin. His status as Drury Lane's most versatile comic actor remained firm, but his influence over Fleetwood was becoming shaky. Like many others in the company, Fleetwood was alienated by Theo's vanity and high-handed, tactless attempts to assert his authority. Theo had reason to object to the patentee's management, however. Initially, Fleetwood had paid serious attention to the playhouse, but he was more interested in capitalizing upon his investment in Drury Lane than in conserving a tradition of serious British theatre. His real passion was gambling and, unknown to the players, he was already "a ruined Man" when he took over the theatre. With his wealth drained away, he was obsessed with doing whatever it might take to turn a profit.[12]

Besides the arrogant Quin, another rival was more stealthily vying for Fleetwood's ear, encouraging his dislike of Theo. Charles Macklin was an Irish actor who had been hired by Highmore during the mutiny, fired by Fleetwood, but then rehired. Macklin, who peppered his speech with oaths, was as hot-tempered as Quin was cool (the two Irishmen would develop their own rivalry, both personal and professional). Already Fleetwood was delegating, not only to Quin, but also to Macklin, some of the duties that had been Theo's responsibility.[13]

For Charlotte, as for her brother, 1734–35 was a season of discontent. Despite all her troubles with the Mad Company, management had given Charlotte a taste of independence and importance. However modest her venue, she had played leading roles of her own choosing, expanding her repertoire enormously. But the Drury Lane company contained many talented—and more senior—actresses, vying for a limited number of good female parts. Furthermore, Charlotte's preference for male roles would never be honoured at Drury Lane, as she was well aware. An actress in a patent company might play a leading male part only as an occasional novelty.

Charlotte did keep her good character roles as Dol Common, Mrs. Otter, and Louisa, and her breeches parts in *The Tender Husband* and *Oroonoko* that year. But she lost other roles to Sarah Thurmond (ironically enough, the actress who had given Charlotte her start by requesting her to perform for her benefit back in 1730), Kitty Clive, Hannah Pritchard, and others.

She did play the new role of Lucy in Congreve's *The Old Batchelor* on one occasion—Tomo-chichi and his party were in the audience again that evening—but when the play was repeated later that season the role went to a different actress, and she had only one other very small part in a pantomime that year. If she had been able to sing as fetchingly as Kitty Clive and Hannah Pritchard, there would have been much for her to do, but her voice, though good, was not exceptional. Charlotte's forte was the comedy of the seventeenth and eighteenth centuries, with its strongly drawn, even grotesque characters; but the majority of new roles clustered in ballad operas and pantomimes.

This was not what Charlotte had come to expect, and certainly not what she thought she deserved. After more than four years of apprenticeship that included very hard work playing an unusually large range of parts in other venues, she felt that she was being treated unfairly. Charlotte had not been caricatured in *The Stage Mutineers* as "Mrs. Haughty" for nothing. She complained to Fleetwood, who smiled sympathetically and told her, with all his gentlemanly charm, that she was an invaluable member of the company and that any troupe in town would be proud to count her among them. He promised with apparent sincerity that she would have better roles soon—but none materialized.

Charlotte did receive some amends for her meagre season, however, perhaps through Colley's or Theo's influence. She was singled out to become, in her words, "Stock-Reader to the Theatre, in Case of Disasters"—that is, a kind of universal understudy.[14] She had to prepare herself to go on at short notice in any of the major female roles in the repertoire that season, if an actress was unable to perform and there was no one else available who had played the part before. This was an immense undertaking, but Charlotte had demonstrated the strength of her memory many times. She was a quick study, learning her lines rapidly and accurately, able to hold a large number of roles in her head, even by the demanding standards of eighteenth-century theatre. Her talent for mimicry also made her a logical choice for this position, since audiences of the time would have expected a stand-in to perform in the style of the actress whom she was replacing.

Disasters were in particularly scarce supply that season. One evening, however, probably the night of February 25, Charlotte abruptly was called to the playhouse and told that Elizabeth Butler had been taken ill. She had fifteen minutes to costume herself to perform the lead role of Queen Elizabeth in John Banks's tragedy *The Unhappy Favourite; or, The Earl of Essex*. The house was already filled with spectators eager to see this popular play, and Fleetwood was anxious not to lose the box-office receipts they represented. The responsibility for keeping the audience rested on Charlotte's shoulders.

Even more dauntingly, playing opposite her as Burleigh was James Quin. As Charlotte flew around Mrs. Butler's dressing room in her shift, calling for the dresser to help her into her gown, wig, and jewels, hastily reciting her lines under her breath, she must have tried to keep her thoughts from dwelling upon Quin's intimidating bulk and his impatient frown. Twenty years later, Charlotte had not forgotten the terror she felt that night: "Had I been under Sentence of Death, and St. Sepulcre's dreadful Bell tolling for my last hour, I don't conceive I could have suffered much greater Agony. I absolutely had not a Joint or Nerve I could command, for the whole Night." The playhouse was packed, but "the Apprehension I laboured under in respect to the Audience," she said, "was nothing in Comparison to the Fright his Aspect threw me into." But Charlotte's training and her memory served her well. However cracked and weak it may have sounded in her ears, her voice held up, she remembered her lines, and she forced her quaking limbs to behave with some semblance of royal dignity. Mrs. Butler graciously showed her appreciation by sending Charlotte a couple of guineas the next morning. Charlotte thought the gesture more than the occasion merited, but she was not in a position to refuse the money even had she desired to do so.

Late that season, Charlotte once again withstood the "Shock," as she characterized it, of performing a leading role at a few minutes' notice under intimidating circumstances. In early May, she was summoned to the playhouse at the end of the second music and told that while the third music played—fifteen or twenty minutes—she had to prepare herself to go on in place of Mrs. Heron as Cleopatra in Dryden's *All for Love.* It was a benefit performance for the actor-playwright James Worsdale, and the Prince of Wales was in the audience. Charlotte survived that shock, too, managing her nerves, allowing Worsdale a good benefit, and acquitting herself "tolerably to the Satisfaction of the Masters and Audience."[15]

Charlotte later wrote that Mary Heron could not perform that night because she had fallen on the stairs in her house and broken her kneecaps. In fact, her indisposition on that occasion must have been more minor, since she returned to perform several more times through mid-June. But in July Mrs. Heron did suffer the disastrous accident that ended her career.[16] Immobilized by her broken knees and thrown into fits by the excruciating pain, Mary lingered for months before she died, the following March.

⤆

Charlotte's two understudy performances were exciting, if stressful, moments in an otherwise long, dreary season. Even with her duty of making herself ready as the stock reader, she was often at loose ends, spending much of her time frustrated, restless, and resentful, conscious that, though she was just twenty-two, her career seemed to be regressing. For the first time since 1731, she did not receive a benefit—both an insult and a significant financial injury. Increasingly, her conversations with Fleetwood erupted into quarrels.

Charlotte's frustration began to show in her behaviour. She started to engage in what she described as "private Misconduct," "Follies," and "Faults" that she made "too conspicuous."[17] Tantalizingly, she did not specify what this private but conspicuous misconduct consisted of, and no external evidence has survived. We can only conjecture the possible forms her misbehaviour might have taken.

She may have had an affair with a man, but that sort of thing was so common among actresses as scarcely to merit comment, even if Charlotte, as a female member of the Cibber family, might have felt that she had to judge (if not guide) her sexual behaviour according to a higher standard. She may have begun a sexual relationship with another woman, though there is no evidence for this at this time. Or she simply may have embraced the London low life that surrounded her, as her brother and her estranged husband had: haunting the dives of Covent Garden (perhaps in company with Betty Careless), gambling, drinking, and carousing, roaming the London streets by night, as she would do later, "in search of Adventure." It may have been at this time that she formed the friendships with the bawds and prostitutes of Covent Garden that would prove invaluable to her later.

Apart from or in addition to these activities, there is one type of private but conspicuous misconduct that Charlotte may well have engaged in. By day as well as by night, she may have appeared on the streets of London, and arrived at the theatre, dressed as a man.

～ 13 ～

CORDELIA; OR,
THE ART OF MANAGEMENT

(1735–36)

Charlotte was at the playhouse when she received a message from her father, commanding her immediate appearance. She must have felt uneasy at this unusual summons as she walked the short distance to Charles Street, and her agitation would certainly have increased when she was ushered into the drawing room to find that Colley was not alone. Seated beside him were her least favourite sisters, Catherine and Anne (whom Charlotte privately called Goneril and Regan). A family tribunal was about to come to order: she, Charlotte realized, was the defendant.

Sitting in judgment that day were the two eldest, least theatrical Cibber children.[1] Though they remained close to their father, Catherine and Anne had little in common with their other siblings, especially Charlotte. Catherine Brown, now a widow and the mother of a young daughter, was approaching her fortieth birthday. Upon the recent death of her husband, James, she had swooped into Charles Street to take up residence with her father, installing herself as Colley's housekeeper (and, from Charlotte's perspective, house harpy). Catherine had quickly made herself indispensable to her ageing father's comfort, and consequently wielded great influence with him. Her marriage into the wealthy, socially prominent Brown family had elevated her importance in her father's eyes, and in her own. Catherine harboured a profound sense of family dignity and propriety, especially feminine propriety—the very thing Charlotte enjoyed flouting.

The second eldest Cibber child, Anne Boultby, was now thirty-five. She had made a success of the Golden Jar, her tea and millinery shop located on Charles Street not far from her father's house. (It is unclear whether she gave up the shop when she married John Boultby in the early 1730s.) Anne and her husband were living close by Colley on Bedford Ground, Southampton Street.[2] Anne seems to have possessed the sense of decorum and self-consequence characteristic of the respectable bourgeoise she had made of herself.

Charlotte gave enough details about the confrontation that day to allow us to imagine the scene. The "Triumvirate" (her term) greeted her stiffly and, when Colley's servant had shut the door behind him, they started in. Catherine probably did most of the talking, enumerating Charlotte's crimes, while the others chimed in. It was disgraceful enough, they declared, that Charlotte was no longer living with her husband, but now she was compounding her disgrace by indulging in reckless, even dissipated behaviour. Their father had heard shocking stories. Not only was Charlotte making a dubious reputation playing men rather than women, her father had been appalled to see her at the playhouse flaunting men's clothes *offstage*. Breeches parts were one thing, but to wear men's clothes in the streets defied decency.

The family was seriously concerned for Charlotte's welfare, but even more concerned about the family name: even an actress needed to maintain some respectability, especially if she was a Cibber, daughter of the poet laureate. Her father had spent his career trying to make his profession more respectable, and now Charlotte threatened to undo all his good. A disreputable woman was despicable, and a woman wearing a man's clothes was an affront against nature.

Charlotte felt "baited like a Bull at a Stake." Tossing her horns, she indignantly fought back. Voice rising in anger, she denied the justice of their charges, refusing to apologize for her conduct and rejecting their demands that she mend her ways. Infuriated by her stubbornness, the others shouted her down. Finally, "perceiving they were resolved to carry their horrid point against me," she said, "I grew enraged and obstinate and, finding a growing indignation swelling in my bosom, answered nothing to their purpose." Charlotte's resistance enraged her father.

"Worked up into a strong fit of impatience," Colley abruptly rose, declaring that he was leaving the house and would not return until Charlotte's departure. Then he stormed out of the room. Catherine, with an air of smug satisfaction, rhetorically asked if they were done, and "in a peremptory manner" turned Charlotte out-of-doors.*

Charlotte later commented that what enraged her was not so much Colley's attempt to enforce his paternal authority, since "it was undoubtedly my duty to satisfy any demand that he should think proper to make." It was her haughty sisters' presumption: "the insolent assistance of those whose wicked hearts were too fraught with my ruin." The scene that day, as Charlotte later wrote, was King Lear goaded by his vicious daughters Goneril and Regan to disown their sister, Cordelia, the one who truly loved him.

Lear as Charlotte would have known it was not quite the grim tragedy Shakespeare had written, however, for public taste had demanded a less bleak outcome. In Nahum Tate's 1681 rewriting of the play, performed under the title *King Lear and His Three Daughters*, Cordelia does not die (although Goneril and Regan do). Instead, she lives to be reunited with her father, who also survives, and to be crowned Queen. But if Charlotte had Tate's sentimental ending in mind, she was envisioning herself in the wrong play. Her situation actually bore more resemblance to the original.[3]

The second blow came quickly on the heels of the first. In late spring or early summer, Fleetwood fired Charlotte from Drury Lane Theatre. Sending her a letter informing her that he would not rehire her for the following season, the manager claimed (in a lie transparent to both of them) that he was forced to take this step in order to save expenses.

Fleetwood had long wished to rid himself of Charlotte. He would have heard the gossip about her rupture with her father (news that would have circulated rapidly, since Charlotte was not one to keep quiet about perceived injustices), and felt emboldened. Fleetwood repeated Catherine's condemnation of Charlotte's "private Miscon-

---

* Charlotte wrote that after her father left the house, Catherine "was pleased to ask the rest of her colleagues if they had done with me," which seems to imply that there was another person present besides herself, Anne, and Colley. This might have been Elizabeth or even Anne's husband, John. (It is hard to imagine that it would have been Theophilus, but this cannot be discounted.) The principal instigator of her father's resentment against her, according to Charlotte, was always Catherine.

*Colley Cibber in his prime, as Poet
Laureate. He served from 1730 to 1757.
(Colley Cibber, coloured portrait bust,
perhaps from the workshop of Sir Henry
Cheere, circa 1740. Courtesy of
the National Portrait Gallery.)*

duct" as further justification for his action (a specious excuse, as his
theatre was hardly a bastion of moral rectitude).

Charlotte was thunderstruck, and, despite her quarrels with
Fleetwood, unprepared. "I confess it was what I did not in the least
expect, as being ignorant of having deserved it," she said at the time,
for "he has often spoke of me as one, whom he thought, worth Acceptance (as a Player) in any Theatre."[4] Later, someone (probably
Theophilus) confronted Fleetwood, but the patentee remained obdu-
rate. This blow came, according to Charlotte, at a time when it was too
late for her to try to secure a position at Covent Garden Theatre or
Goodman's Fields for the following year. Unemployed, with a daughter
to support, she now faced destitution.

Both rejections hurt Charlotte deeply, too. To be fired from Drury
Lane was equivalent to her father's kicking her out of his house: the
theatre had also been her home. She felt that "Ancient Drury," as she
sentimentally called it, was her birthright every bit as much as Theo
considered it his: she had grown up there, anticipating the day when
she, too, would step onto its stage. Her sense of entitlement was so
strong that she had probably never seriously imagined not being part of
the company and carrying on the Cibber legacy. Charlotte viewed the

dismissal as akin to Adam and Eve's expulsion from the Garden: it was a characteristically self-dramatizing analogy, but also a heartfelt one.[5]

Charlotte faced the summer in even worse financial condition than usual. She had not received the additional boost to her income of a benefit that spring; she could not look forward to her salary resuming in the autumn; and this year there would be no lucrative weeks at Bartholomew Fair: authorities recently had moved to suppress the fair's anarchic energy by shortening it to three days. Hunger, the street, and debtor's prison were all real threats.

She certainly could no longer go to her father for aid. Of the two family members to whom she was still speaking, Elizabeth lived a straitened life, and Theophilus had his own creditors. Richard was merely a liability. There would be no end to his whining and railing against Colley's unfairness; Charlotte found his behaviour more obnoxious than ever and in fact had heard that, attempting to ingratiate himself, Richard had been among those whispering about her into her father's ear.

That summer, still fuming, Colley took himself off to the luxuries of Bath, where he ensconced himself as an impeccably dressed ageing rake who delighted in flirtatious banter. Back in town, Charlotte plunged into action. It seemed that her immediate needs were covered, since Theophilus had promised her a good place in Drury Lane's summer company, which he was managing again that year. As she waited, Charlotte gathered together a troupe of players and rented Lincoln's Inn Fields Theatre for a one-night performance on June 19. She advertised it as a "Benefit for a Family in Distress," surely her own. As usual when performing under her own management, Charlotte played a male role. But this time her choice of play and part was particularly significant, for she chose to perform her father's *The Careless Husband*—and to cast herself as Lord Foppington. Charlotte had mimicked her brother on the stage; now, for the first time, she targeted her father.

Charlotte would have imitated Colley's foppish mannerisms in ways that both echoed and parodied him. As she appeared onstage in Lord Foppington's enormous wig, the satisfaction she felt must have been many-layered, incorporating homage, poignancy, and pathos on one hand—and mockery, defiance, and revenge on the other. Charlotte's advertisements promised a "New Epilogue addressed to the Town to be spoken by Mrs. Charke in the Character of Lord Foppington." Perhaps Charlotte used her speech to air some of her grievances against her father and sister, seeking, as she would do again later, the Town's support in her family quarrel.

Charlotte also played Sir John in *The Devil to Pay*—Theo's usual role—and danced twice with Ann Brett that night. Her advertisements announced that among the audience would be "Che-sazan Outsim, Hindy-Gylesangbier, Charadab-sina, Gulgulachem-chemaunim, and Tichucbactey Ormophan, Sacheoutzim-Sinadab Caocormin, the Chineze [sic] Mandarines, lately arrived in England, on a Tour throughout Europe, being the only People of that Nation, who have been in England since the Reign of King James I." Given the inventive transliteration of non-Western names in the eighteenth century, these may have been actual Chinese dignitaries, but the absence of newspaper references to visitors from China at this time strongly suggests that Charlotte may have been using every device available to sell a few more tickets. (She might even have placed some volunteers wearing pseudo-Chinese costumes in one of the boxes, and instructed them to converse among themselves in "Mandarin" for the more credulous to gawk at.)

With a bit of benefit money in her purse, Charlotte could keep her creditors at bay until summer performances began. On July 1, Theophilus's Drury Lane company opened with a revival of *The London Merchant*, with Charlotte as the evil seductress Millwood. Their season began auspiciously: the first performance was met with enthusiasm from a full house and received good notices in the papers. Whatever serious reflections the tragedy may have inspired must have been lightened by the subsequent performance of *The Mock-Doctor*, and completely erased when Theophilus trotted onstage afterward to recite the comic epilogue astride an ass.

Hopes for a good summer ran high, buoyed by the nearly incessant rain that restricted people to indoor entertainments, and a second performance was advertised. But abruptly, with no warning, Fleetwood ordered the performances stopped, saying that he needed the playhouse empty in order to accommodate "several New Preparations for the ensuing Winter."[6] He did have the playhouse repainted that summer, but this alone did not require that the entire season be cancelled. His real reasons for closing Drury Lane's summer company remain obscure, but it was alleged at the time that he had succumbed to pressure from some of the more important players who were not acting that summer and were jealous of the salaries of those who were.

Theophilus, whose income at this point could support him (if not his creditors) throughout the summer, dropped out. The other players rushed to salvage the season by hastily arranging to rent Lincoln's Inn Fields and advertising performances beginning on July 11. They began, logically, with *The London Merchant* (Charlotte retaining her role as Millwood), and spiced their offerings with the promise of a new ballad farce, Henry Carey's *The Honest Yorkshireman*. But this bill, advertised as a benefit for Carey, seems never to have been played. Carey was understandably infuriated, and then something happened at Lincoln's Inn Fields to complicate the situation even further. Newspaper notices signed by Carey complained that he had encountered "Several Difficulties and Inconveniences attending the intended Performance of my Farce" at Lincoln's Inn Fields. Therefore he chose, he said, "to have it acted under my own Direction, for my own Benefit," at the New Theatre in the Haymarket.[7]

The company that followed Carey to the Little Haymarket included many of the original Drury Lane summer players, but not Charlotte. Carey's "difficulties and inconveniences" may have involved her. She had not been scheduled to perform in the farce herself, but Carey's comment that he wanted the farce to appear "under my own Direction" suggests a power struggle for control of the company between Charlotte and either Carey or those aligned with him. In the absence of Theophilus, Charlotte probably moved to assume control of the troupe—not unjustifiably, since she did have experience in management—and she and Carey probably disagreed about the direction of his farce. Now that she had been fired, Charlotte had lost stature, and others may have been reluctant to cast their lot with her. She was left with a reduced troupe at Lincoln's Inn Fields.

Carey was a difficult man, so despite Charlotte's own reputation for obstinacy, not everyone thought the rupture was her fault. He felt compelled to insert a note in the advertisements for his farce, expressing his dismay at learning "that some People (tho' I hope but few) should turn my Misfortune into a Crime, insinuating this Change of Day and Theatre is my own Fault. I beg Leave to assure the Publick, such Informations are entirely false and groundless."[8]

Now there were two companies vying for audiences that unusually rainy summer, and the competition turned nasty: Charlotte was outraged to discover that her playbills were being torn down or plastered over by bills for the Little Haymarket. She publicly warned the bill setters that if caught they would be "prosecuted to the utmost Rigour of the Law."[9]

Again that summer, Charlotte herself played male roles almost exclusively (ten of her thirteen parts). Although she did not repeat her performance as Lord Foppington, she played another of her father's famous roles, the bumpkin squire Sir Francis Wronghead in *The Provok'd Husband*. Calling attention to this performance, she informed the public that "the extravagant Attempt of Sir F. Wronghead gives me painful Apprehensions; but as the Town has given me repeated Instances of their Indulgence," she would do her best. She must have parodied Colley on this occasion, too.

Having emulated her father's and brother's careers to the point of actually parodying them on stage, Charlotte followed them one step further that summer by turning playwright, although the vast majority of people who wrote for the stage in her day were men. Her first effort was a pantomime, *The Carnival; or, Harlequin Blunderer,* in which she played the "French Harlequin," as Theophilus had done; she also wrote and spoke a prologue. Unfortunately, the pantomime was not published and no account of its performance seems to have survived, but it was successful enough to be repeated several times, including on September 5, Charlotte's benefit night, when she advertised that a new Medley Overture written by Richard would be performed by a "large Band of Musick provided for that Night, with French Horns, Kettle Drums, and Trumpets."

When the autumn arrived, Charlotte determined to make a go of her young troupe by extending her summer season into the autumn—in effect, creating a full-time company to rival Drury Lane and the other theatres. She rented the Little Haymarket for her first performance on September 17, a bill consisting of *Jane Shore* and *The Carnival*. But it was the advertisement for the next performance that made the Town take notice.

Fuming over Fleetwood's treatment of her all summer, Charlotte had given vent to her indignation by performing *The Stage Mutineers,* in which she revisited that rebellion against bad management, and played the character, Mrs. Haughty, who was probably based on her in the first place. (She must have taken some heart from her rousing lines calling for "Liberty and Freedom.") That autumn, Charlotte announced her second effort as a playwright, and caught the Town's attention in a much more controversial way.

On September 19, Charlotte advertised a production that, her ad said, had been originally scheduled for an earlier date. The evening would feature *The Beggar's Opera* with Charlotte, unusually, in the role of Polly. But the real focus that evening would be the afterpiece, a new farce written by Charlotte herself called *The Art of Management; or, Tragedy Expell'd,* in which she would make public her case against Charles Fleetwood.

The Art of Management made its debut at "the Great Room" in the York Buildings, a complex of "divers beautiful Streets and Alleys" near the Strand, on a site where the London mansion of the Archbishops of York had formerly stood.[10] As Charlotte explained, her company being "too young a Sett of People to venture at great Expences," she had been forced to move from the Little Haymarket to this less expensive venue.[11] Here, her troupe would seek the favour of the Town, "as we are determin'd to the full Extent of our Power, to endeavour to entertain them."

On the evening of September 24, 1735, the Great Room overflowed with spectators, for gossip about Charlotte's firing by Fleetwood had circulated and they were eager to watch her take her revenge. Interspersed among the audience, however, young men hired by Fleetwood fingered their catcalls and loosened the ties on the bags of rotten onions and oranges they had smuggled in.

The crowd stirred with anticipation as the cast of *The Beggar's Opera* took their bows. A short interlude ensued, during which the ragtag orchestra played and a few songs were sung. Then Charlotte appeared, solemnly walking to the front of the stage draped in the robe and diadem of a tragedy queen. She raised her voice to be heard over the murmuring crowd and spoke, with great but controlled emotion, her autobiographical prologue.

When the first Pair from Paradise were driv'n,
They sigh'd, they wept, and mourn'd their latest Heav'n

With Grief unbounded, left their native Seat,
While resounding Echoes did their Woes repeat,
I, like them from ancient Drury expell'd,
Why I know not, yet helpless to be repeal'd,
To this poor Refuge, unwillingly I flew,
And humbly refer my hapless Cause to you;
When injured then the worst Judges we become,
And partial to our selves heighten our Oppressor's Doom,
No, I rather chuse your Pity than your Scorn
Of all ills that's the hardest to be born,
That I have Faults unlimited, I do confess,
Yet that, makes not the Wrong of others less;
All my Hopes do on your Smiles depend,
Nay, my bounded Wishes ask no other Friend;
Since exil'd thus from my dear native Land,
And cast on Fortune's Stream; afford a saving Hand.
Your friendly Pity I must earnestly implore,
And tenderly assist to waft me to the Shore,
With unwearied Toil I'll hourly strive to please,
If successful think't a Conquest gain'd with Ease,
To your good Nature ever pay a just Regard,
And think each Effort too little for the sweet Reward.

Charlotte spoke her appeal to the spectators so "pathetically," said the next day's *Daily Advertiser,* that she "drew Tears from the whole Audience." The spectators were disposed to favour this young actress who so openly acknowledged her faults and who had been so unjustly treated—not only by Fleetwood but also, gossip had it, by her own callous father. The Town could be hard on sin, but it dearly loved repentance. Having shed tears of sympathy at the mistreated heroine's prologue, the audience happily settled in for the rout to come. They were not disappointed.

The Art of Management told Charlotte's thinly disguised version of the history of Drury Lane Theatre's decline during the 1734–35 season and her firing by the managers, portrayed as corrupt, arrogant blockheads. She satirized Fleetwood as Brainless, the patentee, and Macklin as Bloodbolt, his henchman and deputy. Theophilus was represented as Headpiece,[12] the dedicated actor who leads a player's rebellion, and

Charlotte was the unjustly fired Mrs. Tragic. As the play's subtitle, "Tragedy Expell'd," indicates, Charlotte conflated her own expulsion from Drury Lane with its managers' selling out of serious drama.

Charlotte portrayed Brainless as an incompetent nincompoop who declares to his players, "I find Management so troublesome a Business, that I wish I were fairly rid of you all." Bloodbolt is a blustering, swearing misogynist—"A parcel of senseless Women are to be eternal Plagues to a Man!"—possessing bear-garden tastes and a sadistic delight in flaunting his power over the players.

One of the worst depredations committed by this blockhead and this bully is their firing of Mrs. Tragic, who declaims her lines and explodes into tragedy rants:

> Ha! discharg'd dismiss'd! turn'd out! Death!
> Rage! and Torture! Now mourn ye *Tragic* Muse
> Since Tragedy's expell'd! Now Revenge alone
> Shall sate my Fury!

Charlotte's self-portrait satirized Fleetwood's bad economics of cutting costs at the expense of serious actors like herself and instead spending lavishly on elabourate spectacles, demoralizing most of the remaining players and ruining "ancient Drury." But she also wrote Mrs. Tragic with considerable tongue-in-cheek, self-referential humour. Charlotte stormed around the stage, likening her expulsion to the death of tragedy itself:

> Oh! now farewell the haughty Strutt,
> The Salary that make Actress's extravagant and proud;
> Farewell the spangle Robe, and the tir'd Page, whose
> Akeing Legs that rowl, and Players Pride has oft Supported.
> O farewell, the diadem and crown that
> Make shrill voices squabble for parts of queens.
> Oh! farewell all pride, Pomp, and Circumstance of Self-conceit.
> Farewell all, for *Tragic*'s Occupation's gone!

Such hyperbole makes Mrs. Tragic, too, into a comic figure, but also a sympathetic one, whose self-dramatizing speeches nonetheless contain a kernel of truth. And what satisfying revenge it must have been to stand onstage calling Charles Fleetwood "Blockhead, Tyrant, Ravisher of Merit's Right."

The Art of Management reaches a happy end, when Brainless is imprisoned for debts so massive that he will never be released. (Charlotte's vengeance was thorough.) His patent reverts to his lawyer, who sells it to Headpiece. Headpiece restores Mrs. Tragic and serious drama to the playhouse, banishing Bloodbolt and his pantomimes to the bear gardens where they belong. All the players are delighted that good management has cast out bad, and the play ends with Headpiece embracing Mrs. Tragic, exclaiming, "My Sister! Oh! let me hold thee to my Heart." Mrs. Tragic responds, "There if I grow the Harvest is your own."

The Art of Management was not only an act of revenge but also Charlotte's wish-fulfilment fantasy. She restored to Theophilus the "birthright" of the patent denied him by their father (who is never mentioned in the farce), and created for herself an imaginary Drury Lane where Theophilus reigns unchallenged, a loving brother who cares for his sister as a father should. As a fantasy, the play was profoundly satisfying; as a piece of revenge, it was even more effective.

Fleetwood had been so unable to bear the prospect of being openly mocked that he had circulated reports threatening to bring "Civil Power" against Charlotte "for exhibiting a Satyr on the Managers of Drury Lane."[13] He also hired a band of "young Clerks to raise a Riot" on opening night, but his ruse backfired. The audience hugely enjoyed Charlotte's farce: she had won them over with her prologue and entertained them well with her hilariously scathing caricatures. So when the clerks started to catcall and launch their rotten produce, the spectators rose against them. "Their rude Behaviour was so extraordinary," reported *The Daily Advertiser* the next day, "that several Gentlemen were provok'd to threaten them with the discipline of their Canes, upon which they thought proper to desist."

The same papers that reported Charlotte's opening night success also carried ads for the second performance of *The Art of Management,* on Friday, two nights later. But that performance did not take place. The farce was not performed again until Monday, on account, the papers said, of Charlotte's "indisposition." What was this indisposition, coming on the heels of her humiliation of Fleetwood?

All the stress of writing, rehearsing, and performing the farce—plus the threats of legal action and audience disruption—certainly may have been enough to make Charlotte ill. (Perhaps her nervous energy got her through the opening night performance, and she collapsed afterward.) But it is also possible that the illness was a cover story, devised to delay the next performance because she hoped to negotiate an accommodation with Fleetwood. The exchange would have been simple: she would stop performing the satire if he reinstated her at Drury Lane. (She would have called this justified pressure; he would have called it blackmail.) Charlotte would attempt a comparable negotiation later in her life, so it seems possible that she ventured it here. In any event, whether she recovered from her illness or failed to reach a satisfactory agreement with the patentee, a second performance went ahead, and then a third, this one for her benefit.

The advertisement for the fourth performance, scheduled for October 3, noted that "Printed Books of the Farce will be sold at the Great Room." The text was crudely printed, but this was not unusual for the initial publication of many plays and afterpieces of the time. Charlotte boldly dedicated her play to "Charles Fletewood [*sic*], Esq.," and, dripping with sarcasm, thanked him for her "many Obligations" to him.

Charlotte also wrote a preface to her farce, in which she set out a "just Account" of her dismissal from Drury Lane, introducing it by telling her readers about the threats she had received of legal action against her. She offered a transparently disingenuous disclaimer of any resemblance between her characters and actual people: "Now, Whether any one about Town know such Persons as Squire Brainless, or Mr. Bloodbolt is doubtful; for I solemnly protest I don't."

Announcements of *The Art of Management*'s publication greatly magnified Fleetwood's anxiety: presumably he dreaded the prospect of being immortalized as Squire Brainless. He immediately ordered his minions to buy up every available copy and destroy it. So, thanks to Fleetwood, Charlotte happily sold out her edition. And the patentee's attempts to eradicate the published farce failed: at least seven copies have survived in British and U.S. libraries, where Fleetwood lives on as Brainless to the present day.

But the farce did not go into a second printing, nor was it performed again after October 1. On October 6, Charlotte's "Young Company" advertised that they would defer playing until the "next Wednesday se'nnight," when they would stage Shakespeare's *Two Gentlemen of Verona,* "which has not been acted these 73 Years."[14] But the Two Gentlemen's return to the stage would have to await a later day, for after this notice nothing more was heard from the Young Company. On November 18, Charlotte could be found once again playing Dol Common on the stage of Drury Lane.

Fleetwood rehired Charlotte because, she later said, Colley interceded on her behalf—perhaps, as Koon conjectures, he made his own willingness to perform contingent upon Charlotte's reinstatement. Though Colley was still not speaking to his daughter, he seems to have been willing to give her another chance. His heart was not entirely hardened against her, and her escapade at Fleetwood's expense must have amused him. (Colley was on amiable enough terms with Fleetwood, but he did not respect him. Perhaps he also admired his daughter's pluck.)

Charlotte performed again two days after her return, in her role of Mrs. Otter in *The Silent Woman.* Her reinstatement might have had something to do with her brother's temporary return to power at Drury Lane: Theophilus had resumed authority because a vacuum had presented itself, created by Charles Macklin's absence. The hot-headed Irish actor was still in London, but he had been in seclusion because he was the defendant in a criminal prosecution that would come to trial that winter. The crime he was charged with was murder.

Back in May, a quarrel had erupted at Drury Lane over a wig. The mainpiece was under way, and a group of actors who would perform in the afterpiece had congregated in the green room on benches in front of the fire, already dressed in their costumes. The night before, Macklin had used one of the stock comedy wigs—a stringy, greasy affair—and intended to use it again in the afterpiece. But in the meantime, it had disappeared from his dressing room: one of the dressers had given it to Thomas Hallam.

With his usual temper, Macklin accosted Hallam, demanding "his" wig as if the other actor had stolen it. "Damn you for a rogue," Macklin, according to witnesses, shouted, "What business have you with my wig." Hallam retorted, "I am no more a rogue than yourself; it's a stock wig, and I have as much right to it as you have." "You're an impudent rascal, and ought to be caned for your impudence," spat Macklin.

The actors spoke at such a pitch that they drowned out the players onstage. Mills entered the green room to shut them up, saying, "Hallam, don't be impudent; and give him the wig." Mr. Kitchen, the property man, interjected that he would find Hallam a better one. So Hallam surrendered the disputed wig to Macklin and received another from Kitchen, commenting sulkily that he liked the new one better anyway.

The group sat in uneasy silence for several minutes, while Macklin combed out his wig, muttering to himself. Suddenly, he burst out, "You are a scoundrel for taking my wig." "No more a scoundrel than you are," retorted Hallam. "Damn you, you dog, dare you prate," cried Macklin. Rising up suddenly from the bench, Macklin thrust his cane at the other man, just as Hallam was turning towards him. Macklin's cane caught the other actor in the left eye, pushing all the way through to his brain. Hallam died the next evening.

When he was tried the following December, Quin, Fleetwood, and others testified with straight faces that Macklin was a mild, peace-loving man, and he was convicted of involuntary manslaughter.

While Macklin awaited his trial, Theophilus once again asserted authority at Drury Lane; he may have been partially responsible for the fact that between mid-November and the end of December, Charlotte performed seven times, in the best of her old roles. But when Macklin returned, Theophilus's hard-won authority did Charlotte little good against Fleetwood's resistance and the entrenched, conservative culture of Drury Lane under his management. Though Colley returned to perform in selected plays in late December and again in January, Charlotte did not perform in any of them. The two had not reconciled, despite whatever bargain Colley may have struck for his daughter's return to the theatre. In the playhouse, their encounters were distant and silent.

Colley's attention had become newly engrossed by his daughter-in-law. Having initially disapproved of Theophilus's marriage, the old man had been won over by Susannah's softness and docility—and by what his canny eye discerned as her potential for projecting feminine pathos on the stage. Colley had always thought Susannah's singing voice limited, but now noticed that her speaking voice had promise, particularly for tragedy, and undertook to coach her as an actress, teaching her the singsong delivery he had learned from the master Betterton. Colley devoted a great deal of time to tutoring Susannah, experiencing, he said, "Great Delight in it: for she was very capable of receiving Instruction." (In pointed contrast to Charlotte.) In all his years on the stage, said Colley, "I never knew a Woman at the beginning so capable of the Business, or improve so fast."[15] Colley began to dote on Susannah so obviously that, upon seeing him in attendance upon her, along with another of her devotees (Owen Swiney, a former actor-manager of Colley's generation), a wit remarked, "There go Susannah and the elders."[16]

All this must have increased Charlotte's sense of neglect and injustice. Colley's attentions to Susannah, who was a year younger than she, implied (accurately enough) that he had found in her a daughter more to his liking. Susannah represented just the ideal of modest, deferential womanhood that rebellious Charlotte rejected. That quality attracted powerful men throughout Susannah's life, including Handel, Quin, and, later on, David Garrick.

It must have seemed a cozy scene, with obedient Susannah learning Colley's old-fashioned "intoning" delivery of tragedy, as Theophilus hovered. Susannah's debut as an actress in the lead role of *Zara* (by Aaron Hill, based upon Voltaire's *Zaire*), was a triumph. Although her opening night was marred by a disastrous performance by Hill's nephew as the leading man, the audience made clear that it wanted more of Susannah. Though she was in the last months of pregnancy that winter, Susannah played a heavy schedule of performances.

For Charlotte, however, reinstatement at Drury Lane brought little satisfaction after that first flurry. She must have begun to feel that her career would never flourish under Fleetwood and his henchman Macklin. Rebellious players like Charlotte did not endear themselves to theatre managers. Furthermore, Theophilus wielded less power than before and was less able to promote his sister's career. Besides, he was now much more interested in promoting his wife's, for as her husband he had an immediate financial stake in her success. Charlotte was more overlooked and more friendless at Drury Lane than ever.

Then, as January concluded, she became embroiled in new quarrels with the patentee. Only one performance came her way that winter, her old role of Louisa in *Love Makes a Man* on February 18; her next appearance, it seems, would not have been until the end of March.[17] But, as events transpired, she would not tread the boards of Drury Lane again. Charlotte's career at "Ancient Drury" came to an end that spring, and the catalyst was Henry Fielding.

❧ 14 ❧

ON THE EDGE

(1736)

Tucking her shirt into her breeches and adjusting her wig, Charlotte took five-year-old Kitty by the hand and clambered down the narrow wooden stairs of their lodgings to the sitting room, where she delivered her daughter into the care of her sister. Elizabeth—aside from Theo the only Cibber still speaking to her—had recently allowed Charlotte and Kitty to "swell up the Number of her Family," as Charlotte put it, by moving into a shabby garret at the top of the set of rooms rented by the Bretts in a house on Oxendon Street. Elizabeth, who had just celebrated her thirty-fifth birthday, doted on her younger sister and was amused by her eccentricities. Neither Elizabeth, her husband, Dawson, nor their daughter, Ann, was particularly disturbed by her choice in clothes.

Kissing Kitty good-bye, Charlotte threw on her coat. Descending the remaining steep stairs to the street, she stepped out into the brisk March afternoon, clapping her hat firmly on top of her head. So much cold air habitually seeped through the chinks in the windows of her ill-furnished room, however, that she scarcely registered the drop in temperature. Elizabeth's lodgings were modest, but Oxendon Street itself was a convenient and not undesirable location. Constructed in the 1680s, it was described by Strype as "good, open, well built, and inhabited"; it was (and remains) a short street running parallel to and one block east of the upper part of the Haymarket.[1]

At its northern end, Oxendon Street joined Coventry Street, the eastward continuation of Piccadilly, where the taverns and gambling houses that crowded the street ensured good custom for the large numbers of prostitutes who congregated there.[2] Yet Charlotte could walk with Kitty just a block farther east from Coventry Street and come upon Leicester Fields, a lovely open square filled with flowers and trees, enclosed by painted wooden railings, and surrounded by handsome houses (a picture almost unimaginable to anyone familiar with the crowds and neon of its modern incarnation as Leicester Square). Charlotte's route that day took her south, however, to the Haymarket and the Little Theatre.[3]

Charlotte was now the newest member of the Great Mogul's Company of Comedians, as Henry Fielding called his troupe, thumbing his nose at the "mogul" managers Rich, Fleetwood, and Cibber. Unable during the last year to interest Drury Lane or Covent Garden in consistently staging his work, Fielding had taken matters into his own hands. Renting the Little Haymarket, he had recruited a company of fringe players to open a short season in early March with his new satiric farce, *Pasquin*. Despite performing with a group of players most of whom were inferior or inexperienced or both, and despite operating on a shoestring budget at a small, threadbare theatre, Fielding—who advertised that "the Cloaths are old, but the Jokes intirely new"—was filling the playhouse every night and turning away crowds of disappointed latecomers. He had created a theatrical phenomenon rivalling *The Beggar's Opera*.

Fielding probably had approached Charlotte to join his company in mid-March, after it became clear that his play was a success: her first performance was no earlier than March 18, and Charlotte, always a quick study, would not have taken long to learn her part.[4] At the time of her meeting with Fielding, she would have known of *Pasquin's* success; perhaps she had already gone to see it. For his part, Fielding certainly must have heard the gossip about her quarrels with Fleetwood, her discontent at Drury Lane, and her estrangement from her father. Though Charlotte was only a young, second-tier actress at Drury Lane, Fielding, in wooing her away, had "scored a coup."[5] She would be Fielding's best-known player, and he knew exactly how he could use her. He offered Charlotte four guineas a week and benefits from which house charges were not deducted (a sum virtually guaranteed to be handsome), considerably more than her salary at Drury Lane, making her the highest-paid player in his company.

Charlotte accepted, quitting Drury Lane abruptly in mid-season. Taking "French leave" of Fleetwood, as she put it, she aligned herself with a man who once again was establishing himself as London's leading playwright, a political satirist whose favourite butts included Colley Cibber. She went because of the opportunities he offered, but his delight in poking satiric fun at her father probably had particular appeal to her just then.

Charlotte's move must have elicited many chuckles from those anticipating her delivery of a new, particularly delicious edge to Fielding's satire. *Pasquin* is a farce in the form of a "rehearsal play," that is, a play (or in this case two plays, a comedy and a tragedy) within a play. The action revolves around the "rehearsal" of these two plays; their authors and a critic are present, interrupting the rehearsal periodically to direct the actors and comment on the action. *Pasquin* satirizes the corruption of English politics: the comedy-within-the-play, in which Charlotte appeared, is entitled "The Election," and directs barbs at both the Whigs' and Tories' practice of bribing voters with money and promises of political favours.

Charlotte first came onstage as the (male) Player designated to speak the prologue to the comedy. As the Player recites, he is directed by the author, Trapwit, on his stage action: "Oh! dear sir," Trapwit instructs the Player, "seem a little more affected, I beseech you; advance to the front of the stage, make a low bow, lay your hand upon your heart, fetch a deep sigh, and pull out your handkerchief." Charlotte would have been costumed already as the foppish Lord Place, so Trapwit essentially was telling her to mimic Colley as Lord Foppington. Charlotte's parody of her father here paved the way for Fielding's joke, later in the play, that a laureate is not necessarily a poet.

Fielding recruited Charlotte because she was an able comic actress, possessing the imprimatur of Drury Lane, but he also wanted her, obviously, because of her parentage and her talent for burlesque. Her increasing notoriety as a cross-dresser would have been an attraction as well. Whatever scandal attached to her in public could only enhance the bite of her parody of her father. In Fielding's hands, Charlotte's portrayal of her father's affectations signified his actual corruption; her imitation of Lord Foppington shaded into a direct attack upon Colley himself.

And the enormous success of *Pasquin* testifies that Charlotte's performance did not disappoint. When, on March 30, the company played

INTERIOR *OF THE* LITTLE THEATRE. *HAYMARKET.*

FRONT *OF THE* ABOVE.

The Little Haymarket, where Charlotte satirized her father in the controversial work of satirist Henry Fielding, after its subsequent remodelling. (James Stow, engraving after George Jones, Interior and Exterior Views of the Little Haymarket Theatre, 1815. Courtesy of the Guildhall Library, Corporation of London.)

to still another bursting house that included the Prince of Wales, *The Daily Advertiser* noted (presumably with some exaggeration), that "many thousands of People" were "turn'd away for want of room."

From a career standpoint, Charlotte's decision (however impulsively made) to leave London's most august theatre company for this haphazard band of upstarts was not at all a bad move. Fielding, Battestin observes, "had a talent for a kind of pointed, inventive foolery that audiences had not seen on stage before—a talent for ridicule and brisk dialogue, for deft and emblematic characterization and for devising absurd yet expressionistic plots that have scarcely been matched in the experimental theatre of our own century."[6] His troupe, with Charlotte prominent among them, were quite capable of pulling off his innovative, outrageous, almost surrealistic farces. "Fielding," explains Hume, "was running a company genuinely devoted to contemporary plays. Nothing of the sort had ever been tried in the modern history of the London theatre. . . . Anyone who wanted variety and experimentation would have to seek it from Fielding's company."[7] However much the theatre establishment might have sneered at it, the Great Mogul's Company was the avant-garde of London theatre, and a very successful avant-garde at that.

Charlotte must have viewed her name in capital characters on the playbills for *Pasquin* with great pleasure. Fielding's farces did not require the same skills as the traditional repertoire, but they did call for considerable stage presence, a knack for deadpan or exaggerated satiric gestures, and skill at ensemble performance. Fielding was a hands-on author-manager, working diligently to coach his actors, and his audiences were the most glamorous the Little Haymarket had ever hosted.

Charlotte would have gazed upon these glittering audiences with pride. Beyond her enjoyment of their response would have been the satisfaction of showing both her brother and her father that she, too, could be a great success, acting in her own masculine style. Of course, joining with Colley's enemy to mock him was unlikely to earn his admiration, but it certainly got his attention. Coming after her father had softened enough to get Charlotte rehired at Drury Lane and perhaps to hint at reconciliation (if only she would repent and behave), this was a grave affront. It does seem, however, that Charlotte, while she certainly knew that her association with Fielding displeased her father (and while she took some pleasure in nettling him), genuinely was oblivious to the enormity of the offence. She seems not to have fully realized that ridiculing Colley before large, upper-class audiences night after night might cause him considerable mortification. After all, she could have told herself, his skin was so famously thick.

Pasquin ran for more than sixty nights that spring, a spectacular run that dominated the London theatre, overshadowing even the castrati. Mrs. Pendarves wrote to Jonathan Swift that when she had left London last autumn, "the reigning madness was Faranelli." But upon her return that spring, "I find it now turn'd on *Pasquin*."[8]

Charlotte played roles (predominantly, though not exclusively, male) in several other plays staged that season by Fielding, including George Barnwell in *The London Merchant* and the rake Gaylove in *The Honest Yorkshireman* (the same play that its author, Henry Carey, had pulled from her company the summer before). In Fielding's satiric afterpiece, called *Tumble-Down Dick; or, Phaeton in the Suds,* an attack on pantomimes with particular reference to one currently running at Drury Lane called *The Fall of Phaeton,* Charlotte created the role of "Clymene in the character of an Oyster Wench." Clymene is an adulterous cobbler's wife, a burlesque of the character played by Kitty Clive in Drury Lane's production. Saucy Kitty with the irresistible singing voice had been Fielding's favourite player at Drury Lane, but now he was in the theatrical opposition against her company. Charlotte possessed neither Kitty's coquetry nor her musical abilities, but she was a relatively experienced singer with a good enough voice and a particular gift for "styling songs satirically."[9]

Charlotte's other opportunity to create a role that spring was supplied by George Lillo, the same playwright who had been the occasion of the first role she had created, Lucy in *The London Merchant.* Despite the great success of that bourgeois tragedy, Lillo was unable to interest any of the establishment managers in his new play, *Guilt Its Own Punishment; or, Fatal Curiosity.* Fielding accepted the play, casting Charlotte in the female lead, Agnes Wilmot, who urges her husband (played by John Roberts) to murder a man whom she subsequently discovers to be her beloved only son.

Fielding's generosity as a manager and assiduity as a director are particularly illustrated in the account of the staging of *Fatal Curiosity.*

Tom Davies, who played the role of Agnes's son and victim, said that Fielding treated Lillo "with great politeness and friendship," and that he "took upon himself the management of the play, and the instruction of the actors," rehearsing the players with tact and courtesy.[10] For Charlotte, this must have been a startling change from the bitter conflicts and strutting egos she had experienced (and herself demonstrated) at Drury Lane.

When the play was ready to be performed, Fielding puffed it in a letter to *The Daily Advertiser* on May 25, praising the artistry of Lillo's moral fable and expressing his confidence in the abilities of his young actors. "As to the performers, I shall only say, if the Town will once more waive their Prejudice against a young Company, I believe they will not repent it; and I am deceiv'd, if Mr. Roberts and Mrs. Charke do not convince them, that if they are not equal to some of their Predecessors, they are, at least, so to any of their Co[n]temporaries on the Stage." Charlotte's contemporary tragediennes included Mrs. Porter, so Fielding's compliment, though self-promoting, was nonetheless a high one. Charlotte's part of Agnes, a once wealthy woman embittered by poverty, who colludes in a crime that rebounds horribly against her, required her to convey, said Davies, the emotions of "anger, remorse, despair and horror."[11]

On May 28, *The Daily Advertiser* reported:

Last Night the new Tragedy call'd Guilt its own Punishment, or Fatal Curiosity, was acted at the New Theatre in the Hay-Market, with the greatest Applause that has been shewn to any Tragedy for many Years. The Scenes of Distress were so artfully work'd up, and so well perform'd, that there scarce remain'd a dry Eye among the Spectators at the Representation; and during the Scene preceding the Catastrophe, an attentive silence possess'd the whole House, more expressive of an universal Approbation than the loudest Applauses, which were given to the many noble Sentiments that every where abound in this excellent Performance, which must meet with Encouragement in an Age that does not want both Sense and Humanity.

Its glowing language suggests that this account was written by Fielding. Charlotte's own description was less ecstatic: on opening night, she said, she and John Roberts were "kindly received by the Audience."

Unfortunately, *Fatal Curiosity* was not particularly successful that spring. After the long run of *Pasquin,* explained Davies, the audience had difficulty switching gears. Furthermore, the play's timing in late May, as the London season was ending and people were leaving town, was against it, despite the advertisements that hot spring calling the Little Haymarket "much the coolest House in Town."

Charlotte's benefit came on May 5; she chose the remunerative combination of *Pasquin*—its forty-fifth performance—and *Tumble-Down Dick.* The Great Mogul's Company advertised that it would continue playing twice a week throughout the summer, but the scarcity of newspaper advertisements for their performances suggests that they did not maintain this schedule.[12] Charlotte seems to have supplemented her income that summer by mounting at least two independent productions with a pickup group of actors at the Little Haymarket. Their first performance, on June 26, was *The Beggar's Opera* with Charlotte as Macheath, advertised as a benefit for "a Gentlewoman of Seventy Years of Age" who played Dye Trapes, the tallywoman (a woman who equips prostitutes for their jobs by renting them expensive clothing). As an afterpiece they performed *The Mock-Doctor,* in which Charlotte played the male role of Leander.

For their second performance of *The Beggar's Opera,* on August 2, they advertised with characteristic humour a "New Polly Peachum, just arrived from the Island of Obscurity," with the part of Captain Macheath to be played by Charlotte "and the Rest of the Characters to best Advantage," and a "new Comi-Tragical Interlude" called "The Deposing and Death of Queen Gin," written by "Jack Juniper, a Distiller's Apprentice, turn'd Poet." (The reference was to the highly unpopular Gin Act, which Parliament had passed that spring, raising taxes and licensing fees on the retailers of gin.) Charlotte may also have played in a performance of Susannah Centlivre's *A Bold Stroke for a Wife* on July 14, advertised by the Great Mogul's Company. And she may have managed a "Lilliputian" group that gave at least three performances, originally scheduled for the York Buildings but moved to the larger venue of the Little Haymarket, "there being a greater Call for Box tickets than was expected"; this troupe of children included her niece Ann Brett, who played the leading role.[13]

As the summer trickled to an end, Charlotte had to find a way to support herself and Kitty until the winter, when Fielding promised another season. She had begun the summer with a little money in her purse, but money in Charlotte's purse had a way of rapidly disappearing. Bartholomew Fair, though now drastically truncated, was one opportunity. At the end of August, the "Poet Fustian's Booth" at the fair advertised that *Pasquin* would be acted, with "all the Characters to be perform'd by those Persons who did them originally, when the Play had a run of 65 Nights successively."

Depending upon the meaning of "originally," this could have included Charlotte, who performed the last fifty-three of those nights. But her name also appeared in the ads for Timothy Fielding and John Hippisley's Great Theatrical Booth in the George Inn Yard in West Smithfield. Unless we imagine Charlotte spending the three days of Bartholomew Fair running back and forth between the two booths (a possibility, if an unlikely and frantic one, especially in the heavy rain that fell during the fair that year), she probably performed as advertised with Timothy Fielding and Hippisley.[14] Charlotte went on to perform, for the first time, at Southwark Fair in September—for this was also the first time in her career that she began September with no autumn theatre season to prepare for.

In early October, Charlotte picked up steady work with Henry Giffard's company, formerly of Goodman's Fields but now relocated to the larger venue of the theatre in Lincoln's Inn Fields (much to the displeasure of Fleetwood, for Lincoln's Inn Fields was close enough to Drury Lane to compete for the same spectators). The mood in the green room was unusually somber when she arrived, for the players were consumed with news about a dreadful accident that had just taken place at Covent Garden Theatre.

On October 1, Rich's company was performing the pantomime *The Necromancer; or, Harlequin Dr. Faustus.* One of the "flying machines" Rich used for his spectacles had just reached its utmost height when its wires snapped; the chariot and its four occupants crashed to the ground. The spectators, thinking this was part of the act, screamed with delight until, realizing the truth, they began to scream in horror. The people in the car were servants employed by the theatre, acting as stand-ins for Rich and the other actors. One man was badly bruised and another broke his arm. A third (named James Todd) landed on his head, fracturing his skull, and dying the next day "in a miserable manner." The sole woman in the car broke her thigh and shattered her kneepan.[15]

The young poet Thomas Gray happened to be in the audience that night, and wrote to Horace Walpole that the horrific scene had given him a "surfeit of Mr. Rich and his cleverness." As he was leaving the theatre, Gray saw the actress Elizabeth Buchanan being carried to a sedan chair in "such a fright that as she is big with child, I question whether it may not kill her."[16] (Mrs. Buchanan seems to have recovered from the fright, for she performed again subsequently; but Gray's comment was prescient nonetheless: she died after giving birth to still-born twins in November.)

However wary players may have become of their theatres' machines and contrivances, the accident did not keep plays and pantomimes from going on as usual that autumn. Charlotte had a full schedule at Lincoln's Inn Fields. Her first performance came on October 9, a night when unusually heavy rains and winds may have kept the audience small.[17] In the advertisement for this performance of Centlivre's *The Wonder: A Woman Keeps a Secret,* she was given the desirable final billing: "And the part of Flora, by Mrs. Charke."[18]

Charlotte played regularly at Lincoln's Inn Fields through January of the next year, keeping up a respectable schedule of performances—though not, usually, in roles she would have chosen (most were important, but female). It was enough to sustain her and Kitty until Fielding's new season began. Among her parts were Mrs. Peachum (Charlotte's fourth role in *The Beggar's Opera*), and a part in *All Alive and Merry,* written by the eccentric Samuel Johnson of Cheshire—the creator of Lord Flame on stilts—who, on opening night, true to his reputation as a difficult man, "was for fighting with somebody in the pit."[19] Possibly Charlotte also played Lord Place in the company's staging of *Pasquin* in January. Most interesting to her (we might suspect), was the role of Pistol in an afterpiece called *The Beggar's Pantomime* that was performed numerous times during January. Pistol, of course, was a pantomime parody of Theophilus.

The Beggar's Pantomime made fun of a controversy that roiled much of London in the autumn of 1736, to the consternation of some and the great glee of many more. At the centre of the controversy was Susannah Cibber. The occasion was this: that autumn, word spread that Drury Lane would stage a new production of *The Beggar's Opera,* an idea that had been first broached and then retracted by Fleetwood the previous winter. This new production would star Susannah, who was now established as one of Drury Lane's principal actresses, in the lead role of Polly Peachum.

Fleetwood may have come up with this casting of his own accord, but Susannah's spouse was more likely behind it. Theophilus was enjoying the rewards of being the husband of Drury Lane's newest star and therefore the legal possessor of her large salary, lucrative benefits, and valuable gifts from male admirers smitten by her melting performances of pathetic heroines. Susannah had become celebrated, in the words of her modern biographer, as "a priestess of sensibility."[20]

As usual, Theo's idea combined self-interest with sound theatrical judgment. Polly is a sentimental, romance-reading naïf thrust into a world filled with greedy cynics, most particularly her own parents. She was a perfect role for Susannah, well conceived to exploit her new popularity. The problem was that the part of Polly Peachum belonged to Kitty Clive, who now was cast in the second female lead of Lucy Lockit. Kitty's explosion of outrage resounded throughout London. In short order, troops of Kitty Clive partisans sprang to her defence, only to be countered by troops who took up arms for Susannah. The "Polly War" had begun.[21]

The furor reminded many of the rivalry between the divas Faustina and Cuzzoni ten years earlier. Newspapers bristled with vehement letters that overflowed into pamphlets, while arguments erupted in taverns, coffeehouses, and green rooms. Some of the most incendiary letters, taking Susannah's side and signed "A.Z.," were very likely penned by Theophilus, who loved a good paper fight. But he met his match in Kitty, who published a letter charging that a conspiracy was mounting at Drury Lane to take away all her good parts and give them to Susannah, despite "a receiv'd Maxim in the Theatre, *That no Actor or Actress shall be depriv'd of a Part in which they have been well receiv'd, until they are render'd incapable of performing it either by Age or Sickness.*" Furthermore, she said, everyone knew perfectly well who "A.Z." was.[22]

As the controversy raged on—Kitty contemptuously rejected "A.Z."'s suggestion that she and Susannah play Polly on alternate nights and let the Town decide who was better—Theophilus emerged from his disguise to write under his own name.[23] Little as he wished to "enter the Lists of a Paper War" against a woman, he protested, the dispute had escalated to such a point that he must step in to defend his wife's honour. Susannah was so modest, so in awe of Kitty, that it was only with "the greatest Reluctance and Terror" that she would accept the part, and then only if Kitty resigned it voluntarily. Still, he continued smoothly, it was the manager's prerogative to assign parts, and Mrs. Clive was contractually obligated to take whatever role Fleetwood ordered her to play. To this, either Kitty or one of her partisans retorted snidely that in fact Lucy would be a much more appropriate role for Susannah than Polly, for there is "a certain Narrowness between her Brows, together with a Sharpness of Face that will hit to Admiration that angry Resentment of Wrongs so strong in the Character of Lucy."[24]

Susannah had only recently returned to full-time acting that autumn after giving birth the previous April to a son, christened Caius Gabriel Cibber, who had died two weeks later. Now it seemed that all London—and all the players in every green room in town, especially Drury Lane's—had taken sides for or against her. She tried to keep herself above the fray, mortified by the attacks upon her. Finally, so great was the controversy, so damaging the turbulence within the Drury Lane company, that Fleetwood caved in, handing Susannah's side a defeat. *The Beggar's Opera* was announced with Kitty as Polly and her good friend Hannah Pritchard playing Lucy.

Kitty's victory was not yet secure, however. On opening night, the playhouse was packed with disruptive Cibber and Clive partisans, who howled, clapped, catcalled, and hissed until Kitty came forward, apologized for having been in any manner the cause of a disturbance, and began to cry so movingly "that even the Butchers wept."[25] Then, in the most humble tones, she told the audience that she would perform any role the Town wanted, and asked them if she should continue as Polly. The house burst into affirmative applause: with this masterstroke, Kitty Clive had won.

Charlotte's attitude to the Polly War must have been mixed. Maybe her small remaining quantity of family loyalty drove her into Susannah's camp. But it did not prevent her from drawing upon her powers of burlesque when Giffard, following Fielding's example, cast her as a travesty Pistol and Theophilus impersonator in Henry Woodward's spoof of the Polly War, *The Beggar's Pantomime; or, The Contending Colombines.* Charlotte continued her pantomime mockery in its sequel, *Pistol in*

Mourning, which Woodward added after Kitty emerged the victor. With her performances for her own summer companies, for Fielding, and now for Giffard, Charlotte had established quite a name for herself by parodying the male members of her family.

January 1737 was ushered in by the poet laureate's annual Ode for the New Year. "Grateful Britons! grace the Day, / Give to Godlike George his due; / this alone shall swell the lay; / George is blest, in blessing you. / May years to years the sound repeat, / And sing the mutual bliss compleat," intoned Colley Cibber. Colley's ode (as always) extolled Britain's joyful subjection to George II, and ended by exhorting His Majesty's loyal subjects to raise the song, "That great and glorious, great and long! / Long, long and happy, live the King."[26]

In fact, during December, when rumours had circulated that George had drowned in a shipwreck while returning from his long stay in Hanover, many of his English subjects had remained cheerfully dry-eyed. Some had even begun to celebrate the coronation of his successor, Frederick, Prince of Wales, a response that proved premature when His Majesty landed on English soil in mid-January. The new year began with a feeling that was far from "mutual bliss."

During the previous year, the long-simmering feud between Prince Frederick and his parents had burst into a boil, with Frederick moving into open opposition to his father and establishing his own court with his own supporters. An atmosphere of political discontent pervaded the country.[27] Popular unrest was escalating. The Walpole government was particularly unpopular, with public agitation against the Gin Act, which had taken effect in September 1736, especially vehement. The Gin Act imposed a large duty upon gin sold in small quantities, required an expensive licence to retail the spirit, and stipulated sub-stanstial fines for those who disregarded the Act, while those who could not pay faced prison sentences of hard labour and whippings. Mob violence flared again and again; it took very little for an incident to escalate into a riot.

In the summer of 1736, an opponent of the house of Hanover triggered an explosion in Westminster Hall; two weeks later the eastern precincts of the City erupted into anti-Irish riots. Other parts of the country saw rioting as well. In Edinburgh, unrest exploded when the

English army captain John Porteous, who had been convicted of murder for firing on a Scottish crowd at an earlier disturbance and killing eight people, had his execution postponed by the Queen. In response, a group of armed men broke into the prison and lynched Porteous. As Michaelmas (September 29), the date for the implementation of the Gin Act, approached, the government filled London with armed patrols. No riots occurred that time, but the gin merchants draped their stores with black bunting and held mock funerals for "Queen Genevra."

King George himself spent eight months of 1736 in Hanover, resisting entreaties from his courtiers and his wife to return. The prolonged absence of the King was a popular grievance in itself—the court's absence took business from the tradespeople, and his lavish spending abroad with his German mistress emptied the British treasury. The cry "No gin, no king" could be heard. Queen Caroline, who ruled in George's stead when he was out of the country, was hissed at the opera.

In this fraught atmosphere, a series of disturbances occurred at the playhouses—always highly politicized venues—that rattled the crown and the government. Performances of *Cato* were disrupted at Lincoln's Inn Fields Theatre by groups of hissing, stomping men (the suspected culprit here was Fleetwood, angered by Giffard's move from Goodman's Fields). While Charlotte may not have witnessed any of these uprisings (she did not perform in *Cato*), the general atmosphere was one in which the playhouses came to be seen as potential threats to the country, the monarchy, and Walpole. Attacks on the government and the monarchy became more open. Frederick made a political statement by pointedly attending the theatre with his princess and not the Queen. (On November 16, Charlotte's company was treated by Giffard to a good supper and a concert in honour of the princess's birthday, on which occasion the players drank the health of the Prince and Princess of Wales, "with universal Demonstrations of Joy.")[28]

Charlotte was still performing at Lincoln's Inn Fields at the end of January 1737, when another provocative incident happened, this time at Covent Garden Theatre. While the Prince and Princess of Wales attended Handel's *Parthenope*, the prince's sedan chair was parked nearby. During the performance, Francis Cooke, John Rich's coachman, picked up a prostitute and then tried to break into the sedan chair, intending "to

make, as he was pleased to call it, a Bawdy-house of the Prince's Chair."
When the guard tried to stop him, he struck the man with his horse-
whip, and a mob scene ensued. The Guard was called and only with
difficulty prevented the mob from breaking into the theatre where the
royal couple was seated. (Needless to say, Rich fired Cooke.)[29]

Subsequently, a series of riots erupted at Drury Lane Theatre after
Fleetwood decided to end the long established practice of giving free
seats in the upper gallery to footmen who accompanied their employers
to the playhouse. The upper-gallery spectators were notorious for dis-
ruptiveness, and on February 19 instigated an all-out riot, fighting with
those in the pit despite Theophilus's call for order. Fleetwood thereafter
locked the doors to the gallery, but this attempt to block the footmen
from what they called "their Gallery" produced violent confrontations.
Two nights later, a large number of footmen besieged the theatre, trying
to break down the door and threatening to burn the building with the
audience inside if they were not admitted. Colonel de Veil, the Bow
Street Magistrate, who was particularly unpopular as the enforcer of the
Gin Act (and as an official known for both professional harshness and
personal dissipation), confronted them, and "notwithstanding they
threaten'd to knock his Brains out," read them the Riot Act.[30]

That night the rioters went away, but twelve days later, they returned,
this time armed with "Sticks, Staves, and other offensive Weapons,"
and, with a play in progress, broke down the doors and stormed the
playhouse, wounding nearly thirty people. De Veil, surrounded by a
small group of guards, tried to read the Riot Act again but without
effect, despite the presence in the playhouse of the Prince and Princess
of Wales (who by this point might have been starting to rethink their
patronage of the London theatre). De Veil arrested the ringleaders of
the riot, "the Audience having been put into the utmost Confusion, and
several Ladies greatly frighten'd." The prisoners were taken to a nearby
room and examined; several were committed to Newgate Prison, while
a surgeon attended to the wounded.[31]

In this turbulent atmosphere, the playhouses became bolder in their
offerings. Inspired by Fielding's success with *Pasquin* the season before,
other theatres, including Lincoln's Inn Fields, began to present plays
more openly critical of the government and the crown. Even Fleetwood
at the traditionally pro-Hanover Drury Lane was not above pandering

to the audience's taste for politically insinuating farce. Political satire sold seats, and the prospect of large audiences made even habitually timid managers shed their caution.

This was the political climate in London when Charlotte left Lincoln's Inn Fields Theatre in mid-February to begin rehearsals for her second season with the Great Mogul's Company; performances were scheduled to begin in March. Flush with *Pasquin*'s success, Fielding was actively making plans to compete more directly with the patent playhouses. That winter, he was soliciting investors for the project of building a new theatre, where he planned to establish a permanent company with himself as manager and resident playwright.[32] Charlotte, as his principal player, well schooled in burlesque and satiric farce, would have had every reason to expect that she would continue to occupy an important position in his upgraded company. In the meantime, as she learned her lines and went daily to the morning rehearsals, her spirits must have been high: she faced the prospect of an exciting few months immediately ahead, and a glorious future at the cutting edge of London theatre.

Charlotte's mood was so good that even her sudden awareness of the sad state of her living conditions did nothing to dampen it. She and Kitty were still living harmoniously with Elizabeth and her family, but one "blustering Night," that winter, the howl of the wind about her ears jolted her into an awareness of the chinks in the windows and the wretched condition of her furniture. Her response was to write a poem:

> Good People, for awhile give Ear,
> 'Til I've describ'd my Furniture:
> With my stately Room I shall begin,
> Which a Part of Noah's Ark has been.
> My Windows reach from Pole to Pole;
> Strangely airy—that in Winter, o' my soul,
> With the dear Delight, of—here and there a Hole.
>
> There is a Chest of Drawers too, I think,
> Which seems a Trough, where Pigeons drink;
> A Handkerchief and Cap's as much as they'll contain:
> O! but I keep no Gowns—so need not to complain.

In five more stanzas Charlotte went on to describe her "inch of Stove," which scarcely heated the large room, so that she was frozen by the time she got to her door, the fireplace lacking irons, the ancient bed (which presumably she and Kitty shared, in the custom of the time), whose curtains disintegrated as she breathed, and her lone chair. While most people might take offence at their sister's ensconcing them in her lodgings' worst room, Charlotte's response was wry amusement.

Charlotte appears to have inherited her poetic muse from her father: she was not likely to redeem the Cibber name in the annals of poetry. But Elizabeth found the poem endearing. "Foolish, fond" Elizabeth— Charlotte's affectionate words—saved this bit of doggerel for nineteen years, throughout her own vicissitudes of fortune, until she returned it to Charlotte to copy in her autobiography. We know only a few details about Elizabeth's life beyond her loyalty to Charlotte (including the probability that she paid a high price for her devotion), and this small gesture affords a touching glimpse of the affection she felt for her sister.

But these verses also provide an important clue to the history of Charlotte's cross-dressing: when, exactly, did she begin to wear men's clothes in public on a regular, even exclusive, basis? I think that she had already gained some notoriety as a transvestite when she joined Fielding's troupe—meaning that she was in the habit of cross-dressing by the spring of 1736—and that her reputation as both an onstage and offstage male impersonator developed significantly during her time with him. Most references to Charlotte in breeches outside of the theatre, however, including some of her own, state or imply dates subsequent to this period; one of the few more specific external references suggests that she took up cross-dressing sometime shortly after June 1737.[33]

But in Charlotte's poem, which she could have composed as early as winter 1736 when she first resided with Elizabeth, she says, "I keep no Gowns." The implication is that by this point breeches had become her customary garb, and that the gowns she wore in her few female roles at the Little Haymarket belonged to the theatre stock, not to her. Perhaps Elizabeth had calculated Charlotte's lack of a need for storage space for cumbersome female garments when she gave her that broken-down room with its "pigeon trough" chest of drawers. There were, as it happened, certain advantages to having a cross-dressing sister.

≫ 15 ≪

Bad Acts

(1737)

The date was March 21, 1737, and the Little Haymarket once again overflowed with restless, gossiping spectators. That evening brought the much anticipated debut of Henry Fielding's newest "Dramatick Satire," entitled *The Historical Register for the Year 1736.* This farce, its advertisement announced, would feature "a Pack of Politicians; a Pack of Patriots; a Pack of Ladies; a Pack of Beaus; Mr. Medley, an Author; Mr. Sourwit, a learned Critick; Lord Dapper, a great Critick; Apollo's Bastard Son; Quidam Anglicae, a certain Person; Mr. Hen, an Auctioneer; Mr Ground Ivy, a Laureat," and others, whose names were equally pointed.

Because the demand for tickets was heavy, the ad also warned that "none will be admitted after the House is full; for which Reason, the sooner you come, or secure your Places, the better." Finally, "all Persons are desir'd to cry at the Tragedy, and laugh at the Comedy, being quite contrary to the present general Practice. Mr. Hen gives Notice, that if any Joke is both Hiss'd and Clapp'd, such Division will be consider'd an Encore, and the said Joke be put up again." Mr. Hen, with his gender-confused name, was Fielding's parody of Christopher Cock, the unscrupulous Covent Garden auctioneer. Fielding had written the part knowing that in Charlotte, he had the perfect male impersonator to play the role.

Inside the Little Haymarket, *Fatal Curiosity* was already in its third and final act, with Charlotte onstage, uttering exclamations of sorrow and penitence, and dying rather slowly. Despite the harrowing action, people continued to trickle in to the already full house, finding seats and greeting friends. Once again venturing into enemy territory, Colley Cibber arrived and took his seat in his box. He was here for the premiere of a play that, in advertising a character named "Ground-Ivy, a laureate" (a wreath of ground ivy would be a lower-rent version of the poet's traditional laurels), made clear that he would be a target again.[1] Charlotte must have glanced in her father's direction from time to time; it had been nearly two years since they had spoken.

When the much anticipated afterpiece began, Colley did not have to wait long for the first salvos of satire. In the first act, a character stepped out to sing an "Ode to the New Year" as the audience stirred and giggled, many glancing at the poet laureate. "This is a day in days of yore, / Our fathers never saw before," sang the player. "This is a day, 'tis one in ten, / Our sons will never see again."

> Then sing the day,
> And sing the song,
> And thus be merry
> All day long.
> This is the day,
> And that's the night,
> When the sun shall be gay,
> And the moon shall be bright.
> The sun shall rise,
> All in the skies;
> The moon shall go,
> All down below.
> Then sing the day,
> And sing the song,
> And thus be merry
> All day long.

Once again, the audience turned to see how the poet laureate was taking Fielding's latest mockery of his mundane versifying. As usual under siege, Colley laughed and applauded, while inwardly he was seething—once again.

At least one account maintains that on the opening night of *The*

Historical Register, it was Charlotte who recited the mocking ode in Colley's presence, clad in her customary breeches. (In the subsequent published version of *The Historical Register,* her character does not speak this poem.) Indeed, Fielding could have assigned these lines to Charlotte on the first night, when he would have anticipated his rival's presence. Given this opportunity, he would have been remiss to give the ode to anyone but Charlotte.[2]

Charlotte next appeared in a small part as one of a group of ladies gushing about their lust for Farinelli in a scene that satirized the sexually subversive desire of society women for castrati. But, when she walked onstage for her third appearance, she had changed back into her breeches for her principal part of the evening, Mr. Hen. The scene written around this character is one of the sharpest, funniest satiric bits Fielding ever wrote for the stage. Charlotte stood at an auctioneer's pulpit, auctioning off goods such as "political honesty" and a "piece of patriotism"—to no avail: the courtiers in her auction wanted no part of these goods. She tried to knock down "three grains of modesty," but the ladies, this time, had no use for it, modesty being "out of fashion." "One bottle of courage" was bought by an officer at a bargain price, there being few bidders. "All the wit" belonging to "Mr. Hugh Pantomime, composer of entertainments for the playhouses and Mr. William Goosequill, composer of political papers in defence of a ministry" received no takers. A "very neat clear conscience" that no dirt would stick to likewise garnered no bids. But when Charlotte brought to the block "a very considerable quantity of interest at court," a frenzy of bidding erupted.

Having knocked down court interest for a pretty price, Charlotte then tried to find bidders for cardinal virtues, a great deal of Wit, and a little Common Sense—with no success. Suddenly a report came in that Pistol had run mad, thinking himself a Great Man (a common satirical designation for Walpole), and was marching through the streets with a drum and fiddles. Everyone, including Mr. Hen, ran off the stage to see. "Pistol," the play specified, "is every insignificant fellow in town who fancies himself of great consequence and is of none"—in other words, of course, he was Theophilus Cibber.

With the exception of her possible recitation of the ode on that first night, Fielding's anti-Cibber satire in *The Historical Register* did not use Charlotte directly as a mouthpiece, unlike his use of her in *Pasquin* (although Mr. Hen's scene did satirize the political corruption of the Walpole administration, with which Colley was associated). Nonetheless, Colley's self-control must have been taxed to maintain his habitual mask of insouciance; he certainly could not have been happy about his daughter's highly visible association with the production.

More barbs flew in Colley's direction in subsequent scenes, in which the laureate Ground-Ivy engages in a discussion of altering Shakespeare—a reference to Colley's notorious (but not always unsuccessful) rewriting of plays such as *Richard III* and *King John*. Faulconbridge in *King John* is too "effeminate," Ground-Ivy says, so he cuts him out and gives all his lines to the female character Constance, as "so much properer to speak them." (This Colley actually had done. That he had felt the need to correct Shakespeare's blurring of the lines between masculine and feminine suggests something about his attitude towards Charlotte.)

This scene touched a particularly sensitive nerve. Earlier that spring, Drury Lane had announced that it would stage Colley's old alteration of *King John*, retitled *Papal Tyranny in the Reign of King John*, which had been pulled from production a decade before. The new production encountered much the same ridicule and hostility that had attended the old. Despite a public letter from Colley asking the Town to let it be played, attacks multiplied. (At Covent Garden, Rich staged a production of Shakespeare's original *King John*—implying, rightly enough, that Colley's adaptation would suffer from the comparison.) In fact, opposition to Colley's version mounted so high that finally one March morning, as it was in rehearsal, Colley marched into the prompter's room, snatched his play from the desk, and left.

Fielding seems to have antagonized Colley to a degree that even Alexander Pope never equalled. This must be accounted for in part by personal animosity, possibly inflected with a certain class resentment of Fielding's gentlemanly education and aristocratic connections. (Colley was by far the wealthier and also signed himself "Esq.," but as he knew full well, he was an arriviste.) But a good part of his hatred must have had to do with the fact that Fielding wrote his satires on Colley for the stage. This was both bearding the lion in his den, as it were, and a particularly effective method of inflicting damage. More than printed satire, Colley believed, enacted satire did particularly powerful and lasting damage to the victim's reputation. ("A Character of Disadvantage, upon the Stage," he wrote, "makes a stronger Impression, than elsewhere.") Reading, he argued, was akin to secondhand hearing, but the stage involved the more powerful faculty of sight. ("The Eye is much more affecting, and strikes deeper into the memory, than the Ear. . . . The Life of the Actor fortifies the Object, and awakens the Mind to take hold of it—Thus a dramatic Abuse is riveted, in the Audience.")[3]

Three years later, when Colley published his entertaining, score-settling autobiography, his choice of words conveyed how bitterly he still felt Fielding's insults; he must have experienced his daughter's participation in them not only as disobedience but also as betrayal. We can only imagine what Fielding's cynical cooptation of Charlotte—as Colley would have seen it—may have contributed to Colley's dislike of him.

Refusing to dignify Fielding by using his name, Colley provided his readers with his own history of the Great Mogul's company: a "broken Wit," he remarked, had collected a troupe of "bad Actors" at the Little Haymarket. Eager to make money and knowing that it paid more to be "intrepidly abusive, than decently entertaining," this broken wit "produc'd several frank, and free Farces, that seem'd to knock all Distinction of Mankind on the head: Religion, Laws, Government, Priests, Judges, and Ministers, were all laid flat, at the Feet of the *Herculean* Satyrist!" With so many theatre companies in competition at the time, he continued, inferior companies like the broken wit's "must have starv'd, unless they fed upon the Trash and filth of Buffoonery, and Licentiousness."[4]

Just as Colley refused to name Fielding, he referred to Charlotte only implicitly, as one of Fielding's bad actors. It is impossible to believe that when Colley pictured Fielding's players he did not picture first and foremost his own daughter, energetically impressing these insults into the minds of the audience. When he asserted that Fielding's plays were so bad that "the greatest Dunce of an Actor could not spoil" them, Colley implicitly insulted Charlotte, assigning her a place among a dunciad of actors (a reference that would become unintentionally appropriate, given his own later skewering by Pope as King of the Dunces). Even in castigation, the father uttered a prescient acknowledgment of his daughter's likeness to him.

Colley's retaliation against Charlotte, however, was more immediate than his revenge upon Fielding. Few of Cibber's papers survive; among them is this letter, one of only two extant that Colley wrote to Charlotte.

Tavistock Street
Covent Garden
March 27

Dear Charlotte,

I am sorry I am not in a position to assist you further. You have made
your own bed, and thereon you must lie. Why do you not disassociate
yourself from that worthless scoundrel and *then* your relatives *might* try
and aid you. You will never be any good while *you* adhere to him, and
you most certainly will not receive what *otherwise* you might from *your*
Father.

Colley Cibber

Colley's biographer-frustrating failure to note the year in which he
wrote this makes its application to this period conjectural. But it does
make sense to date it either 1737 or 1736, closely following Colley's
attendance of either *The Historical Register* or *Pasquin*. ("Tavistock
Street" could refer to Anne Boultby's house, which would also date the
letter around this time.)[5] Some commentators have assumed that the
"worthless scoundrel" must have been Richard Charke, but I share
the opinion of others that he was Fielding.[6] (Colley's reference to never
being "any good" could have a moral reading, but more likely he
intended a professional sense—good as an actress.)

Charlotte certainly would have been aware from the beginning that
Fielding's satire would sting her father, and that must have given her a
certain gratification—a bit of revenge for Colley's attempts to control
her, perhaps, or for his continuing refusal to speak to her while he
allowed that viper Catherine to dominate his household, and while he
danced attendance upon ladylike Susannah. But in the flush of her triumph Charlotte seems to have had no suspicion—until it was too
late—that she might be risking permanent alienation. If she had been
unconscious of how deeply the barbs she (and others) delivered onstage
in her performances with Fielding penetrated the Cibber hide, this letter must have given her some indication. But even here, Colley did not
completely close the door on his daughter.

The letter indicates that Charlotte had approached Colley for
money, which she would not have done if she had not had some hope
of receiving it. Charlotte was earning well with Fielding, as she had

presumably done earlier at Lincoln's Inn Fields; but, like Theophilus, she was improvident. She also had Kitty to support. That she would have approached Colley reveals both the extent of her need and her general obliviousness to how much her association with Fielding had angered him.

But it also indicates that despite their "family tribunal" confrontation of almost two years earlier, their long period of not talking to each other, and Charlotte's apparently ungrateful departure from Drury Lane, she did not think a permanent rupture had occurred. She seems to have been correct: even in this letter denying her assistance, Colley clearly suggests that if she were to leave Fielding—if, in other words, she were to toe the line of convention and transform herself into a dutiful daughter—her relatives might try to aid her (this overlooks Elizabeth, who *was* aiding her), and she could receive the support from her father to which, he seems to acknowledge, she is, or at least could be, entitled. For all Charlotte's offensiveness in working with Fielding, Colley blamed Fielding more than he did her—he was the playwright-manager; she was just the player obeying his orders, as players should do—and if she were to transfer her allegiance back to her father, on his terms, she could in time be reinstated into her family.

But Charlotte did not leave Fielding of her own accord. How could she have done? In his way, he had made her a kind of star. Charlotte's independence, her optimism, and her professionalism all dictated that she not sacrifice her autonomy and her career in order to gain her father's blessing. In March of 1736 or 1737, she could have had little idea that, for reasons not in her control, the consequences of her "elopement" with Fielding were to be very grave.

As one of the featured performers of the Great Mogul's Company for the second year in a row, Charlotte achieved a public visibility that spring that she could only have dreamed of at Drury Lane. As Lord Place, Mr. Hen, and other characters she played, especially the playwright Mr. Spatter in *Eurydice Hiss'd,* she became a familiar stage presence, nearly as well known to London audiences as Susannah Cibber or Kitty Clive, if much more uncompromising as a female performer. Her celebrity was unique. She was not a melting, pathetic sufferer like Susannah. Nor was she a pert, flirtatious gamine who dons breeches to

Henry Fielding, later the creator of
Tom Jones, *helped make Charlotte a
leading player in London's avant-garde
theatre.* (Henry Fielding. *Engraving
after William Hogarth. Courtesy of
the National Portrait Gallery.)*

win her man. Charlotte's roles for Fielding, like the roles she usually chose for herself in her own troupes, seem to have bypassed this erotic spectacle in favour of different types of effect. Charlotte in breeches often constituted a deliberate satiric comment upon the masculinity of the characters she inhabited. Though it was inevitable that the outlining of her slender body, revealed to advantage by men's attire, would have been perceived as erotic by some spectators, this effect was incidental to her intentions.

Even at the height of her fame, it is doubtful that Charlotte had to spend much time fending off the advances of male admirers who crowded into the green room after and during performances. Her visibility with the Great Mogul's Company solidified her reputation for eccentricity and farce, and gave her a public identity as a stage transvestite whose transvestism was becoming her offstage identity as well. Whether or not she projected hints at this point in her life of what we now call lesbianism, she certainly did not project conventional eighteenth-century femininity. None of this was calculated to please her father, of course, however much it may have gratified her personal inclination and, in the context in which she performed, the public taste.

All the town was talking about *The Historical Register* that spring, and audiences continued to crowd the benches of the modest playhouse.

The Great Mogul's Company did have its share of failures, but their successes were so great that they more than made up for them. The company performed eleven plays, all of them either new or, like *Pasquin* and *Fatal Curiosity,* revivals of plays premiered the year before. On May 3, Charlotte chose for her benefit *The Historical Register,* "With a Preamble on the Kettle-Drums by Mr. Job Baker"; these were preceded by a new ballad opera called *The Sailor's Opera* ("written in Honour of the Gentlemen of the Navy"), in which she played one of her occasional female roles, Kitty Cable: perhaps in this role she mimicked Kitty Clive. *The Sailor's Opera* has not survived, but one advertisement identifies it as "written by a Female Politician": it is possible that Charlotte wrote this piece herself, but more possible that it was written by another actress new to the troupe that year, the playwright and novelist Eliza Haywood.[7]

Eliza Haywood brought to Fielding's company a notoriety that exceeded Charlotte's, and an aura of disreputable glamour. Twenty years Charlotte's senior, Eliza was already both famous and infamous as the prolific author of popular erotic fiction possessing titles such as *Love in Excess, The Fatal Secret,* and *The Distress'd Orphan; or, Love in a Mad-House.* The runaway wife of a clergyman, Haywood was reputed to have been the mistress of several men and the mother of two illegitimate children. As a writer, she also seems to have posed a threat to literary respectability and high culture, or so its male defenders thought. Jonathan Swift called her a "stupid, infamous, scribbling woman." Pope included her along with Colley Cibber in his population of dunces in *The Dunciad,* where she represents "the profligate licenciousness of those shameless scriblers" (that is, scandalous writers who were the more reprehensible for being female). In comparison to the seasoned Haywood, twenty-four-year-old Charlotte was a mere neophyte as a scandalous woman.

Fielding must have welcomed the well-known and genuinely talented Eliza into his company with the same glee with which he had recruited Charlotte. Haywood not only possessed acting experience, she was also the author of several plays, including several staged at Lincoln's Inn Fields and Drury Lane. It is likely that she wrote some of the pieces, now lost, that the Great Mogul's Company performed that year, and it is also likely that Charlotte acted in some if not all of them. (It is regrettable that neither Charlotte nor anyone else left a record of their encounters, that there was no green-room spy to write up the conversations between the two notorious women: the worldly, scandal-weathered Eliza and the rebellious, cross-dressed Charlotte, her own notoriety still in its infancy.)

Night after night at the Little Haymarket that spring, Charlotte performed to packed, enthusiastic houses. As one of the principal players closely identified with London's most successful playwright, an actress now accustomed to seeing her name in capital characters and singled out as the featured performer, Charlotte had achieved recognition, and she was earning a good salary, too. Fielding's fund of crowd-pleasing invention seemed inexhaustible and he was busily making plans for the future.

Fielding was engaged that spring in setting himself up as a mogul in earnest, meeting with potential investors and exploring possibilities for establishing his permanent company to vie more directly with Drury Lane and Covent Garden. Though it is uncertain whether he ever envisioned running a full September–June season, he was certainly planning a more ambitious schedule than he had attempted in 1736 and 1737. At some point in his planning that spring, he abandoned his earlier idea of building a new playhouse, choosing instead to refurbish and perhaps even extensively rebuild the Little Theatre. To that end, he had already arranged with the playhouse's owner, John Potter, to take a lease on the Little Haymarket for twenty-one weeks beginning in January 1738. But as Fielding moved ahead confidently with his plans, and Charlotte looked forward to a future in an established yet cutting-edge company, Walpole and his allies were planning their attack.

The Great Mogul's Company had encountered troubling omens at the very start of their second season. At the time of the troupe's opening performance on March 14, 1737, ominous rumblings in Parliament were unsettling the entire theatre community. The spate of politically charged plays that had been running at both Lincoln's Inn Fields and Drury Lane since February, along with the general anticipation that Fielding's new season at the Little Haymarket would give voice to even more popular political satire, had spurred the government to renew efforts to discipline the playhouses. Two years earlier, Walpole had introduced a stage censorship bill, but it had failed. Now he tried again.

On March 9, a bill to regulate "rogues and vagabonds" was read in Parliament. That particular bill was not passed, but it sounded a warning: vagabond legislation was the usual method of attempting to suppress actors—used, for instance, to justify the incarceration of John Harper during the mutiny of 1733. Though it was not always successful, "any rogue and vagabond legislation always made the players jumpy."[8] Walpole also threw his support behind the attempts by the universities at Oxford and Cambridge to suppress theatres in their vicinities, an issue that was making its way through Parliament that spring and that he would use as a springboard for a more sweeping attack.

The Great Mogul's Company encountered other problems as well. They had opened their season with a new play called *A Rehearsal of Kings,* scheduled for March 9, in which Charlotte played the male role of "Don Refinando." But on the afternoon of the premiere, she and the rest of the cast found the Little Haymarket's doors barred by a group of men who had stormed and occupied the theatre. The occupiers were duly arrested and committed to Bridewell prison, but they succeeded in canceling the evening's performance. "On this Account," said *The Daily Advertiser,* "several hundred Persons were turn'd away." The play was rescheduled for the eleventh, but this time, the newspaper noted, the play was "put off, by an unforeseen Accident, till Monday next."[9] (The nature of this delay and the identities of the occupiers remain unclear.) Then the play was staged three times without apparent incident and disappeared, never to be revived or printed.

Fielding had asked the critic Aaron Hill to write a prologue and epilogue for this ill-fated play, but Hill declined. He seems to have found *A Rehearsal of Kings* both unintelligible and politically dangerous: the latter could account for the occupation and the "unforeseen Accident."[10] Hill's concerns about political dangers were well founded, as the remainder of the company's season would demonstrate.

The real source of the company's problems that season had to do with Fielding's satires themselves, in the context of the current political climate. Especially in *The Historical Register* and its companion piece, *Eurydice Hiss'd,* Fielding sharpened his focus. Whereas *Pasquin* had been relatively evenhanded in directing its satire against various political parties or alliances and an array of prominent personalities, this spring Fielding assumed a much more specifically and comprehensively anti-Walpole position.

The Historical Register and *Eurydice Hiss'd* contained "the most audacious political satire that had ever appeared on the English stage."[11] That satire was explicitly directed against the prime minister and his supporters, making "him the Laughing-stock of crouded Audiences, for several Weeks together."[12] Satirizing Walpole was risky. In 1733, as he was trying to push through Parliament his hugely unpopular excise bill, an actor in a troupe then playing at the Little Haymarket took the occasion to throw out some unscripted, unflattering lines directed at him. Walpole was in the audience, as presumably the player knew. The Great Man strode behind the scenes and demanded to know whether the lines were in the script. Told that they were not, he then beat the actor up—or, in the more decorous language of the newspaper account, "his Lordship immediately corrected the Comedian with his own Hands very severely."[13]

This time, however, the prime minister's methods were less crude and much more thorough. First the ministerial paper, *The Daily Gazetteer*, printed an attack on Fielding that implied that his satires constituted seditious libel and condemned them as a threat to Britain; the article warned that these sorts of things might "make Restraint necessary."[14] Then Walpole's allies in Parliament introduced a bill to amend the Vagrancy Act as it related to actors, prohibiting the performance of plays everywhere in Britain except those playhouses operating under a royal patent or a licence from the lord chamberlain. A little later, Walpole added an additional clause to this stage-licensing bill that would subject all new or revised plays to censorship by the lord chamberlain.

The bill was hotly contested, in Parliament as in the newspapers, with prominent figures lining up on both sides. Colley Cibber supported the bill, both because it was beneficial to the theatre establishment with which he identified, and because it was inimical to troupes such as Fielding's, which he saw as scandalous and subversive. The bill's opponents, in response to such arguments, raised powerful objections based upon the scope and consequences of such legislation for Britain's vaunted freedoms. But then Walpole made his decisive move.

During one of the parliamentary debates concerning the bill, he pulled out a sheaf of papers. Here, he argued, brandishing the papers, was a prime example of theatre run amok, an eloquent illustration of the need for censorship. The manuscript was a farce called *The Golden Rump,* based on a scurrilous political allegory that had been published in an antiministerial newspaper two months before. Walpole read sections of the farce, which, according to witnesses, "was fraught with treason and abuse upon the government," a libel "abounding in profaneness, sedition, and blasphemy" against the government and the crown. It was "the most barefaced and scurrilous abuse on the persons and characters of the King and Queen and the whole Court."[15] The members of Parliament were shocked.

The Golden Rump was later revealed to have been delivered to Walpole by Henry Giffard, the manager of Lincoln's Inn Fields Theatre, the story being that it had been presented to him for consideration, and that Giffard was alarmed by it and took it to Downing Street. In fact, there is reason to suspect that Walpole had arranged in advance for Giffard, who was apparently experiencing financial difficulties, to "receive" this play, which the prime minister's allies ascribed to Fielding (an attribution he denied), but which in fact may have been written by someone at Walpole's behest. In any event, the prime minister's reading of passages from the play, particularly those openly abusing the King and Queen, had the desired effect of outraging Parliament and reinforcing the legislators' conviction that something needed to be done to discipline the unruly stage. Walpole also made certain to read the offending play to the King and Queen, and thus secured strong royal support of the bill.

On May 23, the day or two before Walpole's dramatic reading of *The Golden Rump* in Parliament, Charlotte performed once again in *The Historical Register* and *Eurydice Hiss'd.* By that time, Fielding's troupe had probably already begun morning rehearsals of two new plays, and on May 25, the first advertisement for their new programme appeared. The Great Mogul's Company announced the performance on May 30 of *Macheath turn'd Pyrate; or, Polly in India* and an afterpiece entitled *The King and TiTi.* The former play, it was obvious, was based upon John Gay's *Polly*—which had been suppressed by Walpole in 1729 as seditious—and the latter was most likely based upon a recent French work that vigorously mocked the warfare going on between the Prince of Wales and his parents. As the historian Vincent J. Liesenfeld comments, the first would have been offensive to the government, the second deeply offensive to both the government and the royal family.[16]

John Potter, the owner of the Little Haymarket, had become an increasingly nervous man as the spring continued. Delighted as he had been to have his playhouse filled with important people, a single troupe using it continually for several months, and a lease already signed with Fielding for the following year, he watched with anxiety the attacks on the Mogul's troupe in the papers and the escalating signs of ministerial and Parliamentary displeasure. He must have seen some of the rehearsals of *Polly* and *The King and TiTi,* and what he saw brought his anxieties to a head. Potter surreptitiously approached the lord chamberlain and Walpole, who assured him that if he could take steps to shut Fielding down—probably illegal ones, since Fielding would still have had some time before his current lease expired—Potter would be reimbursed for the income he lost by closing the theatre, and handsomely rewarded for his patriotism as well.

One morning at the end of May, the players arrived for rehearsals and discovered a scene of devastation. Their sets and scenery were stripped, dismantled, and thrown into heaps. The playhouse was stacked full of heavy construction materials: deal, timber, bricks, and lime. The theatre was unusable—in effect, shut down.[17] Potter seems never to have received his compensation for his ingenious ploy (such were the promises of ministers, as he should have known from seeing Fielding's plays), but he had brought an abrupt, premature end to the company's season of 1737. Parliament and the King then stepped in to ensure that it would be their last.

On June 1, despite passionate opposition in the newspapers and on the floor of Parliament, the House of Commons overwhelmingly passed the Stage Licensing Act of 1737. On June 6, despite an eloquent speech by Lord Chesterfield decrying the dangers to freedom, particularly freedom of the press, of suppressing and censoring the playhouses, the House of Lords passed it also. The King gave his assent on June 21, and the act became law on June 24. It shut down all playhouses not operating by virtue of a royal patent or licence from the lord chamberlain—in effect, in London, all venues other than the Theatres Royal Drury Lane and Covent Garden, and the King's Theatre in the Haymarket (Giffard's Lincoln's Inn Company played a short summer season under Rich's patent, but did not mount a season the following year). The holding of any performance not so licensed was a criminal offence. New or rewritten plays, or new additions to old plays, were to be submitted to the lord chamberlain's office for censorship. "The damage to drama and theatre" done by the Licensing Act, remarks Hume, "is incalculable."[18] The act effectively stifled the development of theatre in London for centuries. (A version of its censorship provision remained in force until 1968.) It served the political establishment by suppressing a vital vein of political discourse; it freed Walpole of irritating dissent; it eliminated most of the competition to the patent houses; it put a large number of actors and actresses out of work; it ended Henry Fielding's theatrical career; and it devastated Charlotte's professional future.

Fielding abandoned his attempts to write for the stage and spent the next two years studying law. A convincing argument has been made, based on his uncharacteristic silence during the heated debates about the bill in June, that he was bought off by Walpole.[19] As Hume says, Walpole "was accustomed to purchasing silence," and Fielding, pragmatic as always, probably exacted a high price for what seemed inevitable. The payoff funded his studies: it would enable him to become the reformist magistrate of Bow Street (founder of the Bow Street Runners, London's first police force), a prolific essayist, and, of course, one of Britain's greatest novelists, the author of *Tom Jones*.

Charlotte, occupying a very different position, possessing different talents, and female, was less fortunate. Her prospects simply vanished. It is difficult to overestimate what a crushing blow this was to the twenty-four-year-old woman, who probably had little money to support herself in this sudden catastrophe. Her father had rejected her request for financial support, since she had refused to leave Fielding. There were now a large number of out-of-work actors who would be desperately vying for employment, and besides, Fleetwood's and Rich's companies worked in concert: having severed her ties with Drury Lane, Charlotte would not be welcome at Covent Garden.

The eighteenth century had no system of unemployment compensation and no official welfare programme except the very unevenly administered, often oppressive parish relief, whose "benefits" ranged from inadequate handouts of food and clothing to the punitive rigours of the workhouses. Private charity, individual and organized, carried much of the burden, but by nature it was haphazard and humiliating. Crime was an option, and some of the newly unemployed players may have turned to it; assuredly, at least some of the unemployed actresses would have become prostitutes (which was often a way of supplementing an inadequate salary even when an actress was working). As May and June progressed, and Charlotte became increasingly aware of the consequences of the Licensing Act for her personally, she must have experienced moments of desperation.

However much responsibility Charlotte had for her alienation from Drury Lane and from her father, her decision to join Fielding had been, professionally speaking, the right one. The gamble should have paid off, and what else could she have done? The stage was not only her life but also her living. She was the only support of herself and her daughter, and she had to look for improvements in income, as well as opportunities to extend herself as an actress, to be challenged creatively, to gain an audience. Henry Fielding gave her all those things. Her participation in his satires of her father was undutiful and impolitic, to say the least, but it was also an assertion of her autonomy and her professionalism.

In fact, Charlotte was not primarily responsible for the circumstances that put her life on a new course in 1737—a point missed by some theatre historians, who seem to delight in blaming her. Had Parliament attended to Lord Chesterfield and others, had it defeated Walpole and his Stage Licensing Act, Charlotte's life probably would have been very different.[20] She might have become an actress known to posterity for the eccentric originality of her performances; a unique, unconventional player well suited to the absurdist genius of the playwright who wrote parts specifically for her; and a key contributor to London's most innovative company, solidly established at the Little Haymarket for many years. Instead, Charlotte plunged, unwillingly but also courageously, into the tumultuous circumstances of the remaining twenty-three years of her life.

PART

THREE

16

PUNCH'S THEATRE

(1737–38)

The splendid engraving by William Hogarth entitled *Strolling Actresses Dressing in a Barn* went on sale in the print shops in March 1738. It portrays a group of itinerant players, identified as "a Company of Comedians from the Theatres at London," preparing for a performance at the George Inn. (At least two of the many venues called the George Inn, one in Smithfield and the other in Southwark, customarily hosted play performances by troupes of London actors during the fairs.)

In the foreground of the engraving, two documents have been tossed onto a low bed. One, resting against a chamber pot, is a playbill, and the other, a scroll partially unrolled, is inscribed "The Act against Strolling Players"—a statute from the Licensing Act outlawing itinerant theatre companies. The playbill states that this evening's entertainment is "the last time of Acting before ye Act Commences," establishing that the scene is set in late June 1737, for the act took effect on the twenty-fourth.

Hogarth began work on the original painting from which he made the engraving in May of that year, when the Parliamentary debates over the Licensing Act were under way, and completed it after the act's passage. (Unfortunately, the painting was destroyed by fire in the nineteenth century; but the black-and-white engraving is beautiful and, despite its satiric edge, moving.)[1]

William Hogarth, Strolling Actresses Dressing in a Barn. *(Courtesy of the Henry E. Huntington Library.)*

The engraving bursts with energy and life, as the players, costumed as mythological characters—Juno, Night, Cupid, Flora, Eagle, Ghost, and an Attendant—go about their preparations. On the left clusters a particularly interesting, and provocative, threesome. An unlovely "Aurora," a star affixed to her flowing headdress, stands in the middle of the group, making some adjustments to the costume of the "Siren," whose fish's tail curls into the air behind her, held in position by a rope. The pretty Siren is gazing compassionately at the third figure in the group, who, handkerchief pressed to jaw, is suffering from a toothache; she tenderly hands the sufferer a dram of gin. (The Siren's sleepy eyes suggest that she has partaken of it already herself.)

The toothache victim at the far left of the engraving, sometimes identified by critics as "Ganymede," balances on the cot.[2] This person is comely, slender, and tall, dressed in a long shirt, stockings, and an unbuttoned coat, and standing on a pair of breeches that lies on the bed. This figure seems at first glance to be a particularly attractive young man. But the long, undressed hair cascading down his back seems an oddly feminine touch (though this detail is ambiguous: men of this period who did not crop or shave off their hair for periwigs wore their "own hair" long and tied back). More definitively, on closer scrutiny "his" exposed thigh and knee are noticeably rounded, shaped like a woman's rather than a man's. This "man" *is* a woman, a cross-dressed actress. And she very well may be Charlotte.

There are some good arguments for this. To think of the Licensing Act was to think of Fielding, who was also a friend of Hogarth: of all the playwrights who offended Walpole, he was the most offensive, the most successful, and the most threatening. To think of Fielding was to think of Charlotte, his leading player, whose roles in the Great Mogul's troupe, especially her most famous ones, were male. And though Hogarth set the scene immediately prior to the Licensing Act's taking effect, he anticipated the fate that would befall a number of London's players. Many did fall into the hand-to-mouth existence of strollers or pick-up actors in quasi-legal (or downright illegal) temporary venues. Many lives were changed for the worse, including Charlotte's.

Christine Kaier, who analyzes the transvestite figure in *Strolling Actresses* as a possible reference to Mrs. Charke, also argues that Hogarth's portrayal of the warm interaction between the "Siren" and the cross-dresser suggests a sexual relationship between them. This interpretation makes sense, she says, because "Charke was a well-known cross-dresser and lesbian in her real life, causing her theatrical transvestism to reflect her sexuality more pointedly than that of the more common, feminine 'breeches part' actresses."[3] Kaier's point that Charlotte's version of theatrical cross-dressing was not the conventional "heterosexual" one is well-taken, but although Charlotte almost certainly was well-known by this time for offstage cross-dressing, there is no solid evidence that she had a reputation for "lesbianism" (or that she had yet had erotic relationships with women) at the time of Hogarth's engraving. (The term "lesbian," in the sexual/social sense, is an anachronism, besides: both the usage itself and the notion that people possess "sexual identities" are historically much more recent developments.)

One additional piece of evidence may bolster the identification of this transvestite actress as Charlotte, however. Art historians' typical identification of the cross-dresser as Ganymede—in classical mythology,

It is likely that Hogarth's figure holding the handkerchief to her jaw was inspired by Charlotte. (Courtesy of the Henry E. Huntington Library.)

the beautiful boy who was cup-bearer to the gods and Jupiter's object of desire—is open to question. The playbill does not include a Ganymede, although it lists all the other characters present in the barn.

Who, then, is this actress supposed to be playing? Unlike every other player depicted, the cross-dresser wears ordinary street clothing, bearing not a single mythological attribute. What if this actress is not—or not yet—in costume? That is, what if Hogarth was portraying an actress for whom male dress was her ordinary attire? She could be just about to change into costume, first having shed her breeches. Or, perhaps more likely, she could be a member of the troupe whose bad toothache has "indisposed" her, making her unable to perform that night. In either case, the actress would not be (or be only) a *stage* cross-dresser, but an *offstage* cross-dresser—and that would point even more directly to Charlotte.

If the cross-dresser is Charlotte dressed in street clothes, we can look at the evident bond between her and the Siren—made more suggestive by the fact that their interaction takes place around a bed—and at least wonder. Did some of the unspecified "misbehaviour" that so incensed her father and sisters and that Fleetwood cited as a reason to fire her in 1734 include erotic relationships with women? Perhaps the Hogarth engraving itself is evidence that Charlotte had such relationships at this point.

In the autumn of 1737, only the opera house, Drury Lane, and Covent Garden opened their doors. For Charlotte, acting was, for the moment at least, a dead end. What was she to do with her life?

For all her impulsiveness, Charlotte also possessed large stores of courage and imagination. Once she recovered from her shock, she cast about for an alternative. At least she had had her benefit performance before Potter closed the playhouse, and she seems to have had a bit of money remaining. Just as, in previous years, Charlotte had followed the path of her father and brother as a player, a manager, and a playwright, now she looked to another member of her family for a model: the only one of her siblings at this point (as far as we know) to have set herself up in an independent nontheatrical career, her sister Anne Boultby.

Anne had worked as a clerk for a grocer in the City before establishing her own tea and millinery business. Characteristically, Charlotte's imitation of her model was selective: she chose to move straight into proprietorship. Taking the lease of a building on Long Acre in Covent Garden, Charlotte and Kitty moved out of Elizabeth's house into quarters on its upper floors, where she also took a boarder, a "Widow Gentlewoman." On the ground floor, she opened an oil and grocery shop. Charlotte does not seem to have approached her sister for advice in her new endeavour.

"The Oil-Shop," said R. Campbell in *The London Tradesman*, typically "is furnished with Oils, Pickles, Soap, Salt, Hams, and several other Family Necessaries."[4] The oilmen Thomas Waddell & Son, for instance, whose shop was located north of Long Acre near St. Giles Church, advertised

> The finest sallet [salad] oyls or virgin Luca [Lucca], Florence and Genoa, Oyl for Scowring Iron or Brass, Oyl for Plaisters and Oyntments, Rape Oyl for Lamps, Mackaronee, vermajelly [vermicelli], salt peter and peter salt, salt prunella [fused nitre, molded into cakes or balls, a treatment for inflamed throats], china soye and ketchup, cavear and pickled oysters, morrells and truffles, bolognia sausages, spruce beer and pearl ashes [potassium carbonate], lemon and verjuyce [acidic juice pressed from unripe fruit, particularly grapes], links and flambeaux, lam-black [lamp-black, a pigment made from soot] cord and pack-thread [package twine].[5]

Oil was to be had from Italian importers, who also traded in goods such as "mackaronee," truffles, and sausage. Charlotte, who would not have attained the Waddells' variety of stock herself, mentions both edible and fuel oils, tea, sugar, and spirits among the goods she sold.

Long Acre, the northern boundary of Covent Garden, dividing it from St. Giles, ran between St. Martin's Lane on the west and Drury Lane on the east. It was known particularly for its coach-makers. Strype described it in 1720 as "a very handsome broad Street, with good Buildings, well inhabited both by Tradesmen and others."[6] Long Acre was not Covent Garden's fashionable shopping street; that was the Strand, to the south. But for a business such as an oilshop, it was not a bad location. Charlotte spent her remaining money on stocking her store: she probably received some assistance from Elizabeth and bought the rest of her stock on credit. It would have been entirely in character, too, for her to spend a large sum on a handsome shop sign.

Charlotte's shopkeeping experiment was a comedy of errors in a highly theatrical sense; she approached her business as an actress playing a part. (Or so she emphasized in telling the story later.) Playing a businesswoman, she paid more attention to the outward forms of such a person than to the substance of her work. She took great pains to fix her "mercantile face," giving her countenance "as conceited an Air of Trade as it had before in Physick" (a revealing allusion to her childhood role-playing). "The Rise and Fall of Sugars was my constant Topick; and Trading, Abroad and at Home, was as frequent in my Mouth as my Meals. . . . I constantly took in the Papers to see how Matters went at *Bear-Key*; what Ships were come in, or lost; who, in our Trade, was broke; or who advertised Teas at the lowest Prices: Ending with a comment upon those Dealers, who were endeavouring to under-sell us." Images of Charlotte spouting medical Latin, toting a horse blanket and grumbling about her nags, or leaning on her gardener's pitchfork and discoursing about planting, echo in this description.

Charlotte immediately conceived grand plans for her business. At one point, she says, she decided that, as a good horsewoman, she would make her country deliveries herself. Fortunately, she was unable to establish any country accounts, for these would have cost her horse-hire and travel time, at little profit. At another point, she decided on scant evidence that she needed a huge scale and beam for trading in hundredweights, and traipsed across town looking for one. Again fortunately, she was unsuccessful, and then was persuaded not to waste her money on this particular expense.

Charlotte's career as shopkeeper proved not much more enduring than her turns as physician, gardener, and groom had been: the realities of business interfered with the role she was playing. The following story is an example. She had bought a hundred pounds of lump sugar, and was allotted the customary bonus of six pounds extra. When a generous friend of hers came to buy twenty-five pounds of sugar—many of her customers were her friends and acquaintances—Charlotte was so excited that she neglected to play her part: "I was so insufferably proud of hearing so large a Quantity demanded by my friend, that I really forgot the Character of Grocer, and, fancying myself the Sugar-Baker, allowed in the twenty-five Pounds the Half of what I got in the Hundred."

Her friend, not realizing that the bargain she had been given would, if repeated, ruin the seller, promised to bring her more customers. If she had done so, Charlotte wryly observed, it "might in due Course of Time have paved the Way for me either to Newgate, the Fleet, or Marshalsea."

Charlotte's lack of business experience and acumen was one liability. Theft was another. Oilshops dealt in links and flambeaux, the pitch and wax torches carried by "linkboys" whose job was to guide pedestrians and sedan chairs through the city at night. Though houses were required to provide outside lighting, London's streets were sometimes impenetrably dark, and always dangerous. Nearly every newspaper carried daily accounts of footpads waylaying unfortunate pedestrians, sometimes badly injuring or killing them as well as depriving them of their money, swords, wigs, watches, and even clothes. Linkboys provided light and theoretically some degree of safety, though stories circulated about linkboys (and sedan-chair men) who were in cahoots with robbers, leading their customers into an ambush.

One particular linkboy became one of Charlotte's most steady customers, dropping by nightly at dusk. Grateful for the loyal custom of the "sooty-colour'd Youth," Charlotte would treat him to an occasional dram of spirits as thanks for his patronage. On one particular evening, the boy backed out of the shop, bowing, and expressing, Charlotte said, "great Satisfaction that even, in his poor Way, he had the Power of serving his good Mistress." A few moments later, Charlotte realized that he had stolen her entire set of brass weights, which she carelessly had left stacked on the corner of the window near the door. (She did not see the thief again until sometime later, when she had the satisfaction, she said, of happening to spot him "making a small tour in a two-wheeled Coach" from Newgate Prison to Tyburn Tree, the gallows.)

One of Charlotte's concerns when she set up her oil business was how to keep any profits out of Richard Charke's hands. This seems to have concerned her more now than it had when she was drawing a theatre salary, since her margin was so narrow and her future so uncertain. Also, she needed her earnings to buy more stock. She solved the problem by having her receipts taken in the name of her widowed lodger, "and I sat quiet and snug with the pleasing Reflection of my Security, though he suspected I had a Hand in the Plot." In any event, Richard was not a concern for long, for he soon left London and sailed to Jamaica.

The story of Richard's departure for the West Indies, as Charlotte told it, is that one day as he sat at dinner with his mistress—the sister of one of Covent Garden's most notorious prostitutes, and Charlotte's neighbour—the bailiffs entered and arrested her for a debt of £100. Richard, "to show his Gallantry," went to the City and borrowed money on the strength of his agreement to join a company of actors bound for Jamaica. The sponsor of the troupe was Henry Moore, later Lieutenant Governor of Jamaica and Governor of New York, and Richard became one of his star attractions.[7] Richard's mistress planned to join him in the West Indies, where they intended to live as a married couple. This, Charlotte said, "she had my Leave to do, [as] though she were a Lady."

For all Charlotte's relief at Richard's absence (she recorded no hint of Kitty's feelings for her father), she also was aware that now, more than ever, Kitty's welfare and her own rested entirely upon her shoulders. Richard had never provided any support before his departure, but his absence was nonetheless disquieting, particularly in light of her other burdens. As long as he was alive, she could not seek a new husband (marriage was by far the most common means of making a living for a woman of Charlotte's class background). Knowing that she "was as liable to Death or Infirmities as any other Part of Creation, which might have disempowered me from getting my own, or my Child's bread," she wondered, "What was to become of us then?"

The British sugar colony of Jamaica, where troupes of actors travelled on occasion to entertain, was a slave economy; British colonists might become rich, if they survived their stay there, though many did not. (A great many more of the tens of thousands of slaves they ceaselessly imported from Africa died.) Jamaica's climate was tropical and, from a northern European's perspective, disease-ridden, its society cruel, violent, and provincial. British citizens such as Richard, who were down on their luck, sometimes travelled there to escape the bailiffs and try their fortunes.

Chetwood told the story of a theatre troupe that went to Jamaica in 1733 and "clear'd a large Sum of Money":

They receiv'd 370 Pistoles the first Night, to the *Beggar's Opera;* but within the Space of two Months they bury'd their third Polly, and two of their Men. The Gentlemen of the Island, for some time, took their Turns upon the Stage, to keep up the Diversion; but this did not hold long; for, in two Months more, there were but one old Man, a Boy, and a Woman of the Company, left: the rest died, either with the Country-Distemper, or the common Beverage of the Place, the noble Spirit of Rum-punch, which is generally fatal to New-comers.

Richard Charke, perhaps undone by rum punch or simply a victim of distemper, died in Jamaica about a year and a half after he arrived there. His mistress had never joined him.[8]

A few months after the incident with the linkboy, Charlotte gave up her shop, despite the £100 worth of paid-for stock she still possessed (presumably she was able to sell most of it). The shop had been a useful, if not particularly profitable, expedient, however; it gave her time to cast about for another way to support herself and Kitty—a way, if possible, to return to the theatre world she loved in the new, post–Licensing Act reality. She came up with a promising, even brilliant, solution: puppets.

In so doing, Charlotte added a small but significant chapter to the history of English puppet theatre, to which she brought a spirit of innovation and artistry. Although she had never operated puppets before, and presumably knew little about them, puppetry was an excellent idea, possessing many advantages for Charlotte. It was, first and foremost, theatrical, an ingenious way for her to return to the only world that really mattered to her. Puppetry allowed her cleverly to evade the Licensing Act (as many out-of-work theatre professionals were scheming, with varying degrees of success, to do): it governed live actors, so puppets were probably exempt. (To be safe, however, she successfully petitioned the lord chamberlain for a licence to operate a puppet show, and advertised her theatre as operating "By Permission.")[9] Hers was the only puppet theatre "in this Kingdom that has had the good Fortune to obtain so advantageous a Grant," she bragged.

Puppet shows were very popular in the eighteenth century, and, under the right circumstances, they could attract well-heeled audiences: they were by no means limited to children, nor were they always restricted to the fairs. Martin Powell, who had operated his famous puppet show in the Little Piazza, Covent Garden earlier in the century, had enjoyed great success among the fashionable with his puppet-parodies of Italian opera. The puppet theatre historian George Speaight remarks, of the eighteenth century, that "never before or since have the puppets played quite so effective and so well publicized a part in fashionable Society; never before or since have puppet theatres so successfully made themselves the talk of the town."[10]

As usual, Charlotte thought big. Her ambition was to keep "a grand Puppet-Show" that would be acclaimed as "the most elegant that was ever exhibited." To this end, she spent a small fortune—some £500—on having her puppets, Punch and his cohorts, carved, clothing them magnificently, and constructing scenery to match. She must have had some money left over from the sale of her shop goods, and was able to borrow or beg the rest from her friends. Puppet historians—who speak respectfully of Charlotte's career as a puppeteer—agree that her puppets were certainly marionettes, manipulated with strings by operators standing overhead, rather than the old-fashioned glove puppets operated from below, the ones we usually envision when we think of Punch and Joan or Judy.

One of Charlotte's most innovative ideas concerned her puppets' faces. Rather than giving her puppet characters their traditional appearance, based upon the Italian commedia dell'arte figures, Charlotte instead purchased a set of mezzotints of famous people of her day, and had her puppets carved in their likenesses, including Farinelli's. (Fidelis Morgan characterizes her idea aptly as the precursor, by 250 years, of television's *Spitting Images*.)[11]

The author of a pamphlet entitled "The Usefulness of the Stage" added, in the second edition (dated April 18, 1738), a set of "Remarks upon Mrs. C—'s new Licensed Figures," repeating the commonplace joke comparing puppets, who spoke in high, squeaking voices, to castrati: "'Tis said she intends, by their artificial voices to cut out the Italians; for it has been found that Punch can hold his breath and quiver much better and longer than Farinelli; I wish this may be true, for then we may expect to have Italian songs at a moderate rate, without the use of a knife." Farinelli was the only living model Charlotte mentioned by name—but would she have been able to resist having one of her Punches carved in the likeness of Colley Cibber?

Instead of the tall, narrow, portable booths used for outdoor glove-puppet shows, marionettes performed in something approximating a playhouse, or at least a large room. Charlotte took a lease on the theatre in the Tennis Court in James Street (the present-day Orange

Street), just around the corner from the Little Haymarket, a venue used occasionally by strolling troupes. It was a theatre she had passed innumerable times during her performances in the Haymarket, and one that she would have scorned not long before. Speaight says it must have been a "horrible little flea-pit."[12]

Tennis court theatres had once been plentiful in London—the large indoor space of an old tennis court could fairly easily be adapted to theatre performances—but the James Street Theatre was at that time the only remaining court still in use as a theatre. (It is not clear whether it was a conversion of the actual tennis court, or a small theatre above or beside an existing tennis court.)[13] Although it was not in continual use, the James Street Theatre was a genuine theatre, with pit, boxes, and two galleries. Perhaps it was not all that despicable.

On March 11, 1738, Charlotte placed an ad in *The London Daily Post and General Advertiser* announcing the debut performance of her company. "*By Permission according to Act of Parliament,*" it read:

> At Punch's Theatre, at the Old Tennis-Court in James-street near the Hay-Market, on Monday March 13, will be presented the Historical Play of King Henry the Eighth. Written by Shakespear. Intermix'd with a Pastoral, call'd Damon and Phillida by C. Cibber, Esq; Poet-Laureat. With the Christning of the young Princess Elizabeth; on which Occasion will be performed a New Ode, written by Mrs. Charke, the Musick compos'd by an eminent Hand; and Entertainments of Dancing by Punch and his Wife; also a new Prologue. The Comedians, Scenes, and Clothes entirely New. To begin at Six o'Clock. Boxes 3 s. Pit 2 s. Rail'd Gallery 1 s. Upper Gallery 6 d. No Money to be return'd after the Curtain is drawn up. The House is newly fitted up.

Perhaps the "eminent Hand" that composed the music was that of Richard Charke, with Charlotte appropriating his work just as she appropriated her father's play—and his capacity as a composer of odes.

Charlotte used her puppets in a way new to the history of English puppet theatre. Rather than following the traditional fare of plays and drolls based upon popular ballad and chapbook legends, she used her marionettes to stage real plays that might be seen at the same time at Drury Lane or Covent Garden. Charlotte was following the letter of the law: her licence, issued with traditional puppet theatre in mind, did not restrict the kinds of plays she could perform. Her stagings of actual plays with puppet performers could compete with the plays offered by the playhouses, at a cheaper price, and offered the added attractions of novelty, farce, and parody—all within the strict bounds of legality.

From various accounts of marionette shows in England and Italy in the seventeenth and eighteenth centuries, we can speculate with some confidence about what Charlotte's spectators encountered when they entered Punch's Theatre. Like a traditional theatre, this had a stage with a proscenium arch, a curtain, and movable sets, as well as the usual array of variously priced seats and a house lighted by candles in sconces. Stretched across the proscenium arch, however, was fine wire mesh, separating the audience from the action onstage; the mesh disguised the puppets' strings, strengthening the illusion that this was some double-jointed Lilliputian troupe performing Shakespeare's play.

Charlotte's puppets were wooden, probably two to three feet tall; perhaps they had leaden legs and hands and flexible arms made of cord; they were attired in silken outfits and completely dressed from hat to shoes. Their operators, standing on bridges above the stage, controlled them by means of an iron rod or thick cord attached to their heads, and threads affixed to hands and feet that allowed the puppets to gesture, walk, skip, dance, even fly through the air.

More cords allowed their eyes to roll and their jaws to move as they "spoke." Charlotte used the traditional tin or wooden tubes called squeakers to create the puppets' voices: the actors manipulating the puppets spoke their part, holding the squeakers in their mouths and speaking their lines in high-pitched screeches and squawks. (Imagine enunciating the language of Shakespeare through a roll of tin in your mouth.)

Punch as a puppet character had already established himself in England, having emigrated from Italy where his ancestor was Pulcinella from the commedia dell'arte tradition. Charlotte's Punch (or Punches, since she had more than one) may have possessed his traditional body shape—protruding belly and humped back (no hooked nose yet)—but to stage her plays she probably worked variations on his traditional costume of big buttons down his front, large ruff, and tall, narrow-brimmed, conical hat. With her puppets carved to resemble actual people—perhaps mostly stage people, like Farinelli; the idea of a Colley-

Punch remains enticing—Charlotte would have dressed her puppets as the characters they "played," and used them in ways that were inevitably parodic, even when playing their roles "straight."

Few spectators would have come away from Punch's Theatre with a deeper understanding of Shakespearean history plays—Charlotte probably rewrote and cut them—but the antics of the puppets, speaking their blank verse in squeaking voices, must have created a very entertaining form of mock-heroic, in which the "high" art of Shakespearean drama met the "low" culture of Bartholomew Fair. The James Street theatre's movable scenes and flying machines, the staples of opera and pantomime, would have assisted in creating that juxtaposition of high and low, not to mention the "intermixing" of *Henry VIII* with Colley's ballad opera afterpiece, in the manner of pantomime.

Between March 13 and May 9, Charlotte undertook an ambitious and exhausting schedule. Punch's Theatre offered a total of ten different plays, two per performance, over that period, and they performed most nights every week. Her puppets danced as well as acted, in the manner of the playhouses, and Charlotte brought in added musical attractions. On their sixth night (March 21), her old acquaintance Job Baker, a very popular drummer, was billed to "perform some Jiggs and Country-dances on the single Kettle-Drum, accompanied with the whole Band." The troupe's ninth performance substituted Fielding's *The Mock-Doctor*—whose lead role was one of Theophilus's standards—as the afterpiece "intermix'd" with *Henry VIII*. The evening was capped by "a grand Dance by Mr. Punch, in a full-bottom Perriwig." Theo probably would not have worn such an old-fashioned wig, but Colley did.

At the end of March, Punch's Theatre held a concert of music, featuring Job Baker, "For the Benefit of a Family in Distress" (perhaps Charlotte's or Baker's). On April 10 the mainpiece changed to *The Unhappy Favourite; or, The Earl of Essex,* and two evenings later, "At the desire of Several Gentlemen of the Ancient and Honourable Order of Free-Masons," she staged another Shakespeare, *King Henry the Fourth,* "With the Humours of Sir John Falstaff, The Part of Sir John Falstaff by Mr. Punch. And all the parts to very great Advantage."[14] (Punch as Falstaff was an inspired idea.)

On April 25, Charlotte mounted an all-Fielding evening, combining

The Mock-Doctor with *The Covent-Garden Tragedy,* the play that had been damned as obscene when performed with live actors because of its representation of bawds and whores. The play is sprinkled with metaphors equating various aspects of human behaviour to puppets: lines such as "man is a puppet which woman moves" would have been particularly funny when squeaked by actual puppets.[15] That evening, under Charlotte's direction, the play added the element of puppet travesty, too, when the part of "Mother Punch-Bowl"—a Covent Garden bawd based on the infamous Mother Needham—was performed by Punch, "being the first Time of his appearing in Petticoats."[16] On the next night, with the same bill, "Punch in Petticoats" danced the Black Joke.

In early May, Charlotte advertised a performance for the "Benefit of Miss Charke, Grand-daughter to Colley Cibber, Esq." The bill that evening featured another Shakespeare, *Richard III,* and the afterpiece *The Beggar's Wedding.* The combination of all these elements in one evening demands comment, for this was an evening devoted, on many registers, to Charlotte's family. Kitty was now seven, old enough to be present at theatre for performances and to participate in various ways, perhaps even helping to manipulate a puppet.

Charlotte's mention of Kitty's grandfather in the bill was an obvious way of distinguishing Kitty and soliciting ticket buyers, but it must also have carried a message of some bitterness, for one of the consequences of Charlotte's estrangement from her father was that her daughter was estranged from him, too. Colley did not acknowledge Kitty or give her money, in marked contrast to his care of Catherine's daughter Catharine, who lived with him, and Theophilus's two daughters from his first marriage, Jenny and Betty. To those who were aware of the situation in the Cibber family—as many people seem to have been—this ad would have had a certain pathos. The invocation of Colley's name for a benefit was, it implied, the only way Kitty *could* benefit from having a wealthy, famous grandfather.

Charlotte seems to have chosen the plays, too, with her family in mind. Richard III was one of Colley's most famous roles, though it was also one of the most infamous examples of both his alterations to Shakespeare and his alleged inability to act noncomic characters. It was his performance of Richard III that Aaron Hill compared to "the distorted heavings of an unjoined caterpillar" (and his Foppingtonian accent apparently transformed Richard's well-known cry into "A harse! A harse! My kingdam far a harse!").

The Beggar's Wedding—while it had practical appeal as a crowd-pleasing ballad opera—also had personal resonance, for it was in this piece that Richard Charke had achieved a measure of glamour when Charlotte met him. Charlotte's audience probably appreciated the self-referential nature of performances such as these: as one modern scholar remarks, "Charke's puppet shows, in their deliberate invocation of her own theatrical notoriety, their incongruous mix of carnivalesque comedy and the fashionable, must have offered a particular theatrical charge to an audience otherwise now limited to the two patent houses."[17]

Charlotte's energy and creativity brought new excitement to marionette theatre in London, but at a very high cost to her. As she had found with her Mad Troupe nearly four years earlier, the demands of management—even when the majority of her players were made of wood—were exhausting. Punch's Theatre maintained a rigorous schedule of near nightly performances, and each evening was long, featuring real plays (even if shortened), in double bills of mainpieces and afterpieces. Playing in a puppet theatre was more physically strenuous than acting *in propria persona,* since the puppets had to be manipulated, and their lines spoken, by a relatively small troupe of operators: there would have been few moments of rest during a performance, for both puppets and operators must have played multiple characters. Speaking ambitious lines of dramatic poetry through a squeaker would have strained the voice, too. At the end of an evening's performance, Charlotte must have been drained. And as the proprietor, she also had to deal with all the other demands of the theatre, from scheduling and rehearsing the plays, choosing the music, and dealing with the human members of her troupe, to placing the advertisements, paying the bills, overseeing the maintenance of the puppets, costumes, scenes, and playhouse, running around to drum up business, and so on. And she had Kitty to care for.

Punch's Theatre initially rewarded these labours, playing steadily to good houses—Charlotte was, as she said, "one of the principal Exhibiters for those Gentry [i.e. puppets]"—and promising soon to repay

Charlotte's investment. On April 29, a puff addressed "to the Author of the London Daily-Post" appeared in that paper:

> I had last Night the Pleasure to be a Spectator at Mrs. Charke's little Theatre in James-street near the Hay-market; and 'twas with infinite Pleasure I passed two Hours there, at the Representation of the Covent-Garden Tragedy, written by Mr. Fielding. I confess the Humour of Mr. Punch in his Petticoats even exceeds real Life; and the whole Play was performed with the utmost Theatrical Decorum. The Expences Mrs. Charke has been at is a certain proof of her Desire to Entertain, in the most elegant manner such a Performance will admit of, the number of People of Quality, as well as Foreign Ministers that were there, gives me hopes the Town will encourage her, as much as so much Industry deserves.

This puff (probably written by Charlotte or one of her friends) mentions people of quality and even foreign ministers (there is no reason to disbelieve that her performances attracted these sorts of spectators, as Powell's had done). Despite her very large outlay, her proceeds promised to soon pay off her debts. Punch's Theatre seemed poised to provide Charlotte and Kitty with a comfortable living, barring unforeseen occurrences.

After rehearsing and presenting ten plays in less than three months, Charlotte included in her advertisements the promise of another ambitious bill for her eleventh offering: "Very speedily will be performed a Comedy called Amphitryon, or the Two Sosia's. The Part of the Two Sosia's to be performed by two Punches." But this performance of Dryden's play, with the enticing prospect of dual Punches, never appeared. Instead, after May 9, Punch's Theatre closed, for Charlotte, having worked herself into a state of nervous exhaustion, had fallen seriously ill.

17

HARD TIMES

(1738–41)

Charlotte had contracted a "violent Fever," which, she said, "had like to have carried me off." Fevers of all sorts flourished in eighteenth-century London, and the possibility of a sudden fall into illness, and if the victim survived, thence into poverty, was evident in the thousands of paupers eking out a miserable existence throughout the city.

How Charlotte managed to support herself and Kitty in the year that followed her illness is not clear. She had earned a good income with her puppet theatre, but now was unable to work; she had contracted debts in order to have her puppets made, and paying them off—if she did pay them off—would have drained her profits. (With Richard's death, Charlotte had become legally responsible for her own debts.) This, and her habit of spending money freely when she had it, must have left her with a very small reserve. Almost certainly she was sustained by small donations from Elizabeth and from friends, and by credit with tradespeople. Colley and Catherine were of no assistance, and Theophilus, even if she was on good terms with him at this time, was dodging his own creditors. As a result of her illness, Charlotte began to accumulate serious debts.

She rented a small, inexpensive house in Marsham Street, Westminster, where, her beautiful puppets piled in a corner, she and Kitty spent her long convalescence, living, she said, "very quietly." Quiet would have been inescapable. Marsham Street today lies within the concrete-and-asphalt neighbourhood south of Westminster Abbey. Then, however, it was at the edge of the city, and nearly rural, an area of dirt roads dominated by large tracts of fields and market gardens. It grew swampy in the winters, but in the summers provided London with some of its best produce. Marsham Street itself was wide and probably unpaved; nearby Horseferry Road led to the Thames and the only ferry in all London capable of carrying horses and carriages. (Prior to the construction of Westminster Bridge in 1750, London had only one bridge—London Bridge—and one horse ferry.) To the immediate west of Marsham Street were market gardens and Tothill Fields, a large expanse of open ground.

Tothill Fields was the site of a Bridewell prison, one of a system of prisons, all called Bridewells, built specifically to incarcerate prostitutes and vagrants, whose crimes against society consisted of joblessness and homelessness. These "rogues and vagabonds" were precisely the category that, under the expanded provisions of the Licensing Act, included players in unlicensed theatres. Prisons like this Bridewell were among London's many threatening reminders of the potential consequences of poverty. Having one so close at hand, at the very time that illness left her unemployed and with her mounting debts, must have made Charlotte uneasy, especially when she considered her responsibility for her daughter.

For the moment, though, she had a roof over her head, and, while she recuperated, she had more time to devote to Kitty than ever before. Their quiet life together on Marsham Street may have aroused tender memories in Charlotte of her own childhood in Hillingdon, when she lived there alone with her invalid mother. On fine days that summer, as her strength returned, mother and daughter could have walked the country roads, along the fields and gardens, or strolled over to the river's edge to watch horses and carriages loaded onto the ferry for the trip across the river to Lambeth.

That summer there was a shortage of fine days, however. Violent rains and hailstorms pounded the city throughout July and August. Even some of the performances in the playbooths at Bartholomew Fair were cancelled on account of rain. The unpaved country roads must have been impassable during much of the summer. Charlotte, protective of her fragile health, probably spent most of her time indoors near the fire; the unseasonable weather took its toll in the increased expenditures on fuel. Perhaps she took this occasion to give Kitty lessons.

Kitty must have received some kind of more formal tutoring during her childhood, but it could not have been much (there is no indication that she ever went to school, as Charlotte had done): probably Charlotte herself, and possibly Elizabeth, gave Kitty what education she had, supplementing it with tutors when she had a steady salary and was still receiving assistance from her father. Now Charlotte may have begun to train Kitty as an actress, one way in which the child would be able to contribute to the family coffers and someday, perhaps, make her own living. Not that Charlotte's own experience was very encouraging on this score.

While Charlotte was convalescing quietly in Westminster, recovering her health but running up debt, other members of her family were experiencing their own vicissitudes. The year of 1738–39 was not a good one for several members of the Cibber family. Charlotte's closest ally in the family, Elizabeth, suffered the death of her husband, Dawson Brett, in November 1738; this loss began a series of financial misfortunes that would plague her for years and that certainly undermined her ability to help Charlotte. Her daughter, Ann, had been married the previous June to William Rufus Chetwood, the Drury Lane prompter and writer, so now Elizabeth was alone. (It is possible that Charlotte left Westminster to take up residence with her in Oxendon Street or elsewhere that winter, or that Elizabeth joined Charlotte and Kitty in Westminster.)

Even Colley, who unlike his two youngest daughters was thoroughly enjoying a comfortable life (he made nightly forays to White's Club), experienced a setback that year. After signing a lucrative contract to return to the stage (Covent Garden), he acted in a series of five plays during August, and continued into the autumn, reprising his most famous comic roles to packed houses. His audiences were nostalgically delighted to see this relic of the old, glorious days of Drury Lane in action once again. In January, however, when he attempted to play Richard III, it was a different story, for, as Benjamin Victor remembered, Colley's "usual Strength and Spirit failed him most unhappily."

The elderly actor floundered so badly that Victor went behind the scenes in the third act to ask him how he was doing. In a rare moment of vulnerability, Colley allowed his mask of insouciance to slip, whispering into Victor's ear "That he wou'd give fifty Guineas to be then sitting in his easy Chair by his own Fire-side."[1] After this season, Colley did not perform again for more than two years.

The Cibber who had the worst year by far, however—and it was a spectacularly bad one—was Theophilus. He had only himself to blame. His personal drama burst into public awareness on Tuesday, December 5, 1738, when at 9:00 A.M., in the Court of King's Bench in Middlesex, the Right Honourable Sir William Lee, Knight and Lord Chief Justice, presiding, a "remarkable Tryal" began. The complaint was criminal conversation. The plaintiff, "Mr. Theophilus Cibber, Gent.," was suing the defendant, Mr. William Sloper, Esq., for damages of £5,000, for "Assaulting, Ravishing, and carnally knowing Susannah Maria Cibber, the Plaintiff's Wife."[2]

The history behind this scandalous lawsuit was this. For the first three years of their marriage, Theophilus and Susannah had seemed happy enough, or so Colley testified at the trial. But the marriage inevitably soured. Theophilus had continued in his dissipated extravagance and spent his wife's income to support it. He lived constantly on the edge of arrest and prison. (A story circulated that Colley had encountered his indebted son wearing a particularly expensive suit, and had reproved him for his extravagance. "The'," said his father, "I pity you." "Don't pity me," replied Theo. "Pity my tailor.")[3]

As Theo's expenses soared, he made increasing demands upon his wife, whose fame—and salary—were growing. Susannah had never attempted to enforce the prenuptial agreement that her mother had insisted on, assuring her the right to dispose of her own income. So Theophilus received Susannah's money as his own, justifying this by custom and the law, and by buying her costly presents and residing in an expensive house in Wild Court that drove them further into debt. Once, when particularly desperate for money, Theophilus even raided Susannah's stage costumes and jewels.

But Susannah possessed, or so Theophilus believed, promising sources of income beyond her Drury Lane salary—namely, her wealthy male admirers, including William Sloper, the married son of a rich and influential Berkshire gentleman. Theophilus, scenting a potentially lucrative mark, encouraged Sloper's attentions and urged Susannah to do the same. The three could often be seen together, dining at Sloper's expense; at some point Sloper began giving Theophilus an allowance of money. During the summer of 1737, the threesome lived handsomely in a house Sloper had taken in Kingston-on-Thames, a resort not far from Hampton Court. So successful was Theophilus in getting money from Sloper that he privately took to calling him "Mr. Benefit."

At some point, Theophilus added new elements to his manipulation of Sloper, adopting a strategy uncannily similar to that of the cynical Mr. Modern in Fielding's *The Modern Husband*. (Fielding must have heard the reports of the trial with amusement.) During their stay in Kingston, Theo made a habit of leaving Susannah and William alone together for long periods. Soon, according to the testimony of their confidential maid, Anne Hopson, Theophilus encouraged Susannah to begin sexual relations with Sloper. According to Mrs. Hopson, Susannah initially was reluctant, but Theophilus forced her at gunpoint into Sloper's bed. Thus Susannah and William became lovers. The three developed a routine: after Theophilus and Susannah readied themselves for bed each night, he would conduct his wife and her pillow into Sloper's adjoining bedroom, making sure to bring her pillow back to his own bed the next morning for the servants' benefit. (They were not fooled, however, being well able to see which bed bore the imprint of one body and which of two.)

Theophilus congratulated himself on this surefire means of securing Sloper's devotion and money; but what he did not anticipate was that Susannah would come to return Sloper's affection. In fact, the sexual relationship blossomed into a genuine love affair. How different William Sloper's steady devotion must have seemed to Susannah, when compared with Theophilus's exploitative abuse.

When they all returned to London for the 1737–38 season, William secretly rented rooms in Leicester Fields so that he and Susannah could be alone together. Theophilus, who employed a spy to follow his wife, was aware of this and uneasy, but he endured it for financial reasons. Despite the boost to his income, however, his debts mounted to such a degree that he had to give up the couple's Wild Street house and pile up his furniture in the street for sale. He convinced Sloper to rent another house for the three of them in Kensington, but this time the ménage-à-trois was short-lived: his creditors closed in, forcing Theophilus to flee to France. Just as he was preparing to leave, in April, Susannah confessed that she was in love with Sloper and requested a separation. It was unlikely that either she or William could get a divorce, for they would need their spouses' consent and, in any case, were unwilling to undergo the public scrutiny a divorce act in Parliament always brought. As it happened, they underwent far worse.

Theophilus chafed in exile in Calais, although he remained confident of his power over Susannah, refusing to acknowledge her desire to leave him. But, when the playhouse closed for the season, Susannah accompanied William to Buckinghamshire, where she discovered at some point that she was pregnant with his child. Theo joined them temporarily after he returned to England in June, but there the matter reached a head. Susannah, with new courage, declared her resolve to stay with William, and Sloper threw Theo out.

Facing the prospect of being stripped of his wife, her income, and Sloper's allowance, Theophilus plotted his counterattack. First, he attempted to create what we would now call a paper trail, a public record that cast a sympathetic light on himself. Susannah's biographer Mary Nash argues convincingly that in late summer Theophilus wrote and backdated a series of letters he later published, claiming to have written them in France.[4] In them he presented himself as a wronged husband, claiming that Susannah alone deceitfully orchestrated her liaison with Sloper. These letters may have been written calculatingly, with the public in mind, as Nash says, but they do seem to shed some light on Theo's emotional state at the time: he was overwhelmed with outrage and loss. The obvious elimination of his scheme for getting money was not the only issue. He seems to have been genuinely distraught at losing his wife.

Finally, Theophilus acted. In early September, as the lovers were having breakfast in their nightclothes in the Buckinghamshire house, Theo appeared at the head of an armed party of men, asserted his legal right to Susannah, and forcibly abducted her. According to witnesses, as she left, Susannah removed an expensive watch that William had given her and returned it to him lest Theophilus confiscate it—an eloquent gesture that later became the subject of a widely circulated engraving.

William dressed and followed, but could do little against an armed party. In London, however, he enlisted Susannah's brother Thomas Arne, who, unlike William, could act in this regard without exposing himself to criminal prosecution. Arne discovered the house where Theophilus was holding Susannah under guard and brought his own armed group of men to the door, where he had the presence of mind to call to Susannah to scream for help, in order to make clear that she was held against her will. Susannah's cries quickly attracted the usual mob, who helped Arne's party free her. Thomas took her to their mother's house in St. Giles (their father was dead by this time), and the next day Mrs. Arne and Susannah swore the peace against Theophilus. This, the eighteenth-century equivalent of a restraining order, removed her from his control. Barred from physically approaching his wife, Theophilus turned to the courts.

On that morning in December 1738, the prosecution opened the trial with witnesses called to prove that there had indeed been a sexual relationship between Mrs. Cibber and Mr. Sloper. The star witness was the husband, apparently foreign-born, of their Leicester Fields landlady, Mrs. Hayes. Perhaps he had been paid by Theophilus to spy on Susannah, or perhaps he was simply an opportunistic voyeur, but Mr. Hayes's testimony was sensational. Having taken the expedient of boring a hole through the wainscoting between their room and an adjoining closet, he said, he had a view of Susannah and William that was "very plain."

> He used to kiss her, and take her on his Lap. On the 22nd Day of *December* I was looking through; he took her on his Knee, lifted up her Clothes, and took down his Breeches, and took his privy Member and put it in his Hand, and put it between her Legs. . . . On the 12 day of *January,* I was lock'd up in the Closet at one o'Clock in the Afternoon . . . he took her upon his Lap, took up her Clothes, took down his Breeches, and put his privy Member between her Legs. I stayed there longer. Between five and six in the Evening, he let down the Turn-up Bed softly, she laid herself upon it, upon her Back, and pulled up her Clothes; her Body was bare. He unbuttoned his Clothes, hung his Bag-wig upon a Sconce, let down his Breeches, took his privy Member in his Hand, and lay down upon her.

"Being a Foreigner," the account of the trial elabourated, the witness "expressed himself as much by Gestures as by Words." At that point, the lord chief justice interrupted Hayes's testimony, commenting that there was "no occasion to be more particular; we are not trying a Rape."[5]

The defence, led by "Mr. Serjeant Eyre," represented the case as the seduction of an innocent young gentleman from the country by two hardened theatre professionals. Eyre asserted that players know how to assume characters, and because they are constantly playing love scenes, are particularly open to love, "without any Confinement of the Passion to a particular Subject." Women of the stage, he continued, "learn all the Allurements that can engage the Eye and Ear, and strike the Imagination of young Gentlemen."[6]

After using the bad reputation of the theatre to denigrate not only Theophilus's character but Susannah's as well, the defence concluded its case. The closing remarks were delivered by a young, relatively inexperienced lawyer named William Murray, who argued that, if the clear evidence of an affair between Susannah and William made it necessary to find for the plaintiff, the jury should give him as small an amount as possible. The jury concurred, finding for Theophilus, but awarding him token damages of a mere ten pounds.[7]

The trial made William Murray's career, sullied Theophilus's, and devastated Susannah's. An eyewitness account was published immediately, so everyone could read and gossip about the graphic, humiliating testimony. The actress who had been celebrated for her pathos-laden performances as innocent sufferers was represented in the most offensive and public way as an immoral schemer who had prostituted herself. But William Sloper's devotion remained unchanged.

Sloper took rooms for Susannah as she approached her lying-in, and he continued to visit her regularly. A daughter was born, whom they named Molly. Theophilus had not yet abandoned his claims on his wife, however, and tracked her down, vowing to sue Sloper again. As Theophilus prepared for a second lawsuit, William took Susannah out of London into the country. She dropped out of sight for nearly two years, her name dishonoured by scandal, her career in tatters.

In early December 1739, exactly a year after the first trial, Theophilus took before the court his second suit against Sloper, this time for "Detaining the Plaintiff's Wife." He asked damages of £10,000, both to punish Sloper and to compensate for his loss of Susannah's income. This time the jury, unsympathetic to Theophilus but faced with the

*Susannah Cibber, Charlotte's sister-in-law and Theo's long-suffering wife, was one of London's great tragic actresses. (*Susannah Cibber, *after* Thomas Hudson. *Courtesy of the Henry E. Huntington Library.)*

Theophilus Cibber, whose attempts to profit from his wife's attractiveness to her fans led to one of London's most scandalous marital imbroglios. (R. Clamp, Theophilus Cibber in the Character of a Fine Gentleman, *after a drawing by Thomas Worlidge. Courtesy of the Henry E. Huntington Library.)*

evidence of Sloper's continued association with Susannah, brought in a verdict of £500.[8]

Charlotte's attitude towards her brother and sister-in-law throughout this scandal must have been mixed. Relations with Theo had been somewhat chilled because of her alliance with Fielding, but there had been no rupture between them, and he had remained, besides Elizabeth, her only other ally in her family. She had had reason to resent Susannah for Colley's attentions to her. But she must have identified with the burden of an unloved and dissolute husband trying to appropriate one's income, and unlike certain other members of her family, Susannah did not abandon Charlotte. In her autobiography, Charlotte publicly expressed her gratitude to her sister-in-law for helping her with presents of money, often unsolicited, on numerous occasions over the years. It is possible that Susannah first came to her assistance after Charlotte's illness brought an end to her puppet show, when Charlotte would particularly have felt the kindness.

It was probably in the summer of 1739 that Charlotte, having largely recovered her health, decided to try to make use of her valuable puppets once again. Since the London season was ended and the modish audiences she desired to attract were out of the city, she determined to go to Tunbridge Wells, a fashionable spa, to stage some shows there. Perhaps she was influenced by her knowledge that her father had taken to stopping by Tunbridge Wells early in the summer before going to his now annual sojourn in Bath (where, word had it, he was writing his autobiography).

Once this idea occurred to her, Charlotte gathered up her puppets, collected a small troupe of operators and her daughter, and marched on Tunbridge Wells without stopping to further investigate the details. When she arrived, however, she found the field already taken: the famous Mr. Lacon had already established himself as a puppeteer there for a number of years, and there was no room for a newcomer. Rather than give up entirely, Charlotte rented a performance venue called Ashley's Great Room, and, with her small company of puppeteers-turned-actors (they probably *were* originally actors), gave a sparsely cast series of plays—a few comedies and *The London Merchant*. (These were illegal performances, but the Licensing Act was much less consistently enforced outside of London, and she did not play long.) Charlotte could not have earned much money from these performances—probably scarcely enough to cover cart hire to bring her puppets and troupe to Tunbridge Wells and take them home again.

Charlotte was too fragile physically to mount a new puppet theatre and more and more desperately in need of money.[9] The weather that winter would not have helped her situation: the Great Frost of 1739–40 hit London on Christmas Day and continued until mid-February. Though the frigid weather occasioned much festivity—booths were erected, coaches rolled, and an ox was roasted on the frozen Thames—the cold air and dense coal smoke must have taken a toll on Charlotte's health, just as the costs of keeping warm further depleted her purse.

Charlotte finally was forced to sell her puppets. The marionettes had cost her more than £500, but she sold them for £20 to a purchaser who, she said bitterly, "knew the original Expence of them, and the Reality of their worth." This buyer was Isaac Fawkes, a well-known conjurer and showman who used the puppets at the fairs beginning in 1740, advertising them, rather gallingly, as "Mr. Punch's celebrated comedians . . . formerly Mrs. Charke's from the Theatre in the Haymarket."[10]

Charlotte must have been very sad indeed to see her magnificent puppets go, and with them her hopes for a stable and successful—even "genteel"—business. The fact that they were now the property of a mere showman rather than a genuine actor like herself (in terms of the hierarchy that governed the theatre world and her own thinking), made the sale all the more painful. Speaight imagines the fate of the puppets in these terms, too: "no doubt they played up and down the country for many years, a sad and pale reflection amid the violent fairground drolls of Charlotte Charke's elegant and ill-fated enterprise."[11]

Charlotte was still in mourning for the loss of her puppets when, she says, she entered into one of the more mysterious relationships of her life. Its details remain obscure, but in one respect this episode followed a pattern that was starting to become all too characteristic: hopes raised and then disappointed. The account she gives of this relationship in her autobiography is worth quoting at length.

> Not long after I had parted from what might really, by good Management, have brought me in a very comfortable Subsistence, and in a gen-

teel Light [her puppets], I was addressed by a worthy Gentleman (being then a Widow) and closely pursued 'till I consented to an honourable, though very secret Alliance; and, in Compliance to the Person, bound myself by all the Vows sincerest Friendship could inspire, never to confess who he was. Gratitude was my Motive to consent to this Conjunction, and extream fondness was his Inducement to request it.

The mystery of this "honourable, though very secret Alliance" was increased by Charlotte's refusal to identify the worthy gentleman even fifteen years later: "nor shall any Motive whatever make me break that Vow I made to the Person, by a Discovery of his Name."

Commentators have tended to assume that this was Charlotte's second marriage (which she contracted in 1746) and that she misdated it by five or six years in her autobiography.[12] But that would have been an unusually large mistake for her. And when she discussed the relationship in the body of her text, she did not call it a marriage. Though "alliance" was a word that could signify marriage—as well as other sorts of relationships and affinities—why would she not have been specific about the nature of this alliance, if she was willing to acknowledge it at all?

The term "alliance" (and a very secret, if honourable, one at that) could also imply that this was a lover, or, in the balder contemporary term, a "keeper"; a man with whom she contracted a sexual relationship in exchange for his financial support of her and Kitty. This is not to deny that there could have been a serious emotional attachment between them, as Charlotte says: "extream fondness" existed on his side; gratitude on hers. (It is interesting, and revealing, that she avoids implying that she herself was actuated by desire for this man.)

The exchange of sex for money, whether sanctified by marriage or not, was the most common livelihood for women of Charlotte's day and class, and "keeping" was prevalent among actresses. Perhaps her lover was a married man; still, some extenuating circumstances seem to have allowed Charlotte to justify this as an "honourable Alliance": if not a clandestine marriage, it may have been a relationship with a man who was estranged from his wife (as was common enough in an era of arranged and mercenary marriages), even formally or informally separated from her. He may have had a wife who was chronically ill or even incarcerated in Bedlam (or a more genteel private asylum). In an era virtually without divorce, there were many ways to rationalize an adulterous alliance as honourable. (One can find many permutations on this thinking in the pages of Defoe's novels of intrepid women such as Moll Flanders and Roxana—Charlotte's fictional counterparts in many ways.)

One other element of Charlotte's account is particularly provocative: she implied that this relationship was responsible for her dressing, as she expressed it, "en cavalier." How shall we understand this? It seems nearly certain that Charlotte was already a well-established cross-dresser by this point (in her autobiography, she gave several motivations for her adoption of men's clothes). Perhaps the nature of her cross-dressing was changing, as it became more important as a means of hiding her identity. Perhaps she was now trying seriously, on occasion, to pass as a man.

Passing as a man would have had obvious benefits in an illicit affair or secret marriage, allowing Charlotte to come and go incognito from their meeting place. In any event, her lover seems to have had enough money to provide for her and Kitty, and to sustain her both financially and emotionally at a difficult time. Charlotte's spirits began to rise, as she allowed herself to hope that she had "secured myself far above those Distresses I have known." But once again, that promise of security and relief, seemingly so close at hand, proved elusive—for, not long after they had begun their alliance, the man suddenly died.

It was an emotional blow and a financial disaster. Charlotte said that "by the unexpected Stroke of Death [her expression suggests something very sudden], I was deprived of every Hope and Means of a Support." Not only was Charlotte deprived of support—an additional indication that this was not a legal marriage, since the man seems to have had money that she had no legal claim to—but it placed her in a more precarious position than ever: "I was left involved with Debts I had no Means of paying."

Perhaps Charlotte had taken the lodgings where she met with her lover in her own name and, upon the expectation of his paying the bills, had furnished and supplied them comfortably; perhaps she had bought herself and Kitty new, expensive clothes upon the same supposition. As a result, upon "the villainous Instigation" of a "wicked drunken Woman," Charlotte was arrested for a debt of £7 "when, as Heaven shall judge me, I did not know where to raise as many Pence."

Charlotte now underwent the terror and mortification of being seized by a bailiff, who had found her easily because, though she was dressed as a man, he had been given a precise description of her "very handsome lac'd Hat" (revealing the limitations of this kind of disguise if one's taste in male clothing was particularly showy). Visions of Southwark's dreaded Marshalsea Prison loomed before her, "the Gates of which I thought, though at that Time in the Middle of Covent-Garden, stood wide open for my Reception." Charlotte envisioned the all-too-real horrors of debtor's prison: its extortionate jailors, its often vicious prisoners, its stench, its vermin, its damp, seeping walls, its jail fever (typhoid), which could put a quick end even to someone whose health was not fragile.

Eighteenth-century law gave creditors the right to press warrants against their debtors. The obvious irony, of course, was that an imprisoned debtor was not necessarily ever able to pay off the debt, especially since incarceration was expensive. Prisoners paid a "garnish" to other inmates when they entered the prison, at risk of losing their clothes if they did not; they paid for accommodation in the less foul quarters of the prison; they paid for some kind of straw bedding to place on the cold, often wet ground; they paid for food other than bread and water—sometimes, as in the Marshalsea, they had to pay even for that.

Prisoners who could not pay fared horribly, even to the point of starving to death; if you walked past a prison, you would hear the inmates begging for money from its windows. Creditors—who were legally responsible for paying to maintain debtors imprisoned on their account, but often ignored that requirement—could keep a debtor in prison for life. "For debt only," wrote Defoe (who knew what he was talking about), "are men condemned to languish in perpetual imprisonment, and to starve without mercy, redeemed only by the grave. Kings show mercy to traitors, to murtherers and thieves . . . but in debt we are lost to this world. We cannot obtain the favour of being hanged or transported, but our lives must linger within the walls, till released by the grave."[13] In 1759, according to an outraged article in *The Gentleman's Magazine*, there were some 20,000 debtors in prison, where one fourth of them died every year.[14] Charlotte envisioned these horrors when she imagined herself forced to "linger out a wretched life in Prison," while Kitty was "despised only for being mine; and, perhaps, reduced to Beggary."

The bailiff who arrested Charlotte, however, was compassionate. More cynically, it might be said that he was in fact self-interested, for it was to his advantage not to remand her to the Marshalsea or the Fleet, since money might be made by keeping her at his house. Bailiff's houses, which served as prisons themselves, were known as "sponging houses," and bailiffs had the power to imprison debtors there and even, for a fee, to allow them to live outside the prison as long as someone stood security, or bail, for them. Charlotte's bailiff, swayed by "a trifling Favour" given to him by a friend of hers, set her free for two days to try to find two "bails," financially respectable people who would act as security for her.

The friend who came to Charlotte's assistance with the timely bribe was herself far from respectable, for it was none other than Betty Careless, occasional actress, former keeper of a bagnio, and just about this time, proprietor of a coffeehouse in Playhouse Passage, Covent Garden.[15] Betty had an attorney friend arrange for "a note of indemnification" from one Mr. Mytton, who ran the Cross-keys Tavern. Mytton thus became one of Charlotte's bails. Given the tendency of her friends to be in financial trouble themselves, she could not have expected finding the second one to be easy. Indeed, a frantic day of scouring London proved fruitless, and Charlotte had to turn herself in to the sponging house.

She had not been there an hour when Betty Careless returned at the head of a contingent of women. These were coffeehouse (and brothel) keepers of Covent Garden, who tried to offer money for the release of "poor Sir Charles," as they called her. But they were unable to raise enough money to pay both the debt and the bailiff's fees, though they offered to stand as security themselves, an offer the bailiff declined.

The picture of this highly disreputable band of prostitutes, bawds, and keepers of rowdy houses coming to the aid of their cross-dressed friend Sir Charles conjures up an image of the sort of low-life female society caricatured in satires such as *The Covent-Garden Tragedy*, *The Beggar's Opera*, and *The Rake's Progress*. It offers us, too, a glimpse of a very real female solidarity that existed outside the bounds of respectable society: a particular example of the mutually supportive "credit networks" that existed among the poor.[16]

All the time that Charlotte was combing the city to find a second bail, Kitty (whom Charlotte later identified as eight years old then, but who was more likely ten), was left alone at their lodgings throughout the night, wondering desperately what had become of her mother.[17] When Charlotte did send for her the following morning, the girl arrived, "with her Eyes over-flowed with Tears, and a Heart full of undissembled Anguish."

Spurred by her daughter's distress, Charlotte promptly wrote letters to thirty-eight people—including, certainly, members of her family—and sent poor Kitty out to deliver them. It was not her relatives who came to her relief, however, but the Covent Garden ladies once again—this time with an additional two guineas from Elizabeth Hughes (who ran a coffeeshop in Playhouse Passage, where she also sold and rented masquerade costumes "of the Genteelest and best Sort"), and another guinea from Mrs. Jane Douglass, known, in John Gay's words, as "that inimitable Courtesan."[18] Mother Douglass kept a particularly elegant brothel in the Covent Garden Piazza; after the death of Mother Needham—who was stoned to death in the stocks—she had assumed her place as Britain's best-known bawd, catering to an illustrious clientele.[19] Together the prostitutes and bawds covered Charlotte's debt, took her out for a good dinner, and sent her home with the present of a guinea for Kitty.

Charlotte nonetheless remained at risk of arrest for her other debts. The bailiff—once again displaying compassion mixed with self-interest—advised her to rid herself of her easily identifiable silver-laced hat (of the currently fashionable smaller style), offering to exchange it for his own coachman-styled hat, bedecked with heavy crape against the cold. The bailiff, Charlotte said, could have played Falstaff without the padding, and the two made a comical contrast: he with her tiny hat perched atop his head (he undoubtedly sold it later), and Charlotte obscured to the eyes in his oversized, tobacco-fouled one. The image of Charlotte dwarfed by a man's hat conjures up the picture of her four-year-old self-display in her father's hat so many years before: the difference between Colley's elegant laced hat and the bailiff's coarse one speaks volumes about the turn Charlotte's life had taken in the intervening twenty-three years.

Charlotte's brief imprisonment in the sponging house and her rescue by the Covent Garden ladies probably took place in 1740, when Charlotte was twenty-seven. She holed up with Kitty in a gloomy set of rooms in Great Queen Street (the street on which Richard's former mistress had lived, and perhaps still did, to Charlotte's disgust). The ramshackle old house seemed liable to collapse at any moment. She now lived the fearful, backward-glancing life of a debtor, a life lived by thousands in eighteenth-century London, including at different times her grandfather, her brother, and her husband. Skulking indoors during the week, she became a "Sunday man," the cant term for "one who goes abroad on that day only, for fear of arrest."[20] (Debtors could not be arrested on Sundays.) Poor Kitty, wretched with fear of penury and of losing her mother, fell seriously ill. This time, Theophilus reached into his own nearly empty purse to pay for an apothecary to examine her. Perhaps he felt a new sense of connection to his younger sister, now that she was a fellow debtor.

18

DOWN AND OUT IN LONDON

(1741–44)

One Sunday morning during Kitty's illness, Charlotte left her daughter in the care of their landlady while she went out to "prog for her and myself," as she put it, by selling her clothes. That morning she convinced an acquaintance to buy her "beautiful Pair of Sleeve-Buttons"— at a fraction of their value, no doubt. Returning to Great Queen Street two hours later, Charlotte discovered that soon after she had left, Kitty had gone up to their room and not come down again. The landlady supposed (without bothering to check) that she had fallen asleep. Alarmed, Charlotte rushed upstairs, and discovered her daughter writhing on the floor in convulsions.

As her horrified mother hung over her, Kitty's contortions suddenly ceased, and she lay still. Charlotte pulled Kitty into her arms, where she slumped, her body a dead weight. Panicked, she dropped the girl with a thud and ran into the street, screaming and distracted, "with my Shirt-Sleeves dangling loose about my Hands [she had just pawned her buttons], my Wig standing on End, 'Like Quills upon the fretful Porcupine,'"

And proclaiming the sudden Death of my much-beloved Child, a Crowd soon gathered round me, and, in the Violence of my Distraction, instead of administering any necessary Help, [I] wildly stood among the Mob to recount the dreadful Disaster. The People's Compassion was moved, 'tis true; but, as I happened not to be known to them, it drew them into

Astonishment, to see the Figure of a young Gentleman, so extravagantly grieved for the Loss of a Child. As I appeared very young, they looked on it as an unprecedented Affection in a Youth, and began to deem me a Lunatick, rather then [*sic*] that there was any Reality in what I said.

Finally someone from her lodgings came to find Charlotte and take her home. Kitty had not been dead, just unconscious. The child's convulsions recurred throughout the night, but she survived.

This scene, as Charlotte recounted it in her autobiography, is both harrowing and funny (Charlotte often struck this combination of notes when she told the story of her life: the detail of her *wig*'s hairs standing on end is particularly amusing). But the passage also reveals much about Charlotte's self-presentation: she portrayed herself, in her genuine distress for Kitty, suffering as a mother but behaving as an actress. (Her choice of a quotation from *Hamlet*—updating the original "porpentine" to "porcupine"—to describe her terror compounds the story's theatricality.) Instead of securing help from the crowd, Charlotte enacted a scene of maternal anguish worthy of Agnes or Andromache—with one difference: her men's clothes.

The crowd did not know Charlotte or anything about her, so their response provides an indication of how she appeared to strangers on the street: that is, to most people she encountered in London. They interpreted Charlotte according to her dress—which, even in its disordered state, signified that she was a man—rather than according to her behaviour. (A father would not have been expected to grieve so extravagantly and publicly the death of a child.) Likewise, Charlotte's smooth, beardless face signified not that she was a woman in her late twenties, but that she was a "very young" gentleman. And if her behaviour signified anything, it was that "he" was mad.

As Charlotte nursed Kitty back to health, she was spared further decimations of her wardrobe by the timely assistance of an old friend. Adam Hallam was an Irish-born actor whom she had met when she began at Drury Lane; he had been one of the mutineers, and his professional path had crossed Charlotte's frequently ever since. Hallam was close to Charlotte's age. He, like she, was a member of an extended theatrical family (it was his father, Thomas, who had been run through the eye by

Charles Macklin in Drury Lane's green room). Unlike Charlotte, Adam was employed, for he had been established in the patent theatre companies at the time of the Licensing Act. (Through spring 1741 he was at Covent Garden; he went back to Drury Lane beginning the next autumn.)

Hallam lived next door to Charlotte's lodging house in Great Queen Street. His wife had lived with him there, but she had died in June 1740, and now he opened his doors to Charlotte, not only sending her a present of money, but also inviting her to become a regular guest at his table. There, in delicate consideration of her feelings, he often put aside other engagements to join her rather than leaving her to dine with the servants, or alone as an obvious "pensioner."

Ever mindful of the bailiffs, Charlotte came and went surreptitiously by Hallam's back door, through the garden. This fact, along with her great fondness for Adam—she referred to him as a "sincere Friend"—led Holland to speculate that they were lovers. It is certainly possible: Hallam was a kind and very good-looking man. But Charlotte's autobiography gives no hint of any amorous involvement. Theirs could have been a brief, friendly affair—perhaps along the lines of her earlier one: fondness on his part, gratitude on hers—but the detail of her sneaking into his house through the back door can be adequately explained by her need to avoid arrest. (Adam remarried in 1743.)[1]

Hallam's largess helped Charlotte's little family through the worst of Kitty's illness, but once Kitty was recovered enough, her mother again had to leave her in the landlady's care while she looked for work. Charlotte landed a job as a waiter with one Mrs. Dorr, proprietor of the King's Head tavern and "ordinary" (eating house) in Marylebone. It was probably at this time that her ability to pass as a man offstage first became crucial to her employment. An old friend of the Cibber family had persuaded her husband to recommend her to Mrs. Dorr as "Charles," a "young Gentleman of a decay'd Fortune," who needed employment.

Mrs. Dorr's only concern, as she sympathetically noted the "melancholy Aspect" of Charles's face, was that he would find it unpleasant to serve the tavern's lower-middle-class clientele, who were his social inferiors. Charlotte, without repudiating her status as a gentleman, responded that she was ready to undertake any kind of honest labour. In her new career as a waiter—she was, she says, "the only Appearance of a Male" in the house, excepting the customers—she greatly pleased her employer with her agility in carrying trays of food and ale up and down the ordinary's steep stairs. When Mrs. Dorr found that Charles also was fluent in French and could converse with the French tailors and German wig makers who made up a significant part of the tavern's customers, she was overjoyed, for heretofore they could communicate only by gestures.

Mrs. Dorr became so fond of her new waiter that she regularly invited him to dine with her. Indeed, she soon came to look on him, Charlotte said, as "rather her Son than her Servant." Not only was Charles better bred than the others, but he also possessed an unusual sensitivity. When Charles told her that he had a ten-year-old daughter and that his wife had died giving birth to her, Mrs. Dorr was amazed "to hear a young Fellow speak so feelingly of a Child." She asked to meet Kitty and kindly commiserated with the girl over "her's and her supposed Father's Unhappiness." (That Kitty was able, at such a young age, to play this scene without revealing her "father's" secret testifies to her promise as an actress.)

Marylebone in the 1740s was a semirural area in northwest London, largely consisting of fields punctuated by an occasional farm, sewage dump, burial ground, or tavern. Fidelis Morgan locates the King's Head Tavern at the Tottenham Court Turnpike, a cluster of buildings at the top of Tottenham Court Road at the intersection of the Hampstead and Euston—then called New—Roads. (The tavern is one of those pictured by Hogarth in *The March to Finchley*.)[2]

Every day Charlotte walked between Marylebone and Great Queen Street. She would arrive at the King's Head in the morning and not leave until ten or eleven at night, when she would try to disappear into the crowds as she entered Covent Garden. Bailiffs were not Charlotte's only worry. Her route took her through long stretches of dark, sparsely populated country where footpads lurked, and then through the squalid, dangerous neighbourhoods of St. Giles. But since she "used to jog along with the Air of a raw, unthinking, pennyless 'Prentice," she passed unscathed.

Charlotte settled into a routine, responding warmly to Mrs. Dorr's maternal affection and spending her time on less busy weekdays working in the garden. If Mrs. Dorr found her employee an attractively unusual young man, so, apparently, did a young kinswoman of hers. One day as Charles was in the garden planting some Windsor beans, the maid approached him and, in a tone of excited confidence, told him that he could make his fortune by marrying the kinswoman, who had taken a fancy to him. (It seems that the maid had concocted this story, though there may have been some truth in it; she had also told the kinswoman that Charles was enamored of her.) Charlotte's reaction to this news is telling: she felt repugnance—not at the idea of *a* woman falling in love with her, but at the idea of *that* woman doing so. She, Charlotte said, "had no one Qualification to recommend her to the Regard of any Thing beyond a Porter or a Hackney-Coachman." The issue was not gender, but class: however low her fortunes had fallen, Charlotte still clung to her identity as a gentleman.

As if the maid's meddling had not created complications enough, shortly thereafter someone came into the tavern and "hinted" that Charles was a woman. With her identity exposed, Charlotte had to leave Mrs. Dorr and search for new employment. (Mrs. Dorr, who regretted the departure of her Charles, not long thereafter lost her entire business thanks to some shady dealings by her relatives. She stayed in contact with Charlotte, however, and visited her later, when she professed herself still unwilling to believe that such an appealing young man could be a woman.)

Charlotte's employment at the King's Head, though hard to date conclusively, probably covered the spring and summer of 1741, when she was twenty-eight.[3] Shortly after that, for the first time since her puppet theatre collapsed, she returned to acting. Enterprising managers of unlicensed troupes were testing the limits of the Licensing Act. In 1740–41, Henry Giffard reopened Goodman's Fields Theatre and played a full season there, using the "concert formula": he announced a concert for which admission was charged; at the concert, the audience would be treated, "gratis," to a play as well. Giffard owned a small share of the Drury Lane patent, and the authorities did not interfere. His example opened the way for smaller theatres, and from this season on, brief runs of plays would appear at places such as the James Street Tennis Court. And the various spas on the outskirts of town—the New Wells in Clerkenwell and Sadler's Wells near Islington, for instance—featured programmes of "entertainments," including music, dancing, and pantomimes, also without effectual interference.[4]

Hogarth's depiction of the King's Head Tavern captures Mother Douglass (lower right) and her prostitutes leaning from the windows. (William Hogarth, The March to Finchley, *1750. Courtesy of the Henry E. Huntington Library.)*

Now Charlotte became more than ever a denizen of the night— "Owl-Light," she called it—when she would "creep out, in Search of Adventures." Risky adventures these were, even under cover of darkness, since at any moment she might be recognized by her creditors. But plays were again being acted and there were opportunities to perform, however brief and marginal. Charlotte frequently crept to the James Street Theatre, where "with trembling Limbs and aching Heart," she would try to pick up a role. But even inside the theatre, she had to exercise extreme caution, for the bailiffs frequently lurked in these venues.

One night in late September 1741, Charlotte was hiding in the green room as the cast prepared to perform *The Recruiting Officer,* when the actor playing Captain Plume confessed that he did not know a single line of his part.[5] Seeing her advantage, Charlotte whispered to the manager that she could play it—perhaps. "To be sure, Ma'am," she craftily told the manager, "I'd do any thing to oblige you: But I'm quite unprepared—I have nothing here proper—I want a Pair of White Stockings, and clean Shirt." (In fact, this was a negotiating strategy: "in Case of a lucky Hit," Charlotte had "all those Things ready in my Coat-Pocket; as I was certain, let what Part would befal me, Cleanliness was a necessary Ingredient.") Hearing the audience noisily "clattering for a Beginning," Charlotte held out for a guinea, and the manager was forced to agree. Afterward, in order to get home without being arrested, Charlotte traded clothes with an even more tattered friend, making her way home unrecognized in his rags.

But opportunities to perform were still in short supply. So, for the first time, Charlotte's search for acting jobs took her outside of London, where she could occasionally make a pittance performing with actors whose abilities she despised. Another old acquaintance, "Jockey" Adams (a "strange, unaccountable Mortal," Charlotte called him, who got his nickname for dancing the Jockey Dance to the tune "Horse to Newmarket"), offered her a position with his temporary touring company. He seems to have been in the same financial straits as Charlotte.

On this occasion, Charlotte assumed, for the first time, the name Charles Brown. This was probably a way to dodge her creditors, since Adams was not going to travel far enough from London for safety, but perhaps she was also ashamed of having fallen so low as to join a troupe of strolling players. Brown, of course, was her sister Catherine's surname, signifying her marriage into a wealthy, influential family. Charlotte must have appropriated it as an affront to her sister, but often Charlotte's affronts (such as her burlesques of Colley and Theo, or even her attempts to be a shopkeeper like Anne) seem also to have been assertions of kinship, even some peculiar kind of homage. They were Charlotte's way of insisting upon family ties that her relatives could not undo, however much they tried.

Charlotte travelled with Adams to a town within four miles of London, where her "courtship" of the young heiress (recounted in the prologue to this book) occurred.[6] Had she been really what she pretended to be on that occasion, Charlotte observed, she "might have rid in my own Coach, in the Rear of six Horses." Instead, she returned from her visit to the young woman unbetrothed, disappointing some male members of her troupe who had offered "to supply my Place in the Dark, to conceal the Fraud." What action of her life, Charlotte asked them contemptuously, "had been so very monstrous, to excite them to think me capable of one so cruel and infamous?" (And illegal.)

After her tour with Adams ended, Charlotte briefly returned to London, but was soon summoned by another manager to join his troupe at Dartford, Kent, about twenty miles from London. Unable to afford a coach, Charlotte had to walk there through a "dreadful Shower of Rain" that soaked her thin shoes and left her so hoarse that she was unable to perform after the first night. Whereupon the manager fired her, "an excellent Demonstration," she said, "of those low-lived Wretches! who have no farther Regard to the Persons they employ . . . and look upon Players like Pack-Horses, though they live by 'em."

Charlotte and Kitty were again reduced to pawning their clothes, until they were "stripp'd to even but a bare Change to keep us decently clean." But then she met a woman who had scenery and clothes in pawn that could be redeemed for two guineas. Charlotte would have been hard pressed to come up with twopence, but she wrote to a friend pretending to be incarcerated in a sponging house, and had the note delivered by a player who looked rough enough to be a bailiff. Getting the money, she and the woman redeemed the costumes, cobbled together a troupe, and sailed down the Thames to Gravesend, the port at the river's estuary. There, and afterward at nearby Harwich, they enjoyed some success for several weeks, until the woman left the troupe, taking the props with her. Her husband was in Newgate Prison about to be transported to the colonies, and she found it too onerous to travel back and forth to visit him.

Now Theophilus came up with a characteristically offbeat idea, introducing Charlotte to one of his rakish friends, who introduced her to another rake, who happened to be seeking a manservant. This was the libertine Richard Annesley, sixth Earl of Anglesey, "chiefly distinguished," according to the *Dictionary of National Biography*, "for the doubts which hung about his title to the barony of Altham and the legitimacy of his children."[7] (In addition to the usual complement of mistresses, Lord Anglesey appears to have had more than one wife at the same time.) His lordship had recently arrived from Ireland to his London house, and wished to employ a valet who was well bred and could speak French. Charlotte fit those requirements admirably, and Anglesey hired her. He was perfectly aware that his new valet was a woman: the idea of having a transvestite valet helping him dress and undress obviously appealed to him.

Charlotte's employment by Lord Anglesey may have had salacious overtones, but it came as a welcome relief from her struggles. She was now the "superior Domestick" of his household, entitled to certain perquisites. She had her own table each night with a bottle of wine and a cooked dish of her choosing as well as the leftovers from his lordship's meal, and she was paid a guinea a week. In consideration of Kitty, Anglesey did not require Charlotte to sleep at his house, but allowed her to arrive each morning and depart late each night.

The earl's London household consisted of himself and his Irish mistress.[8] When there was "extraordinary company" for dinner, the mistress sat with Charlotte at her table, and when there was no company Charlotte joined the two of them at his lordship's. "Many agreeable Evenings I passed in this manner," she said, since Anglesey, for all his libertine ways, was cheerful and pleasant, and his mistress was "a sensible Woman, whose Understanding was embellished by a Fund of good Nature."

Best of all was the protection serving a peer gave Charlotte from her creditors. She could strut freely in the streets, proud "to cock my Hat in the Face of the best of the Bailiffs, and shake Hands with them into the Bargain." These happy circumstances lasted for about five weeks, until some of the earl's less liberal-minded friends interfered, convincing him that he was culpable for "entertaining one of an improper Sex in a Post of that Sort." So, reluctantly, he discharged her.

The loss of this position must have hit Charlotte hard. She and Kitty moved to Red-Lyon Square, a relatively inexpensive neighbourhood north of High Holborn and Lincoln's Inn Fields. From there, Charlotte wrote to a neighbour, the renowned tenor and actor John Beard, who within fifteen minutes of receiving her letter sent her a generous sum of money. Beard was living in Red-Lyon Square with his recent wife, the daughter of Earl Waldegrave, who had scandalized polite society by marrying him despite the earl's disapproval. (The marriage of an aristocratic male to an actress was deplorable but it did sometimes happen; the marriage of a noblewoman to an actor was an unpardonable offence.) Beard's kind gift was all the more generous since he and his wife, who had been disowned by her father, themselves were living beyond their means.[9]

With Beard's money, Charlotte bought at Newgate Market a quantity of pork, which she made into sausages. Taking Kitty with her, she ventured out to sell them at the houses of her acquaintances, and soon, she said, she "disposed, among my Friends, of my whole Cargo." Encouraged, Charlotte threw herself into her new profession as a "higgler" of sausages and poultry, trudging from door to door with her heavy basket of links.

But now she was exposed to rumours that even she considered slanderous. When she was seen with a hare that Lord Anglesey's cook had ordered, word spread that she was walking around with a string of rabbits on a pole and—here was the heart of the slander—crying them on the streets. To Charlotte this was a vicious slur: she had an honourable door-to-door business, and was *not* a street vendor. However colourful and characteristic the "cries of London" may have been, the criers themselves were stigmatized as low-life nuisances. (Newspapers at this time were publishing commentary indicating a rise in public sentiment against street vendors as disturbers of the peace.)

Charlotte could undertake the occupation of higgler without shame both because she could consider herself superior to common street vendors, and because she could transform the job into a kind of theatre. As a seller of sausages, she performed for a selected audience the sentimental character of the struggling but virtuous woman who is trying to make an honest livelihood rather than succumb to the common expedient of prostitution. Indeed, Charlotte said that when she visited her friends to sell them her meats, they "applauded" (a revealing choice of words) her attempts. She remained, first and foremost, an actress.

Charlotte soon heard reports that her door-to-door sausage business outraged her sister Catherine almost as much as her stint as a valet had done. If Catherine was so offended by her attempts to make a living, Charlotte said, all she had to do was to use her influence to bring Colley around, or simply give her money. Perhaps Catherine's outrage was intensified by the rumour mill her youngest sister seemed so adept at cranking. The image of Colley Cibber's estranged youngest daughter as a door-to-door seller of meat proved irresistible to storytellers. (Their rupture was obviously the source of some wickedly inventive gossip.) Two often-repeated anecdotes must have been even more offensive to Catherine—and certainly to Colley—than the hare-higgler story.

One story reported that Charlotte had become a fishmonger. (Fishwives, notorious for their profanity and raucousness, were the most colourful and intimidating of all vendors.) One day, according to this account, Charlotte was crying a load of fish on the street when she spied her father, whereupon she stepped up to him and slapped him in the face with a flounder. In her autobiography, Charlotte hotly denied this allegation—but in so doing she repeated it in writing, deftly offering the tale up for her readers even in the act of protesting its untruth.

The second story was more glamorous. In this account (invented, she said, by a playhouse hanger-on), Charlotte turned highwayman. She hired a "very fine Bay Gelding," borrowed a brace of pistols, and rode out to confront her father in Epping Forest.

> I stopp'd the Chariot, presented a Pistol to his Breast, and used such Terms as I am ashamed to insert; threaten'd to blow his Brains out that Moment, if he did not deliver—Upbraiding him for his Cruelty in abandoning me to those Distresses he knew I underwent, when he had it so amply in his Power to relieve me: That since he would not use that Power, I would force him to a Compliance, and was directly going to discharge upon him; but his Tears prevented me, and, asking my Pardon for his ill Usage of me, gave me his Purse with threescore Guineas, and a Promise to restore me to his Family and Love; on which I thank'd him, and rode off.

"A likely Story," exclaimed Charlotte, after she had recounted it in full, graphic detail, "that my Father and his Servants were all so intimidated, had it been true, as not to have been able to withstand a single stout Highwayman, much more a Female, and his own Daughter too!" She was enraged when she heard it, she said, less on her own account than because of the "impudent, ridiculous Picture the Scoundrel had drawn of my Father." So angry was she at this picture of Colley blubbering tears of terror, she claimed, that she ambushed the story's perpetrator and knocked him to the ground with a club.

As if humiliating gossip were not enough, Charlotte was featured in the paper war against her father, too. In 1742, an anonymous satire pictured Colley flanked by his two notorious children, Theophilus and his "Daughter Chark": "In Day-light breech'd a bullying Spark, / But a mere *Female* in the Dark."

"*G—d d—n my Liver!* cry'd She-He,
"Down, Father, with your *Dust,* dy'e see;
"I must have *Rhino, by the D—v—l,*
"So, *'Sblood!* You may as well be civil."

"Rhino" was a cant term for money. Colley, known for punctuating his conversation with oaths, seems here to have bred a foul-mouthed daughter (how much this satire exaggerated her customary speech, we cannot say). In a footnote, the author of these lines reminded his readers that Charlotte as an actress had "play'd off her Father and Brother with surprising Humour to the high Recreation of many audiences," and that she "chose to communicate herself to the Publick by Day-light in Men's Cloaths."[10]

Charlotte at first made a success of her sausage business. But, as so often when her imagination and energy seemed about to put her on a track that would sustain her, circumstances intervened to undo her tenuous equilibrium. Privation, hard labour, stress, and possibly an inherited tendency to pulmonary disorders once again took their toll: Charlotte fell ill.

Kitty, eleven or twelve at this time, had literally to bear the burden of their business by delivering the meat herself, and she was not strong enough to carry much. Charlotte was forced to neglect most of her customers. Little money came in, and her stock dwindled. Yet when she recovered, she still possessed three pounds of pork, the means of restoring her business. But once again haplessness and bad luck intervened: Charlotte left the meat on the table unattended while she went out to take the air in Red-Lyon Fields, and returned to find a dog devouring the last of it. Her rent for the previous month was due the next day, and she had no money: her landlady would surely call in the bailiffs.

Fortunately, Charlotte reported, she encountered an old gentlewoman whom she had known as a child, who sympathetically asked why she looked so sad—and why she was wearing men's clothes—and gave her enough money to pay her rent. Though the woman's generosity allowed her to avoid prosecution for a new debt, Charlotte and

Kitty still had to move out of their lodgings. Now they were cast onto the streets, destitute.

Desperate, Charlotte may have steeled herself to approach her father for relief. And if she did, it may have been on this occasion that she received in response the following letter:

September 21

To Mrs C. Charke
Madam—

The strange career which you have run for some years (a career not always unmarked by evil) debars my affording you that succor which otherwise would naturally have been extended to you as my Daughter. I must refuse therefore—with this advice—try Theophilus.

Yours in sorrow,
Colley Cibber[11]

Theophilus was in debt himself, so Colley's suggestion that Charlotte seek help from him must have been ironic. Certainly it reflected his opinion that his two youngest children deserved each other.

Once again, the absence of a specific year makes it impossible to date this letter with certainty, but it does seem to have been written later than Colley's other surviving letter to Charlotte. The tone has changed: Colley's accusation of "evil" and his flat refusal to help strike harsh notes of finality. This letter may actually have been written by Catherine: its angular script seems less to resemble Colley's usual hand than it does Catherine's (insofar as a surviving example of her signature allows us to judge her handwriting).[12] But the letter must have been written on Colley's authority, if not actually by him.

In the place of Charlotte's family, a young female friend came to her aid. This woman, though not well-to-do herself, took her and Kitty into her home, and in so doing literally saved Charlotte's life. Within a few days, Charlotte's fever had returned with such severity that she hallucinated; those tending her "hourly expected" her death. "Had it not been for the extensive Goodness" of her woman friend who nursed her, Charlotte said, "my Child must have either begged her Bread, or perished for the Want of it."

The fortunes of the other members of the Cibber family varied widely during these years of Charlotte's struggles. Elizabeth remarried, sometime after 1742 (at which point she was still being called Mrs. Brett), a man named Joseph Marples. Though Charlotte liked Joseph because of his devotion to her sister, his ability to support his wife, unfortunately, was not equal to his affection for her. Joseph later went bankrupt, and even early on the Marpleses probably were not doing well.[13] Elizabeth's daughter, Ann, and her husband, William Rufus Chetwood, were struggling financially, too: in the autumn of 1740, Chetwood was imprisoned at the King's Bench for his debts. Colley raised the money to free him by playing a benefit for him at the Covent Garden Theatre.

Charlotte would have seen virtually nothing of her sister-in-law, Susannah Cibber, in the early 1740s, but Susannah was undertaking her professional rehabilitation after having lived in seclusion with William Sloper for nearly three years. She first reappeared on the stage in Ireland, under the auspices of her longtime defenders, the actor James Quin and the composer George Frideric Handel. These powerful men began to restore Susannah's reputation and career by casting her in a series of plays and musical performances they staged in Dublin during 1741–42, the most important of which was the debut of Handel's oratorio *The Messiah*. On April 13, in its first official performance, Susannah sang one of the arias Handel had written specifically for her, the beautiful, brooding "He Was Despised." In the audience for that performance was Dr. Patrick Delany, the chancellor of St. Patrick's Cathedral, who was mourning the death of his wife. As Susannah sang in her plaintive voice the melancholy words of the aria—"He was a man of sorrows, and acquainted with grief"—Dr. Delany, moved beyond decorum, sprang to his feet and exclaimed, "Woman, for this all thy sins be forgiven thee!"[14] And, indeed, Susannah's "sins" would be forgiven her—by British theatre audiences, at least, if not by her estranged husband.

Theophilus was progressing rapidly, if unevenly, on a downward course largely of his own making. In the immediate aftermath of the first trial, he was hissed and pelted with vegetables when he showed himself onstage. He nonetheless continued to perform at Drury Lane that season, but after many more quarrels with Fleetwood, Quin, and

Macklin, he left to join John Rich's troupe at Covent Garden the following year. By 1741–42, he was back at Drury Lane. (Fleetwood was on the verge of financial collapse himself, his "body as . . . impaired by an excessive Gout, as his Fortune by his Misconduct."[15] Towards the end of 1744 he was forced to sell the Drury Lane patent.)

In the spring of 1742, Theo sought to exploit a potentially lucrative source of revenue in the person of another female member of his family: he arranged the stage debut of his older daughter. Jenny, twelve, was named after her deceased mother, Jane: she was well positioned to win the audience's sympathy, and she did. On March 20, she spoke an epilogue, and on April 28, she played Cordelia for her benefit and that of her younger sister, Elizabeth. Theo probably would have planned a theatrical career for his other daughter, too, but Betty seems to have been mentally handicapped in some way (according to the actress George Anne Bellamy, who was later asked by Colley to serve for a time as the girl's caretaker). In May 1743, Theo performed in Dublin for the first time.

Throughout the 1740s, Theophilus continued to live as sunk in debt, as profligate, and as dissipated as ever. He was not always able to flee to France or Ireland to escape his creditors, so he ended up in sponging houses and in prison. Because he spent so much of this time either in hiding or in jail, his daughters went to live with Elizabeth. Colley, who had endured so much from Theophilus, remarked to a friend that he would never have believed him his son, "but that he knew the mother of him was too proud to be a whore."[16]

The friend to whom Colley made this comment was Laetitia Pilkington, an Irishwoman and former friend of Jonathan Swift. Colley had met her in Dublin, but after a scandalous severance from her obnoxious husband (who divorced her for adultery), she moved to London to try her fortunes, setting herself up in rooms directly opposite to White's Club. Mrs. Pilkington was a poet of some talent, but her name has endured for posterity because she wrote (with Colley's encouragement) a lively memoir that recounted vivid anecdotes of her friendship with Swift. Colley Cibber figured prominently in the memoir, too, for Laetitia understood exactly how to manage him for her own benefit. She made herself for a time the foremost of the younger women upon whom he enjoyed lavishing his attention (and money). He generally had one or more such protégées, whether she was the alluring actress Peg Woffington, then making her name on the London stage, or one of the stylish ladies of Bath.

Laetitia wrote poems; Colley praised them, bestowed upon her gifts of money, and encouraged the gentlemen of White's to do the same. The club rather adopted her for a time—as she must have hoped when she chose the location of her lodging. In the context of Charlotte's story, Laetitia Pilkington provides an interesting point of comparison, a woman who also struggled with her place in patriarchal society, but who was very much what Charlotte was not: an alluring figure who traded upon her feminine wiles to get by. Laetitia's was a more typical story of an often hapless eighteenth-century woman who made a precarious living by her wits and, while it lasted, by her attractiveness. She suffered her own grim struggles to survive, but it is impossible to imagine Laetitia Pilkington, however desperate, knocking on doors with a string of sausages.

Colley continued to relish making the rounds at White's, dining well, associating with noblemen, and spending more and more time in Bath, where he twinkled as a genial old rake, an ageing celebrity—an elder statesman, as it were, of pleasure. It was there, in the spring of 1744, at the age of seventy, that he suffered a bout of illness serious enough to mislead *The Gentleman's Magazine* into reporting his death. But Colley recovered to continue enjoying good health, his beautifully dressed figure spry, his face belying his years. His grandson-in-law Chetwood described him at seventy-five: "As to his Person, he is strait, and well made; of an open Countenance, even free from the conspicuous Marks of old Age. Meet or follow him, and no Person would imagine he ever bore the Burden of above two Thirds of his Years."[17]

In 1742, Colley gave up his home in Covent Garden, moving himself, Catherine, and her daughter westward into a large, expensive house in newly built Berkeley Square, a genteel address. Colley's house still stands today (it is number 19) on the east side of the square at the south corner with Bruton Street.[18] He was to live in these elegant quar-

---

*Colley used the term "apology" in the now rare sense of explanation or vindication; there was nothing, in the modern sense, "apologetic" about it.

ters, whose interior Charlotte never saw, for the rest of his life. In the 1740s, Colley returned to the stage on occasion, without repetition of his earlier embarrassment. Most important, he enjoyed a new kind of public notice when, in 1740, he published his autobiography, *An Apology for the Life of Colley Cibber, Comedian, and Late Patentee of the Theatre-Royal. Written by Himself.** As an exceedingly lively, informative, and often charming narrative, a cheerfully vain account of someone who had a great deal of interest to say about the recent history of the English stage, Colley's book was a significant achievement. (It also made him fifteen hundred pounds richer.) Even Jonathan Swift, otherwise no admirer, admitted that he stayed up all night to read it.

Colley's *Apology* is especially valuable for its critical remarks upon the performances of players such as Thomas Betterton, whose stage presence would otherwise have vanished from history. It likewise contains a great deal about Colley Cibber (much more, his enemies declared, than any one would ever want to know). But, writing as a public personage rather than a private man, Colley said virtually nothing about his family: he lauded his wife (not by name) in passing, for her prodigious production of "I think . . . about a Dozen" children. Except for alluding to her as among the half of his offspring who survived childhood, Colley did not mention Charlotte at all (nor, to be sure, any of the rest of her siblings).

The only clouds on Colley's cheerful, ageing horizon were the many attacks on him, which increased in fervour after he had the effrontery to publish his *Apology*. Fielding, whom Colley attacked in the autobiography, now wrote periodical essays and was turning to the new genre of the novel, where he continued his mocking offensive against the laureate. Colley had won the war against Fielding on the theatre front, or so Colley saw the Licensing Act: Fielding's barbs stung less, relegated as they now were to print. But another enemy was resurgent, whose blows in print would prove more damaging: Alexander Pope.

Colley's customary response to Pope's sporadic attacks over the years had been silence, but in the *Apology* he characterized the poet as an adversary filled with malice and jealousy, envious of Colley's success (including his sexual success, something that the frail, hunchbacked Pope could never attain). Colley condescendingly explained that Pope attacked him in his satires in order to profit from dropping the laureate's famous name. Pope retaliated with a derogatory reference to Colley in his *New Dunciad* of 1742. Now, despite his earlier policy of silence, Colley was provoked to strike back.

He published an open letter to Pope in which he recounted the story of a visit he claimed that he and Pope (in the days before their enmity), along with an aristocratic friend, had paid to a "House of Carnal Recreation." The nobleman set Pope up with a prostitute—a woman attractive enough, said Colley, to tempt even the "little-tiny Manhood of Mr. Pope." After the poet had been ensconced with her for a time, Colley, according to his account, suddenly thought to fear for Pope's fragile health (lest he contract syphilis). So he rushed to the door and threw it open, revealing "this little hasty Hero, like a terrible *Tom Tit,* pertly perching upon the Mount of Love!" Such was his surprise, continued Colley, "that I fairly laid hold of his Heels, and actually drew him down safe and sound from his Danger." Thus he saved the great poet from cutting his life short with "a Malady, which his thin Body might never have been cured of."[19] As one of Pope's biographers observes, publishing this cruel anecdote "was a shrewd gambit, brilliantly executed."[20] Colley struck unerringly at the heart of the crippled poet's deepest vulnerabilities—his small, misshapen body and his stunted sexuality. Pope vowed vengeance.

Pope would die in 1744, but not before he got his revenge, which was great and enduring. In 1743 he published his revised *Dunciad,* in which he enthroned Colley as the King of Dunces, creating the seemingly indelible picture of a buffoonish Cibber that has shaped the laureate's image to the present day. And he made sure that a copy of the relevant passages made its way to Colley months in advance, so he could stew over its imminent publication.

≫ 19 ≪

A MIND TO GET MONEY

(1742–46)

"For the Benefit of a Person who has a Mind to get Money," announced the advertisement for a concert at the James Street Theatre in November 1742. Sandwiched between the two halves of the concert would be a performance of *Fatal Curiosity*, with the part of Agnes "by Mrs. Charke, who originally performed it at the Haymarket"; the other roles, announced the ad with equal forthrightness, would be played "by a set of people who will perform as well as they can, if not as well as they would, and the best can do no more." The programme would include the ballad opera *The Devil to Pay*, with "the part of Nell by Miss Charke, who performed Princess Elizabeth at Southwark [Fair]." The troupe, promised their advertisement, would take "particular care . . . to perform with the utmost decency, and to prevent mistakes."[1] The money-minded person, it seems, was Charlotte.

Charlotte's fallback position was always the stage. Throughout the early 1740s, she had recourse to a variety of venues (probably many more than appear in the records, which are often nonexistent for fringe performances). In the summer of 1742, she may have acted in a pantomime at the New Wells spa in Clerkenwell; she did perform at Bartholomew Fair and probably Southwark Fair as well. The latter was a memorable occasion, when eleven-year-old Kitty made her acting debut. Their performance at James Street may have been one of a series she possibly staged at that theatre during the 1742–43 season.[2] Charlotte was certainly there on March 16 when her company performed for the benefit of "the author, Mrs. Charke," a farce entitled *Tit for Tat; or, Comedy and Tragedy at War*. (Her advertisements suggested that this piece might have been a puppet show, but this is uncertain, since Charlotte never published it: it is unlikely that she could afford puppets.) Her troupe had at least some human actors: Charlotte herself played the lead role of the rake Lovegirlo in her farce. Around that time, she also joined forces with a "Master of Legerdemain" to stage entertainments in Petticoat Lane near Whitechapel. The bailiffs continued to haunt her, however. At one point, Charlotte was pursued for owing £25—a debt that might have been £250, for all her ability to pay it.

On January 13, 1743, Charlotte turned thirty years old, facing an uncertain future. Acting was the one thing she wanted to do, but even with Kitty performing it did not provide enough to live on. So in late 1743 or early 1744, weary of living in constant fear of her creditors, Charlotte reached for help beyond her immediate relatives to the only other surviving family member of her parents' generation, her uncle John Shore. It was Uncle John who had given Charlotte her globes when she was an ambitious geography student, but the family relationship had become strained after Katherine's death. Shore had had the misfortune to split his lip some years earlier, which ended his career as a trumpeter. He had become irascible and quick to take offence, to the point of fistfights; he had embroiled himself in a series of lawsuits.[3] And he had quarrelled with Colley. But his sense of responsibility to other Cibbers apparently had not completely vanished.

Charlotte approached Shore with a request that he bankroll her new scheme—to open an eating house. (Perhaps her experience at the King's Head lay behind this ambition.) She told her uncle frankly that she would never be able to repay any money he gave her, so he would have to consider it a gift. Charlotte was asking for a large sum. Uncle John, perhaps surprisingly and certainly very generously, agreed to give it to her but he asked her to take the lease on a house first, to show that she was serious. "As I have been in a Hurry from the Hour of my Birth," Charlotte said, she rushed out to look for houses for rent, and took a lease on the first one she found. It was in Drury Lane—specifically, in Prince's Court, at the corner of Drury Lane and Colson's Court, a small street extending eastward from Drury Lane south of Great Queen Street and northeast of the Theatre Royal.[4]

In her hurry and excitement, it was almost inevitable that Charlotte would choose badly. (The place, she found later, had "been most irregularly and indecently kept by the last Incumbent, who was a celebrated Dealer in murdered Reputations, Wholesale and Retale.") Charlotte galloped back to Uncle John in a hackney coach with proof of her lease, and received a generous amount of money in gold and a bank bill. Just barely managing to contain her enthusiasm enough to thank him adequately, Charlotte rushed away, but could not resist stopping at a tavern to count the gold and read the bank note over and over. Immediately she dealt with her greatest torment, by settling with her principal creditor.

Then, liberated from the anxiety that she had lived with so long, Charlotte "flew, with impatient Joy, to all the Brokers in Town" to buy furniture, paying the asking price for everything and buying many things she had no use for. It is easy to understand her sheer dizzy joy— she had been freed, at least temporarily, to walk the streets without fear, and she had a new plan under way.

Within two days, after she had "cluttered an undistinguishable Parcel of Goods into my House," Charlotte opened for business as "Mrs. Charke's Stake and Soup House." She must have hired a small waitstaff and a cook, and probably waited on tables herself—her experience with Mrs. Dorr served her well. On her first day, as was customary on such occasions (or so she believed), she gave away "an Infinity of Ham, Beef and Veal, to every Soul who came and call'd for a Quart of Beer, or a single Glass of Brandy. . . . Though I afterwards found, I had successfully run myself out very near seven Pounds, in less than twenty-four Hours, to acquire, nothing at all."

Despite her consistent lack of business sense, Charlotte undoubtedly assumed to perfection the *appearance* of a proprietor of an eating house. But, as she had done before, she made bad judgments, giving away too much and extending credit to customers (including strolling players) who never paid her. Theft was endemic to all businesses, eating houses as well as oilshops. Innkeepers in the parish of St. Giles painted their bedsheets with their names to keep them from being stolen and fenced: the sheets of one inn bore the legend in large red characters: JOHN LEA, LAWRENCE LANE, STOP THIEF. In the Maidenhead Inn, in Dyot Street, "the shovels, pokers, tongs, gridirons, and purl pots" were chained to the fireplace. In the local cookshops, it was not unusual to find knives and forks fastened to the table.[5] Drury Lane was not as desperately poor and squalid a neighbourhood as St. Giles, but it contained as active a set of thieves.

Charlotte rented to lodgers three rooms of her house, two on the second floor and the garret. This arrangement turned out badly: the tenants had to draw their water in the cellar where the beer kegs were located, and they carried pails of beer to their rooms instead. When she was finally alerted to the pilferage going on under her nose, Charlotte found not only that her kegs had been drained, but also that her candlesticks, saucepans, pewter mugs, and coals were missing. And she acquired a new understanding of why so many "dogs" had been able to make away with so many joints of meat.

On March 28, 1744, Charlotte put on a performance for her own benefit of *The Fair Penitent* (she played the rake Lothario) at the James Street Theatre. This suggests that she was once again in need of money, having run through all of Uncle John's. Shortly after her benefit, she took the furniture and stock from her rooms and quitted the premises, leaving her tenants with a deserted house and an empty cellar.

John Shore must have been seriously displeased; it is doubtful that he and Charlotte ever had any contact again. To everyone's horror (including Charlotte's), Shore later married his maid, an act that firmly cemented his reputation for "madness" within the Cibber family. When he died in 1753, he left his wife everything, except for an insulting one shilling apiece to be given to each of the Cibbers, because of "their evil behaviour to me."[6]

Her most recent disastrous experiment behind her, Charlotte returned to the stage. During Mayfair, the first two weeks of May, she and Kitty, along with her old friends Betty Careless and Jockey Adams, performed in a company managed by one of the Hallam family. Charlotte's parts in the drolls they performed at the fair included many repeat performances of her brother as Ancient Pistol.

When the fair ended, Charlotte rented another building in the area to stage a short June season, during which she played a series of leading roles, all male; her company included Kitty, Jockey Adams, and Betty Careless. Her innovative solution for evading the Licensing Act that month made a lasting mark upon British theatre. She advertised her theatre as, in essence, a tavern: "Each Person to be admitted for Sixpence at the door, which entitles them to a Pint of Ale, upon delivering the ticket to the Waiter." (Morgan suggests that this was an ingenious way of using up the leftover stock of ale from her ordinary.)[7] While they drank, her customers would be treated to a play free of charge. "This tactic," says *The London Stage*—its editor's tone slightly less condescending and irritated than it usually is when he mentions Charlotte, whom he elsewhere calls an "irrepressible nuisance"—may be "the unfortunate Charlotte Charke's most permanent contribution to the English stage."[8]

During the following September, 1744, Charlotte and Kitty returned to the Little Haymarket, for Theophilus had received permission to stage a limited season of plays there. He opened with a flourish of controversy by staging a performance of *Romeo and Juliet,* in his own adaptation. As Juliet he cast his fifteen-year-old daughter, Jenny, and as Romeo, he cast himself. Much of London shuddered in disgust.

Perhaps this was owing to Theo's unsavoury reputation, or perhaps the incestuous overtones were too unsettling to pass without comment. Aaron Hill judged that Jenny's performance possessed "considerable merit," but she would have been better, "if there had been some gay young fellow for her lover, instead of a person . . . too old for her choice, too little handsome to be in love with, and into the bargain, her father."[9]

But spectators filled the house, and among them on opening night was David Garrick, who was then establishing himself as the most influential figure in British theatre. (Garrick would assume the management of Drury Lane Theatre in 1747.) At his London debut in 1741, he had exploded onto the English stage as a revolutionary whose "naturalistic" style of acting came as a rebuke to the earlier tradition of highly stylized performance handed down from actors such as Thomas Betterton to Colley Cibber to Theophilus Cibber and James Quin.

Garrick's acting emphasized individuality, emotional expressiveness, and a delivery that rejected sonorous intoning and the striking of attitudes in favour of more natural cadences. His groundbreaking performances of Richard III and Hamlet made the earlier styles seem outdated and even preposterous, and those who had been molded in the earlier tradition began to look antiquated. Charlotte was one of them.

Garrick's description of the performance that evening was filled with loathing and contempt for Theophilus, condescension to his company, and a personal and ideological abhorrence of all things Cibberian. He wrote to a friend, "[Theophilus] spoke a prologue, letting us know, that his daughter was the grand-daughter of his father, who was a celebrated poet and player, and that she was the daughter of his first wife by him who had formerly met with their approbation. I never heard so vile and scandalous a performance in my life, and, excepting the speaking of it, and the speaker, nothing could be more contemptible." (Theo's invocation of Jane's memory was intended, of course, not only to add pathos to Jenny's debut but also to underscore the bad behaviour of his second wife, Susannah—who would return to stardom as Garrick's leading lady.)

"The play," continued Garrick, "was tolerable enough, considering Theophilus was the hero. . . . Mrs. Charke played the Nurse to his daughter Juliet; but she was so miserably [*sic*] throughout, and so abounded in airs, affectation, and *Cibberisms,* that I was quite shocked at her: the girl, I believe, may have genius; but unless she changes her preceptor, she must be entirely ruined."[10] (Jenny's career, in fact, would be brief.)

So decreed the new monarch of London's theatre establishment. His characterization of Charlotte's acting as affected and "Cibberian" sounded the death knell for her prospects of ever rejoining Drury Lane. At the age of thirty, she was already becoming outmoded and out of step. Yet there is a puzzle about Garrick's comment: the advertisements for all of this company's performances of *Romeo and Juliet* billed an actress named Mrs. Hill as the Nurse. Charlotte was listed as Escalus, the Prince. Unless Garrick was mistaken about the identity of the actress playing the Nurse, Charlotte must have assumed this role at the last minute that night. Her performance could have reflected her lack of preparation for this part, and indeed her unfamiliarity with the play itself: *Romeo and Juliet,* according to Theo's advertisements, had not been acted by any company "these 100 Years."

Still, Garrick was complaining about Charlotte's acting *style.* Her years—seven, now—out of regular theatrical employment, and her even longer time away from performing the standard repertory at a patent theatre, had left her entrenched in the old style of acting that she had learned from her father. She had had little opportunity to develop as an actress in classical roles, to modernize herself. Had Fielding been permitted to establish his theatre, Charlotte might have made a respected, even renowned, place as a specialist in satire, farce, and travesty, her principal talents. Had she never left Drury Lane in the first instance, she might have been able to evolve an acting style more in tune with the newly favoured one. But now, her chances were virtually nonexistent.

Throughout the tragedy's run, Charlotte continued to be billed as Escalus (never as the Nurse), and all her other roles for this company were male as well. Always, she appeared not under her own name but as "Mr. Charles." (The reason is not known; perhaps one of her creditors had sworn a warrant against her.) "Mr. Charles" was particularly well received as the sentimental hero Young Bevil in Steele's *The Conscious Lovers;* cast as the female romantic lead, Indiana, Jenny now played the lover of her cross-dressed aunt.

While the performances continued throughout September and October, Charlotte and Kitty lived with Theophilus, who remained as arrogant, hot-tempered, and dissolute as ever, but who continued to be a good, caring brother to her. This was all the more remarkable given Theo's interest in remaining on speaking terms with Colley, and his loyalty must have been deeply comforting to his sister. Living with him, Charlotte said, "I passed my Time both cheerfully and agreeably." The family's two black sheep recognized their common bond, a passion for the theatre.

But, as Charlotte commented glumly, her "Happiness was never of very long Duration." Soon Theophilus's short-term licence expired; the lord chamberlain closed down his troupe in late October. Theo emerged again shortly afterward with a new strategy for bypassing the Licensing Act: an "Academy" of acting that provided "free" plays. But this tactic did not work and he was forced by the magistrate to desist. So Theophilus joined the Covent Garden Theatre, where his sister was not welcome. Charlotte was on her own once more, "left suddenly," she said, "and in Distress."

She planned a series of performances to begin that winter (using the concert formula to evade the Licensing Act), and Theophilus gave his permission for Jenny to act with her. Charlotte ambitiously envisioned herself playing a series of male leads, with her niece in the complementary "tender, soft" female parts: they were a promising duo, she thought, since "our Figures were agreeably match'd." Colley, however, intervened—prompted, Charlotte believed, by Catherine—ordering Theophilus to remove Jenny from Charlotte's troupe in order to save her reputation from the taint of association with her aunt. Charlotte said that her family thought "'Twould be a Scandal for her to play with such a Wretch as I was. 'Twas letting her down, to be seen with me."

At that moment, Charlotte and her company were rehearsing "a play not acted these sixty years," Elkanah Settle's tragedy *The Female Prelate: Being the History of the Life and Death of Pope Joan*.[11] This rather disreputable late-seventeenth-century play dramatizes the legend of Joanna Anglica, a young ninth-century Englishwoman who supposedly disguised herself as a man and was elected pope, and whose imposture was only exposed when she gave birth to a child.

A little flurry of notices appeared in *The Daily Advertiser* surrounding this impending production. On February 27, a letter appeared, signed "Q.Z.":

> I find by the Daily Papers, that there is an old Play reviving, (and which is to be performed on Monday next at the Hay-Market Theatre) called POPE JOAN, wherein Mrs. Charke represents the Character of the Pope. I must confess it gave me great Pleasure when I read her Name for a Female Character, and take this publick Manner of congratulating her on her appearing in her proper Sphere; and hope there will be a crowded Audience to encourage her to persevere in the Resolution of laying aside the Hero, and giving them the Pleasure of her Performance for the future as the Heroine. I hope this friendly Hint will be received, as it is meant purely to serve her, having been informed, that her throwing herself into Male Characters have proved detrimental to her; if so, allowing that she is sensible of her Error, I think 'tis Pity she should be lost to the Town, having sufficient Merit, in my Opinion, to entitle her to its Favours.

The letter might have been placed in the paper by Charlotte herself, or by a friend. In any case, its warning about the "error" of her transvestite performances seems firmly tongue-in-cheek, given that the "female character" it compliments her for playing is a woman who disguised herself as a man and became the Pope.

Charlotte responded on February 28:

In your Paper, Yesterday, I had the Pleasure of reading a Letter, which convinces me I am not quite forgotten. I am certain it must come from a Friend, and therefore receive the Hint as it was intended; but at the same Time must take this Opportunity to inform the Town, that Misfortunes were the original Cause of my Change of Dress; and my appearing in Male Characters at the Haymarket this Winter, was occasion'd from a Scarcity of Actors who should have supplied those Parts I, but at best, pretended to make shift with; and since there are Friends left me, who are willing to be pleased with my Endeavours to entertain in a proper Light, I hope, with their Encouragement, to manifest how much I have it at Heart to oblige the Town, who have kindly receiv'd me formerly, as well as good-naturedly excus'd any Attempt to get a Livelihood that Misfortune or Conveniency have forc'd me to. On Monday next the Play of POPE JOAN will be performed at the Hay-Market, where I shall be proud, in the best Manner I can, to entertain my Friends, and ever acknowledge myself, Their most obedient Servant . . .

It may have been a mark of Charlotte's desperation—or calculation—that she chose on this occasion to explain publicly her theatrical cross-dressing as an expedient "forc'd" upon her by "Misfortune or Conveniency." Even had this been true, it did not account for her billing as "Mr. Charles" for those Haymarket performances. And, most strikingly, it left entirely unaddressed both Charlotte's long history of playing male roles in a large variety of contexts, and her offstage transvestism. Charlotte's promise to "entertain in a proper Light"—again some irony entered here, given the play she had chosen—called upon the Town's good nature but did little to indicate her own reformation. She gave no hints here of larger explanations for her conduct, and while she engaged in a certain amount of pleading, she struck no real note of repentance, either here or in the similar letter she published two days later.[12]

Despite the pains Charlotte had taken to ensure a good audience, her company played only one night, to a "dreadful House." Many who had bought tickets for the purpose of encouraging Jenny had returned them. Ten years later, Charlotte's memory of her family's intervention, their "rancorous Hate to me" and their "low Malice," would still rankle. What "mighty Degree of theatrical Dignity" did Jenny have, Charlotte

Charlotte's father with one of his granddaughters (probably either Jenny Cibber or Catharine Brown). (Edward Fisher, Colley Cibber, *after J. B. Vanloo. Courtesy of the Department of Special Collections, University of California, San Diego.)*

asked, as compared with herself as an actress? Why was she such an unfit companion for the girl, whose blood, after all, she shared? "The only Disgrace was, my being under Misfortunes; the very worst Reason for my Family's contributing to a Perpetration of that, which Nature and Humanity should rather have excited 'em to have helped me to overcome."

During November 1745, Charlotte picked up some acting work with a company run by four members of the Hallam family (not including Adam) at Goodman's Fields, playing a series of roles that month, all female. Returning to perform at one of London's larger playhouses, Charlotte would have become aware of changes since her last appearance in a comparable theatre. There was the spate of anti-Catholic plays that all the companies seemed to be performing. Audiences were thin everywhere. Sometimes the playhouses were so sparsely populated that performances were cancelled. Revenues plummeted; actors went unpaid. And a novel custom had arisen: every night, the audiences rose from their seats to sing a new song, whose title was "God Save the King."[13] Britain now had, in effect, a national anthem, and its citizens sang it through throats tight with anxiety and fear.

That July, a small invasion force had landed in the Hebrides. At its head was the Young Pretender, Charles Edward Stuart. Grandson of the deposed James II and son of the Old Pretender, he was known to his supporters as Bonnie Prince Charlie, or simply as the heir to the thrones of England and Scotland, the rightful future King Charles III of Great Britain. The son of the current "King across the Water" had returned to claim his family's crown, surreptitiously backed by France. Mustering some support among the Highland chiefs hostile to Hanoverian England, Charles had marched his army across Scotland, taking the city of Perth and arriving in the vicinity of Edinburgh, where in August he shocked the country by defeating George II's forces in the Battle of Prestonpans. Then, mustering an army of about five thousand, he crossed into England.

During the autumn of 1745, the Jacobite forces were advancing south through the English countryside on their march towards London. Jacobitism was not dead in England, and one of the causes of anxiety among the Hanoverians was uncertainty about how much support Charles would muster from the English people during his advance. There seemed a real possibility that the invaders would gain in strength as they progressed. With a portion of the King's troops committed overseas, Londoners were in a panic that their city might be taken. They were not in much of a mood to attend the theatres, even to see anti-Catholic plays. (That most of these plays were ludicrously bad even by the standards of patriotic jingoism did not help matters.)

While she must have followed the deployment of the armies with the same anxiety as other Londoners—like her father, Charlotte was a staunch Hanoverian—she was also pressed by the more immediate concern of sustaining herself and Kitty. Her one-month stint during November with the Hallams, whose theatre was struggling, would have brought in little. But then she happened upon an opportunity that seemed, even in those uncertain times, to give her hope.

John Russell was having more success than the playhouses attracting audiences with a puppet show he was staging in Hickford's Great

Room, in Brewer's Street above Piccadilly, a well-to-do area. His show seems to have offered parodies of Italian opera in the manner of Martin Powell's puppet theatre at the beginning of the century, charming his wealthy spectators. He had an orchestra of ten, and some of his female puppets wore real diamonds, lent to Russell by his patrons. Though his marionettes were small—much smaller than Charlotte's had been, and lacking the caricature carving that had made hers unique—they were difficult for the inexperienced to manipulate. So Russell was eager to secure Charlotte's expertise in puppetry, and her knowledge of Italian was an additional advantage. Russell hired her at a guinea a day— a very handsome salary—particularly to operate Punch.

This was a boon to Charlotte. News that the Jacobite army, failing to muster the popular support Charles had expected, had turned back towards Scotland in early December, pursued by government forces, added another dimension of hopefulness. Charlotte was again perse- cuted by her creditors, which meant that she had to take care to avoid the bailiffs, leaving home between five and six o'clock every morning, skulking up and down St. James's Park until Hickford's maid arose to let her in, staying inside all day, and then "mingling with the thickest of the Croud at Night to get Home." Still, her prospects seemed to brighten. Happily, she proceeded to "new rig" herself and Kitty, redeeming their clothes from the pawnbrokers.

But Russell's show lost its appeal. His expenses, which were consid- erable, outstripped his income, and his wealthy subscribers abandoned him to his rapidly accumulating debt. His former friends "cast him off in two or three Months," Charlotte said, "with as much Contempt, as an old Coat made in Oliver [Cromwell]'s time," and he was sent to Newgate.

There Charlotte visited him with a proposition. Russell had written a promising comic play or farce, still unproduced. She suggested that she gather a troupe and stage it at the Little Haymarket, offering to manage the company and act in the play for no salary, while he would stipulate those who would keep the receipts. Russell could pay his debts and gain his release; only then, if his receipts were large enough, would he pay Charlotte. This was an appealing idea, fruit both of Charlotte's genuine friendship for Russell and of her irrepressible inge- nuity, her almost astonishing ability to continue to rally in the face of adversity.

Instead of embracing her plan, however, Russell reacted with offended suspicion. As she continued to talk with him, Charlotte became increasingly aware that his intellect had become disordered. She left him then, and when she returned two days later, she found him "absolutely changed from the Man of Sense to the driv'ling Ideot."

In early July, Charlotte went again to visit her friend and found that he had been transferred to the Fleet Prison (he had been moved there on May 31).[14] Arriving at the complex of buildings that constituted the Fleet, Charlotte expressed her concern for Russell to a woman there, who politely desired her to walk up to his room to see him. After wandering around the warren of rooms, Charlotte came upon Russell's quarters, where she found him—lying dead in a coffin. The woman had naturally enough thought that Charlotte wished to pay her last respects. The shock was considerable.

Russell's deterioration had progressed over several months, from the winter into the summer of 1746. During this time, the tide turned against the Jacobite forces; they had retreated into Scotland, where they experienced more setbacks, pursued by an army under the command of William, Duke of Cumberland, the twenty-five-year-old third son of George II. Their final defeat came on April 16, near Inverness in the plain at Culloden, where the exhausted Jacobite force was overrun by a Hanoverian army twice its size, and slaughtered. Culloden brought an end to the Stuart threat. Charles escaped the slaughter and was hidden by his Highland allies until he eventually was able to steal out of the country. He returned to France, where he spent the rest of his life in bitterness and alcoholism.

Charlotte shared the relief that many others in London felt at the end of the Jacobite danger, but she also turned it to her advantage. Once again obliged to scrounge acting gigs, she got a role playing Silvia in a benefit performance of *The Recruiting Officer* on April 30 for one Mr. Scudamore, a sergeant of dragoons who had recently returned from the Battle of Culloden. At his request, Charlotte also provided a prologue for him to speak, which she reprinted in her autobiography. "I don't pretend to have any extraordinary Talents, in regard to Poetry in Verse, or indeed in Prose," she admitted (accurately enough as regards the poetry, though modestly underplaying her vivid, lively prose). But "as it speaks the Warmth of my Heart towards the Royal Family," she gave it to her readers.

"From Toils and Dangers of a furious War, / Where Groans and Death successive wound the Air; / Where the fair Ocean, or the chrystal Flood / Are dy'd with purple Streams of flowing Blood," her prologue begins. Written in the first person to be spoken by Scudamore, the poem lauds "Great William": "With steady Courage dauntless he appears, / And owns a Spirit far beyond his Years." Charlotte's fulsome tribute to the man known to history as the Butcher of Culloden may jar modern ears (as, we must acknowledge, her verse does too), but as most eighteenth-century Londoners saw it, Cumberland did "save this Nation from a Papal Throne," defending his country so that, in Charlotte's ringing conclusion: "NONE BUT GREAT GEORGE SHOULD FILL THE BRITISH THRONE." As Charlotte said of this prologue, "Though my Poetry may be lame, my Design was good." Even better, Scudamore rewarded her handsomely for her effort.

Charlotte managed to squeeze more revenue from her prologue than this single performance. She began to perform at the New Wells spa, where, along with the tumbling, rope dancing, singing, and dancing featured at each performance, she recited her prologue "in the character of a Volunteer," as the ads put it; perhaps she held a prop musket at her side, or engaged in a few soldierly manoeuvres. Her performance anticipated by four years an act momentarily popular at the New Wells in Goodman's Fields of another well-known female cross-dresser, Hannah Snell, "the female soldier," who rose to fame in 1750 when she published her life story.

Snell, who had disguised herself as a man in order to join the army, both out of a long-cherished desire to be a soldier and in order to pursue her absconded husband, served undetected as a marine for nearly five years at sea, travelling as far as the East Indies. Although she spent much of that time on a ship where her fellow tars nicknamed her Molly (suggesting an effeminate homosexual man), although on two occasions she was stripped and flogged (somehow managing to conceal her breasts), and although she was once wounded in her legs and groin (allowing doctors to treat her legs, but herself extracting the musket ball from her groin), she preserved her disguise. Returning to England in 1750, she theatrically disclosed her identity to the amazement of her mates, received a small annuity from the Duke of Cumberland for her

Amazonian heroism, and collabourated with a bookseller (Snell could read but not write) to publish her sensational story, which celebrated her as a true British heroine. Snell capitalized upon her moment of fame by becoming an attraction at the New Wells, where, dressed in her regimentals, she performed military manoeuvres and displays of musket handling.

Charlotte acted at the New Wells, Clerkenwell through the summer of 1746, taking roles in pantomime entertainments as well as continuing to recite her prologue. But now she was billed as "Mrs. Sacheverel, late Mrs. Charke."[15] On May 2, she had married a man named John Sacheverell.

In a life story so many details of which remain obscure, the mystery of Charlotte's marriage to John Sacheverell is one of the most tantalizing. Virtually nothing is known about him. He appears in the marriage register as belonging to the parish of St. Andrew's, Holborn, not a particularly elegant parish but one where businessmen, lawyers, and theatre people might live (the Fleet River and Lincoln's Inn Fields were both nearby). He does not seem to have been an actor, but perhaps he had some other connection with the playhouses. Charlotte's own entry in the register describes her home at the time of her marriage as Kensington. Perhaps she lived there while she worked for Russell, or shortly thereafter; perhaps she moved there in search of better air to protect her health or Kitty's. (She was familiar with Kensington, since her mother had lived there.)

Charlotte married her second husband in the parish of St. George's, Hanover Square, but not in the handsome parish church itself. The officiant was one of the curates associated with the notorious Dr. Alexander Keith, who ran a thriving trade in cut-rate, clandestine weddings at St. George's Chapel, Hyde Park Corner, known as the Mayfair Chapel.[16] By 1746, Dr. Keith himself had been prosecuted by the rector of St. George's, Hanover Square, and committed to the Fleet Prison, where his business if anything increased, since the prison was the site of the most flourishing clandestine marriage trade in all London.

In her autobiography, Charlotte does not say a word—at least, not an explicit word—about Sacheverell. Only the survival of the marriage register and the newspaper advertisements for her New Wells performances reveal his existence. The implication is unavoidable that she wished to forget, even to deny, it. She later resumed the name Charke. But during the summer of 1746, she apparently had no qualms about having herself billed as "Mrs. Sacheverel," with the addition of "late Mrs. Charke" to make her identity clear.

It is difficult even to speculate about this relationship. Possibly, as most commentators have assumed, the "honourable secret alliance" Charlotte mentions in her autobiography refers to Sacheverell. But the uncharacteristic discrepancy in the apparent date she assigns to that event, and her vagueness about it, make any secure identification impossible. So John Sacheverell remains a shadowy figure in Charlotte's life. Perhaps he was the earlier honourable alliance, or a new companion, who also died, at the end of the summer, 1746, leaving Charlotte disappointed, destitute, and in debt once again. Or perhaps this was a marriage hastily contracted and almost as hastily repented, so that they separated within months. Perhaps Charlotte discovered that her new husband already had a wife still living. Bigamy occurred often enough, not only in the pages of *Moll Flanders*. Clandestine marriage venues were notorious for register-fiddling: for a price, they might report the death of a living spouse, or erase an entry of a previous marriage.

Whatever the truth of the mysterious marriage of Charlotte Charke and John Sacheverell, it did not last long and it was not a part of her life that Charlotte subsequently wanted herself, or anybody else, to remember. The marriage was over by late September when, the New Wells season having ended, Charlotte left the city altogether to escape her creditors and to try her fortunes in the country.[17] She was thirty-three. She would not return to London for more than eight years.

20

A LITTLE, DIRTY KIND OF WAR

(1746–53)

Charlotte's once handsome coat was threadbare, its row of buttons tarnished; her shoes were badly worn, and her wig was bedraggled. Her dusty hat retained a bare semblance of its former shape. It was an evening in the spring of 1749, and Charlotte, Kitty, and Charlotte's friend Mrs. Brown had just arrived in the Devonshire village of Cullompton to join a strolling troupe playing there. Already Charlotte was on the makeshift stage for her first performance with the company, in Farquhar's comedy *The Beaux' Stratagem*. She was beginning the scene in which her character, Mr. Archer, and the servant Scrub get drunk together. Scrub had just hoisted a tankard of ale.

Suddenly, a third figure marched onto the stage—the actress playing Mrs. Sullen, entering much earlier than she was supposed to. Striding over to the startled Scrub, she grabbed the tankard and raised it in a toast to Charlotte, pledging their better acquaintance. Then, ordering Scrub to bring a fiddler onstage, she insisted that Archer join her in dancing a minuet. Charlotte, too astonished to protest, conducted her in the stately dance, while the upstaged Scrub slumped in a chair watching them, morosely finishing off the tankard.

The audience, however, noticed nothing amiss. In the front row sat "a Range of drunken Butchers," most asleep, their snores resounding while their wives chattered to each other so loudly that the players had to raise their voices. Charlotte looked at the spectators, shrugged, and threw herself into the spirit of the occasion.

Archer and Mrs. Sullen romped wildly through the rest of the evening, entertaining all with speeches from every play they could remember. Archer addressed Mrs. Sullen with Jaffeir's passionate words to his wife, Belvidera, in *Venice Preserv'd*; Mrs. Sullen tenderly responded with the soliloquy from *Cato* in which the hero determines to commit suicide. And they went on in this way, taking, Charlotte said, "a Wild-goose Chace through all the dramatic Authors we could recollect." Finally, Mrs. Sullen brought the evening to a close by reciting the tercet in which Jane Shore bemoans woman's fate in a man's world. The performance was "all to the universal Satisfaction of that Part of the Audience," said Charlotte, "who were awake." Just another evening in the life of a strolling player.

Upon leaving London in the autumn of 1746, Charlotte and Kitty first made the twenty-five-mile trek to Sunninghill, a town south of Windsor, where they were contracted to perform. (Charlotte had probably been approached by the troupe's manager in town, possibly at one of the inns doubling as theatrical employment offices.) As she and Kitty travelled through the lush Berkshire countryside, skirting the edges of Windsor Great Park, the prospect must have been soothing after a summer of the dirty city and John Sacheverell. Perhaps the proximity of Sunninghill to the royal castle and the nearby Ascot racecourse lifted Charlotte's spirits, too. A more sophisticated audience than was usual in the country seemed certain. But there are greater curses than unrefined tastes.

Cast in a familiar role as Captain Plume in *The Recruiting Officer*, Charlotte discovered shortly before the performance was to begin that the actress playing the part of Silvia was, she said, "unable to speak a plain Word, or indeed to keep her Ground." Presumably, she was drunk. The company being tiny, Charlotte had to assume both roles. She knew the part of Silvia; that was not the problem. The problem was that Captain Plume and Silvia are the comedy's leading romantic couple, and are on stage at the same time, playing bantering love scenes together. The evening required all the theatrical ingenuity that Charlotte could summon.

As she would learn over the course of the next few years, such episodes were not unusual in the world of the strolling player. Elizabeth Elrington, the actress who played Mrs. Sullen in Cullompton, told Charlotte that she had been forced on one opening night of *The Beggar's Opera* to play the parts of both Polly and Lucy, who have a big confrontation with each other—while the actress assigned to play Lucy snored drunkenly in her bed. Had she accomplished this, Charlotte wondered facetiously, with a magic lantern?

Strolling companies occupied the despised underbelly of the theatrical profession in the eighteenth century, although some acclaimed players began their careers acting with such troupes in the provinces.[1] The difference between a country stage and the patent theatres of London, Charlotte sniffed, was the difference between "a Mouse-trap and a Mountain."

Having once acted at Drury Lane—a fact that would have been proclaimed in the playbills for her performances—Charlotte had considerably higher status than most of her fellow itinerant thespians, and considerably more talent. "'Tis a pity," she wrote, "that so many, who have good Trades, should idly quit them, to become despicable Actors; which renders them useless to themselves, and very often Nusances to others. Those who were bred up in the Profession, have the best Right to make it their Calling; but their Rights are horribly invaded by Barbers 'Prentices, Taylors and Journeymen Weavers; all which bear such strong Marks of their Professions, that I have seen Richard the Third murder Henry the Sixth with a Shuttle, and Orestes jump off the Shopboard to address Hermione."

There was, however, one thing that the provinces shared with the metropolis: ego. William Templeton quickly learned an unwelcome lesson when he joined his first itinerant troupe. "From their humble merit," he commented of the strollers, "I expected to find in them nothing but modesty and diffidence; but I was deceived—a company composed of GARRICKS could not talk more largely . . . they talk loud in the streets, are overbearing in public company, and at the theatres break out into all the insolence of self-importance."[2] Charlotte's sensibilities suffered.

Several eighteenth-century strollers wrote accounts of their careers, and they reported tensions and rivalries within the strolling companies that could make the conflicts at Drury Lane seem almost restrained.

Not all companies were equally tempestuous: many groups of strollers developed a strong camaraderie, supporting one another and remaining philosophically cheerful in the face of great privation. But Charlotte seems to have encountered more petty rivalry than good nature. In her experience, bad actors were despised, she said, but good actors were resented even more. "The least Glimmering or Shade of Acting, in Man or Woman," Charlotte wrote, "is a sure Motive of Envy in the rest . . . I think, that going a Strolling is engaging in a little, dirty Kind of War, in which I have been obliged to fight so many battles."

Many strollers' sense of self-importance contrasted, often ludicrously, not only with their performances but also with the conditions in which they performed. They plied their trade in purpose-built theatres, the great rooms of public buildings, and the halls of local manor houses, but also in inns, courtyards, barns (where haylofts often served as galleries), and old stables. A disused pigsty, still redolent of its previous occupants, might be pressed into service as a dressing room.[3] Often only a board drilled with holes to hold tallow candles as footlights separated the players from the orchestra (or what passed for one), and only a few token slats of wood separated the orchestra from the pit and the pit from what passed for the boxes. In such "theatres," performers might swelter or freeze.

Audiences ranged from cultivated local gentry to farmers, butchers, hostlers, and other provincial townsfolk, who might snore, shout, or brawl throughout a performance. Some rustic spectators genuinely enjoyed the plays, but lacked, as it were, a sense of genre: Charlotte reported that one evening an enthusiastic fan—who had previously praised her Hamlet because she "so frequently broke out in fresh places"—interrupted her in the middle of *The Distress'd Mother* to call for the servant's speeches from *The Beaux' Stratagem*. The audience liked her performance of Pyrrhus very well, he explained, but if she were to mix in a few of Scrub's lines too, they would like it all the better.

It was a gruelling life. Managers hired players capable of learning a large number of "lengths" nightly: a "length" was forty-two lines. Players often had to master a new play within two or three days; and the principals might be expected to perform five or six different roles in an evening, and to perform nearly every evening of the week. But the evening's profits were shared equally among the players, with those who did not play many roles—or even play at all—making the same amount as those who had been almost constantly onstage. Managers received five shares of the earnings—one for acting and four for other duties and expenses. For every fair-minded and generous manager, there seem to have been many unscrupulous ones, who misrepresented the solvency of their companies when hiring new actors, who exaggerated the size of the company's expenses in order to pocket more money, and who dined well while their players starved. Even in honest companies, players often went hungry.

Actors' wages were usually a pittance—the stubs of the tallow candles used in each performance were included in their pay. Players really earned money only from their benefits, when they would be forced to go door to door, cap in hand, to plead for largess from the local gentry and, as Rosenfeld says, "cringe in gratitude thereafter."[4] At times a player had to solicit the gentry's support more on the basis of her hard-luck story than her performance. (There often seems to have been only a slender distinction between benefits and beggary.) Furthermore, strolling was outlawed by the Licensing Act, although the law was generally ignored in the country far from the lord chamberlain's view. (If prompted by a complaint filed by an informer, however, magistrates were legally bound to imprison the players as vagrants.)

Sometimes the troupes found good audiences, but often they sold barely enough tickets to make their performances worthwhile. Strolling players paraded into towns accompanied by the beating of a drum, dressed in whatever colourful costumes their threadbare wardrobes could muster. A goddess's scarf might spangle with a few paste jewels; a copper crown or a gilt diadem would glint in the sun (or drip in the rain); an officer's uniform flashed a bit of crimson through its stains; a kingly robe's frayed hem dragged along the ground. The actors' coats were tattered, their buttons tarnished, their wigs greasy, their stockings ribbed with runs. Yet the principal players strutted in front of their prospective spectators as if they had just stepped off the boards of Drury Lane, while some of the lesser members handed out copies of the playbill for the evening's performance.

Trailing them, the carthorses, ribs visible under their unkempt coats, strained to pull a couple of heavily laden wagons, in which a large green curtain might lie rolled up, beside a few battered Roman helmets. Miscellaneous paraphernalia jutted out—a papier-mâché arch, a couple of ragged banners, the long shark-toothed cylinder of a wave machine, several of its waves missing. We can imagine Charlotte reenacting this scene over and over during her years in the country, when she trudged along as one of the men, in worn breeches, a faded coat, and a hat topped with bedraggled lace; Kitty, a young woman now and a full-time player, might have walked beside her. Another actress closer to Charlotte's age would also frequently have been at her side; occasionally they would glance at each other, and exchange weary smiles.

The first strolling troupe that Charlotte mentions joining during her period in the country belonged to Mr. Linnet, who may have been the manager who invited Charlotte from London to Sunninghill.[5] Linnet's troupe was one of the more respectable strolling companies, possessing a good wardrobe and properties, and performing a repertoire of standard plays Charlotte knew well.[6] With Linnet, she and Kitty moved from town to town in the south of England: she mentions locations in Gloucestershire and Wiltshire. Charlotte seems to have travelled under the name of Charles Brown, permanently putting an end to her brief identity as Mrs. Sacheverell, and suspending, in most situations, the name Charlotte Charke.

The privations and stresses of Charlotte's last several years in London had weakened her health even before she plunged into the rigours of itinerancy. She had suffered two serious bouts of prolonged illness since 1737, one of which had been life-threatening. She may have inherited a susceptibility to respiratory disorders from her asthmatic mother: recent studies have suggested a genetic factor in asthma and related conditions. After a short period of travelling with Linnet's company, she became ill again. Charlotte endured "a nervous Fever and Lowness of Spirits, that continued upon me for upwards of three Years."

She continued to perform, but, when the troupe was approaching the town of Cirencester in Gloucestershire, she collapsed. For a time she hovered on the brink of death: "my Dissolution was every Moment expected." But Charlotte's crisis passed: the faithful ministrations of a woman friend saved her life. Charlotte later spoke feelingly of her friend's "tender Care in nursing me in three Years Illness, without repining at her Fatigue, which was uninterrupted."

Charlotte's friend was a fellow actress, whom Charlotte may have first met in London: she speaks later of having known her for "many years." This woman was generous and kind. Charlotte relayed an anecdote that illustrated what she considered to be her friend's "Superfluity of good Nature." One night, while not onstage herself, she stood in the scenes intently watching her friend perform in the role of the Queen in Dryden's *The Spanish Friar*; it may have been her friend's first performance in this role, for Charlotte felt anxious for her success, and could not understand her inexplicable behaviour.

> I found she spoke sensibly, but, to my great Surprize, observed her to stoop extreamly forward, on which I concluded she was seized with a sudden fit of the Cholick, but she satisfied me of the contrary; and, on her next Appearance, I remarked that she sunk down very much on that Side I stood between the Scenes, on which I then conjectured her to be troubled with a Sciatick Pain in her Side, and made a second Enquiry, but was answered in the Negative on that Score.

The mystery was solved when, as the Queen descended from the stage into the dressing room, Charlotte glimpsed "a Pair of naked Legs." The truth emerged that, having noticed that the actor in the part of Torrismond had "a dirty Pair of Yarn Stockings, with above twenty Holes in Sight," the actress—figuring that she had her hoop and petticoat to cover her own legs—had kindly stripped them "of a fine Pair of Cotton, and len[t] them to the Hero." At this discovery, Charlotte owned, she was "both angry and pleased. I was concerned to find my Friend's Humanity had extended so far as to render herself ridiculous, besides the Hazard she run of catching Cold: But must confess, I never saw so strong a Proof of good Nature, especially among Travelling-Tragedizers; for, to speak Truth of them, they have but a small Share of that Principle subsisting amongst them."

Charlotte formed the most enduring partnership of her life with this kind, thoughtful actress, who lived and travelled with her for many years. This woman's real name is unknown. She exists in Charlotte's story only as Mrs. Brown, for she shared, while they travelled, at least, Charlotte's pseudonymous name: they identified themselves as Mr. and Mrs. Brown. (It is possible, of course, that her name really *was* Brown, but it seems more likely that she adopted Charlotte's chosen surname.) While their fellow actors knew that they were two women, many of the outsiders they met thought that they were what they appeared to be, a married couple.

Were they lovers? Probably, but Charlotte herself did not say so. Much tenderness is evident in her references to Mrs. Brown, and she often speaks of her "Friend" in a lovingly proprietary kind of way. Their connection was undeniably deep and long-lasting (much longer than Charlotte's marriages). Charlotte seems to have made the significant decisions about their shared life: while Mrs. Brown sometimes greeted her plans reluctantly and tried to talk her out of her more reckless schemes, she nonetheless abided by Charlotte's decisions. Charlotte played a masculine role to Mrs. Brown's feminine one, according to the conventions of her day; she behaved as a husband, Mrs. Brown as a wife.

Linnet's troupe played a relatively lengthy engagement in Cirencester, and during this time Charlotte recuperated. While Mrs. Brown was performing at night, Charlotte was kept agreeable company by a new friend, a "reverend-looking Elder, about sixty Years of Age" who, along with a young man identified as his nephew, made himself a companion to "the Browns." When Charlotte's apothecary recommended riding as a restorative to her health, this gentleman loaned horses to Mr. and Mrs. Brown. He filled Charlotte's head with stories of his estate in Oxfordshire, where, he promised, he would settle her and Mrs. Brown, making Charlotte the manager of his overseas affairs and allowing them to quit the strolling life. Surely, Charlotte thought, "this Man was dropped from Heaven, to be my kind Deliverer from all the Sorrows of Life." Here was a substitute father who gave her the care and affection that her real father denied her.

This delightful plan being agreed upon, Charlotte, Mrs. Brown, and Kitty gave Linnet a month's warning; and in token of their compact, the old gentleman gave Mrs. Brown a valuable present, a heavy gold necklace and locket worth at least £20, Charlotte calculated. Fearful of losing it or having it stolen, and also leery of attracting attention (this expensive necklace not being the sort of thing customarily seen on itinerant tragedy queens), she insisted that he keep the necklace in his possession until they left town. In the meantime, she and her little family indulged in comforting dreams of being settled and provided for. Her depression lifted, and gradually she regained her health.

But not long before they were due to leave, Charlotte's new friends began to behave strangely. The "nephew" went away and stayed away for some days, throwing the old gentleman into a violent passion until the younger man returned. Then suddenly the men received a communication from the magistrate ordering them out of town on pain of jail. While Charlotte and Mrs. Brown were puzzling about what this might mean, Linnet rushed in to tell them that he had heard from the townsfolk that the two men were "Gamblers and House-breakers," and that the horses and necklace were stolen goods. It turned out that all the old man's professions of friendship and promises of a happy future had been a part of a scheme to steal the "Browns"' baggage, which contained good linens and a set of clothes Mrs. Brown had just received from relatives. Even more frightening, had Mrs. Brown been seen wearing the necklace by someone who could identify it as stolen, both she and Charlotte could have been hanged for the theft. Instead, it was the old man who was hanged about a year later; his "nephew," Charlotte later heard, died "raving mad in a Prison in or near London."

Back with Linnet's company again, Charlotte and her family travelled in February 1749 to play at Chippenham in Wiltshire, a market town on the Bath road known for its woollen manufacture and its large number of taverns.[7] Here, Charlotte said, she made "many Friends," but then Linnet took his troupe to Corsham four miles away. In the unpredictable, precarious way of itinerant acting, business proved bad in this town; unpaid and therefore unfed, Charlotte, Kitty, and Mrs. Brown "had little else to do than to walk out and furnish our keen Stomachs with fresh Air."

Tempers wore thin among the starving, ragged players, and the company erupted in quarrels. The sight of her daughter and companion hungry while Linnet ate well was more than Charlotte could bear. She confronted him and demanded an advance. Linnet refused, and they quarrelled. Outraged, Charlotte determined to leave his company. Another manager, Richard Elrington, had approached her earlier about playing for him, so Charlotte now wrote him to say that if he would send three guineas, "my Friend, Daughter and Self would immediately join him." They quickly received an effusive response accompanied by two and a half guineas, hired a pair of horses, and left Linnet's troupe for Tiverton in Devonshire, nearly seventy miles away. This probably occurred sometime in the spring of 1749.[8]

But the Elringtons' troupe, it turned out, was in even worse circumstances than Linnet's. They, too, were starving and quarrelsome; they, too, were decimated in numbers. It was at Tiverton that Mrs. Elrington had been forced by a fellow actress's drunkenness to act Polly and Lucy simultaneously, which had not made a very good opening-night impression on the audience. When Charlotte and her party arrived after their long journey, they found to their dismay that the troupe had been forced to begin playing three times a week at the village of Cullompton, five miles away, "that they might have a Probability of eating once in six Days." Charlotte borrowed enough to get there, but as her trio approached the town they encountered a prosperous-looking farmer who identified them as players, and told them sincerely that, if they had any pity for themselves, they should turn back, or starve. This threw Mrs. Brown into such alarm that she dropped her reins (she being, Charlotte said, "not the best Horsewoman in the World"), and her horse ran into a hedge, throwing her, fortunately unharmed, into a ditch.

The three continued to Cullompton, where the Elringtons greeted them with great joy, delighted by the prospect of supplementing their diminished numbers with more players, particularly one of Charlotte's stature. Charlotte was immediately pressed into service to play Archer in *The Beaux' Stratagem;* it was that night that Mrs. Elrington, playing Mrs. Sullen, intruded on her scene and inspired the madcap recitation of the medley of tragic speeches. Elizabeth had done this because she had feared that seeing the condition of their troupe, Charlotte might have been inclined not to stay. The playful absurdity of this performance and Charlotte's immediate affection for Mrs. Elrington probably did contribute to Charlotte's decision to remain, but so did the lack of alternatives.

The farmer's warning had been accurate. The troupe went such a long time barely eking out a living that, Charlotte said, "I at last gave up all Hopes and Expectations of ever enjoying a happy Moment." The vicissitudes of fortune in the country were much greater than Charlotte had ever experienced in London: not only were there few places to pick up acting work, but also she lacked the network of friends and acquaintances whose timely guineas had so often saved her from ruin in the past.

Kitty shared her mother's and Mrs. Brown's situation for several years. She had developed into a talented actress, capable of handling a variety of parts. Charlotte judged that she had genuine, if uncultivated, theatrical gifts, good enough to play at the patent theatres in London. Kitty was particularly good, Charlotte thought, in low comedy, which was "agreeable to her Figure, and entirely so to the Oddity of her humourous Disposition." By "humourous," Charlotte could have meant either capricious and whimsical or funny and mirthful: it is likely both sets of definitions fit Kitty, who perhaps resembled Charlotte in certain ways, though she was increasingly defying her mother (in which behaviour, of course, she also resembled Charlotte).

On January 6, 1750, Kitty, then twenty years old, married John Harman, another strolling player, who may have been at one time a member of Linnet's or Elrington's troupes. Whether Charlotte and Kitty's conflicts began before he entered the scene is uncertain, but certainly the marriage drove a wedge between them. Charlotte experienced it more as losing a daughter than as gaining a son, for Kitty married very much against her wishes. Harman, Charlotte believed, was irresponsible and improvident—Richard Charke all over again. She thought him not Kitty's equal in any way, and found Kitty much too deferential to her husband. Though she had no fortune, Kitty was a good match, her mother felt, for she was level-headed and responsible (notably, in these respects, unlike Charlotte). "Had she met with as sober and reasonable a Creature as herself," said Charlotte, they might have assembled their own strolling company and made enough money to set up in a respectable business. (This was a recurrent fantasy of Charlotte's, one she was never able to realize.) But Harman, in Charlotte's opinion, was neither sober nor reasonable. When she heard of "the unpleasing Knot's being tied," she would have immediately "unmarried" them had she been able. As it was, she adapted to her own situation the lines of Brabantio, Desdemona's father, as he unhappily resigns his daughter to Othello: "I here do give him that with all my Heart, / Which, but that he had already, / With all my Heart I wou'd keep from him." (And we know how *that* marriage turned out.)

The Charke-Harman nuptials took place in the church of St. Thomas in Lymington, a coastal town in Hampshire southwest of Southampton. Perhaps Kitty was still with Charlotte, performing in the area at this time, but it is probable that they had parted ways some time before. Unsurprisingly, Charlotte was not present at the wedding; she wrote of having "heard" about it. The Harmans joined another strolling troupe that also travelled around the south of England.

In the autumn of 1750, Elrington's troupe made its way to Cirencester, with all its bad memories for Charlotte. Then, without informing the players, Mr. Elrington suddenly left them, going off to London to play at Covent Garden Theatre and leaving Mrs. Elrington alone with the company. Charlotte, who believed that Elrington had abandoned his wife, came to her assistance with the duties of management. Though she was tempted by an offer from Linnet to join him in Bath, Charlotte's loyalty and affection for Elizabeth Elrington—who said she depended upon Charlotte as her "Right-hand"—made it impossible to abandon ship. She soon discovered, however, that her loyalty was misplaced. Elizabeth had known of her husband's intentions all along, and soon she also abandoned the strollers to join him in London. Charlotte was left with the tattered company—six players besides herself, "one Scene and a Curtain, with some of the worst of their Wardrobe," and "an inexhaustible Fund of Poverty."[9]

Suddenly, Charlotte was once again manager of a company. The duties of a provincial manager were onerous: not only did she have to deal with play selection, casting, and maintaining the stock, she also had to oversee a continual round of packing and unpacking, and getting the company from one town to another. They were so poor that they probably had to travel on foot, the players carrying pieces of scenery or costumes on their backs.[10] Charlotte had the critical responsibility of choosing where they would visit next and then "taking the town": that is, going to secure a licence from the mayor or magistrate, which might involve buying him a glass or two of wine to put him in a receptive mood. She had to find a venue for their performances, secure lodgings for the troupe, and find musicians. She had to try to solicit bespoke performances from the mayor or other wealthy citizens. Upon arriving at the town, she had to write the playbill, and perhaps even print it up herself.

At the beginning of the following summer, 1751, the Elringtons reappeared, Covent Garden having closed for the season.[11] Charlotte does not record in what mood she received them, but she was not angry enough to quit. The summer season began hopefully, for the troupe travelled to the small Cotswold village of Minchinhampton in Gloucestershire, where they were invited by a local landowner, Samuel Sheppard, to perform.[12] They had not been in Minchinhampton very long, however, before Charlotte and two of her fellow players were arrested for vagrancy under the terms of the Licensing Act. They had fallen prey to an extortion scheme practised by a "decayed Relation" of a councilor at the nearby market town of Stroud, who had been granted by his relative a "special Warrant" to apprehend those deemed vagrants under the law. The idea was to extort money from the troupes and the gentry who patronized them. Charlotte and her fellows were seized as representative of the company (Charlotte was assumed to be a man), conducted fourteen miles north to the sessions court in Gloucester, and then thrown into jail.[13]

The effect on Charlotte was devastating. The Gloucester jail was filled, she said, with more than two hundred condemned prisoners (all male), who were awaiting execution or transportation. The manacled felons' "hedious Forms and dreadful Aspects, gave me an Idea of such Horrors, which can only be supposed to centre in Hell itself. Each had his Crime strongly imprinted on his Visage, without the least Tincture of Remorse or Shame." Their language was brutal and blasphemous; they were dressed in filthy, vermin-ridden rags; they stank.

Working herself up into a frenzy of despair, Charlotte dramatically exclaimed to the other players that if they were sentenced to remain in the prison she would offer to cut their throats and then her own—an offer they declined. After spending all day in that ghastly prison (they had been incarcerated at nine o'clock in the morning), Charlotte was horrified to hear the clock strike eight, the signal for closing the prison gates. She realized that they would spend the night there—and who knew how many nights thereafter.

She was terrified, too, lest they be thrown into the men's condemned hold with the condemned—a loathsome prospect, and one that carried a serious threat of rape. Her fears were eased by a young warder who took pity on them and arranged to have the strollers join two shoemakers in the otherwise unoccupied women's condemned hold. The cell's floor and walls were made of flint and were cold and damp, but Charlotte, fortunate to be wearing boots and a greatcoat, rolled herself up in a piece of the shoemakers' leather and settled into misery. After a gloomy silence, one of the other players, Mr. Maxfield, tried to rally her spirits by remarking that he had often seen her play Captain Macheath in a stage prison, but now she could give them the authentic thing; wouldn't she entertain them all with the relevant scene from *The Beggar's Opera*? Charlotte pulled herself out of her melancholy long enough to sing Macheath's medley of songs as he confronts his imminent execution. Perhaps the reminder of Macheath's last-minute reprieve came as some solace.

At nine the next morning, Charlotte and the others appeared in court and, assisted by a letter from Sheppard containing a large amount of gold, had their case dismissed. Charlotte and her fellow players were free, but they had to pay for their incarceration, being charged a guinea each plus horse hire to cover the expense of transporting them to Gloucester. "I have often heard of People's paying Money to avoid a Jail," she remarked, but *she* had to pay "for going into one."

In the autumn, the Elringtons once again left their company, this time to play in Bath, leaving Charlotte in charge, officially, this time. Charlotte led her troupe into south Wales, where she made a group of friends (presumably all of them knew that she was a cross-dressed woman, though this is not certain) and found a new support system to replace the one she had left behind in London. A Chepstow widow and her family extended their generous hospitality, and another younger lady, the heiress of a considerable property near Chepstow, became her friend.

From Chepstow, the troupe went on to Abergavenny, where her heiress friend corresponded with her. (This woman, at least, must have been aware of Charlotte's sex; to correspond with a man not related to her would have been indelicate for a woman, especially a single woman, as Charlotte's friend appeared to be.) Charlotte's dream of a settled country life, so cruelly played upon by the old criminal in Cirencester, had not left her, and her kind reception in Chepstow inspired in her "a firm Design, at that time, to quit all Thoughts of Playing." Charlotte was heartily sick of "Vagabondizing (for such I shall ever esteem it)." With Mrs. Brown's reluctant consent, Charlotte and she quit the company and took a house together in the country.

21

THE FEMALE HUSBAND

(1752–54)

On October 7, 1746, Mary Hamilton went on trial at the quarter sessions court in Taunton, Somersetshire. Calling herself Dr. Charles Hamilton, she had married Mary Price at St. Cuthbert's Church in Wells on July 16, and the newlyweds had travelled around Somersetshire for two months before Hamilton was arrested in Glastonbury on September 13, her new wife giving evidence against her. In Hamilton's deposition, made shortly after her arrest, she said that she had been dressing as a man since she was fourteen, when she first put on her brother's clothes, and that she had continued to wear men's apparel ever since (she was then about twenty), wandering around Devonshire and Somersetshire practising as a quack doctor. Mary Price in her deposition testified that she and Charles Hamilton had "lain together several Nights" after their marriage and that he "had entered her Body several times" (presumably with a dildo) which made her believe him to be a "real Man." Later, however, she began to suspect otherwise, and Charles confessed to her that he was a woman.[1]

In prison, Mary Hamilton became a tourist attraction: "Great Numbers of people flock to see her in Bridewell" (where she did a brisk trade selling her quack medicines), reported *The Bath Journal*. She "appears very bold and impudent. She seems very gay, with Perriwig, Ruffles, and Breeches; and it is publickly talk'd, that she has deceived several of the Fair Sex, by marrying them." A later newspaper account reported (surely with some exaggeration) that Mary Price was the *four-teenth* woman Hamilton had fraudulently married, "using certain vile and deceitful Practices not fit to be mentioned." A few London news-papers picked up *The Bath Journal*'s report; but the story got much wider circulation when a heavily fictionalized account of it was pub-lished later in November, entitled "The Female Husband." This pam-phlet was published anonymously, but in the twentieth century it was definitively identified as the work of Henry Fielding. Fielding must have thought of his old cross-dressing colleague Charlotte when, in need of money as always, he rushed his sensational account into print.

During Hamilton's trial, the Somerset court spent a considerable amount of time debating "the Nature of her Crime." Finally resolving to call it fraudulent, the court determined that Hamilton was "an uncommon notorious Cheat" and sentenced her to six months at hard labour, and during that time to be publicly whipped in four towns in Somersetshire: Taunton, Glastonbury, Wells, and Shepton Mallett.[2] The sensation produced by Mary Hamilton's crime was simultaneously salacious and moralistic: the trial proceedings themselves, the newspa-per accounts, Fielding's pamphlet (and, indeed, her punishment itself), all combined moral outrage with erotic titillation. But Hamilton was convicted not for her sexual conduct but for fraud. By posing as a man and marrying Mary Price, Hamilton had assumed the legal position, the privileges and power, of a man vis-à-vis his wife—entitlement to her income, representing her under the law, and so on. This was Hamil-ton's crime: falsely entering into a marriage with its attendant legal sta-tus, not her imposture as a man per se, and not what we would now call her lesbianism. Though sexual relations between women were con-demned as unnatural in the eighteenth century, there was no law against them.*

Somersetshire was in the vicinity of the circuit Charlotte began trav-elling as a strolling player in autumn of 1746. Perhaps she saw news-paper accounts of the case, or came across a copy of "The Female Husband." On more than one occasion thereafter, Charlotte and Mrs. Brown were in Wells, the town in which Mary Hamilton had been mar-ried and one of those in which she had been publicly whipped. Her story certainly must have given Charlotte pause.

*Male "sodomy" was illegal.

Mary Hamilton was not the only female husband to be tried and punished in the eighteenth century: another cross-dresser named Ann Marrow, for instance, was convicted for marrying three women and sentenced to the pillory and six months in jail.[3] Though contracting a fraudulent marriage was particularly dangerous, cross-dressing itself risked running afoul of the law: one woman discovered "travelling to Uxbridge in a Sailor's Habit" aroused suspicion because her "odd Shape" made three Gentlemen who stopped her suspect an "evil Design." She was taken before the justice, and, when she could not give any "satisfactory" reason for being in men's clothes, committed to "Tothill-Fields Bridewell to hard Labour in the same habit."[4] In her case, her sailor's outfit seems to have raised suspicion that she was plotting criminal activity.

Some cross-dressers were celebrated, especially "female soldiers" such as Hannah Snell and Christian Davies ("Mother Ross"), who, like Snell, published an account of her military service. Davies put on her soldier's uniform in order to pursue her wayward husband, whom she did find (though in the arms of another woman). Davies lived some time with her husband posing as his brother, but when she was wounded in battle her sex was discovered (unlike Snell's), and she reverted to a female identity.

The stories of both of these female soldiers emphasize their relationships with men. Snell did engage in flirtations with women, but this is presented as something she had to do to make her disguise convincing. Her narrative often stresses her remarkable ability to preserve her "virtue" while serving as a marine, meaning that she neither was raped nor engaged in consensual liaisons with men. Accounts of much less virtuous women who dressed as men and went to sea—the female pirates Mary Reade and Anne Bonney, for instance—still show them in amorous relationships with men. But for every celebrated story of a woman who put on men's clothes and went into battle, there were other, more threatening cross-dressers, such as the ambiguous Uxbridge sailor and the female husbands, who transgressed (or seemed as if they *might* transgress) the law.

Three important factors differentiated Charlotte from female husbands such as Hamilton and transgressors such as the female sailor, however: Mrs. Brown's knowledge of her sex, the fact that they did not undergo a wedding ceremony, and Charlotte's identification as an actress. There was no fraud or "cheat" involved (neither of Mrs. Brown nor of a clergyman deceived into marrying them), nor did Charlotte break any laws governing marriage and property. And while a strolling actress was vulnerable to the enforcement of the Licensing Act as a vagrant, her profession also gave her cross-dressing a context: in a situation comparable to the female sailor's, she could have come up with an explanation that probably would have "satisfied" a magistrate, even if he considered her cross-dressing offensive.

For us today there is another important difference between Charlotte and Mary Hamilton: whereas the intimate details of Hamilton's marriage became public in the trial, we have little information about the relationship between Mr. and Mrs. Brown. Though Charlotte wrote about her friend in very tender tones, making it clear that they had established some kind of partnership founded upon a strong attachment between them, the nature of that attachment remains unspecified.

Some modern readers have been anxious to "protect" Charlotte from the imputation of lesbianism, arguing that there is no proof that her relationship with Mrs. Brown was sexual. (Why should the absence of proof require us to assume that they were not lovers rather than that they were?) Some argue that a woman like Charlotte would have many reasons to want to pass as a man: employment opportunities, safety, and economy (in not having to carry a change of clothes for her men's roles), for example. And all these certainly were relevant to Charlotte—but they are inadequate to explain the extent of her cross-dressing even when it was obviously not to her advantage, her strong investment in male theatrical roles (not just breeches parts) in the first place, and her long relationship with Mrs. Brown.[5]

Our ability to understand that relationship is complicated not only by the absence of definitive information but also by the difference in the way people then thought about sexuality. When we speculate about whether Mr. and Mrs. Brown were "lovers," it is not even clear what that might have meant. Genital sexual contact? A chaste but passionate emotional bond? Or something in between? Same-sex desire among women in the eighteenth century might have been expressed in diverse ways. There were women who did "have sex," as we would say, with other women, who now probably would be called lesbians or bisexuals, and who then might have been called tribades (which Charlotte does not appear to have been called) or, later, Sapphists: the female counterparts to male sodomites or Mollies.

But there also were women who engaged in intensely passionate "romantic friendships" with other women that might have not expressed themselves in genital sex but might have involved some degree of physical intimacy. Queen Anne was passionately attached to Sarah Churchill, the Duchess of Marlborough, and openly expressed her passion in her letters; Anne's sister Mary addressed her dear friend Frances Apsley as "Husband." The bluestockings Elizabeth Carter and Catherine Talbot, neither of whom married, sustained a devoted friendship for thirty years. Eleanor Butler and Sarah Ponsonby, the "Ladies of Llangollen," who lived together for fifty years, were the eighteenth century's most famous romantic friends, visited by many respectable people.

Our consideration of Charlotte's sexuality is further complicated by the anachronism of the nomenclature and categories we use today. Our modern notions of "lesbian" "identity" (or, for that matter, "heterosexual" "identity"), for instance, did not exist as such in Charlotte's world; how eighteenth-century people *did* understand their own and others' sexuality is a topic vigorously debated among historians.[6] This presents a difficulty in labeling Charlotte as "a lesbian" or "a bisexual" according to our modern ideas, not only because we do not know the nature of her relationship with Mrs. Brown, but even more because, even if they were sexually intimate, they would not necessarily have thought of themselves as possessing an identity based upon that sexual conduct. The notion that what we do sexually confers on us a social (and political) identity—gay/lesbian, straight, bisexual, and so on—belongs to our time, not to theirs.

On the other hand, even if Charlotte and Mrs. Brown did not "have sex," their relationship still could have been founded upon mutual desire that we would call homoerotic. My own judgment is that Charlotte and Mrs. Brown were the eighteenth-century forebears of what we would call today a lesbian couple, and that whatever they actually "did in bed," their relationship involved strong feelings for each other that included erotic desire. After her unfortunate relationships with men, Charlotte finally found a loving, loyal companion to relieve her loneliness and to share her exile. Their long-term relationship—it may have continued for the rest of Charlotte's life—seems to have been a tender partnership that for both women superseded sexual relationships with men. Charlotte and Mrs. Brown occupy an important place in lesbian history as one of the few historically visible same-sex couples from two hundred and fifty years ago, even if we cannot say for certain how closely the modern term "lesbian" characterizes their experience.

When she and Mrs. Brown quit Elrington's company and returned to Chepstow, Charlotte immediately took a lease on a house belonging to the father of her heiress friend, where, with Mrs. Brown's assistance, she proposed to turn "Pastry-Cook and Farmer." These professions are rather odd ones for a woman who has spurned the feminine domestic arts, and who, despite her youthful experimentation with gardening, was so utterly urban. But oddity, after all, was Charlotte's trademark. So she and Mrs. Brown moved into their "very handsome House, with a large Garden" of nearly three quarters of an acre. Its desirability was somewhat attenuated by the fact that it was completely empty and they had no furniture. Charlotte was "without a Shilling in the Universe, or really a positive Knowledge of where to get one"; she could not afford to buy even a bed. The house did have an oven, but she had no money to purchase fuel for a fire, either.

Charlotte, however, had committed herself. Since they had nothing to sleep on, she and Mrs. Brown had to stay in lodgings and pay daily visits to their empty house. Wandering through the rooms, Charlotte began to suffer doubts, but she kept them to herself. Then, once again, a friend came to her rescue. The Chepstow widow gave Charlotte enough money to purchase fuel and the ingredients to make pies, so she and Mrs. Brown could turn their hands to baking.

At first, they did extremely well. Their friends supported them, and curiosity drove others to buy their wares. Elated by her success, Charlotte was all for rushing out to buy a horse (before she had bought a bed) to carry her pies to markets around the area—exactly the same reckless plan she had made in the first flush of her oil shop fifteen years earlier. This time Mrs. Brown, for once, successfully dissuaded her, which was a good thing, since after the novelty wore off a few weeks later, business precipitously declined. Presumably their pies were not all that tasty (certainly when pitted against the products of the experienced bakers who must have operated in the area).

But now another wealthy friend stepped in to offer assistance. This was Valentine Morris, a local gentleman, who gave Charlotte enough money to furnish her house and to put her farming scheme into effect. With Morris's gift, Charlotte rushed off to buy a breeding sow that turned out, after she waited for three months for the promised piglets to arrive, to have been "an old Barrow." She had to sell it for less than she had paid for it, her loss compounded by the costs of feeding the animal all this time.

Next she made do by selling the fruits from the trees in her garden, which brought in some income until vandals invaded her orchard, stealing her fruit and pulling the trees up by their roots. (What was behind this vandalism can only be conjectured. Random violence? A rival farmer? An indication that some of the locals were hostile to, or suspicious of, Mr. Brown?) Once again, theft proved the last straw: Charlotte was forced to admit that her experiment had failed. Selling their new furniture and taking their pastry-making implements, she and Mrs. Brown set out for Pill, a small seaport near Bristol, where she took a little shop and put up her sign: BROWN, PASTRY-COOK, FROM LONDON.

Pill, where Charlotte and Mrs. Brown stayed for six months, turned out to be an even worse disaster than Chepstow. At first the move seemed to have been a good idea. Their trade flourished during the summer, when the ships from Ireland docked. But in the winter the ships did not sail, and trade declined to almost nothing.

The town itself would not have been unpleasant, Charlotte thought, if not for its residents—the "Savages who infest it, and are only, in outward Form, distinguishable from Beasts of Prey." Hardened swearing by boys of ten, rampant drunkenness, and downright criminal activity made Pill like nothing so much as "the Anti-Chamber of that Abode we are admonish'd to avoid in the next Life, by leading a good one here." As they began to appreciate the extent of her neighbours' ruthless greed and lack of any charitable impulses, Charlotte and Mrs. Brown began to fear for their safety, especially when they found themselves sinking further into debt as the winter progressed with no kind-hearted, generous friends around to relieve them. Just when their plight looked desperate, however, Mrs. Brown got the news that she had received an inheritance from an uncle. The question was how to get to Oxfordshire to collect it.

Charlotte showed the letter to their landlord, asking for the loan of a guinea so that she (acting as the husband) could travel to pick up the money, leaving Mrs. Brown there as kind of a hostage, but the innkeeper suspected that it was forged and refused. So, said Charlotte, "I consulted on my Pillow what was best to be done, and communicated my Thoughts to my Friend." She and a very reluctant Mrs. Brown sneaked out together, despite the fact that they had no money and Charlotte no hat, having pawned it. Mrs. Brown shed tears of distress over the prospect of "so daring an Enterprize, to set out, without either Hat or Money, fourscore Miles on Foot." Charlotte had to promise to ask a friend in Bristol for some money before she would go. At Bristol, Charlotte got the money and borrowed a spare hat from a fashion-conscious young journeyman; the women went on to Oxfordshire. They secured the inheritance and celebrated by renting a horse to carry them part of the way back, paying farmers for rides on their wagons the rest of the way.

When the women arrived back in Pill, they were greeted with surprise, for word had circulated that they had absconded (this being the only interpretation that occurred to anyone). But returning with money in her purse, Charlotte paid off her landlord, got her hat out of hock, and "as long as the Money lasted, was the worthiest Gentleman in the County." Memories of their recent struggles slipped away, despite the onset of winter and the falloff in trade. Charlotte, who like a legal husband took control of her wife's money, spent the inheritance freely and enjoyed the popularity it gave her, only to find herself, once the money ran out, "as disregarded as a dead Cat." Mrs. Brown, who had probably tried her best to rein in Charlotte's expenditures as the money streamed away, apparently exerted no more control over it than any legal wife forced to watch her reckless husband gamble and drink away her dowry.

That January, 1753, Charlotte turned forty, destitute once again with the winter hard upon them. She was filled with remorse for her squandering of Mrs. Brown's inheritance, money that could have seen them through. As she cast about once again for a way to get by, Charlotte seized upon another new idea: she would become a journalist.

Charlotte wrote "a little Tale" and got a friend to introduce her to Edward Ward, printer and proprietor of *The Bristol Weekly Intelligencer* newspaper, who generously engaged Charles Brown as a proof-reader and occasional writer.[7] Had he known who she really was (and who her father was), Charlotte said, he might have been more self-interested in securing her services, but employing "Charles Brown" was an act of kindness to a needy and not untalented stranger.

The walk from Pill being long, dirty, and dangerous, Charlotte and Mrs. Brown determined to move to Bristol. But they were in debt by eighteen shillings to their landlord. So one night they locked up their shop and stole away, leaving £5 worth of stock behind; in Bristol, Charlotte mailed the key to the landlord, telling him to keep the stock as (over)payment of their debt. Now she had work. But the pay was so slight that if they had not been fed dinners by sympathetic friends, she and Mrs. Brown would have gone as hungry in the city as they had in the country.

After a month of struggling, Charlotte asked Ward for more money and was turned down, so she decided to stage a benefit of *The London Merchant* for herself at the Black Raven tavern in the High Street, despite the fact that theatre was outlawed in Bristol. She quietly brought in a group of strolling players from nearby Wells, including Kitty and her husband. Many people promised to attend, but on the night in question they did not appear, leaving Charlotte with a poor house that did not begin to cover the debts she had incurred to mount the performance. The next morning she was "obliged," she said, "to strip my Friend of the ownly decent Gown she had" and pawn it in order to pay the players a pittance. Not only did her failure once again rebound on the long-suffering Mrs. Brown, this time it once again affected her formerly long-suffering daughter (and subjected Charlotte to her son-in-law's complaints).

So Charlotte resumed strolling. At least there was the consolation of a reunion with Kitty, since she and Mrs. Brown joined the Harmans' company at Wells. Charlotte could have gone elsewhere but wanted to be with Kitty, despite her dislike of John. However, a smallpox epidemic was raging in Wells at that time; people were too sick or too frightened to attend the theatre, and if it were not for the kindness of some of the town gentry, who gave them presents of good clothing, "the poor Exhibitors might have been glad to have shared the Fate of the Invalids, to have been insured of a Repository for their Bones." After Wells, Charlotte and Mrs. Brown travelled with Kitty and John through a tour of six towns. Their run was not without success, but friction intensified between Charlotte and her son-in-law who, she thought, treated her with great "Impertinence." (John must have been well aware of her opinion that her daughter could have done much better.)

In the sixth town, Honiton in Devonshire, Charlotte was pleasantly surprised to receive a letter from Theophilus, writing to tell her that Mr. Simpson, who managed one of the two principal theatre troupes in Bath, wished to hire her as prompter. The chance to settle down in Bath with a relatively established troupe was irresistible. The brief taste of strolling in company with her son-in-law had reawakened all Charlotte's contempt for him and for the itinerant life. She accepted Simpson's offer, and she and Mrs. Brown went off to Bath, where he welcomed her warmly. He specified a condition of her employment, however: Charlotte would have to give up wearing men's clothes and start dressing as a woman. He advanced her a sum of money so that she could "equip" herself in her "proper Character."

Simpson stipulated that Charlotte give up her breeches in order to maintain respectability in a resort that was the most fashionable venue outside of London. But his insistence that Charlotte appear in petticoats probably had a more specific rationale, which is that Bath was acquiring a reputation as a hotbed of female homosexual behaviour. Hester Thrale later called the town "a cage of these unclean birds."[8] This might explain the manager's anxiety to have Charlotte respectably in petticoats: to attenuate her masculinity and to forestall the gossip that would have arisen had she and Mrs. Brown continued to present themselves so visibly as husband and wife.

It must have felt horribly uncomfortable, even like a self-violation, for Charlotte to squeeze her body into stays and a hoop knowing that she was sacrificing the freedom of breeches not just for an evening's performance but for the foreseeable future. She had to do it to eat. And perhaps she was beginning to feel that the costs of defying propriety had become too great. Whether she suspected it or not at the time, this was a decisive moment for her. Her cross-dressing days were over. It was October 1753.

Bath was a modish destination year round, though the flood of elite pleasure seekers increased in the summer, when the London season ended. They came ostensibly to drink from and bathe in the spa's supposedly restorative hot mineral springs, but they also came to see and be seen. The town had been a resort in Roman times and in the eighteenth century was undergoing a renaissance, with new, imposing buildings being erected in the prevailing neoclassical style. The social demands of Bath were onerous. You bathed, you made your appearance in the Pump Room to drink the water, you visited coffeehouses, you shopped, you strolled in the streets and the parks, you dined in elegant company, and in the evenings, when not engaged in card parties at private houses, you attended plays, concerts, and balls in the Lower and Upper Assembly Rooms. Colley Cibber had been a fixture at Bath for many years, where he enjoyed a friendship with the master of ceremonies, the dandy Beau Nash ("the King of Bath"), told his stories of the bygone glory days of the theatre, and flirted with the ladies. (Colley at eighty-two was beginning to slow down a little, however, and he does not seem to have been at Bath that year; his usual season at the spa was the summer, in any event, so Charlotte would not have run much risk of encountering him.)

Charlotte's work as a prompter gave her steady employment, but it proved exhausting and, she discovered, exasperating. Besides sitting behind the scenes during performances to feed the players their lines when necessary, Charlotte was responsible for attending rehearsals, keeping the promptbooks and a diary of performances, placing the advertisements, and overseeing the printing of the playbills. She also had to deal with the actors.

They bombarded Charlotte with their complaints against the manager: she was often unhappily caught in the centre of disputes. Simpson's personality made matters worse. He was a very genial man, but a poor manager. He "ought to have been MASTER OF THE HOUSE," said Charlotte, "but his good Nature, and Unwillingness to offend the most trifling Performer, made him give up his Right of Authority, and rather stand neuter, when he ought to have exerted it." As a result, discipline in his troupe was nonexistent.

Charlotte's fragile health suffered, and she also became a victim of her fellow players' corrosive envy and back-stabbing. Some patrons of the theatre, who remembered Charlotte from London, desired that she reprise her old role of Lord Foppington in *The Careless Husband*. Charlotte must have been delighted to be recognized and acknowledged like this; the idea was all the more attractive because her performance would be a benefit for her. Simpson initially assented—until two actors complained. Each of them wanted the part for himself although, Charlotte thought, neither was qualified to play it, for they could neither act with the ease required in the role of the aristocratic fop nor speak a word of French, with which Foppington sprinkles his conversation. Simpson, weak as ever, cancelled the performance. So sickened was Charlotte by the collapse of this opportunity that she could scarcely bear to enter the theatre: "I as much abhorred to go to the House as some People do to undergo a Course of nauseous Physick."

In March 1754, when "an old Scoundrel" lodged a complaint with the magistrate against both Simpson's troupe and the rival company performing at the Orchard Street Theatre, temporarily closing both playhouses, Charlotte decided that it was time to quit. Her six months in Bath, coming after seven years of constant privation and uncertainty, wandering from place to place, had left her exhausted and frail. Prompting, she now said, was more a job for a man than a woman— an indication of how worn down she had become, she who had confidently taken on so many "men's jobs" before.

Charlotte turned her back on Bath with relief. To her disgust, however, a story immediately spread that she had been forced to leave because she "designed to forsake my Sex again," and that she "positively was seen in the Street in Breeches." It is a measure of how dispirited she had become that she responded to this rumour with indignant denials, as a falsehood that made her "look ridiculous." She was particularly upset to find that the rumour had spread to London, where an actress (whom she characterized as "half-mad") had made a point of delivering the story to her family. Charlotte wanted to avoid anything that would further discredit her in the eyes of her family, who seem to have been informed that she had resumed women's dress. Probably she herself had made sure they heard the news (Theo would have been the most likely conduit), for she was beginning to lay the groundwork for an attempt at reconciliation.

Leaving Bath, Charlotte and Mrs. Brown still had to eat, so they first engaged themselves with a "most deplorable set of non-Performers" at nearby Bradford, players whose feeble acting was complemented by an almost nonexistent wardrobe. After Bradford, Charlotte and Mrs. Brown joined with another manager, "about as rich and wise as him we left," and went to Devizes. From there, Charlotte determined to head for Rumsey in Hampshire, where she had heard Kitty was playing; they had four shillings in their pockets to take them on a journey of forty miles over the Salisbury plain, and they would have to go another twenty miles out of their way in order to pass through villages that offered lodging. It was "a most deplorable, half-starving Journey, through intricate Roads and terrible Showers of Rain," a "tedious, painful March" through heat and thirst, but after three days, they arrived at Rumsey. They had been forced to spend their last three half-pence on a wagon ride at the end, because their aching legs could carry them no farther.

After all that effort, their time with Kitty and John was brief. The friction between Charlotte and her son-in-law revived more intensely than ever; it was clear they could not live together. (Poor Kitty must have been caught in the middle, though she seemed to her mother always to take her husband's side, too obedient to that "inconsiderable Fool" she had married.) Charlotte was laying other plans, anyway. She had begun to write a novel, calling it *The History of Henry Dumont*, and her ambition of turning author required her to go where there was the largest congregation of booksellers who might be interested in publishing her work: London.

They were on the Isle of Wight when Charlotte told Kitty and John that she and Mrs. Brown would be leaving. Her announcement precipitated another upheaval. Both Kitty and John were offended at this defection of two of the players from their tiny company; they saw themselves as injured. They quarrelled. (We can imagine Kitty hurling deeply felt accusations of selfishness and irresponsibility at her mother.) To make matters worse, another member of the company, who feared the smallpox in that area, left with them, probably increasing the ill will.

Charlotte and Mrs. Brown first went to Fareham, as part of a company of six; there, on the pretence of bringing them assistance, John Harman came and wooed away two of their players, greatly injuring the troupe—acting entirely, Charlotte thought, out of petty vindictiveness against her, though he hurt her less than he did their innocent manager. From there they went to Portsmouth, where they hoped immediately to catch the wagon for London, but found they had just missed it. So they had to spend more of their small amount of money on lodgings while they awaited the next one.

Finally, in December 1754, a month before her forty-second birthday, Charlotte, "transported with Joy," once again set foot on the streets of London. She had been away from her city for more than eight years. Never again, she vowed, would she leave town to chase her fortunes through the countryside. Worn out by the "general Plagues of disappointment and ill Usage, that are the certain Consequences of a strolling Life," she felt "not only sick, but heartily ashamed" of having been a strolling player. It had been a "contemptible life," she thought, "rendred so, through the impudent and ignorant Behaviour of the Generality of those who pursue it; and I think it wou'd be more reputable to earn a Groat a Day in cinder-sifting at Tottenham-Court, than to be concerned with them." Strolling was in her past. Charlotte now had a new plan to earn her living: she would become a writer. And she would see what she could do to repair her relationship with her father.

≫ 22 ≪

THE PRODIGAL DAUGHTER

(1755–56)

Madam,

Tho' Flattery is universally known to be the Spring from which Dedications frequently flow, I hope I shall escape that Odium so justly thrown on poetical Petitioners, notwithstanding my Attempt to illustrate those WONDERFUL QUALIFICATIONS by which you have so EMINENTLY DISTINGUISHED YOURSELF, and gives you a just Claim to the Title of a NONPAREIL OF THE AGE.

With this dedication, Charlotte began her autobiography, *A Narrative of the Life of Mrs. Charlotte Charke, Youngest Daughter of Colley Cibber, Esq., Written by Herself.* The joke was that the "Madam" she addressed was not some wealthy noblewoman (the typical dedicatee) but Charlotte herself. In mock-effusive language, she complimented herself on "the thoughtless Ease (so peculiar to yourself) with which you have run thro' many strange and unaccountable Vicissitudes of Fortune." You, she told herself, are one of the age's "*greatest Curiosities* that ever were the Incentives to the most *profound Astonishment.*" If this book achieves success, she said to herself, "I shall, for Novelty-sake, venture for once to call you, FRIEND; a Name, I own, I never *as yet have known you by.*"

When Charlotte and Mrs. Brown returned to London in December 1754, Charlotte moved ahead with her plans for her novel, *Henry Dumont*. She hoped to publish it in installments—a popular and inexpensive method of publishing at the time—which would allow her to earn money with the parts she had already written while she finished writing the final chapters. So she made arrangements with the printer William Reeve to publish the novel in eight parts. The first installment appeared on March 1, 1755. But rather than plunge into the novel itself, Charlotte chose first to give her audience "a short Sketch of my strange Life." To her surprise, "on the Appearance of the first Number, I was enjoin'd (nay 'twas insisted on) by many, that if 'twas possible for me to enlarge the Account of myself to a Pocket Volume, I should do it." A novel would be enjoyable, they must have told her, but her autobiography was unique and fascinating. The public was always hungry for sensational experiences, and they loved reading "true stories." Readers would flock to buy Charlotte's own account of her extraordinary, entertaining adventures.

Charlotte was powerfully attracted to this idea. She needed money badly. The idea of imitating her father's famous autobiography (as her brother had already done) was compelling, too.[1] By telling her own story, she could attempt both to revive her name in the public mind after her absence from London and to reshape her public image. She could use the book to make explicit overtures to her father that might be all the more convincing for being public. But would her book restore her fortunes and repair her public image, or would it backfire?

If Charlotte wished to restore her reputation or at least invoke sympathy for her outcast plight, writing her life story was risky. Publishing one's personal history without a religious justification (as in an account of Christian conversion or spiritual reawakening) or a political one (as in memoirs concerning important people and historical events) was a new and controversial idea in eighteenth-century England. The term "autobiography" had not even been coined yet. Many felt that there was something shameful about exposing one's life in print for its own sake. Colley, who was successful, secure, and inured to political attacks, had been roundly accused of unpardonable vanity when he published his *Apology* fifteen years earlier. For a woman to do such a thing was even more provocatively immodest: it was a public exposure more disreputable than acting, a kind of literary striptease that might make her more notorious.

Yet, with characteristic boldness, Charlotte threw herself into her task, confident that she could tell her story and that it would sell. (In her impoverished state, the latter was her first consideration.) Despite moralists' castigation of autobiography, the public devoured books promising to provide intimate details of others' lives. Readers loved collections of supposedly genuine private letters bearing titles such as *The Post-man's Pacquet Broke Open*. They savoured sensational life stories recounted by condemned criminals to the officiating clergyman (the "Ordinary") of Newgate Prison. They pored over the sexual escapades confessed by disreputable women such as Delariviere Manley and Teresa Constantia ("Con") Phillips, and snapped up the first-person novels that told, in extended narratives or in letters, the stories of apparently real people such as Moll Flanders and Pamela Andrews.

So Charlotte once again defied the forces of narrow-minded propriety. Her newest performance, played as tragicomedy, gave the public a "Serious but Comic" self-portrait, combining the pathetic heroine of she-tragedy with both the sentimental comic heroine and the clown. To this end, for her epigraph she slightly misquoted a couplet from the prologue to John Gay's play *The What D'ye Call It*: "This Tragic Story, or this Comic Jest, / May make you laugh, or cry,—As you like best." She hoped to make her readers do both.

After the initial March 1, 1755, number, the series that was originally planned to tell the life of Henry Dumont instead told the author's own, evolving into *A Narrative of the Life of Mrs. Charlotte Charke*, published in eight parts, each affordably priced at threepence.[2] Charlotte pronounced herself an "odd Mortal" and cast herself as the picaresque heroine of her life's adventures. She promised to amuse her readers with her zany, hapless exploits—no one in the world was "more fit than myself to be laughed at," she said—and at the same time sought to win their sympathy, portraying herself as a victim of misfortunes, misjudgments, and the malice of others. As she unfolded her story—she seems to have written each week's installment as the previous one was being printed—Charlotte wrote of her days as a promising young actress at Drury Lane; she recounted her quarrels with management and her performances in many other venues after she quit. She denounced Richard, his whores, and his mistress, then forgave him; she described her plight as a single mother, scraping to support her daughter and herself. She recounted her nighttime adventures roaming the dangerous streets of London in men's clothes, befriending prostitutes and dodging bailiffs.

Charlotte both acknowledged her cross-dressing and wove a web of mystery around her reasons for dressing (and sometimes passing) as a man, at one moment seeming to ascribe it to a predilection she carried from infancy and at another stating that she had a specific reason for doing so that involved another person and must forever remain a secret. She described her sad yet comical misadventures as oil merchant, sausage seller, innkeeper, pastry cook, gentleman's valet, waiter, and puppeteer. She told of the women who fell in love with the dashing "Charles Brown" and proposed marriage to him/her. And with particular vigour, since the memory was so fresh, she exposed the desperate, ludicrous lives of strolling players, their big egos, their ragged stockings, and their drunken, snoring audiences.

Not surprisingly, Charlotte made her estrangement from her father a central theme of her story. She presented herself as a repentant sinner, who, having seen her errors (and forsworn her breeches), wanted only to be taken back into the family fold. To this end, she underplayed her time with Henry Fielding, eliding that significant cause of Colley's anger with her, and also glossed over her frequent performances of male roles. Casting herself as a prodigal daughter seeking forgiveness from her father, Charlotte attempted to script the corresponding part for Colley, inviting him in the full glare of public opinion to kill the fatted calf in celebration of his wayward child's return. (She implied that if he considered himself a Christian, he had to pardon her.) In her first installment, she pleaded dramatically for forgiveness. "If strongest Compunction and uninterrupted Hours of Anguish, blended with Self-conviction and filial Love, can move his Heart to Pity and Forgiveness," she swore, "I shall, with pride and unutterable Transport, throw myself at his Feet, to implore the only Benefit I desire or expect, his Blessing, and his Pardon." She hoped, she told the public, that "ere this small Treatise is finish'd, to have it in my Power to inform my Readers, my painful Separation from my once tender Father will be more than amply repaid, by a happy Interview." Thus she introduced a note of suspense into her story: how would this family drama play out? Would it be a sentimental comedy, or a tragedy? Only the future installments would tell.

Charlotte's eagerness to make this public attempt at reconciliation with her father was probably intensified by a recent event. In October 1753, a month before his eighty-second birthday, Colley had made his will (while the wags at White's continued to lay bets on how long he would live). Charlotte had heard the terms of it (as she made clear in her second installment); though not surprising, they probably came as a shock to her. Colley left Theophilus's daughters Jenny and Elizabeth very considerable legacies of £1,000 each; he left Theophilus and Anne (designated in his will as a widow) £50 each. All the rest of his personal estate (he owned no property) he left to his daughter Catherine, with the exception of "five pounds [each] and no more" to be given to his daughters Elizabeth and Charlotte. He made no mention at all of Kitty or of Elizabeth's daughter, Ann.[3]

What Elizabeth had done to provoke Colley's displeasure is not clear; perhaps her crime had been to befriend and defend Charlotte. (The fact that many years before, Colley had gone to court to appropriate Elizabeth's inheritance from her aunt Rose obviously had no weight with him.)

Colley had now officially disowned Charlotte by all but disinheriting her, making her, she said, "an Alien from the Family." Perhaps she hoped that if she could reconcile herself with him he might give her a more favourable place in his will—perhaps enough of a legacy to set herself up in a business. But as early as the second installment of her *Narrative,* Charlotte had to inform her readers of "one of the most tragical Occurrences of my Life, which but last Week happened to me." As her readers would remember, she said, she had made a public confession of her faults in her first installment. And at that time she had expressed the hope that she would soon be able "to ease the Hearts of every humane Breast, with an Account of a Reconciliation." To that end, she had sent a letter to her father, dated March 8, 1755, which she now published in its entirety. "Honour'd Sir," her letter began,

I Doubt not but you are sensible I last Saturday published the First Number of a Narrative of my Life, in which I made a proper Concession in regard to those unhappy Miscarriages which have for so many Years justly deprived me of a Father's Fondness. As I am conscious of my Errors, I thought I could not be too publick in suing for your Blessing and Pardon; and only blush to think, my youthful Follies should draw

so strong a Compunction on my Mind in the Meridian of my Days,
which I might have so easily avoided.

In the remainder of the letter, Charlotte apologized to her father for her
indiscretions, implored his forgiveness, and asked permission to visit
him in order "to throw myself at your Feet." She signed her letter,
"Your truly penitent / And dutiful Daughter."

Charlotte engaged a friend, whom she described as a compassionate
young lady—probably this was Mrs. Brown—to deliver the letter and
await a reply. But the only reply was Charlotte's letter enclosed "in a
blank"—that is, returned unread. So shocked was Charlotte at this
rebuff, she told her readers, that she took to her bed with a fever. She
played out her "inexpressible Anguish," as she had her bid for reconciliation, in public. This unkind blow from her father's hand, she feared,
would prove "the heaviest and bitterest Corrosive to my Mind." Yet she
did not entirely blame Colley: Catherine, "his cruel Monitor," who, she
claimed, had hated her from her birth (and who, she implied, sought to
protect her own financial interest in her father), had no doubt persuaded
him to return her letter. (Charlotte does not acknowledge that Colley
might have acted alone, nor does she seem to consider the possibility
that Catherine had intercepted the letter before Colley even saw it.) "I
hope," declared Charlotte, "my Father's Eyes, for the sake of his Family who are oppressed, may be one Day opened. For my Part, I cease to
think myself belonging to it."

Charlotte, playing the role of the humble prodigal daughter, had
gambled that public opinion might assist in pushing her father into a
reconciliation. Had she also calculated that Colley might have felt
coerced into paying her off in order to prevent her publishing the next
potentially embarrassing installments of her autobiography? If so, she
should have known better. Thick-skinned Colley Cibber had withstood
much heavier artillery than Charlotte could muster.

So Charlotte completed her autobiography unimpeded by intervention from her father. Preserving the guise of repentant daughter to the
end, she never openly attacked him, but she did create an image of him
as hard-hearted and indifferent to her fate (accurately enough, it seems).
She also humiliated him by implication, repeating, for instance, the
rumour about her robbing him at gunpoint in Epping Forest and his
breaking into tears, and the story of her accosting him in a London

street and slapping him in the face with a flounder. And she more subtly assigned guilt, implying that Colley Cibber had permitted, even encouraged, his daughter to grow up into the woman she had become, and then disowned her for it.

The *Narrative*'s final installment appeared on April 19, when buyers also received "a curious Copper-plate of Mrs. Charlotte Charke" (the illustration of her as a four-year-old wearing her father's periwig, page 54, above). Painful as her father's indifference was for Charlotte, posterity must be grateful to Colley for his refusal to pay her to cease writing. Her most recent editor justifiably calls *A Narrative of the Life of Mrs. Charlotte Charke* "a minor masterpiece."[4] Charlotte's quirky prose makes the book a most entertaining read. Her funny-sad autobiography not only gives us the details of a fascinating woman's life that would otherwise largely have been erased by time, it was also groundbreaking from a literary-historical point of view. Hers was one of the earliest British autobiographies written by a woman that was secular rather than religious; it was also the first English autobiography written by an actress.

These reasons for valuing her story, and our appreciation of her lively voice, are relatively recent, however. While readers of her own day clearly enjoyed her story, for readers from the later eighteenth century to the late twentieth, her autobiography cemented her status as a notorious, even immoral, woman. Dr. Burney (who took great pains to instill a sense of propriety in his daughter, the novelist Frances Burney) spoke for subsequent generations when he exclaimed that while Charlotte was "a female not without talents as an actress," she was "of such an eccentric and indecorous character, that the memoirs of her life, though written and softened by being her own biographer, could never be read by persons of her own sex, not wholly abandoned."[5]

Fortunately for Charlotte, in her day there were enough men and presumably abandoned women to make her narrative a success. Her autobiography appears to have been very popular, its combination of confession and sensationalism being much to the public taste. It was immediately reprinted in a single volume that went into a second edition the same year, and it was issued again four years later.[6] The well-regarded *Gentleman's Magazine* also published a condensed, third-person rendition in three monthly installments from October through December 1755, calling it "the entertaining Life" of Mrs. Charke. (This version also appeared in *The Magazine of Magazines,* published in Limerick, Ireland.)[7] The public's imagination was aroused by her adventures, and its sympathy was stirred by her misfortunes.

Her autobiography made Charlotte some money—enough, for instance, to splurge by subscribing to the publication of Edward Miller's *A Collection of New English Songs.*[8] (It is possible that she knew Miller and wanted to support him; or she may have bought the songs with an eye to their use in the theatre.) In the nature of publication in the eighteenth century, though, the publisher-booksellers would have profited more than the author, and it is uncertain how much money Charlotte received either from her book's serial publication or its appearance in bound editions. But for a time, she and Mrs. Brown must have enjoyed the luxuries of coach hire and good meals.

Charlotte had never been successful at managing what little money she had, and her subsequent life suggests that she was as reckless with the proceeds of her *Narrative* as she had been with Mrs. Brown's inheritance. But if she was characteristically improvident, she was also characteristically engaged in plotting her next ventures. She used the *Narrative* to publicize her schemes, in fact: she mentioned more than once the immediate publication of her novel *Henry Dumont* at the conclusion of her *Narrative,* and she informed her readers that in the future she planned to earn part of her living by her pen. She also said that she designed very soon to establish an acting school that would be open three days a week from ten in the morning until eight at night, "where Ladies and Gentlemen shall be, to the utmost of my Power, instructed both in the Art of Speaking and Acting." She spoke of her plans to stage for herself a yearly benefit performance, presumably to supplement her income from her academy and her writing. She outlined other plans, too. She promised to sue her uncle John's widow (the former housemaid), who had "artfully deprived his Heirs at Law of a very considerable Fortune." And she ended her *Narrative* with the hope that she would yet succeed in reconciling with her father.

Few if any of these plans materialized. *Henry Dumont* did not appear immediately on the heels of the *Narrative.* Nothing more was heard about the lawsuit or the academy. But Charlotte's plans to act again were realized, if in a context different from her idea of staging her own yearly benefit. That September 1755, Theophilus got a licence to perform a short run of plays at the Haymarket, and asked Charlotte

Charlotte, as author, in 1755 upon the publication of her autobiography. (Anon., "Mrs. Charlotte Charke," frontispiece to A Narrative of the Life of Mrs. Charlotte Charke, *1755. Courtesy of the Henry E. Huntington Library.)*

to join him. With his company were their niece Ann Chetwood and "Mary Midnight"—the writer and satirist Christopher Smart, performing in petticoats.

In Charlotte's first two performances (September 1 and 3)—in her customary parts of Roderigo and Gaylove—she was billed again as "Mr. Charles" (as she had been in 1744). But in her third role, that of Agnes Wilmot in *The Fatal Curiosity,* she was billed as Mrs. Charke. The advertisement in fact called attention to her: "and the part of Mrs. Wilmot by Mrs. Charke, who originally performed it." This was her benefit performance, a good choice that probably brought in a decent house. But there must have been an element of sad nostalgia in that performance, too. Charlotte had created that role with the Great Mogul's Company. And that night Theo combined *Fatal Curiosity* with the afterpiece *The Tragedy of Tragedies,* billed as written by "the late Mr. Fielding." The witty, improvident, pleasure-loving Henry Fielding had died, probably of cirrhosis of the liver (or possibly of cancer), in October 1754 in Lisbon, where he had sailed in an attempt to recover his health.

One gray morning in late 1755 or early 1756, after a night of heavy rain, two men picked their way along one of the muddy unpaved roads that ran northwest from Clerkenwell into the country. They approached their destination, a dwelling that one of them later described as a "wretched thatched hovel" situated on the outskirts of town in the ragged rural neighbourhood of Cold Bath Fields. Before them across the undeveloped expanse of land, the men could see the New River Head, source of much of London's water supply. Closer by loomed the vast mound where the street cleaners and night soil collectors dumped their foul-smelling accumulation of garbage, offal, and excrement. The neighbourhood's ironic nickname—Mount Pleasant—survives to this day, though the "mount" itself was levelled for the construction of Cold Bath Prison in the 1780s.[9]

The two men, outsiders to the neighbourhood, must have held their handkerchiefs to their noses as they slogged through the shin-deep mud, but they were not to be deterred. Henry Slater, Jr., whose father ran a publishing business in Drury Lane, had opened his own office in Holborn Bars along with his friend Samuel Whyte. Slater and Whyte were on their way to make a deal with Charlotte. Perhaps they had decided to make this trip up from Holborn together for protection against the footpads, pickpockets, and other petty criminals for which Clerkenwell's streets were notorious.

Nearly forty years later, Whyte published an account of his visit to Charlotte in her thatched hut. It is worth quoting a sizeable portion:

> We knocked at the door (not attempting to pull the latch string) which was opened by a tall, meagre, ragged figure, with a blue apron, indicating, what else we might have doubted, the feminine gender. A perfect model for the copper captain's tattered landlady; that deplorable exhibition of the fair sex, in the comedy of Rule-a-wife. She with a torpid voice and hungry smile desired us to walk in. The first object that presented itself was a dresser, clean, it must be confessed, and furnished with three or four coarse delf [sic] plates, two brown platters, and underneath an earthen pipkin and a black pitcher with a snip out of it. To the right we perceived and bowed to the mistress of the mansion sitting on a maimed chair under the mantelpiece, by a fire, merely sufficient to put us in mind of starving. On one hob sat a monkey, which by way of welcome chattered at our going in; on the other a tabby cat, of melancholy aspect! and at our author's feet on the flounce of her dingy petticoat reclined a dog, almost a skeleton! he raised his shagged head and eagerly staring with his bleared eyes, saluted us with a snarl. "Have done, Fidele! These are friends." The tone of her voice was not harsh; it had something in it humbled and disconsolate; a mingled effort of authority and pleasure—Poor soul! few were her visitors of that description—no wonder the creature barked!—A magpie perched on the top rung of her chair, not an uncomely ornament! and on her lap was placed a mutilated pair of bellows, the pipe was gone, an advantage in their present office, they served as a succedaneum for a writing desk, on which lay displayed her hopes and treasure, the manuscript of her novel. Her ink-stand was a broken tea-cup, the pen worn to a stump; she had but one![10]

Whyte's anecdote has a mean-spirited tone ("clean, it must be confessed"). Published in 1794 as a note appended to his didactic long poem on the dangers of the stage ("The Theatre; or, Mirrour for Youth addicted to the Theatro-mania"), Whyte's description of Charlotte's down and out situation was an object lesson in the perils of a theatrical life. Whyte showed Charlotte undoubtedly poor, but suggested that her poverty was a moral condition as well.

Whyte probably did not write down this account until many years after his visit occurred. But however distorted by time and moralizing, his anecdote is one of our last glimpses of Charlotte as well as the only detailed description of her domestic life not provided to us by herself. Reading between the lines of Whyte's sanctimoniousness, we do see Charlotte, and even her poverty has a certain flair to it.

Charlotte may have been cast out by her father, but she shared her dilapidated shack and battered furniture with a family of her own choosing. The "tall, meagre, ragged figure" who opened the door was surely Mrs. Brown (misogynistically caricatured), still sharing Charlotte's life. Whyte's details of the perched magpie, the chattering monkey, the melancholy tabby cat, and the emaciated watchdog named Fidele might have been calculated to catch the attention of children, but they do not seem out of character for Charlotte. We can imagine her finding a sad, ironic satisfaction in referring to Mrs. Brown and this menagerie as her *true* family.

Though she possessed only battered implements for writing, Charlotte had something to sell worth buying: the completed manuscript of her novel, *The History of Mr. Henry Dumont, Esq.; and Miss Charlotte Evelyn*. Why Charlotte did not go ahead with her earlier plans to publish this novel in serial form is a mystery, after her success with her *Narrative*. Perhaps while she had money from her autobiography she did not wish to undertake a demanding new schedule of weekly publication, or she thought that she could get more from the outright sale of the copyright and therefore waited until she had finished the novel to seek a publisher. Perhaps she needed money desperately right then for food or rent, or to placate a threatening creditor.

Charlotte's novel was a worthwhile investment for the booksellers, who would pay her a fixed amount for the manuscript and then reap whatever profits there were to be had. Her autobiography had put her once again prominently before the public and proved her a good storyteller. Publishers of her novel could expect that her name alone would suffice to turn them a tidy profit. Using a "rough deal board with three hobbling supporters" as a desk, Charlotte read her manuscript, negotiated alterations, and asked a price of thirty guineas plus fifty copies of the book. This was a fairly high price, but not unprecedented.

Slater, in turn, offered five. Charlotte refused indignantly. After "some altercation" that threatened to result in a stalemate, Whyte intervened, convincing Slater to raise his offer to ten guineas along with the fifty copies; Charlotte accepted. The copies added a potentially significant source of revenue: she could sell them or she could give some as presentation copies to wealthy potential patrons, hoping for a generous gift in return.[11] The novel was duly published by Slater, Slater and Whyte in February 1756.

The History of Henry Dumont, Esq.; and Miss Charlotte Evelyn features two exemplary protagonists who grow up together and eventually, after various interferences including first marriages to other people, fulfil their destinies by marrying each other. Henry is the orphaned grandson of a French count who has moved the family to England. Charlotte Evelyn is the daughter of the count's friend who served as tutor to both Henry and his deceased mother, after whom she is named. Henry may have lost his parents, but his grandfather is a loving, generous replacement for them both. So ample is the count's paternal love that it expands to include Charlotte, whom he in a sense adopts, paying for her education, though Charlotte's own worthy parents are living (they all live together harmoniously as a kind of extended family). Charlotte, then, is showered with parental love; she has not only a doting mother but also, as it were, two loving fathers.

Even if the author had not given her heroine her own name, it would be obvious that Charlotte Charke's fictional world, replete with the idealized characters not unusual in eighteenth-century fiction, was a fantasy counterpart to her own reality. The central families in the novel are happy models of virtue and mutual love; fathers cherish and protect their children. In a series of subplots involving both the main and peripheral characters, Charlotte introduces scenes of repentance and forgiveness, displays of generosity, relief of both financial and emotional distress, and misfortunes overcome. There are several instances of transformations from poverty to affluence and from wickedness to repentance: those who have fallen low are raised high by the kindness and forgiveness of others.

Based upon a plot line of childhood companions united in marriage that became formulaic in the eighteenth century, the novel is unlikely to appeal to modern readers. But Charlotte unsurprisingly shows particular strength in the drawing of highly theatrical characters and the creating of energetic comic scenes. The Blunder family, centre of an extended comic subplot, consists of a booby country squire and his children, all of whom might have stepped straight off the stage. Charlotte's novel also contains one unusual sequence that has intrigued readers in recent years: a rare depiction of openly homosexual characters in the persons of Billy Loveman and his valet and lover Mr. Turtle. These characters are not well treated: they are roundly condemned by everyone in the novel, and apparently by the author as well. Henry calls the two men "a set of unnatural wretches who are shamefully addicted to a vice, not proper to be mentioned."

There are various ways we might explain this attitude: Charlotte may have not considered that she herself had any affinity with "sodomites," or she may have been a masculine woman contemptuous of effeminate men. Maybe she was trying to assert her credentials as a reformed woman by presenting herself as a moralist, or perhaps she hoped to mask her own same-sex inclinations by attacking them in men. But if Charlotte's attitude towards sodomites disappointingly appears not to transcend the bigotry of her times, on another front she does express an opinion that is "progressive" for her day, a condemnation of the treatment of West Indies slaves: "These unhappy wretches were employed in dreadful tasks in the extremity of the sultry heat," she writes, "frequently receiving cruel stripes from the merciless hands of their overseers."

Henry Dumont was popular enough to go through three editions in 1756, despite a reviewer's judgment that the novel might give "a few hours entertainment to such romance-readers as, fortunately for this class of authors, pay little regard to language, style, nature, imitation, contrivance, or, in short, to proprieties of any kind, provided they are amused with a variety of *surprizing* events."[12] (The reviewer went on to observe that "the defects of her performance are the more pardonable" because Charlotte wrote not by choice but out of "cruel necessity.")

She probably supported herself and Mrs. Brown for a time on the ten guineas and whatever else she gleaned from the sale or presentation of her fifty copies: she must have spent some of her time that winter and spring disposing of them. Charlotte next can be definitively placed at Bartholomew Fair that September, performing at the Great Room in the George Inn Yard with a company advertised as "Mrs. Charke and the King's Company of Comedians" playing a "new Droll" called

England Triumphant.* As usual, her hours would have been long—the company performed from noon to ten P.M.—but her proceeds for the few days of the fair relatively good.

Also at Bartholomew Fair that year, performing not far from Charlotte's venue at the Swan Inn in West Smithfield, were Kitty and John. They played with a troupe managed by one of the Hallam family (probably William, who was a good friend of John's). Kitty and probably John also played at Southwark Fair in mid-September that year, so they were in London from at least September 3 through September 23.[13]

Charlotte and her daughter must have seen each other. Perhaps they were able to assuage the ill feelings remaining from Charlotte and Mrs. Brown's desertion (as the Harmans saw it) from their company in the Isle of Wight two years earlier. If they were able to spend time alone together, they might have renewed something of their old bond. Kitty may have told her mother that she and John, weary of the strolling life in Britain, had been discussing the possibility of accompanying their friend William Hallam to the West Indies. (Members of the Hallam family had for several years been performing in the North American and Caribbean colonies.) Charlotte would have reminded Kitty of her father's disastrous encounter with Jamaica's deadly climate (and its equally deadly rum). She must have seen this plan as ill advised, another irresponsible scheme of her harebrained son-in-law to take her daughter away from her, ruin Kitty's fortunes, and even endanger her life.

But Kitty and John did sail to the West Indies, where they joined a company that William Hallam co-managed with David Douglass. When they left England is uncertain, but they were certainly there by August 1758, when William Hallam lay dying and named "my Trusty and well beloved friend John Harman" the sole executor of his last will and testament.[14] It is likely that September 1756 was the last time Charlotte ever saw her daughter.

After Bartholomew Fair ended, Charlotte began to perform again with Theophilus, who had taken the challenge of circumventing the Licensing Act to new, imaginative heights: he had opened a "Snuff Warehouse" out in Richmond that also happened to double as a "Histrionic Academy,"

---

*In 1752, the British calendar had changed from the "Old Style" Julian to the "New Style" Gregorian, eliminating eleven days from September. Starting in 1753, the truncated Bartholomew Fair began on September 3 (Morley: 350).

whose mission was to instruct young persons in the art of acting. "Rehearsals" of plays were presented entirely free, while customers would buy wares from "Cibber and Co., Snuff Merchants," who sold, not ordinary snuff, but "The Famous Cordial Cephalick Snuff."[15] Advertisements promised that the substance, when "taken in moderate quantities (in an evening particularly), will not fail to raise the spirits, clear the brain, throw off ill humours, dissipate the spleen, enliven the imagination, exhilarate the mind, give joy to the heart, and greatly invigorate and improve the understanding!"[16]

The first recorded appearance of Charlotte here was in mid-September, when she was billed as Mercury (a male role) in Garrick's *Lethe*.[17] Mrs. Brown was also billed as Lady Bountiful in *The Beaux' Stratagem*. It is likely that the two women moved from their Clerkenwell hovel out to Richmond for these September performances; otherwise, they would probably have made the long daily trip by boat.

During the years that had passed since his highly self-publicized loss of his wife, Theophilus had lived a "theatrical odyssey."[18] Sometimes he would play at Drury Lane and Covent Garden when the management would have him, at others he would stage his own performances at the Haymarket or elsewhere, either getting permission from the lord chamberlain or devising creative ways around the Licensing Act. His improvidence persisted at legendary proportions, though he remained a talented actor whom audiences enjoyed seeing on the stage. But his unfailing ability to alienate theatre managers continued to limit his acting options. It was not only his own abrasive personality that put him in an uncertain position, however, but also the influence of his wife. Susannah had overcome her disgrace to return to the London stage in 1742, where she rapidly rose to a position of eminence as London's most celebrated and best-paid actress. When Garrick became manager of Drury Lane in 1747, one of his first deeds was to give the role of Polly Peachum to Susannah, forcing Kitty Clive to play Lucy Lockit. Susannah had waited a long time since the first Polly War, but now she won the second without firing a shot. Kitty Clive's fortunes, as she grew older and fatter and less convincing in her gamine roles, were on the decline, while the continuing expressive force of Susannah's pathetic heroines propelled her to fame, power, and riches.

Susannah still lived with Sloper but she was now a wealthy woman in her own right: "She had an elegant town house at 65 Scotland Yard and a suburban villa at Hammersmith for short retreats when West Woodhay [Sloper's country seat] was too far to travel. She had the equipage and wardrobe of a great lady, and an income, independent of Sloper's, of £700 a year."[19] The one thing she lacked was respectability, since she and Sloper remained married to other people. But among theatre managers and audiences, she reigned as a queen. So when Mrs. Cibber made it a condition of her performance that Theophilus not be allowed in the theatre while she was there, managers obeyed.

Whenever Susannah was performing in one or the other of the patent theatres, Theophilus was barred from the playhouse, even if, as happened in the case of Covent Garden, he was a member of the company that year. This must have been a humiliating and frustrating situation, as Theophilus ceaselessly tried to reclaim his wife, or at least her income, to no avail.

In 1750, finding London's theatres unwelcoming and the creditors too close upon his heels, Theophilus sailed to Dublin again to act in the Smock-Alley Theatre, a playhouse of considerable repute whose manager was Thomas Sheridan, father of Richard Brinsley. Theophilus found a degree of success and acceptance when he visited Dublin. Laetitia Pilkington's son John, who knew him there, said that when Theophilus first arrived in Ireland he was entertained in some of the best houses. The Irish had not heard much about what Pilkington delicately called his "domestic strife," and, he said, "his being rather the gentleman than the comedian in private conversation, made him doubly acceptable."

But in Dublin Theophilus found himself involved in a new quarrel, this time with Thomas Sheridan—though, Pilkington observed, the fault was more Sheridan's than Cibber's. Sheridan saw Theo as a rival who was stealing the applause from him. Their rivalry escalated. At one point Sheridan rallied a number of students at Trinity College with claims that Theophilus was trying to wrest away the management of the theatre from him. The lads showed up to Theo's next performance, "bred a great disturbance, broke up the company, and obliged Theophilus to procure the safety of his life, by making his escape through a window."[20] The quarrel broke out into the inevitable pamphlet war, in which, Pilkington said, Theo acquitted himself with wit and humour, unlike his surly adversary. Sheridan made sure that all of Dublin learned the unsavoury details of Cibber's marriage.

While he was in Dublin, Theophilus also made the acquaintance of one Mrs. Pockrich, the widow of a Dublin citizen (who had been the son of Thomas Pockrich, often credited as the inventor of the musical glasses or "glass harp"). They fell in love. The widow Pockrich was, said Pilkington, "a woman possessed of many accomplishments, and some fortune. She had unaccountably attach'd herself to this unhappy man, who often acknowledged himself highly oblig'd to her excellent counsels, and unalterable affection for him; declaring, that she had, by her superior good sense, and amiable prudence, reclaimed him from many of his irregularities." She also had a small child of whom Theo became "inexpressibly fond." Indeed, under the widow's loving influence, Pilkington said, Theo became "greatly reformed."[21]

Theophilus may have been undergoing a reformation, but when he returned to London in 1753 he was arrested again and incarcerated. When a publisher approached him about lending his name to a series of *Lives of the Poets* (which antedated Samuel Johnson's much more famous essays), Theo sold his name for ten guineas. Once out of debtor's prison, he went back to his rounds of scratched-together theatre performances, a series of lectures (which he called "dissertations" on the theatre), and entertainments. He offered a series of "summer medley" concerts that included himself as a lecturer and comic auctioneer: presumably this latter idea was borrowed from Henry Fielding's Mr. Hen. In this instance, Theophilus followed in Charlotte's footsteps (she having created that role) rather than the other way around.

Though Theophilus was not as unkindly treated in his father's will as were the two youngest daughters, he nonetheless had been effectively disinherited, too. He still felt his father's presence in his life to be an oppressive one, even as he made use of Colley's name whenever possible. He had probably heard of Colley's remark that, had he not known his wife too proud to be a whore, he would have thought that Theophilus was someone else's son.

That witticism was disingenuous, of course, since Colley's most disreputable children were the two who most resembled him. Theophilus's sense that his birthright had been denied must have been a constant goad and reproof to him. Surely it must have underlain at least a portion of this talented, creative man's difficult personality, his often appalling behaviour, and his abiding sense that he had been wronged.

⁓ 23 ⁓

Curtain Calls

(1757–60)

Sauntering cheerfully into old age, Colley Cibber remained remarkably spry and fit: the novelist Samuel Richardson commented that he was "as gay and lively at seventy-nine as he was at twenty-nine."[1] The gamblers at White's continued to have fun laying wagers on his death, though by 1755, when Horace Walpole encountered the eighty-four-year-old laureate looking "still hearty and clear and well," Colley had already outlived two of the men who had bet on his demise years before.[2]

Colley continued to write his odes and an occasional prologue; he authored a few books and pamphlets, including a book about Cicero and, ironically enough, *The Lady's Lecture,* a book of father-to-daughter advice on marriage written in the persona of his sentimental rake Sir Charles Easy. (Samuel Richardson, who had become a friend, nonetheless found Colley's ideas on paternal authority irresponsibly lax: "the piece is calculated as it stands at present to throw down all distinction between parents and children," he complained.)[3] Did Colley think of his own independent-minded youngest daughter as he created the bantering, peculiarly equal relationship between Sir Charles and his daughter? Was he tacitly justifying his own conduct in allowing her so disastrously to choose her own husband when she married Richard?

Once, in 1750, Colley fell so seriously ill that his demise was widely expected, but he recovered: "Though Death has been cooling his heels at my door these three weeks, I have not had time to see him," he wrote to Richardson. "The daily conversation of my friends has kept me so agreeably alive that I have not passed my time better a great while."[4] He passed the next seven years in this agreeable manner. On November 6, 1757, Colley celebrated his eighty-sixth birthday, surrounded, no doubt, by his little "Cluck of Chickens," as he called the "female fry" who lived with him.[5] He probably spent the next month as usual, with his friends, with the members of his family he acknowledged, and with his pleasures. On the morning of Sunday, December 12, Colley awoke at six and exchanged a few words with his manservant, saying that he would doze some more and wished his chocolate brought to him at nine. When the servant returned at that time, he found his master, still reclining on his pillow just as he had left him, dead. Colley was buried not far from Berkeley Square in the churchyard of Grosvenor Chapel on South Audley Street.[6]

What must Charlotte have felt when she heard the news that put an end to any fantasy of reconciling with her father? Of all the blows she had withstood, this must have been one of the worst. She probably attended the funeral, perhaps accompanying Elizabeth and Theophilus, certainly keeping a silent distance from Catherine and Anne.

With this hope (however faint it had been) dashed, Charlotte turned back to her pen. Sometime around this period, probably between 1757 and 1759, she published three short narratives. (They are undated, but they were certainly written after *Henry Dumont,* for it is mentioned on the title pages.) All three were printed by Thomas Bailey's Printing-Office, "where Tradesmen's Bills are Printed neat and Reasonable." It seems likely that she had them cheaply printed herself and peddled them to booksellers. The use of Bailey for all three suggests, though it does not prove, that she wrote them at around the same time. They were entitled *The Lover's Treat, The Mercer,* and *The History of Charley and Patty.*

In the first of these fictions, Charlotte again turned to her own family as a point of reference. Her problems with her father had always been coloured by her bad relationship with her eldest sister. For Charlotte, Catherine now loomed larger than ever as the central villain of her story. *The Lover's Treat; or, Unnatural Hatred* (the best of the three) concerns sibling rivalry and the "unnatural hatred" of a malicious older brother for his younger brother and sister. "In this last Century there has been no Vice more generally rooted in the Minds of Men than a Discordency in Families," Charlotte wrote in the preface, "and which flows from the very Springs, from which we should naturally expect to find the most agreeable Harmony; but Interest whose Power is invincible, too frequently creates us Enemies where we are most nearly and Consanguinity, which ought most especially to endear to each other, is now become a standing Maxim to forget those tender Principles which Nature claims, and the World must necessarily approve."

This forty-page narrative, though more complex than the other two, seems very hastily written, with less striving for literary quality than *Henry Dumont* or the *Narrative*. Marred by long, unwieldy sentences and a perfunctory plot, it is typical hackwork of the time, crudely printed, with many typographical errors. It is hard to believe that Charlotte could have made much money from it, but perhaps it supported her for a few weeks.

Charlotte may have written her other two pieces of hack fiction in the winter of 1758–59. *The Mercer; or, Fatal Extravagance,* which exposes the dangers "of Living beyond our Fortunes," features another loving father who cherishes his daughter. (Things turn out badly nonetheless.) *The History of Charley and Patty; or, The Friendly Strangers* is breathlessly narrated in sentences that run on for a full paragraph, even an entire page: Charlotte seems to have written this story in even more haste than usual. Here the eponymous orphan lovers withstand attempts by greedy, malevolent relatives to keep them apart, suffering abduction, imprisonment, extortion, and "several other surprizing Occurrences," before their final happy union.

At the end of the summer of 1758, Charlotte travelled to Canterbury, where, between late August and the end of September, she performed a series of entertainments. *The Kentish Post* announced her arrival on August 30: "We hear that last Saturday, Mrs. Charke, Daughter to the late Colley Cibber, Esq.; came to this City, with a design, next Week (for one Night only) to entertain the Ladies and Gentlemen here with a comic Medley; after which will be a Ball, as will be farther expressed in printed Bills." The one night extended into others: on September 2, the paper noted that the mayor has "been so obliging as to grant Mrs. Charke the Liberty of the Town-Hall for her Dissertation and Auction on Wednesday next." On September 30, the paper carried a letter from Charlotte herself, giving her "grateful Acknowledgments to my worthy and much esteemed Friends in this City for the Favour lately conferr'd on me at the Town-Hall."

Charlotte's performances seemed to be versions of Theophilus's medley entertainments, a hodgepodge of music, dancing, singing, dramatic enactments, and a mock auction. The paper does not name her troupe members, but Mrs. Brown could have been among them. At Canterbury Charlotte seemed to have had little trouble getting permission to play and to have experienced some success. The weather was unusually wet in the late summer of 1758, so more people may have been encouraged to seek their pleasures inside than was usual at that time of year. In early October, Charlotte returned to London, turning over the Canterbury stage to Mrs. Midnight.

Charlotte probably arrived back in London in time to wish bon voyage to Theophilus. Theo, along with Mrs. Pockrich, who had joined him in London, was embarking for Dublin again. With the London theatres closed against him—he had tried and failed to get a licence to perform that summer (he suspected, probably correctly, that David Garrick was behind the refusal)—Theo accepted a return engagement at the Smock-Alley Theatre. He would turn fifty-five in November, and there was nothing for him in London. It would be interesting to know whether he tried to persuade Charlotte to accompany him (a possibility she might have entertained, for she was fond of the Irish), but she did not leave London.

Theophilus, Mrs. Pockrich, and the wire performer Anthony Maddox set sail in late October on a crowded ship called the *Dublin Trader*. But it did not arrive in Dublin at its expected time. Days went by, and word started to trickle back that she had been caught by a violent storm, and had last been seen being swept past the Isle of Man. Finally definitive news reached Dublin and London: the *Dublin Trader* had foundered, taking everyone aboard down with her. Some days later, the body of a passenger named Mrs. Ford washed up on the Scotland coast, where it was discovered lying beside a chest containing Theophilus's clothes and books. A boat sent out to search for signs of the wreck brought back a playbook inscribed with his name.[7]

Many people who had heard Theo tell his story of his birth during the Great Storm commented on the ironic appropriateness of his death.

Born in a tempest, he had lived in a tempest, and he had died in a tempest. Saddest of all, Theophilus perished just as the skies of his personal life were beginning to clear.

Charlotte must have mourned her brother deeply and sincerely. Losses of various sorts seemed to be compounding themselves in her life in recent years. Theophilus had been disliked by many people and for good reason, but he had been a caring brother to Charlotte. For all his instability and arrogance, his assistance to her had been real and had extended over many years. He had not turned against her as their father had done. Charlotte was one of the few people who actually had liked and admired Theophilus—with her, he dropped the aggressive posturing that was the only side of him so many others saw. (Mrs. Pockrich, too, had seen this better aspect.) Now he was gone—another member of her family dead, or dead to her.

In August 1759, Charlotte was forty-six. Her father and her brother were dead and her daughter had emigrated. Kitty had recently left the West Indies for New York, where their manager intended to open a new playhouse. She was out of reach, and she seemed likely to stay that way. The only members of the Cibber family with whom Charlotte still had contact were her sister Elizabeth Marples (who had opened an eating house in Fulwood's Rents, near Gray's Inn) and Elizabeth's daughter, Ann Chetwood, whose own family was perpetually in debt. Charlotte's hopes of making a living by her pen were little more than fantasies, as so many hack writers have discovered. Acting, as always, was her recourse, the one thing that might earn a little money. But her fragile health meant she could perform only in the warmer months. So one more time, Charlotte returned to her recurrent idea of setting herself up in a business.

Capital was necessary for this scheme, however, and this time there was no Uncle John or obliging Welsh heiress to help out. So on August 7, Charlotte wrote to the Duke of Devonshire, the reigning lord chamberlain.

> May it please your Grace
>
> I must confess this Liberty may be deemed a peice of presumption which wou'd stand a terrible Chance of being render'd Innexcusable from many others of An Equal Rank with Your Grace, And might naturally have prevented my making so bold an attempt in Intruding on

your Grace's Retirement, but as your Humanity is too well known to admit of a Doubt of being forgiven when prompted by necesity, I have ventur'd to Earnest Implore your Graces permission in this vacant Season of the year to perform for ten nights only at the Haymarket Theatre And humbly hope for Sake of the memory of my Late Father Colley Cibber you will permit the Daughter who was bred to the Stage to take an honest Chance for those few nights of establishing her self in a way of Business which will make her happy and greatly add to the numerous Blessings Heaven has Inspired your Grace to bestow on many others. An ill state of health obliges me to decline my profession in the winter, And as the Houses are both Shut up it can be no Detriment to those whose happier Fortunes receive the general advantage of that Season of the year which renders me incapable of Striving for a Support, if your Graces wonted tenderness to the Distress'd will extend it Self to me in this case, I beg you'll give an Immediate order to any of yr Servants to write your pleasure directed to Mrs. Charke at Mrs Hinds in Leicester Street near Swallow Street Piccadilly if yr Grace conceiv'd how happy I may be made by yr favourable Compliance I dare believe you'd both pity and forgive this Trouble from your Graces Most Devoted and obedt Servt

Charlotte Charke formerly Cibber

Please yr Grace in case tis necessary I shall call at Devonshire house to know yr Graces Commands[8]

Charlotte at this time lodged in one of the less attractive neighbourhoods north of Piccadilly. Leicester Street was in the parish of St. James, Westminster, a once fashionable district that had begun to change for the worse. In the second half of the eighteenth century, "the parish had come to be roughly divided into a poorer, relatively insalubrious northern zone . . . and a southern district that had largely retained its high status and voguish popularity with society's elite, with Piccadilly forming the approximate boundary between the two halves."[9] Charlotte's lodgings, unsurprisingly, were in the northern, insalubrious half. Swallow Street was "dark and narrow," running in a straight line up to the intersection now called Oxford Circus. "The road was cobbled, with primitive kennels to carry off the rain-water and to accommodate household refuse for the parish scavengers. . . . The shops were small and unimportant."[10]

Our heroine's poignant letter to the lord chamberlain was designed to obtain his permission for a final performance. (Charlotte Charke, letter to the lord chamberlain, the Duke of Devonshire. August 7, 1759. Courtesy of the National Archives.)

Perhaps moved by her anxious letter and influenced by Colley's memory, certainly confident that she posed no danger to the patent theatres, the lord chamberlain granted Charlotte's request on August 29, though not before Charlotte, waiting impatiently, had sent a second message to Sir Robert Wilmot, the duke's secretary: "I beg pardon for this trouble; but hope as my interest is Concern'd you wont be offended, I shall be much oblig'd if you will let me know by my Friend if the Licence is come or when I may expect it."[11] (The friend who bore the message could have been Mrs. Brown.)

She worked quickly to take the lease on the playhouse, gather her players and her musicians, and begin rehearsals. In early September the newspapers began to carry advertisements for the performance, "By Authority," of an "English Burletta called Galligantus" at the Little Haymarket. After a delay of a week occasioned by the death of Princess Elizabeth, performances began on September 17.[12] *Galligantus* was a two-act piece of musical burlesque adapted from Henry Brooke's ballad opera *Jack the Gyant Queller;* it had been performed once in 1749, at the Smock-Alley Theatre in Dublin, and twice at the Haymarket, in December 1758. (It is unlikely that Charlotte was involved in these winter performances, given her health, though it is always possible that she had tried and could not sustain the effort. Most of the cast list for the earlier Haymarket performances has not survived, but one remaining detail stands out—they starred "a real Giant.")[13]

Burlettas were comic operas—the form originated in Italy—and in 1759 were catching on with the English public via a series of performances of English translations staged at the pleasure gardens in Marylebone. Like the true operas they burlesqued, these burlettas were entirely sung, in often musically fine recitative and aria, with large doses of farce and clowning thrown in: one critic called them "a strange mixture of Buffoonery and Grotesque, with good Musick, [and] Scenery."[14] Burlettas were joke-based, fast-paced, high-spirited, light-hearted, sexually suggestive, highly physical entertainments that delighted their audiences with frenetic foolery, absurd lyrics, and elabourate finales. Charlotte anticipated by several years the explosion of the English burletta's popularity that would occur in the 1760s. But the performances—both the fast-moving physical comedy and the strenuous singing—must have been particularly hard on her health.

On September 28, "the seventh night of performing here," the company interrupted its run of *Galligantus* to perform Susannah Centlivre's *The Busy Body* as a benefit for Charlotte, in which she cast herself in the lead role as the foppish (male) bumbler Marplot. In her advertising for *Galligantus*, Charlotte did not list her name (or those of any of the players). But a few days before her benefit performance, which did list her name, she published a direct appeal to the public. Using some of the same language as she did in her letter to Devonshire, she invoked the memory of her father (and perhaps also the memory of her publicly staged failure to soften his heart) as she implored the Town's favour.

> I take this Method of informing my worthy Friends and the Town in general, that Friday next the 28th inst. I propose taking a Benefit at the Haymarket Theatre; and as my Motive for so doing is to settle me in Business, being at present intirely dependant on Chance for Subsistence, I humbly refer myself to the Nobility and Gentry, who have given many Proofs of their readiness to assist the Indigent, and humbly hope this additional Favour to those already received, and that in regard to the Memory of my late Father, they will kindly contribute to fix me in a happy Situation of Life than I now enjoy, which will ever be most gratefully acknowledged.

She signed herself, "Daughter of the late Colley Cibber, Esq."[15] On September 28, the day of her benefit, her advertisement in *The Public Advertiser* reiterated both the name of her father and her plea for the Town's kindness, repeating that she was "entirely dependent upon Chance for Subsistence, and desirous of settling into Business." Charlotte's weariness and the precariousness of her situation can be heard in these plaintive appeals.

For the last three performances permitted by her licence—on October 1, 5, and 10—Charlotte returned to *Galligantus*, adding to her cast "the Staffordshire Giant."[16] The October 3 issue of *The Public Advertiser* carried a letter concerning her production:

> Sir, On seeing the Burletta of *Galligantus* at the Little Theatre in the Haymarket, I was agreeably surprised to see a Performance of the Kind carried on in so genteel a Manner, no way inferior to any Opera; and

after the nicest Inspection of the whole Performance, I have the Pleasure to inform the Nobility, Gentry, &c., I found all the Performers were English, their Dresses very completely adapted, their Voices excellent, and their Actions quite genteel and comic, their Music charming and set without the Assistance of any Foreigner, it being composed by Mr. J—D—, a Native of Ireland, whose Excellency in that Art needs no Encomium. I am, yours, a True Briton.

This puff, stressing the burletta's lack of foreignness, may have been inserted by a well-wisher or by Charlotte herself: the praise of the composer strikes a philo-Irish note familiar from her *Narrative*. But for all her efforts, these performances did not bring her the financial respite she desired. Setting up in a business remained an elusive dream, and Charlotte's fears of the consequences of "Infirmity or Age" were not assuaged.

On November 15, Charlotte sent another letter to the lord chamberlain's secretary, Sir Robert Wilmot, in which she requested that he present to the duke her petition for a new licence allowing her to perform for "Six nights or mornings." In her previous performances, she said, she had not had "the Desir'd success, thro the heat of the Season, and the Nobility out of Town, Conjoin'd with great Expences." *Galligantus* must have left her more in debt than ever. If she were allowed to play these additional six times, Charlotte promised, she should "stand a happy chance of effecting my former Design of settling my self in Business, and after this Clemency added to the former shall never more presume to trouble his Grace." She remarked that she had thought of trying to reopen the theatre in Goodman's Fields, but found that "Impracticable." Acknowledging her indebtedness to the duke, Charlotte requested that Wilmot mention her petition to him. "I shall Sir wait yr answer to morrow or what time will be most agreeable."[17] But the duke was apparently unmoved. There is no mention of another licence for her in the lord chamberlain's archives, and no record of further performances.

Her November letter to Sir Robert is our last glimpse of Charlotte Charke during her life. What she did between November and the following spring, as the winter came with its wet cold, its smoke, and its increase in the incidences of respiratory illnesses, remains obscure. Perhaps a timely gift from a sympathetic acquaintance allowed her to begin to formulate her plans to start her business. One nineteenth-century history of Islington says that Charlotte ran an eating house there in 1760, but it is possible that the historian confused one daughter of Colley Cibber with another, and that this was Elizabeth at Fulwood's Rents, not far away.[18] More likely, Charlotte continued to eke out a living, as she had put it, "according to Chance," surviving through charity and a small income earned from her writing. The faithful Mrs. Brown may have been with her still.

Charlotte probably did not move from her lodgings with Mrs. Hind, or not very far. She remained near the Little Haymarket, once the scene of her greatest success as an actress, when audiences crammed themselves together on the hard wooden benches to laugh and cheer her parodies of her father. Now on most nights that playhouse remained dark and bolted, an unhappy reminder of how London's theatre world had changed, and Charlotte's life along with it.

On January 13, 1760, Charlotte turned forty-seven. Sometime that winter or early spring, she fell ill. She could have contracted one of those "fevers" endemic in London whose incidence increased in the winter: there were various types of respiratory infection, and typhus. Such "winter diseases" were particularly associated with poverty and crowded living conditions.[19] Charlotte's chronic frail health and her vulnerability to respiratory diseases would have made her particularly susceptible to an illness whose intensity was compounded by privation. If Mrs. Brown was there to nurse Charlotte once again, this time her efforts were in vain. Charlotte had contended gamely against great odds for much of her adult life, and now, weak and exhausted, she could fight no more. In the middle of April, she died.

The London newspapers issued on and around Friday, April 18, 1760, carried reports on the progress of the war between England and France, the end of the drought in Barbados, which saved the sugar crop, the unanimous conviction of the Earl of Ferrers for the murder of his servant, the usually large number of children left at the Foundling Hospital, the eleven prisoners sentenced at the Old Bailey to transportation for theft of items such as a linen handkerchief, a pair of stays, and a sack of malt, and the names of the horses that would be racing at Newmarket. Covent Garden Theatre was playing Shakespeare's *Coriolanus* that night; Drury Lane was presenting Congreve's *Love for Love*. Unusually, the Little Haymarket was to be open that night, too, with a short-term troupe playing, "By Authority," a "pastoral" called *Patie and Roger.*

Inserted among these items was another notice, carried in several of the London papers:[20]

A few Days since died at her Lodgings in the Haymarket, the celebrated Mrs. Charlotte Charke, Daughter of the late Colley Cibber, Esq., Poet Laureat; a Gentlewoman remarkable for her Adventures and Misfortunes.

EPILOGUE

For an Englishwoman to die at the age of forty-seven was less surprising in the eighteenth century than it is now. Given Charlotte's hard life, her bouts of illness, her desperate circumstances, and the intensity with which she lived and worked, it is rather remarkable that she survived as long as she did. Her tenacity, her resilience, and her courage kept her going.

If Charlotte did indeed die in her Swallow Street lodgings, as seems probable, she would have been buried by the parish of St. James Piccadilly, probably in its churchyard. Her burial records have not been located in any parish, however, and the newspapers do not specify the location of her grave. Charlotte's fate probably resembled that of the unfortunate puppeteer Mr. Russell, who, she was shocked to hear, would be removed from the handsome shroud and coffin in which his body was laid out, and buried as a pauper in a cheap one. But unlike Mr. Russell and, indeed, unlike the great majority of the players of her day, whose names survive as little more than letters on a few old playbills or passing references in someone else's story, Charlotte left an enduring monument in the form of her autobiography.

Soon after Colley's death, Catherine Brown placed a notice in the newspaper offering to let, "Elegantly Furnish'd, the House of the late

Colley Cibber, esq."[1] (She continued to pay rates on the house until 1760.)[2] Catherine and her daughter, Catharine, moved to lodgings not far away in Half-Moon Street, Piccadilly. On June 4, 1761, her daughter married John Thomas, Esq. Charlotte's eldest sister and nemesis died not long afterward, leaving the Cibber estate under the control of Catharine Thomas.

Jenny Cibber married a man named William Ellis and seems to have died before 1762; Koon speculates that she died in childbirth. The fate of Theophilus's other daughter, Betty Cibber, is unknown. Susannah Cibber reigned as London's leading tragic actress until her death on January 30, 1766. She and Sloper stayed together until the end, though they were never able to marry, for Sloper's wife outlived them both. Susannah was buried in the north cloister of Westminster Abbey.

The last years of Anne Boultby and Elizabeth Marples are obscure. Elizabeth probably followed the path of her sister Charlotte and died in poverty. Her daughter, Ann Chetwood, had a rough time of it, too: in 1760, William Rufus Chetwood was once again in debtor's prison. It was said of Spranger Barry, one of the new generation of leading actors contemporary with Garrick, that though he was indebted to Chetwood "for most of his merit & reputation as an actor in his principal characters" he nonetheless "refused him relief in his deepest distress."[3] At some point after Charlotte's death, Ann wrote a letter to the Duke of Devonshire, still the lord chamberlain, in which, obviously in great distress, she asked for help, invoking her aunt Charlotte's name. Ann's letter is semiliterate (even by the less exacting standards of the day), but very moving:

> May it please your Grace
>   I am an unfortuante Granddaughter of the Late Colley Cibber whose unhappiness was never to feell for the distreses of his own family otherwise then by a Partiall Judgement the aflictions of his Children was greatly owing to his unfeelingnes my Mother my Lord never Commited She Could Say it on her Death Bed an Act of Disobeadeince: to her and my Aunt Charke he Left but five pound Each to there Children nothing the Bulk of his fortune my Aunt Brown had and my Uncle Theophilus Daughters had a thousand pound Each worn down by Afliction and growing in years not brought up to Earn my Bread by Servile Busines a wrong Judgement in parents who flatter us with Hopes we never Tast

The old Nobility all dead who usd thro pity to Aleavate the Distresses of my family inforces me to plead to your pity in this hope that my Aunt Charke shard in your Compasion I never and please your grace Intreated your Assistance before but as I am informd your Benevolence at this Season of the year Releavs many distresd persons permit me to plead to be in the Number as my distress is great and all I am Capable to do is with my Needle and there is no imploy all Publick Charity taking it in—that Heaven with its Choisest Blessings may await you shall ever be the fervant wish and prayer——

of your Most Obeadant Sert
Ana Cheetwood[4]

When she says that "my aunt Charke shard in your Compassion," Ann could be referring to Devonshire's granting Charlotte the licence to play in 1759, but she could also mean that the duke had given Charlotte money on some occasion. We can only hope that Ann's desperate appeal was successful. William Rufus Chetwood died in 1766.

More fortunate than her cousin Ann, Kitty Harman lived out the rest of her years in the American colonies. The husband Charlotte so disdained had actually helped her establish a career that would sustain her for the rest of her life. From New York, the Douglass company moved to Philadelphia in 1759. When the troupe moved south from Philadelphia at the beginning of 1760, however, the Harmans remained in Philadelphia. During this time they may have tried other ways of earning a living—opening a business, perhaps, as her mother had wanted her to do—or picked up acting gigs in New York. Perhaps Kitty was pregnant and underwent her lying-in in Philadelphia. (If so, the child did not survive, for Kitty was childless at the end of her life.) She is next heard from in late 1763, when she was back with the Douglass company, now renamed the American Company of Comedians, which had just arrived in Charleston, South Carolina. John's name disappeared from the playbills around that time. He probably died (unless he and Kitty split up and he quit acting); in any event, he vanished from the records.

Kitty never remarried. She remained with the American Company for the rest of her life, travelling from one colony to another: Maryland, Virginia, Rhode Island, Barbados, Philadelphia, and New York.[5] When Kitty died, in New York City on May 27, 1773, she was younger than her mother had been at her death. Kitty Harman received the rare (perhaps the first) tribute for an actress of having her obituary published in the colonial papers. *The New York Mercury* reported: "departed this life in her 43rd year, Mrs. Catharine Maria Harman, grand daughter to the celebrated Colley Cibber, Esq; and one of the American Company of Comedians, by all of whom she was much esteemed: The Saturday following her remains were decently interred in Trinity Church Yard." *The Pennsylvania Chronicle* added: "she was a just actress, possessed much merit in low comedy, and dressed all her characters with infinite propriety, but her figure prevented her from succeeding in tragedy, and in genteel comedy. In private life, she was sensible, humane, and benevolent, her little fortune she has left to Miss [Margaret] Cheer [a fellow actress], and her obsequies were on Saturday night attended by a very genteel procession to the cemetery of the Old English Church."[6] Charlotte would have been gratified—though perhaps a little envious, too—that Kitty had achieved this degree of status and respect.

Charlotte Charke's own reputation sank for more than two centuries, as the generations that succeeded her own became increasingly proper. In her own day, people thought that she was outrageous, eccentric, and sometimes scandalous, but they also found her entertaining and even sympathetic, as her obituaries demonstrated. Dr. Burney's judgment that no respectable woman should read her *Narrative* suggested a narrower moral compass, however, especially for women. As the eighteenth century gave way to the nineteenth and the early twentieth, commentators (usually journalists, theatre historians, and literary critics) began increasingly to brand Charlotte Charke as a bad woman, immoral, dissolute, even mad. She was accused of being an ungrateful, undutiful daughter, an unrestrained, promiscuous wanton, an unnatural, depraved profligate. Occasionally more sympathetic voices were raised to insist that she was only misguided and feckless, a sad case, a "twisted and distraught human soul."[7] Mostly, Charlotte Charke faded from sight. She never completely vanished, however.

Charlotte always retained a small but important place in the history of the theatre, however disapprovingly its historians judged her. Her autobiography has remained often in print, a useful source for theatre scholars and an entertaining account of a lively, unconventional woman. Two authors wrote fanciful fictional accounts of her, George Graveley [Edwards] in his comic play *The Wild Girl* (which gives her a male love interest) and Leila Sterling Mackinlay in *The Vagabond Daughter.* The last two decades have seen a resurgence of interest in Charlotte Charke, sparked by new attention to women's history, lesbian/gay history, and the history of sexuality. Two modern editions, one by Fidelis Morgan in 1988 and the other by Robert Rehder in 1999, have introduced her *Narrative* to a new generation of readers and added a great deal to our knowledge of the circumstances of her life. Maureen Duffy incorporated Charlotte's story into her experimental lesbian novel, *The Microcosm,* and excerpts from Charlotte's writing appear in new anthologies of lesbian literature. Scholars such as Philip Baruth, Terry Castle, Emma Donoghue, Robert Folkenflick, Kristina Straub, Cheryl Wanko, and many others have written about her perceptively in academic books and journals.

Charlotte Charke's unaccountable life may have been marked by misfortunes and misjudgments, but she lived it with great creativity and courage. It is possible now to look back on the little girl who paraded through the English morning in her father's wig, and perceive in her performance the extraordinary woman she would become.

NOTE TO THE READER

In quoting from eighteenth-century sources, I have made certain changes, especially in typography, in order to minimize the jarring effect on modern readers. The eighteenth century used italics much more liberally than we do today, so I have largely eliminated them, as well as words that are entirely capitalized, unless either device seems particularly necessary for emphasis. I have occasionally adjusted punctuation, but I have preserved eighteenth-century capitalization.

In 1752, England adopted the Gregorian calendar, losing eleven days in September and beginning the new year in January rather than in March. Without attempting to adjust the days of the month, I have cited years prior to 1752 according to the New Style: thus the Old Style January 1712/13, for instance, becomes January 1713.

One of the most significant difficulties confronting Charlotte's biographer is that, although a great deal of information can be uncovered surrounding her life and, especially, her career as an actress, the only source of many more personal events is her own autobiography, *A Narrative of the Life of Mrs. Charlotte Charke*, published in 1755, when she was forty-two. Like all forms of writing about oneself (including letters and even diaries), autobiographies are self-serving in some way, and this one certainly was, as she tried (though not always consistently) both to repair her rift with her father by emphasizing her reform, and to make money by emphasizing her notoriety. I have tried to keep her agendas in mind, while necessarily relying on her account for many details about her experiences during her life. Incomplete and partial as it may be, the *Narrative*'s modern editors have demonstrated that it is reliable about many of the things she did, and often about when she did them, insofar as they can be checked. (I have found additional verification that this is true.) Whenever I have been able to correct or modify her account, I have done so, but in other instances I have accepted her own chronology and descriptions of events.

Since I often quote from the *Narrative,* I decided that inserting page references for all these individual quotations would be obtrusive. Several editions of the *Narrative* may be found in libraries throughout the United States and the United Kingdom; I have quoted from the facsimile reproduction of the second edition (1755), edited by L.R.N. Ashley, as the version closest to Charlotte's original text. Unless otherwise noted, all quotations from Charlotte Charke in this book refer to this edition of the *Narrative.*

The most comprehensive modern compilation of eighteenth-century London theatre performances is *The London Stage,* an invaluable publication but one that is not free of errors; as often as possible I have tried to check its listings against the newspaper advertisements. (Most of the eighteenth-century newspapers I cite are available on microfilm from the British Library and/or the Library of Congress.) But newspaper records are not necessarily accurate themselves, nor are they complete. Many performances, especially in lesser venues, simply went unrecorded. So my account of Charlotte's stage career can be at best only an approximation, but I hope a representative and revealing one, of her actual experiences within the London theatre world.

Notes

PROLOGUE

1. Charlotte wrote of her encounter with this unnamed young woman in her autobiography, *A Narrative of the Life of Mrs Charlotte Charke.* My version of the "Mary Harlowe" story elaborates somewhat upon her account.

INTRODUCTION

1. In the paragraphs that follow, I have taken liberties in imagining Charlotte's walk across Covent Garden on an afternoon in March 1736; she left no such description. But she would have walked these streets on many occasions, and would have encountered these or similar scenes.

2. Henderson: 33.

3. Quoted in Bayne-Powell: 13.

4. Brown: 22.

5. *The Daily Advertiser,* March 19, 1736. The ads stopped calling particular attention to Charlotte in the ad for the April 22 performance.

6. Cibber said that he attended a play by Fielding that poked fun at him, and applauded it while everyone watched him (*Egotist:* 27–28). He was most likely referring to *The Historical Register* of the following year, but it is highly likely that he would have gone to see *Pasquin,* too—especially once his daughter had joined the cast—and that he would have behaved, under public scrutiny, in a similar way.

7. Many modern scholars have tended to view Cibber through Pope's lens, as in the early biography by Senior and in Barker's somewhat more measured study. More balanced assessments are offered by Sullivan and Ashley's *Colley Cibber,* while Koon offers a sympathetic account that might err in the opposite direction but is also the most comprehensive study of Cibber and provides a welcome counterbalance to the stream of hostile, one-sided criticism. Gámez argues rightly that we need to undo our "conditioning" to see Colley Cibber "as merely Pope's Dunce and Fielding's buffoon."

8. Hill, *The Prompter*, no. 3, November 19, 1734.

9. Battestin: 59.

10. Colley Cibber, *An Apology for the Life of Colley Cibber, with an Historical View of the Stage during his own Time* (1740). Ed. B.R.S. Fone. Ann Arbor: University of Michigan Press, 1968. Future reference to this text will be cited as *Apology.*

1: CIBBERS (1660–1712)

1. I follow Koon's carefully considered account of the family name here.

2. The statue was removed in the nineteenth century, but later donated back to the square by its owner, Lady Gilbert, widow of the Victorian lyricist. Prominent landmarks outside the city contained Caius's sculpture as well: Hampton Court; Trinity and King's Colleges, Cambridge; Winchester School; and Chatsworth.

3. Faber: 12–13.

4. *Apology:* 8. Nothing is known about Caius's first wife, Elizabeth, except that the couple apparently had a son who died in childhood; Tupper finds evidence to suggest that another son from this marriage, named Gabriel, survived at least into young manhood (396). Elizabeth died in July 1670, and Caius married Jane the following November.

5. Quoted in Faber: 8–9.

6. Vertue: 39; 91.

7. Koon: 194, n. 13; 8.

8. "The History of the Life, Manners and Writings of Aesopus the Tragedian," in *The Laureat.*

9. Koon notes that although Grantham was a "Free School" it was really free only for residents of Grantham. Either Caius managed to scrape together the tuition, or Colley benefited from the largess of a relative or one of his father's patrons.

10. Unless otherwise noted, the details of Colley's education and youth are based upon his *Apology:* 9–37.

11. Aston: 3–4.

12. *Apology:* 61–65.

13. Wilson: 112, quoting Downes.

14. *Apology:* 92.

15. Both references: Howe: 30.

16. *Apology:* 97–98.

17. Pepys, *Diary*, January 7, 1661; quoted in Howe: 25.

18. Kynaston's teeth: *Apology:* 71; Joy as actor: *Apology:* 46.

19. Aston: 16.

20. Earle: 59.

21. Details about the Shores from Hawkins, II: 752–54.

22. Thomas Davies, *Dramatic Miscellanies*. 3 vols. Dublin: 1784. Rpt. New York: Benjamin Bloom, 1971. III: 249. Colley said that at the time he actually married, his salary had become twenty shillings a week (*Apology:* 104).

23. Uffenbach: 130.

24. *Apology:* 104; Koon: 22.

25. Koon: 21–22.

26. *Apology:* 139.

27. Davies, *Dramatic Miscellanies*, III: 248.

28. Koon, 30–50.

29. *Laureat:* 53.

30. *Apology:* 166–67.
31. Davies, *Dramatic Miscellanies,* III: 258.
32. Lafler: 5–6.
33. Sullivan, Introduction to Cibber, Colley, *Three Sentimental Comedies:* xiv.
34. *The Prompter,* no. 3, November 19, 1734.
35. Lucas: National Archives: LC7/3, 6 October 1697; MJ/SR (W), no. 113; WSP/1697/Oct/1. Osbourne: Middlesex Record Office WJ/SR/2192, 11 June 1712 (all cited in Morgan: 23).
36. Spence: 202; Davies, *Dramatic Miscellanies,* III: 432.

2: THE IMPERTINENT INTRUDER (1712–13)

1. Avery, Emmet L., Arthur H. Scouten, William Van Lennep, George Winchester Stone, Jr. *The London Stage 1660–1800,* 1: 486. References to this 6-volume publication will henceforth appear as *London Stage.*
2. Bowers: 39; 48.
3. Stone, *Family, Sex and Marriage:* 422–23.
4. *Apology:* 146.
5. The rates books for the parishes of St. Martin-in-the-Fields and St. Paul Covent Garden indicate that in June 1713 "Colley Siber" was still paying rates in Spring Gardens; for September 29, 1714, the scavengers rates book lists the name "Colley Ciber" with a line crossed through it and "Dorothy Parker" written in above. Colley appears in the rates books for Southampton Street West beginning March 17, 1714.
6. All quotations from Charlotte herself, unless otherwise noted, come from her autobiography, *A Narrative of the Life of Mrs. Charlotte Charke* (1755), in its facsimile publication edited by Ashley.
7. In 1714, in a suit in Chancery, Katherine referred to her two sons, one of whom presumably was James; the suit identified him as blind. Charlotte never mentioned him among her siblings, suggesting that he died when she was quite young.
8. Sulloway, *passim.*
9. Hawkins, II: 752. August 8, 1715.
10. *Weekly Journal,* May 27, 1721, quoted in Plumb: 42.
11. Quoted in Hatton: 63.
12. Hatton: 158.
13. Koon: 77.
14. Cibber, Wilks, and Doggett first became actor-managers of the theatre troupe in 1709, at which point the Drury Lane Theatre was temporarily closed, and most of the company performed at the Queen's (aka the King's) Theatre in the Haymarket (cf. Koon: 57–65).

3: A PASSIONATE FONDNESS FOR A PERIWIG (1717–20)

1. *Theatre-Royal Turn'd into a Mountebank's Stage:* 32; *Original Weekly Journal,* late January 1718 (quoted in Koon: 89); *A Lash for the Laureat:* 6.
2. Koon: 206, n. 82.
3. *Applebee's The Original Weekly Journal,* August 16 and August 30, 1718.
4. Charles Johnson, letter in *The Original Weekly Journal,* March 1, 1719. Cited in Morgan: 25; Koon: 88.
5. Davies, *Dramatic Miscellanies,* III: 268.
6. Defoe, *Tour:* 173–76.
7. *London Stage 2,* 2: xxxi.

8. In 1719, Drury Lane had staged Dennis's *The Invader of His Country* at, he thought, an inopportune time after a long delay; he was particularly angry at Cibber for making cuts in the text. Dennis, *Critical Works,* II: 184–85.

Another anonymous letter, published in Steele's *The Theatre,* defended Colley: "you . . . tell a notorious lie in saying he lost £6000 in one season without providing for his family, when everyone that knows him can tell you he settled £300 that very year upon his children." Quoted in Koon: 97.

9. Katherine's brother John, acting with Colley in a 1714 lawsuit, deposed at that time that Cibber looked after his family responsibly, providing for each "according to his means." National Archives, C 6/392/12. The lawsuit, in which Colley and Katherine were nominal antagonists, has sometimes been cited as proof of Colley's unprincipled greed at the expense of his children (the lawsuit concerned Elizabeth's inheritance from her aunt Rose Shore), but both Tupper and Koon argue convincingly that this was a necessary legal strategy to enlist the court's help in, Tupper says, "straightening out two tangled legacies": the complete evidence "indicates pretty clearly that there was no grave quarrel over the estates between Cibber and his wife and that Cibber, for a time at least, adequately financed his family": 395; Koon: 204, fn. 36.

10. Koon dates the Cibbers' move to Charles Street in August 1720 because letters to Colley at this time were directed to a holding address, suggesting that they were in transit during August. Others, for example Rehder, date the Cibbers' residence in Charles Street from 1721. He was rated at his Charles Street address beginning in 1721.

4: EDUCATING CHARLOTTE (1720–27)

1. *Covent-Garden: A Satire.*
2. Richardson: 12.
3. Burford: 67.
4. Strype, I: 173. Parish records show a substantial property held in Westminster at this time by a "Madame Draper."
5. *The Refusal* was, most directly, a rewriting of Thomas Wright's *The Female Virtuosos* (which was itself an adaptation of Molière's *Les Femmes Savantes*).
6. Cf. Hunter, *passim.*
7. Their rather eccentric house is described by Grant as it was in the early nineteenth century.
8. Earle: 304.
9. *Pharmacopoeia Pauperum:* 9.
10. Porter and Porter: 117; 25.

5: LAUREATE (1720–30)

1. The description of court dress styles circa 1730 is based upon Cunnington and Cunnington, and Brooke and Laver, *passim.*
2. Pope, *Epigrams from the Grub-Street Journal:* "V. On the Candidates for the Laurel," in *Poems:* 811.
3. Paulson, *Fielding:* 50.
4. Barker: 138.
5. Barker: 140.
6. Cooke: 23–24.
7. Davies, *Dramatic Miscellanies,* III: 261–62.
8. Victor, II: 105.

9. Davies, *Dramatic Miscellanies,* III: 261.

10. Cooke: 16.

11. Chetwood: 93.

12. Hervey, June 13, 1727, in *Lord Hervey and His Friends:* 18–19.

13. Quoted in Winton: 108.

14. Highfill, Philip H. Jr., Kalman A. Burnim, and Edward A. Langhans, *A Biographical Dictionary of Actors, Actresses, Musicians, Dancers, Managers & Other Stage Personnel in London, 1660–1800.* 5: 221–22. References to this 10-volume publication will henceforth appear as *Biographical Dictionary.* Fenton's birthdate has recently been corrected; she was two years younger than previously thought. See Baldwin and Wilson: 72.

15. Koon gives a vivid account of this scene: 120–22.

16. Lafler: 162.

17. Lafler: 1.

18. Macklin, quoted in Cooke: 24–25.

19. Davies, *Dramatic Miscellanies,* III: 258.

20. "Epistle I. To Richard Temple, Viscount Cobham: Of the Characters of Men," ll. 242–47. *Poems:* 558.

6: THE PROVOKED WIFE (1729–30)

1. *London Stage 2,* 2: 1037.

2. Burling calls this a "review" of earlier performances; *Biographical Dictionary* calls it a "quaint puff" printed *prior to* what appears to have been Charke's first appearance in this role on June 17 (3: 166). The play was first performed on May 29; *London Stage* does not list the name of the actor playing Hunter until June 17, when it lists Charke as Hunter on his benefit night. In the absence of other information, it seems likely, as Burling assumes, that June 17 was not Charke's first performance in this role, and that *The Daily Post* comments refer to earlier performances (while puffing subsequent ones).

3. *Apology:* 211.

4. Barbier: 17.

5. Burling: 94. There is uncertainty about the number and personnel of companies who played at the Little Haymarket during the late 1720s and early 1730s, since the theatre was essentially a "road house" (Hume, *Fielding:* 57) rented by various groups, and had no fixed company. However, it does appear that the company that played in the summer of 1729 was essentially the same one that played "for some 115 performances" (Burling: 93) during the preceding winter season, though there was considerable shifting of the players. Charke seems to have joined this group initially as a dancing master and then began to perform in the summer.

6. *London Stage* 2: 2: 987.

7. *London Stage* 2: 2: 1042.

8. Chetwood: 127.

9. *Daily Post,* August 12, 1729.

10. This exchange appeared in the *Daily Post* between August 6 and 14, 1729.

11. Burney, *Memoirs:* 184.

12. Sir John Hawkins, *A General History of the Science and Practice of Music* (1776), quoted in Burney, *Memoirs:* 184, fn. 6.

13. Marriage register, St. Martin-in-the-Fields: February 4, 1729 (OS: i.e., 1730 NS): "Richard Charke of this parish and Charlotte Ciber of St. Paul's Covent Garden."

14. Morgan speculates that Richard might have been the Richard Charke born in Bodmin in March 1703 (Morgan: 48), which would make him nearly twenty-seven at the time of their marriage; *The New Grove Dictionary* suggests a 1709 birthdate for him, making him about twenty-one at the time. *Biographical Dictionary* cites a reference to a Mr. Charke as a singer sometime around 1720 (3: 165) which, if this indeed referred to Richard, would make the older age more probable. He could have had an early, unrecorded career as a strolling player or in provincial theatre. On the other hand, supporting the younger age is Charlotte's description of *both* of them as too young for marriage, and the absence of performance records for Richard before this year.

15. *The Daily Courant*, February 5, 1730. *The Grub-Street Journal*, a Tory paper, reprinted a notice of the marriage published in the *Morning Post*—"On the beginning of this week, Mr. Charke, a Comedian to the Theatre Royal in Drury-lane, was married to the youngest Daughter of Mr. Cibber"—and commented sarcastically, "The Three Members of this Society are deputed to wait on the learned Mr. Cibber, to congratulate him on this happy occasion." This paper also published the following correction in the same issue: "The Courant and Daily Post in the Article of Miss Cibber's marriage differ from the Morning Post of Saturday, in reading Clark for Chark [sic], and Miss Charlotte Cibber, Daughter to Mr. Cibber, for the youngest Daughter of Mr. Cibber" (February 12, 1730). (Misspellings of Charlotte's new surname bedevil the historical record.)

16. Genest III: 244.

17. *Biographical Dictionary*, 15: 435.

18. Victor, II: 53.

19. Victor, quoted in *Biographical Dictionary* 11: 51. Norris was given his nickname for his role in George Farquhar's *Constant Couple; or, Trip to the Jubilee.*

20. Davies, *Dramatic Miscellanies*, III: 254–55.

21. Davies, *Dramatic Miscellanies*, I: 103–104.

22. Victor, II: 4.

23. *Daily Post*, April 28, 1730.

24. Charlotte was mistaken when, in her *Narrative,* she indicated that this was Jane's first performance in this character: she played the role on at least two prior occasions, though the most recent was November 1727, more than two years previously. *London Stage* 2, 2: 882; 943.

25. Burney, *Memoirs*: 1003, fn. d (Burney's footnote).

7: CHAMBERMAIDS AND PRETTY MEN (1731–32)

1. The cast list does not survive for the season's first performance of *Greenwich Park* on November 12, but upon its repetition on December 17, the playbills listed Charlotte as Mrs. Raison, and she was billed in this role again when the play was performed on May 6. It is probable that she had played this part in the earlier performance.

2. *London Stage* 3, 1: 132.

3. In a performance of Thomas Cooke's *The Triumphs of Love and Honour.*

4. *Daily Post*, July 22, 1731.

5. *The Grub-Street Journal*, July 8, 1731.

6. Chetwood: 29; Victor, II: 58.

7. Modern accounts, following newspaper articles, say that she broke her thighbone, but both Cibber and Chetwood, who were in a position to know, say that

she dislocated it. Either injury would have been very serious, very painful, and very slow to heal.

8. Davies, *Dramatic Miscellanies*, III: 120–21; 276–77.

9. Hill: 150.

10. My discussion of Fielding's career at Drury Lane is based upon Hume's thorough account in *Fielding*: 104–164.

11. *The London Evening Post* and *The Daily Journal*, cited in *The Grub-Street Journal*, July 15 and 29, 1731.

12. There is some reason to think that Fielding accepted a bribe to withhold his ballad opera, *The Grub-Street Opera*, which not only mocked Robert Walpole but also satirized, though rather gently, King George and Queen Caroline and, much less gently, Frederick, Prince of Wales. For attempts to untangle the events concerning Fielding's troupe that summer, see Hume, *Fielding*: 78–80 and 93–104, and Paulson, *Fielding*: 33–34 and 49–53.

13. Quoted in Battestin: 80.

14. Battestin: 128.

8: SHOW, SHOW, SHOW, SHOW! (1732)

1. *The Daily Advertiser*, August 24, 1732.

2. *The London Spy*, chapters 10 and 11.

3. *The Prelude*, 7: 686–87; 718.

4. *The London Spy*, chapter 10.

5. *The Daily Advertiser*, August 25, 1732.

6. Rosenfeld, *Fairs*: 37–38.

7. *The Daily Advertiser*, August 29, 1732.

8. There is some confusion about the actual history of Charlotte's performances of Alicia. In her *Narrative*, Charlotte says that Alicia was her "second Character" (meaning her next major role after Madamoiselle) and that Andromache during the summer season was her third, implying that she had performed Alicia sometime before that year's summer season. She also says that Mrs. Porter's accident "was the Means by which I was possessed of that Part." This comment implies that she played the role sometime during the 1731–32 season (since Mrs. Porter did not perform during the summers, the role would have been vacant then in any event). However, the *London Stage* lists no performances of *Jane Shore* at Drury Lane during that period. It is possible, as Morgan assumes, that records are missing for a regular season performance, or that Rowe's play was substituted for another, advertised play at the last minute. It is also possible that Charlotte, writing twenty-three years after the fact, simply misremembered the sequence in which she played Andromache and Alicia. In saying that she owed her part to Mrs. Porter's accident, she may have been thinking of her subsequent performances of the role during the regular season: Charlotte played Alicia twice more in April 1733, and could have misremembered the year as 1732.

9. Aaron Hill, quoted in *Biographical Dictionary* 12: 94–95.

10. Stone, *Road*: 141–230.

11. See Milhouse and Hume, 2: 781–82.

12. Victor, II: 3.

13. Victor, I: 7.

14. *The Daily Advertiser*, September 28, 1732.

15. Newspaper reports quoted in *The Grub-Street Journal*, October 12, 1732.

16. Victor, I: 9.

17. Theophilus paid his father £442 for the lease. "A Letter from Theophilus Cibber, Comedian, To John Highmore, Esq."

9: STORMY WEATHER (1732–33)

1. Chetwood: 118.

2. *Biographical Dictionary,* 3: 242–60.

3. *The Weekly Journal,* February 19, 1726, quoted in *Biographical Dictionary,* 3: 243.

4. In his pamphlet, "A Letter from Theophilus Cibber, Comedian, To John Highmore, Esq." [1733], Theophilus refers to his "four years" of directing the summer company, saying that the first was the year in which they staged *Sir Thomas Overbury* (which was 1723) and the others the three years immediately prior to the date of his writing (late spring/early summer 1733).

5. October 5, 1732.

6. Davies, *Dramatic Miscellanies,* I: 164–65.

7. *Reflections upon Reflections* (anonymous: 1726), quoted in *Biographical Dictionary,* 3: 260. Her character was Polyxena in Richard West's tragedy *Hecuba.*

8. 79.

9. Clarion: 192.

10. *The Daily Advertiser,* quoted in *London Stage,* 3, 1: 235.

11. Chetwood: 60.

12. *The Daily Advertiser,* September 2, 1732.

13. *The Grub-Street Journal,* citing *The Daily Courant* and the *Daily Post,* November 23, 1732.

14. *The Daily Advertiser,* December 9 and 15, 1732.

15. January 18 and January 23, 1733. *Lord Hervey and His Friends:* 154–55.

16. Undated clipping, quoted in *London Stage,* 3, 1: 245.

17. Clarion: 192.

18. Baptismal record, St. Paul's Covent Garden.

19. Friday, January 26, 1733. The *Daily Post* says that Jane had given birth about a week before her death.

20. *Apology for the Life of Mr. T——C——:* 100.

10: MUTINY (1733)

1. Folkenflick ("Images") and Holland identify this figure as Charlotte; identifications of other figures in the illustration come from Folkenflick and Paulson.

2. "Letter from Cibber to Highmore."

3. *London Stage,* 3, 1: lxxxix.

4. *London Stage* does not identify an author of this unpublished farce, but *The Grub-Street Journal,* May 24, 1733, attributed it to Theo.

5. Victor, I: 10.

6. Davies, *Garrick:* 2: 382–83.

7. *Daily Post,* March 5, 1733.

8. *The Grub-Street Journal,* June 7, 1733: quoting the *St. James's Evening Post* of June 2.

9. Koon: 134.

10. *The Grub-Street Journal,* May 24, 1733.

11. Hume, *Fielding:* 158. For a thorough discussion of the actors' rebellion, see 155–87.

12. "Letter from Cibber to Highmore."
13. Hume, *Fielding*: 158.
14. *The Daily Advertiser,* June 27, 1733.

11: WEARING THE BREECHES (1733–34)

1. Hogarth originally titled it simply, "a Fair." Paulson, *Hogarth*: 154.
2. Morgan: 222. Folkenflick, "Images," does not rule out the possibility that this may be a representation of Charlotte cross-dressed for her role as Haly.
3. Hume, *Fielding*: 162–63.
4. *Daily Post,* August 18, 1733. All quotations of the Bartholomew Fair advertisements are taken from issues of this newspaper from late August and early September, 1733.
5. See Hume, *Fielding*: 168–69.
6. Vaughan: 10–11.
7. Hume, *Fielding*: 174–75.
8. Entry for "Catherine Cibber," Burial Register, St. Martin-in-the-Fields; Morgan states that Katherine died on January 17, but the date of death is not specified in the burial register.
9. Victor, I: 20.
10. By the time Harper's trial date arrived, Highmore was no longer manager of Drury Lane, and the case was apparently dropped. See Hume, *Fielding,* for a complete account of these events. Hume points out that while most people, following Colley's account, thought that Highmore's prosecution of Harper fell apart because as a householder Harper could not be a vagrant, in fact that was not the point at all, because it was his status as an actor in an illegal troupe rather than his status as a property holder that was in question.
11. Fleetwood paid Highmore £2,250 for his half share, and Mary Wilks £1,500 for her third share, which was just slightly more than Hester Booth had received for her sixth share, which she sold to Henry Giffard several months earlier. Hume, *Fielding*: 179.
12. *The Daily Advertiser,* March 9, 1734.
13. Hume, *Fielding*: 180.

12: MAD COMPANY (1734–35)

1. Nash: 74.
2. *Tryal for a Cause*: 7.
3. Victor, III: 7–8.
4. Burling: 285, fn. 60.
5. Clipping dated May 13, 1734. Theatre Museum Study Room collection, Charlotte Charke folder.
6. *The Daily Advertiser,* August 12, 1734.
7. Cibber, *Apology*: 184.
8. *London Daily Post and General Advertiser,* December 12, 1734. Quoted in *London Stage,* 3, 1: 439.
9. Davies, *Garrick,* I: 35.
10. Appleton: 34.
11. *Apology for the Life of Mr. T——C——, Comedian*: 109.
12. Victor, I: 34.

13. Hume says that Theophilus remained in charge at the beginning of Fleetwood's "regime," and that Macklin did not officially assume managerial responsibilities until 1738 (*Fielding:* 186), but Appleton says that Macklin did successfully start to curry favour that autumn (28–29). And Charlotte implies in *The Art of Management* (published around October 3, 1735), that Macklin, whom she satirized as Bloodbolt, was in fact making (bad) management decisions. Quin seems to have had some managerial position, too, for it was he who assumed responsibility for placating the audience in the disturbances surrounding the dancers Roland and Poitier's failure to appear on December 7, 1734. See *London Daily Post and General Advertiser,* 12 December 1734; quoted in *London Stage,* 3, 1: 439.

14. This is Morgan's definition: 33.

15. In her autobiography, Charlotte appears to date her period as stock reader to the 1732–33 season, but the external evidence supports a dating of 1734–35, after Quin had joined Drury Lane. Charlotte says in her autobiography that her first understudy performance was Cleopatra in Mary Heron's place opposite Quin as Ventidius, that this performance was Worsley's benefit, and that her performance for Mrs. Butler as the Queen in *Essex* came after this. But she seems to have the sequence reversed. Mary Heron was billed to play Cleopatra for Worsley's benefit on May 5, 1735, and Quin was not in the advertised cast. He was billed, however, opposite Butler's Queen Elizabeth in *The Unhappy Favourite; or, The Earl of Essex* earlier that season; Butler was billed to play that role on two occasions, on October 12, 1734, and in February 1735, the last Drury Lane performance of *The Unhappy Favourite* until the following October, subsequent to Charlotte's remark about playing the role in *The Art of Management*. It seems likely that Charlotte replaced Butler in February, and this was the occasion on which she had the daunting experience of playing opposite Quin. If this sequence is correct, she would have played Cleopatra on May 5, which was billed as Worsley's benefit. (She says in *The Art of Management* that "I at a Quarter of an Hour's Warning, twice read two capital Parts, viz. The Queen in Essex, and another Night Cleopatra," implying that she played Cleopatra second.)

16. *The Daily Advertiser,* July 23, 1735.

17. Preface to *The Art of Management,* 1735.

13: CORDELIA; OR, THE ART OF MANAGEMENT (1735–36)

1. Charlotte says that Catherine and Colley were present, but does not identify the other participants; Anne was the most likely of her siblings to participate. Though Anne would appear on the stage briefly in 1740, she could not be said to have pursued a theatre career.

2. John Boultby paid rates on a substantial property there between 1733 and 1739.

3. Charlotte's account of this family confrontation does not specify when it took place, but late spring 1735 is a likely date. In her autobiography Charlotte speaks of a moment when she was "newly under the displeasure of her father," and the context of her *Narrative* places that moment in the summer of 1735; since Colley was out of town during most of the summer, and since Charlotte says that he summoned her to the confrontation from the playhouse, spring 1735, when she was still at Drury Lane, seems most likely. Charlotte's account leaves ambiguous the nature of the offences that inspired this confrontation, though in her *The Art of Management* (1735), she makes it clear that she had committed "misdeeds." (The other plausible dates for this confrontation would be the spring of either 1736 or 1737, when she had committed new offences against her father.)

4. Preface, *The Art of Management.*

5. Prologue, *The Art of Management.* In her autobiography many years later she would claim that she quit, but her comments at the time make it clear that she was fired.

6. *The London Daily Post and General Advertiser,* July 4, 1735.

7. *The Daily Advertiser,* July 10, 11, 12, 1735.

8. *The Daily Advertiser,* July 14, 1735.

9. *The London Daily Post and General Advertiser,* July 21, 1735.

10. Maitland, II: 1344.

11. *The London Post,* advertisement for the September 24, 1735, performance.

12. "Looby Headpiece" was a character who had been played by Theophilus in James Miller's *The Mother-in-Law.*

13. Preface, *The Art of Management.*

14. *The London Daily Post and General Advertiser,* October 6, 1735.

15. *Tryal for a Cause:* 7.

16. Koon: 139.

17. *The Silent Woman* was announced for Johnson's benefit two months prior to the performance.

14: ON THE EDGE (1736)

1. Strype, 1: 68.

2. According to Weinrab and Hibbert, Coventry Street had a "bad character" from the time it was built in the previous century: 205.

3. This imagined sequence is based upon Charlotte's statement in her autobiography that she lived with Elizabeth in Oxendon Street during her time with Fielding's troupe.

4. See Hume, *Fielding:* 207.

5. The expression is Robert Hume's. *Fielding:* 207.

6. Battestin: 83.

7. Hume, *Fielding:* 229.

8. Mrs. Pendarves to Jonathan Swift, April 22, 1736; quoted in Hume, *Fielding:* 209.

9. Roberts: 32.

10. Davies, *Lillo:* 11–12.

11. Davies, *Lillo:* 11–12.

12. *The Daily Advertiser,* June 18, 1736; *The London Daily Post and General Advertiser,* June 19, 1736. It is unclear how much involvement Fielding had with them that summer. Records of performances are scanty for this period. See Burford: 101.

13. *The London Daily Post and General Advertiser,* July 27; July 14; June 26, 1736.

14. *The London Daily Post and General Advertiser,* August 27, 1736, mentions "the great quantity of water" that fell that week.

15. *The Daily Advertiser,* October 4, 1736.

16. *Walpole Correspondence,* I: 113–14 (October 6, 1736).

17. *Daily Post,* October 11, 1736; *The London Daily Post and General Advertiser,* October 12, 1736.

18. *The London Daily Post and General Advertiser,* October 9, 1736.

19. Byom, quoted in *London Stage,* 3, 2: 63.

20. Nash: 97.

21. Nash (94–102) gives a lively account of this controversy.

22. *The London Daily Post and General Advertiser,* November 19, 1736.

23. *The Grub-Street Journal,* December 15, 1736, quoted in Nash: 100–101.

24. *The Daily Journal,* December 16, 1736; quoted in Nash: 101.

25. *The London Evening Post,* January 1, 1737; quoted in Nash: 102.

26. *The Gentleman's Magazine,* January 1737.

27. The King's high-handed and parsimonious behaviour to his son earned Prince Frederick considerable public sympathy. In the meantime, the King's favoured minister Walpole faced strengthening opposition within the whig party itself and in the House of Lords. Doing everything they could to brand his regime corrupt, the opposition emphasized the prime minister's self-enrichment while in office, his system of patronage for friends and allies, and his support of highly unpopular forms of taxation that fell particularly heavily upon merchants (as opposed to landed interests). For a further account of the political unrest during 1736, see Liesenfeld: 60–70.

28. *The London Daily Post and General Advertiser,* November 20, 1736.

29. *The Craftsman,* February 5, 1737.

30. *The Craftsman,* February 26, 1737.

31. *The Craftsman,* March 12, 1737. Two of the footmen were discharged and handed over to prosecution by the "noble Lords" their masters, while a third, "belonging to a Lady of Quality," was bailed out. (After a seven-hour trial at the end of April, the two footmen were found guilty, and sentenced to six months of hard labor. *The Craftsman,* April 30, 1737.)

32. *The Daily Advertiser,* February 4 and 19, 1737, published notices about the plans for this theatre. Hume, *Fielding,* discusses the project: 224–28.

33. *Sawney and Colley* (1742) implies that Charlotte took her cross-dressing into the streets subsequent to ("since") her performances with Fielding, which would date it sometime after May 1737: fn. p. 4.

15: BAD ACTS (1737)

1. Cibber, *Egotist:* 29. Colley said that he attended the first performance of one of Fielding's plays. His wording suggests that it was *The Historical Register* whose premiere he saw. In *The Egotist,* Colley stages a dialogue between the Author and Mr. Frankly:

> AUTH: Don't you remember, at the little Theatre in the Hay-Market, upon the first Day of acting some new Piece there? when a personal Jest upon me flew souce [sic] in my Face, while I sat in the Eye of a full Audience, was not I as suddenly loud in my Laugh and Applause, as any common Spectator? . . .
>
> FRAN: Well! to do you Justice, now I remember it, 'twas in some Farce of What-dee-callums! The—The—
>
> AUTH: O! no matter what! if you remember the Fact I want no more of you.
> (27–28)

Frankly tries to recall the title by beginning "The—The—" Neither of the other plays by Fielding that were likely—*Pasquin* and *Eurydice Hiss'd*—begins with "The."

2. The report that she did play this role that evening comes from an account late in the century, written by John Mottley, quoted and accepted by Battestin: 219 ("what was shocking to every one who had the least Sense of Decency or good

Manners, the Part was performed by his own Daughter"). It has been argued that the published version shows that Fielding does not assign these lines to Charlotte's character, and that this anecdote could have been manufactured or assumed as part of a tendency shared by many critics to paint Charlotte as a deviant, unnatural daughter (e.g., De Ritter: 14–15). That many commentators have had such an agenda is indisputable. On the other hand, Fielding, who had hired Charlotte specifically to parody Cibber in *Pasquin,* could well have found irresistible the temptation of having her recite the ode in *The Historical Register,* at least on opening night. Published versions of plays often differed, sometimes substantially, from the plays as they were actually performed, especially in the early performances.

3. *Apology:* 157.

4. *Apology:* 155–56.

5. Between 1733 and 1739, the Boultbys lived on Bedford Ground, Southampton Street, later known as Tavistock Row (cf. City of Westminster Archives Center parish catalog); it seems to have been located very close to Tavistock Street.

6. Koon, for instance, who also dates this letter as 1737: 143.

7. *The Daily Advertiser,* May 5, 1737.

8. Thomas Lockwood, "Fielding and the Licensing Act," quoted in Hume, *Fielding:* 241.

9. *The Daily Advertiser,* March 10, 1737.

10. Hume, *Fielding:* 230.

11. Lewis: 203.

12. *The Craftsman,* May 28, 1737.

13. *Applebee's,* March 31, 1733; quoted in *London Stage,* 3, 1: 280.

14. May 7, 1737. My account of the passage of the Stage Licensing Act draws heavily upon the work of Liesenfeld and on Hume, *Fielding.*

15. Quoted in Liesenfeld: 130.

16. Liesenfeld: 136.

17. Letter from John Potter to the Lord Chamberlain, the Duke of Grafton, January 7, 1738, and a bill submitted February 24, 1738. Hume, *Fielding,* discusses the probable events and Potter's motivations: 244–47.

18. Hume, *Fielding:* 253.

19. Thomas Lockwood, quoted in Hume, *Fielding:* 252–53.

20. Fidelis Morgan was the first person, to my knowledge (besides John Holland in his unpublished biography of Charlotte), to stress what a catastrophe the Licensing Act was to her career and her life: 63.

16: PUNCH'S THEATRE (1737–38)

1. The information about the history of this engraving, and my reading of it below, are based upon Paulson, *Hogarth's Graphic Works,* and Kaier.

2. Paulson so identifies this figure; in most other respects, my own reading of this engraving follows his: 182–83.

3. Kaier: 96–97. Kaier cites Lichtenberg and Nichols as two earlier commentators who each, in his individual uneasy way, saw suggestions of eroticism between these two figures.

4. 281.

5. Heal: 55.

6. Strype, 1: 74.

7. Cf. Wright: 20, 340–44.

8. Though I place Richard's immigration to Jamaica during Charlotte's brief oil-selling career, it is in fact hard to pin down precisely when Charlotte became a widow, because the time at which Richard first departed for Jamaica is uncertain. In her autobiography, Charlotte gives three different dates for Richard's departure from London for the West Indies. At one point, she says that he went about a year after her mother died, which would place his departure early in 1735. But on June 16, 1736, the theatre at Lincoln's Inn Fields advertised a violin solo by Master Oates, "scholar to Charke," which implies that Richard was still in London, teaching violin. Elsewhere Charlotte says that he went abroad when she was at Lincoln's Inn Fields, just before she went to Fielding's company, which would place his departure in autumn 1736 or early winter 1737. But she clearly indicated that Richard was still in London when she set up shop, no earlier than summer 1737, so that her income-guarding subterfuge with the widow was necessary. However, she said, "he did not stay long enough to trouble me on that score." This would probably place his departure in the autumn of 1737.

9. Her licence "to perform, exercise and act a puppet show" was dated March 10, 1737/8 [OS, ie. 1738 NS]. National Archives LC 5/161, Warrant Book, p. 8.

Charlotte seems to have hired Mr. Yeates—who also may have been the person who carved her puppets—to help her master the art of puppet manipulation. She may also have had the assistance of a puppeteer named Hill (Speaight: 347).

10. 93.

11. Morgan: 64.

12. 105.

13. When Yeates performed his puppet shows there in 1739, his advertisements specified "Punch's Theatre, adjoining to the Tennis Court." *The London Daily Post and General Advertiser*, December 22, 1739.

14. *The London Daily Post and General Advertiser*, April 12, 1738.

15. Shershow: 157.

16. *The London Daily Post and General Advertiser*, April 25, 1738.

17. Shershow: 157.

17: HARD TIMES (1738–41)

1. Victor, II, 48. This performance took place on January 31, 1739.

2. *The Tryal for a Cause*: 3. My account is drawn principally from this contemporary pamphlet, written by someone who was in the courtroom taking notes; I also draw upon the thorough retelling of these events in Nash: 93–149, and the discussion in Koon: 145–47.

3. Quoted in Koon: 145.

4. Nash: 119–22.

5. *Tryal for a Cause*: 14–15.

6. *Tryal for a Cause*: 24.

7. Years later, the novice lawyer William Murray became the first Earl of Mansfield, Lord Chief Justice of the King's Bench, and author of the historic Mansfield decision that began the process of abolition in England. Lord Mansfield commented that he owed his career to that scandalous Cibber-Sloper trial (Nash: 147).

8. *The Tryals of Two Causes*: 2; 32.

9. She rented her marionettes and licence to Yeates, who used them to revive Punch's Theatre at the James Street Tennis Court during December and January 1739–40, but his show closed not long after the holidays ended.

10. *London Stage* 3, 2: 845.

11. 106. McPharlin has suggested that her puppets might eventually have made their way to New York.

12. In the overview of her autobiography—placed at the end of her narrative—she referred to having been "privately married, *which, as it proved, I had better have let it alone.*" Though here she seems to put this private marriage in the context of other events occurring around 1740—rather than 1746 when she did remarry—in the body of the *Narrative* she does not refer to another "marriage" at all.

13. Quoted in Bayne-Powell, *Life:* 216. The description of debtor'ss' prisons also draws from Turberville, I: 324–27; Schwartz: 154–62; and Picard, *Johnson:* 73–74.

14. January 1759; quoted in Picard, *Johnson:* 74.

15. Rehder: 155.

16. Hitchcock: 12.

17. Rehder points out that Richard Mytton, who provides Charlotte with one of her bails, kept the Cross-keys Inn between 1741 and 1744. If we place this scene in 1741, Kitty would have been ten (she turned eleven in November of that year). Furthermore, if this scene took place, as Charlotte says, after she sold her puppets, it would have had to take place no earlier than late winter of 1740.

18. Theatre Royal Drury Lane Scrapbook of Cuttings: British Library C 120 h1. Undated (1735?).

19. Burford: 128.

20. Francis Grose, *A Classical Dictionary of the Vulgar Tongue,* 1785. Quoted in Picard, *Johnson:* 74.

18: DOWN AND OUT IN LONDON (1741–44)

1. *Biographical Dictionary,* 7: 32. The death of Hallam's wife on June 9, 1740, and his second marriage on November 2, 1743, in Canterbury provide some boundaries for dating this episode in Charlotte's life. It probably took place sometime in 1741.

2. Morgan: 123. See Paulson, *Hogarth's Graphic Works,* I, 279–80, for a discussion of the Hogarth engraving. Among the prostitutes sticking their heads from the windows is Charlotte's benefactor, Mother Douglass, her hands raised prayerfully to heaven.

3. Different dates have been suggested for Charlotte's employment at the King's Head. Morgan thinks that her mention of Longacre might date this episode to 1737–38, but this is when Charlotte had her oil business there, and then her puppet theatre, and would not have been looking for work as a waiter. Rehder thinks that Charlotte's mention that Mrs. Dorr visited her in Drury Lane dates the King's Head episode in 1744, but it is clear from the context of her comment that the visit took place well after she had left her position at the King's Head, that it occurred when she was keeping her own eating house there (spring of 1744) and after Mrs. Dorr had lost her business.

Although Charlotte said at one point she worked for Mrs. Dorr "about a year" before she kept her own eating house (which we know she had in March 1744), there are reasons for dating this employment in 1741. Charlotte also said that Kitty was "about ten" at the time. Though her memory of Kitty's age was not always accurate, in this case it probably was: this would place the employment at Mrs. Dorr's between November 1740, when Kitty turned ten, and November 1741, when she turned eleven. Charlotte also said that when she left Mrs. Dorr she looked for acting work, and soon found it in a performance of *The Recruiting*

Officer with the army veteran Scudamore, on which occasion she recited the preface; but this performance took place on April 30, 1746, well after she had given up her eating house and therefore well after she had worked for Mrs. Dorr. But Charlotte earlier played a role in *The Recruiting Officer* on September 29, 1741. Perhaps she confused this performance with the one she later did with Scudamore.

Rehder points out perceptively that her working in the garden at Mrs. Dorr's would place the episode in the spring or summer. I would date her time with Mrs. Dorr to the spring/summer of 1741, when Kitty was ten and Charlotte was desperate for any kind of work, and just before she played in *The Recruiting Officer* and then had a little flurry of acting roles again. Her Longacre reference could be explained by her having moved back to that street by 1741 or, as I suggest, that it encompassed the adjoining Great Queen Street where she lived around 1740, and where she remained at that time.

4. See *London Stage*, 3, 2: 847.

5. Charlotte said that they played for the benefit of a young lady who had never acted before. On September 29, 1741, this theatre advertised this play for the benefit of a Miss Rogers, her "first time on any stage."

6. Morgan suggests a town such as Clapham, whose Common bears a marker locating it four miles from Westminster Abbey.

7. Quoted in Rehder: 161.

8. Morgan dates this episode to 1742—with which I concur; Anglesey was in London 1741–42—and identifies the mistress as Juliana Donovan, who may have been at this time one of his bigamously married wives: 123–24.

9. Cf. Halsband: 465–66.

10. *Sawney and Colley:* 4. "Sawney" is Alexander Pope.

11. In the collection of the Theatre Museum Study Room.

12. Document of Cibber's assignment of the copywright of *The Provok'd Husband* to John Watts, September 15, 1727, witnessed by Anne Cibber and "Cath. Brown." British Library: ADD Ms. 38728.

13. Marples declared bankruptcy in 1753. *The Gentleman's Magazine,* "Bankruptcies," July 1753.

14. Nash: 175–76.

15. Victor, I: 62.

16. Pilkington: 168.

17. Chetwood: 188.

18. Colley paid rates in Charles Street in 1741, but had established himself in his new house prior to July 23, 1742, when he wrote to a friend in Bath, giving his address as "Berkly Square near Bruton Street" (Vincent: 3). The current no. 18 was probably part of 19 until it was divided in 1786 (Phillips: 303).

19. Cibber, *A Letter from Mr. Cibber to Mr. Pope:* 47–49.

20. Mack: 779.

19: A MIND TO GET MONEY (1742–46)

1. *The London Daily Post and General Advertiser,* November 22, 1742.

2. Morgan and Rehder say that she played a season: the plays include, among others, *The Miser, The Mock-Doctor,* and *The London Merchant.*

3. Hawkins, II: 752.

4. Rehder: 162, fn. 175.

5. Smith: 51.

6. Quoted in Koon: 176.

7. Morgan: 127.

8. *London Stage,* 3, 1: lv; 999.

9. *The Actor,* quoted in Rehder: 164, fn. 195.

10. To Somerset Draper, September 16, 1744. *Letters,* I: 43–44.

11. *The Daily Advertiser,* March 4, 1745.

12. This third letter, published on Saturday, March 2, and probably placed by Charlotte herself, wished for the performance's success, "for Mrs. Charke's sake, who had long labour'd under many Misfortunes, which the Success of Monday Night may be a Means to extricate her from."

13. The origins of "God Save the King" are rather unclear, but the rise of the national anthem at this time is not disputed.

14. Rehder: 165, fn. 203; Morgan: 129. Charlotte says she visited Russell about a "fortnight" after his transfer to the Fleet (via a writ of habeas corpus), but Morgan quotes a note in the Fleet committals register that he died in July (probably early July). Morgan: 129.

15. Advertisements in *The General Advertiser* for New Wells, Clerkenwell include Mrs. Sacheverell's name, though somewhat sporadically, throughout the summer into late September, when the spa's season ended.

16. St. George's Chapel, May Fair, *Register of Baptisms and Marriages.* Harleian Society, 1889: viii. Marriages were solemnized in the "little Chapel" at the nearby house on Curzon Street, opposite to the Great Chapel. Marriages here were widely advertised in the newspapers: they cost one guinea, and did not require the publication of banns, the securing of a licence, or, for the underaged, parental consent. These marriages were, nonetheless, legal.

17. Charlotte writes that she played at Bartholomew Fair in August, but her name is not included among the very incomplete lists of fair players that summer. She may have played there, but she was still playing at New Wells, too, and may have simply misremembered the spa performances as taking place at the fair.

20: A LITTLE, DIRTY KIND OF WAR (1746–53)

1. The account of strolling players in this chapter is based upon Charlotte's *Narrative,* Mozeen, Templeton, and especially Rosenfeld, *Strolling Players,* Ch. I and *passim.*

2. Templeton, I: 39; 49.

3. Rosenfeld: 21, quoting George Parker, *A View of Society and Manners,* 1781.

4. Rosenfeld: 31.

5. Charlotte and Kitty seem to have been members of Linnet's company between the autumn of 1746 (or the winter of 1747), and sometime in late 1749 or early 1750.

6. Holland: 165.

7. Holland: 167. Morgan cites *The Bath Journal*'s report of the performance of *Cato* in Chippenham, February 27, 1749: 151.

8. Exactly when Charlotte joined Elrington's company is difficult to determine, but since she suggests that it was soon after her Chippenham and Corsham performances, it would likely have been in the spring of 1749. She says that she, Kitty, and Mrs. Brown together joined the troupe, which would place it before Kitty's marriage in January 1750. Both of the Elringtons seem to have been in London performing at Covent Garden Theatre in the spring of 1750. Mrs. Elrington performed

on April 19, being billed as a "Young Gentlewoman who never appeared on this stage before" (*London Stage*, 4, 1: 192, 194) and Mr. Elrington seems to have been given benefit tickets in early May (*London Stage*, 4, 1: 198). Presumably they began their strolling performances after Covent Garden Theatre closed for the season in mid-May. Charlotte must have joined them that spring or summer; she was certainly in the company by the autumn of 1750.

9. Richard Elrington appeared at Covent Garden Theatre as Bernardo in *Hamlet* on October 25, 1750.

10. Cf. Rosenthal: 19, quoting Petronius Arbiter [pseud.], *Memoirs of the Present Countess of Derby*.

11. Elrington's benefit at Covent Garden had been May 9, and the company's last performance was May 21 that year. Morgan discovered that Charlotte's old friend Jockey Adams was acting in Bristol at that time, including a piece called *Tit for Tat*, the title of Charlotte's own unpublished farce, and suggests that Charlotte might briefly have acted with him in Bristol in June. Morgan: 152. There is no concrete evidence for this, however, and Charlotte was still with Elrington's company in the autumn.

12. So identified by Holland: 172, and Morgan: 153.

13. Charlotte does not specify her location, but her reference to being taken to court and her description of a prison filled with "upwards of two hundred" condemned prisoners must refer to the quarter-sessions court at Gloucester: she refers to the "Sessions-House" and its jail. She later refers indignantly to being charged for being conducted to "G—" and speaks of their return from "G—."

21: THE FEMALE HUSBAND (1752–54)

1. Somerset Quarter Sessions Rolls, Ref. No. 314.7(5) and 314.7(6). Quoted in Baker: 219.

2. Reports on Mary Hamilton from *The Bath Journal*, September 22 and November 3, 1746; quoted in Baker: 221–22.

3. *The Gentleman's Magazine*, July 1777; quoted in Friedli: 258, fn. 66. Dekker and van de Pol report several eighteenth-century cases throughout Europe: 58–62.

4. *Fog's Weekly Journal*, October 15, 1737.

5. The first modern editor of Charlotte's autobiography, Fidelis Morgan, has come in for considerable criticism recently for her efforts in her 1988 edition to maintain that Charlotte was not a lesbian, even to the extent of misquoting the sentence in which she describes herself as making a decision, "I consulted on my pillow what was next to be done, and communicated my thoughts to my Friend," as having a period after "done" ("And" beginning a new sentence). This, Morgan argues, shows that the two women did not sleep together. (Actually, they almost certainly *did* sleep together, but that is no evidence one way or another, for sharing a bed was common at the time, even for the wealthy and certainly for the poor; at inns, even strangers of the same sex might have to share a bed.) In fairness to Morgan, whose service to Charlotte Charke's memory has been admirable and invaluable, she was reacting to earlier twentieth-century commentators who had no doubt that Charlotte *was* a lesbian and who saw this as more reason to condemn her either as unnatural and downright evil or as damaged and pathological.

Charlotte's most recent editor, Robert Rehder, surveys the factors that might indicate that she was "homosexual": her masculinity, her cross-dressing, her relationship with Mrs. Brown, her family disowning her, various moments in her life in which she was accused (and accused herself) of undefined misbehaviour, her father's use of the word "evil" to describe something she had done, and a passage mocking effeminate men in a novel she wrote (to be discussed later). Rehder necessarily concludes that while suggestive, these details are not definitive.

Emma Donoghue comments, accurately, I think, on the "love between women" evident in Charlotte and Mrs. Brown's relationship and their partnership as both "working women": 164–67.

6. As just a small sampling of this important body of scholarly literature, see Castle, Donoghue, Faderman, Garber, Halberstam, Traub, Trumbach, and Vicinus.
7. The relevant issues of this newspaper seem not to have survived.
8. Miller, Carl: 235.

22: THE PRODIGAL DAUGHTER (1755–56)

1. *A Serio-comic apology, for part of the life of Mr. Theophilus Cibber, comedian. Written by himself.* London: 1744. Published along with his adaptation of *Romeo and Juliet.*
2. None of the individual installments of the *Narrative* is known to have survived. The ad for the third installment ran: "This Day is published, Price 3 d. Number III of *A Narrative of the Life of Mrs. Charlotte Charke* (youngest Daughter of Colley Cibber, Esq.); both Serious and Comic, Written by HERSELF . . . To which will be added, The History of Henry Dumont, Esq; and Miss Charlotte Evelyn; containing many surprising Adventures, and a great Variety of Characters. Likewise written by Mrs. Charlotte Charke. The Whole will be contained in Eight Numbers, at 3 d. each; and with the last Number, a curious Copper-plate of Mrs. Charlotte Charke, and a general Title will be presented to the Subscribers gratis. Sold by W. Reeve in Fleet-street; A. Dodd, opposite St. Clement's Church in the Strand; E. Cooke, at the Royal Exchange; by the Booksellers in most of the Cities and great Towns in England and Wales, and by the Persons who carry News" (*The Public Advertiser,* Friday, March 21, 1755). Apparently Charlotte at this point still intended to include *Henry Dumont* as part of her autobiography, perhaps thinking that she would not have enough to say to fill up eight numbers.
3. Colley's will is reprinted in Koon: 188.
4. Rehder: ix.
5. Burney, *Memoirs:* 184–85.
6. The earliest advertisement I have located for the first edition of the bound volume, price 2 shillings 6 pence, is in *The Public Advertiser,* dated Monday, June 2, 1755. It was sold in London by W. Reeve, in Fleet Street; A. Dodd, in the Strand; and E. Cooke, at the Royal Exchange. It is impossible to tell whether Charlotte made any changes from the serial version.
7. Vol. 10, 1755.
8. Published in 1755. British Library: Music G.806.i(8). "Mrs. Charke" appears among the names on the subscription list.
9. My gratitude to Colin Thom, assistant editor of the *Survey of London,* for this information and his help in identifying this location: personal correspondence with Edward Lee, June 9, 2004. The location of Charlotte's dwelling is deduced from Samuel Whyte's identification of it as "situated on the way to Islington in the purlieus of Clarkenwel [sic] Bridewell, not very distant from the new River Head, where at that time it was usual for the scavengers to leave the cleansings of the streets, and the priests of Cloacina to deposit the offerings from the temples of that all-worshipped Power."

10. Whyte's account continues: "A rough deal board with three hobbling support-ers was brought for our convenience, on which without farther ceremony we con-trived to sit down and entered upon business—The work was read, remarks made, alterations agreed to and thirty guineas demanded for the copy. The squalid hand-maiden, who had been an attentive listener, stretched forward her tawny length of neck with an eye of anxious expectation!—The bookseller offered, five!—Our authoress did not appear hurt; disappointments had rendered her mind callous; however some altercation insued. This was the writer's first initiation into the mysteries of bibliopolism and the state of authorcraft. He, seeing both sides pertinacious, at length interposed, and at his instance the wary haberdasher of lit-erature doubled his first proposal with this saving provisoe, that his friend present would pay a moiety and run one half the risk; which was agreed to. Thus matters were accommodated, seemingly to the satisfaction of all parties; the lady's original stipulation of fifty copies for herself being previously acceded to. Such is the story of the once-admired daughter of Colley Cibber, Poet Laureate and patentee of Drury-lane, who was born in affluence and educated with care and tenderness, her servants in livery, and a splendid equipage at her command, with swarms of time-serving sycophants officiously buzzing in her train; yet unmindful of her advan-tages and improvident in her pursuits, she finished the career of her miserable existence on a dunghill. The account given of this unfortunate woman is literally correct in every particular, of which, except the circumstance of her death, the writer himself was an eye-witness." Whyte presumably exaggerates the luxury of Charlotte's former life for the didactic effect of its contrast with her, perhaps also exaggerated, fallen state.

11. Charlotte's asking price was well within bounds of high-level trade practice at the time. Charlotte's demand for fifty copies, however, seems to have been fairly high for the trade (Tierney: 31–34). But "the bulk of popular novels, including those by women, were probably sold to their publishers for around . . . five guineas" (Turner: 114).

12. *The Monthly Review,* May 1756: 445. Benjamin Nangle identifies the writer of this review as William Bewley, a close friend of Dr. Burney's.

13. They played in *The Intriguing Captains* at "Bence's great theatrical booth." *The Public Advertiser,* September 20, 1756.

14. Johnson and Burling: 185–87.

15. *The Kentish Post, or Canterbury News-Letter,* August 5–9, 1758.

16. *The General Advertiser,* July 8, 1756, quoted in Walford, II: 363.

17. Issues of *The Public Advertiser,* Sepember 18–25, 1756, list Charlotte in per-formances through September 27.

18. Mann: xliii.

19. Nash: 265.

20. Pilkington: 168–69.

21. Pilkington, 2nd. edition: 108–110. The second, Dublin edition of Pilkington's book is expanded from the first, and contains the information about the widow Pockrich.

23: CURTAIN CALLS (1757–60)

1. Richardson, VI: 65.

2. Barker: 257–58.

3. Richardson, III: 319.

4. Richardson, II: 174.

5. Letter to Richardson, May 30, 1753. Copy in Harvard University Theatre Collection: bMS Thr 357 (10). His "female fry" included Jenny and Betty Cibber, as well as Catherine and her daughter.

6. Koon: 178. Generally, his biographers assume that Colley died at home in his house in Berkeley Square, and that seems to be verified by the newspapers. But one different report is worth mentioning: John Nelson's 1812 *History of Islington* reports that Colley Cibber was said to have had a lodging on Colebrook Row, where he was said to have died on December 12, 1757.

7. Victor, I: 249–51.

8. National Archives LC 7/3.

9. Henderson: 68. I could find no entries for Mrs. Hind or Hinds in the relevant Leicester/Swallow Street rates books, though several of the properties there are marked as inhabited by tenants. Possibly Mrs. Hinds was herself a tenant who rented rooms to Charlotte.

10. Phillips: 85, 240.

11. Derbyshire Record Office, Wilmot-Horton Family Archive, D3155 M/C2256 (transcription courtesy of Joanne Ichimura, archivist). The licence issued to "Mrs. Charlotte Charke & Company" gave her permission to perform between "the date hereof [August 29] and the twenty first Day of September next 1759, the Burletta called Galligantus thus and such other Theatrical Performances as have been heretofore permitted . . ." Warrant Book, National Archives LC 5/162: 148.

12. Advertisements and notices concerning *Galligantus* appeared in *The Public Advertiser* beginning September 7, 1759.

13. It was performed in Dublin on March 27, 1749 (Dircks: 44); at the Haymarket on December 26 and 28, 1758 (*London Stage*, 4, 2: 703). Dircks does not seem to be aware of the London performances.

14. Quoted in Dircks: 17.

15. *The Public Advertiser*, September 26, 1759. On September 27, Charlotte published another notice, soliciting the "Favour of her Friends To-morrow Night" for her benefit: "She farther hopes that her Address to the Public in Yesterday's Paper will prove a tender Incentive to their Patronage, as it may be the happy Means of settling her above the Fears of Distress, e're Infirmity or Age may render her Incapable of providing for herself."

16. The story of Charlotte's last recorded performances has been muddled, with the *London Stage* listing only one performance by her—*The Busy Body*—in the records and the *Biographical Dictionary* assuming that though she received permission to stage ten plays, she was only able to mount one performance. As Morgan, Holland, and more recently Burling have noted, ads for *The Busy Body* make it clear that it was the seventh performance of the series of ten, the rest being performances of *Galligantus*. Charlotte completed the run she had been granted.

17. The letter to Sir Robert, in its entirety, reads: "I hope you'll forgive this Importunity, but not having the Desir'd success, thro the heat of the Season, and the Nobility out of Town, Conjoin'd with great Expences, I am oblig'd to Implore the favour of obtaining a new Licence for either Six nights or mornings, by which means I shall stand a happy chance of effecting my former Design of settling my self in Business, and after this Clemency added to the former shall never more presume to trouble his Grace. I was in hope to have got a Liberty for the Theatre at Goodman's Fields but as that is Impracticable, humbly Intreat that in tenderness to my Circumstances yr Honor would be so good as to mention the above proposal

to the Duke to whom I acknowledge myself most Infinitely oblig'd. I shall Sir wait yr answer to morrow or what time will be most agreeable and with profound respect subscribe [,] Sir yr most oblig'd humble Servt Charlotte Charke." The letter is marked: "rec^d 15 Novr 1759." Derbyshire Record Office: Wilmot-Horton Family Archive, D3155 M/C2297 (transcription courtesy of Joanne Ichimura, archivist). This letter, which I recently discovered, has been mislabeled as a letter from "Mrs. Clarke."

18. John Nelson, *History of Islington* (1812): 385. "[Cibber's] daughter Mrs. Clarke [*sic*], than whom few women ever passed through a greater variety of adventures and occupations, kept a public house in Islington, where she died in great distress in 1760."

19. Landers, Chapter 6: esp. pp. 240–41.

20. *The London Evening-Post*, April 17–19, 1760; *The London Chronicle*, April 17–19, 1760; *The Public Ledger*, April 18, 1760.

EPILOGUE

1. *The Public Advertiser*, January 12, 1758; quoted in Koon: 180. All the rest of the details concerning the subsequent history of the Cibber family, unless otherwise noted, are taken from Koon: 180–81.

2. Phillips: 303.

3. Charles Burney, notes in his copy of *The Companion to the Playhouse*, vol. II: British Library 11795.t.30. *The London Chronicle*, May 17, 1760, reports a "Prologue spoken at Smock Alley Theatre for the Benefit of Chetwood then a Prisoner for Debt."

4. Copy in the Harvard University Houghton Library Theatre Collection.

5. Records gathered in Johnson and Burling, *passim*.

6. May 31–June 7, 1773. Quoted in Johnson and Burling: 443.

7. Speaight: 107. Morgan quotes this and an array of other such assessments: 192–93.

BIBLIOGRAPHY

Allderidge, Patricia. *The Bethlem Royal Hospital. An Illustrated History*. Bethlem and Maudsley NHS Trust, 1995.

An Apology for the Life of Mr. T—— C——, Comedian. Being a Proper Sequel to the Apology for the Life of Mr. Colley Cibber, Comedian. With a View of the Stage to the Present Year. Supposed to be written by Himself. In the Stile and Manner of the Poet Laureate. London: 1740.

Appleton, William W. *Charles Macklin: An Actor's Life.* Cambridge, Mass.: Harvard University Press, 1960.

Ashley, Leonard R. N. *Colley Cibber.* Rev. ed. New York: Twayne, 1989.

Aston, Anthony. *A Brief Supplement to Colley Cibber, Esq. His Lives of the Late Famous Actors and Actresses.* London: [1747?].

Avery, Emmet L., Arthur H. Scouten, William Van Lennep, George Winchester Stone, Jr. *The London Stage 1660–1800.* 5 vols. Carbondale: Southern Illinois University Press, 1960–68.

Baldwin, Olive, and Thelma Wilson, "Lavinia Fenton's Birthdate." *Theatre Notebook* 57, 1 (2003): 72.

Baker, Sheridan. "Henry Fielding's *The Female Husband*: Fact and Fiction." *PMLA* 74, 3 (June 1959): 213–24.

Barker, Richard Hindry. *Mr. Cibber of Drury Lane.* New York: Columbia University Press, 1939.

Baruth, Philip E., ed. *Introducing Charlotte Charke: Actress, Author, Enigma.* Urbana: University of Illinois Press, 1998.

Battestin, Martin C., with Ruth R. Battestin. *Henry Fielding: A Life.* London: Routledge, 1989.

Bayne-Powell, Rosamond. *Eighteenth-Century London Life.* London: John Murray, 1937.

Bowers, Toni. *The Politics of Motherhood: British Writing and Culture, 1680–1760.* Cambridge, Eng.: Cambridge University Press, 1996.

Brewer, John. *The Pleasures of the Imagination.* New York: Farrar, Straus and Giroux: 1997.

Brooke, Iris, and James Laver. *English Costume in the Eighteenth Century.* London: A. & C. Black, 1931.

Brown, Thomas. *Amusements Serious and Comical.* London: 1700.

Buck, Anne. *Dress in Eighteenth-Century England.* London: B. T. Batsford, 1979.

Burford, E. J. *Wits, Wenchers and Wantons. London's Low Life: Covent Garden in the Eighteenth Century.* London: Hale, 1986.

Burling, William J. *Summer Theatre in London, 1661–1820, and the Rise of the Haymarket Theatre.* Madison, N.J.: Fairleigh Dickinson University Press, 2000.

Burney, Charles. *A General History of Music: From the Earliest Ages to the Present Period* (1789). Ed. Frank Mercer. 2 vols. New York: Dover Publications, 1957.

——. *Memoirs of Dr. Charles Burney, 1726–1769.* Ed. Slava Klima, Garry Bowers, and Kerry S. Grant. Lincoln: University of Nebraska Press, 1988.

Campbell, R. *The London Tradesman.* London: 1747.

Castle, Terry. *The Female Thermometer: Eighteenth-Century Culture and the Invention of the Uncanny.* Oxford: Oxford University Press, 1995.

——, ed. *The Literature of Lesbianism.* New York: Columbia University Press, 2003.

Charke, Charlotte. *The Art of Management; or, Tragedy Expell'd.* London: 1735.

——. *The History of Charley and Patty; or, The Friendly Strangers.* London: n.d. [1759?]

——. *The History of Henry Dumont, Esq; and Miss Charlotte Evelyn.* 3rd ed. London: 1756.

——. *The Lover's Treat; or, Unnatural Hatred. Being a True Narrative as deliver'd to the Author by one of the Family who was principally concern'd in the following Account.* London: n.d. (BL catalogue suggests: 1758?)

——. *The Mercer, or Fatal Extravagance: Being a True Narrative of the Life of Mr. Wm. Dennis, Mercer, in Cheapside.* London: n.d. (BL catalogue suggests: 1755?)

——. *A Narrative of the Life of Mrs. Charlotte Charke, Youngest Daughter of Colley Cibber, Esq., Written by Herself.* [2nd. ed., London: 1755] Ed. Leonard R. N. Ashley. Gainesville, Fla.: Scholars' Facsimiles and Reprints, 1969. (Other modern editions of this text are listed in this bibliography under the editors' names.)

Chetwood, William Rufus. *A General History of the Stage.* London: 1749.

Cibber, Colley. *An Apology for the Life of Colley Cibber, with an Historical View of the Stage during his own Time.* Ed. B.R.S. Fone. Ann Arbor: University of Michigan Press, 1968.

——. *The Egotist; or, Colley upon Cibber. Being His own Picture retouch'd, to so plain a Likeness, that no One, now, would have the Face to own it, But Himself.* London: 1743.

——. *A Letter from Mr. Cibber to Mr. Pope,* London: 1742.

——. *The Plays of Colley Cibber.* Ed. Rodney L. Hayley. 2 vols. New York: Garland, 1980.

——. *Colley Cibber: Three Sentimental Comedies.* Ed. Maureen Sullivan. New Haven, Conn.: Yale University Press, 1973.

Cibber, Theophilus. *Four Original Letters, viz. Two from a Husband to a Gentleman: and Two from a Husband to a Wife.* 3rd ed., London: 1739.

————. "A Letter from Theophilus Cibber, Comedian, To John Highmore, Esq." n.d. [London, 1733].

Clarion, Hippolyte. "Reflections Upon the Dramatic Art." *The Monthly Mirror*, March–May, 1801.

The Complete Newgate Calendar. London: Navarre Society, 1926.

Cooke, William. *Memoirs of Charles Macklin, Comedian*. London: 1804. Rpt. New York: Benjamin Bloom, 1972.

Covent-Garden: A Satire. London: 1756.

Cunnington, C. Willett, and Phillis Cunnington. *Handbook of English Costume in the Eighteenth Century*. Boston: Plays, Inc., 1972.

Davies, Christian. *The Life and Adventures of Mrs. Christian Davies, commonly call'd Mother Ross*. London: 1740.

Davies, Thomas. *Dramatic Miscellanies*. 3 vols. Dublin: 1784. Rpt. New York: Benjamin Bloom, 1971.

————. *Lillo's Dramatic Works, with Memoirs of the Author* (1775). London: 1810.

————. *Memoirs of the Life of David Garrick*. 2 vols. London: 1808. Rpt. New York: Benajmin Bloom, 1969.

Defoe, Daniel. *A Tour Through the Whole Island of Great Britain*. Ed. Pat Rogers. New York: Penguin, 1978.

Dekker, Rudolf M., and Lotte C. van de Pol. *The Tradition of Female Transvestism in Early Modern Europe*. London: Macmillan, 1989.

Dennis, John. *The Critical Works of John Dennis*. 2 vols. Ed. Edward Niles Hooker. Baltimore: Johns Hopkins University Press, 1939–43.

DeRitter, Jones. " 'Not the Person She Conceived Me': The Public Identities of Charlotte Charke." *Genders* 19: 3–25.

Dircks, Phyliss T. *The Eighteenth-Century English Burletta*. Victoria, B.C.: English Literary Studies, 1999.

Donoghue, Emma. *Passions Between Women: British Lesbian Culture 1668–1801*. New York: HarperCollins, 1993.

Downes, John. *Roscius Anglicanus* [1708]. Ed. Judith Milhous and Robert D. Hume. London: Society for Theatre Research, 1987.

Earle, Peter. *The Making of the English Middle Class: Business, Society and Family Life in London, 1660–1730*. Berkeley: University of California Press, 1989.

Faderman, Lillian. *Surpassing the Love of Men: Romantic Friendship and Love between Women from the Renaissance to the Present*. New York: William Morrow, 1981.

[Fielding, Henry.] *The Female Husband*. London: 1746.

————. *The Historical Register for the Year 1736*. Ed. William W. Appleton. Lincoln: University of Nebraska Press, 1967.

————. *Pasquin*. In *The Complete Works of Henry Fielding*. Ed. William Ernest Henley. Vol. 4. New York: Croscup & Sterling, 1902.

Folkenflick, Robert. "Charlotte Charke: Images and Afterimages." In *Introducing Charlotte Charke*. Ed. Philip E. Baruth. Urbana: University of Illinois Press, 1998: 137–62.

————. "Gender, Genre, and Theatricality in the Autobiography of Charlotte Charke." In *Representations of the Self from the Renaissance to Romanticism*. Ed. Patrick Coleman, Jayne Lewis, and Jill Kowalik. Cambridge, Eng.: Cambridge University Press, 2000: 97–118.

Friedli, Lynne. " 'Passing Women'—A Study of Gender Boundaries in the Eighteenth Century." In *Sexual Underworlds of the Enlightenment*. Ed. G. S.

Rousseau and Roy Porter. Chapel Hill: University of North Carolina Press, 1988: 234–60.

Gámez, Luis R. "Histrionics and Authority: Colley Cibber and Performance-Influenced Variants in the 1713 *Cato* Duodecimo." *Papers of the Bibliographical Society of America* 91, 1 (1997): 5–29.

Garber, Marjorie. *Vested Interests: Cross-dressing and Cultural Anxiety.* New York: Harper, 1992.

Garrick, David. *The Letters of David Garrick.* Ed. David M. Little and George M. Kahrl. Vol. I. Cambridge, Mass.: Harvard University Press, 1963.

Genest, John, ed. *Some Account of the English Stage from the Restoration in 1660 to 1830.* 10 vols. Bath: 1832. Rpt. New York: Burt Franklin [1964].

George, M. Dorothy. *London Life in the Eighteenth Century.* New York: Capricorn Books, 1965.

Grant, Elizabeth. *Memoirs of a Highland Lady* [1898]. Ed. Andrew Todd. London: Canongate, 1988.

Gwynn, John. *London and Westminster Improved, Illustratred by Plans.* London: 1766.

Halberstam, Judith. *Female Masculinity.* Durham, N.C.: Duke University Press, 1998.

Halsband, Robert. "The Noble Lady and the Player." *History Today,* July 1968: 464–72.

Hare, Arnold, ed. *The Theatre Royal, Bath: A Calendar of Performances at the Orchard Street Theatre.* Bath: Kingsmead Press, 1977.

Hatton, Ragnhild. *George I: Elector and King.* Cambridge, Mass.: Harvard University Press, 1978.

Hawkins, John. *A General History of the Science and Practice of Music.* 2 vols. London: 1853.

Heal, Ambrose. *London's Tradesmen's Cards of the XVIII Century.* New York: Dover, 1968.

Heaney, Peter. *Selected Writings of the Laureate Dunces, Nahum Tate (Laureate 1692–1715), Laurence Eusden (1718–1730) and Colley Cibber (1730–1757). Studies in British Literature* 40. Lewiston, N.Y.: The Edwin Mellon Press, 1999.

Henderson, Tony. *Disorderly Women in Eighteenth-Century London: Prostitution and Control in the Metropolis 1730–1830.* London: Longman, 1999.

John, Lord Hervey. *Some Materials Towards Memoirs of the Reign of King George II.* 1931. Rpt. New York: AMS Press, 1970.

Highfill, Philip H. Jr., Kalman A. Burnim, and Edward A. Langhans, eds. *A Biographical Dictionary of Actors, Actresses, Musicians, Dancers, Managers and Other Stage Personnel in London, 1660–1800.* Carbondale: Southern Illinois University Press, 1973.

Hill, Aaron. *The Works of the Late Aaron Hill, Esq.* 4 vols. London: 1753.

———, and William Popple. *The Prompter: A Theatrical Paper.* Ed. William Appleton and Kalman Burnim. New York: Benjamin Bloom, 1966.

Hill, John. *The Actor: A Treatise on the Art of Playing.* London: 1750. Rpt. New York: Benjamin Bloom, 1971.

Hindley, Charles. *A History of the Cries of London* [1884]. Rpt. Detroit: Singing Trees Press, 1969.

Hitchcock, Tim. Introduction to *Chronicling Poverty: The Voices and Strategies of the English Poor, 1640–1840.* Eds. Tim Hitchcock, Peter King, Pamela Sharpe. New York: St. Martin's Press, 1997: 1–18.

Holland, John D. *My Name Was In Capitals: Charlotte Charke (1713–1760).* Unpub. ms. in Theatre Museum Study Room, London. PN2598.C28.

Howe, Elizabeth. *The First English Actresses: Women and Drama 1660–1700.* Cambridge, Eng.: Cambridge University Press, 1992.

Hume, Robert D. *Henry Fielding and the London Theatre 1727–1737.* Oxford: Clarendon Press, 1988.

Hunter, David. "Margaret Cecil, Lady Brown: 'Persevering Enemy to Handel' but 'Otherwise Unknown to History,'" *Women and Music* 3 (1999): 43–58.

Johnson, Odai, and William J. Burling. *The Colonial American Stage, 1665–1774: A Documentary Calendar.* Madison, N.J.: Fairleigh Dickinson University Press, 2001.

Kaier, Christina. "Professional Femininity in Hogarth's *Strolling Actresses Dressing in a Barn.*" In *The Other Hogarth: Aesthetics of Difference.* Ed. Bernadette Fort and Angela Rosenthal. Princeton, N.J.: Princeton University Press, 2001: 76–99.

Koon, Helene. *Colley Cibber: A Biography.* Lexington: University Press of Kentucky, 1986.

Lafler, Joanne. *The Celebrated Mrs. Oldfield: The Life and Art of an Augustan Actress.* Carbondale: Southern Illinois University Press, 1989.

Landers, John. *Death and the Metropolis.* Cambridge, Eng.: Cambridge University Press, 1993.

A Lash for the Laureat: Or An Address by Way of Satyr; Most Humbly Inscrib'd to the Unparallel'd Mr. Rowe, On Occasion of a late Insolent prologue to the Non-Juror. London: 1718.

The Laureat: or, the Right Side of Colley Cibber, Esq. London: 1740.

Leacroft, Richard. *The Development of the English Playhouse.* Ithaca, N.Y.: Cornell University Press, 1973.

Letters from a Moor at London To His Friend at Tunis. London: 5th ed. [n.d.].

Lewis, Peter. *Fielding's Burlesque Drama.* Edinburgh: Edinburgh University Press, 1987.

Liesenfeld, Vincent J. *The Licensing Act of 1737.* Madison: University of Wisconsin Press, 1984.

Loftis, John, Richard Southern, Marion Jones, and A. H. Scouten. *The Revels History of Drama in English.* vol. V., *1660–1750:* 90–91.

Mack, Maynard. *Alexander Pope: A Life.* New York: Norton, 1985.

Maitland, William. *The History of London. Continued to the Year 1772, by the Rev. John Entick.* 2 vols. London: 1775.

Mann, David. Introduction to *The Plays of Theophilus and Susannah Cibber.* Ed. David Mann. New York: Garland, 1981.

McPharlin, Paul. "Charlotte Charke's Puppets in New York." *Theatre Notebook* 1 (1947): 111–13.

Miller, Carl. *Stages of Desire: Gay Theatre's Hidden History.* London: Cassel, 1996.

Miller, Edward. *A collection of new English songs and a cantata set to music by Edward Miller.* London: 1755.

Morgan, Fidelis, "with Charlotte Charke." *The Well-Known Troublemaker: A Life of Charlotte Charke.* London: Faber & Faber, 1988.

Morley, Henry. *Memoirs of Bartholomew Fair.* London: Routledge, 1892.

Mozeen, Thomas. *Young Scarron.* Dublin: 1752.

Nangle, Benjamin Christie, ed. *The Monthly Review.* First Series, 1749–1789. Oxford: Clarendon Press, 1934.

Nelson, John. *History of Islington.* London: 1812.

Paulson, Ronald, ed. *Hogarth's Graphic Works*. Rev. ed. 2 vols. New Haven, Conn.: Yale University Press, 1970.

Paulson, Ronald. *The Life of Henry Fielding: A Critical Biography*. Oxford: Blackwell, 2000.

Pharmacopoeia Pauperum: Or, the Hospital Dispensatory. Containing the Medicines Used in the Hospitals of London, By the Direction of Dr Coatsworth, Dr. Mead, Dr. Cade, Dr. Wadsworth, Dr. Hales, &c. With Suitable Instructions for Their Common Use. London: 1718.

Philips, Teresa Constantia. *The Happy Courtezan: Or, the Prude demolish'd. An Epistle from the Celebrated Mrs. C—— P—— [Constantia Philips] to the Angelick Signior Far—n—li [Farinelli]*. London: 1735.

Phillips, Hugh. *Mid-Georgian London*. London: Collins, 1964.

Picard, Liza. *Dr. Johnson's London*. London: Weidenfeld & Nicolson, 2000.

Pilkington, John Carteret. *The Real Story of John Carteret Pilkington. Written by Himself*. 2nd ed. Dublin: 1762.

Plumb, J. H. *The First Four Georges*. London: Fontana/Collins, 1956.

The Polite Lady; or, A Course of Female Education. In a Series of Letters From a Mother to a Daughter. London: 1760.

Pope, Alexander. *The Poems of Alexander Pope*. Ed. John Butt. New Haven, Conn.: Yale University Press, 1963.

Porter, Dorothy, and Roy Porter. *Patient's Progress: Doctors and Doctoring in Eighteenth-Century England*. Stanford Calif.: Stanford University Press, 1989.

"The Proceedings of the Old Bailey. London 1674–1834." *http://www.oldbaileyonline.org/*.

Register of Baptisms and Marriages, St. George's Chapel, Hyde Park Corner. London: Harleian Society, 1889.

Rehder, Robert, ed. *A Narrative of the Life of Mrs. Charlotte Charke*. London: Pickering and Chatto, 1999.

Richards, Sandra. *The Rise of the English Actress*. New York: St. Martin's Press, 1993.

Richardson, John. *Covent Garden*. New Barnet, Herts.: Historical Publications, 1979.

Richardson, Samuel. *The Correspondence of Samuel Richardson*. Ed. Anna Laetitia Barbauld, 1804. 6 vols. Rpt. New York: AMS Press, 1966.

Roberts, Edgar V. "The Songs and Tunes in Henry Fielding's Ballad Operas." In *The Eighteenth-Century English Stage*. Ed. Kenneth Richards and Peter Thomson. London: Methuen, 1972: 29–50.

Rosenfeld, Sybil. *Strolling Players and Drama in the Provinces, 1660–1765* [1939]. Rpt. New York: Octagon Books, 1970.

———. *The Theatre of the London Fairs in the 18th Century*. Cambridge, Eng.: Cambridge University Press, 1960.

Saussure, Cesar de. *A Foreign View of England in 1725–1729*. Trans. and ed. Madame Van Muyden. London: Caliban, 1995.

Sawney and Colley (1742) and Other Pope Pamphlets, Ed. W. Powell Jones. Los Angeles: Augustan Reprint Society no. 83, 1960.

Schwartz, Richard B. *Daily Life in Johnson's London*. Madison: University of Wisconsin Press, 1983.

Senior, F. Dorothy. *The Life and Times of Colley Cibber*. London, 1928.

Shershow, Scott Cutler. *Puppets and "Popular" Culture*. Ithaca, N.Y.: Cornell University Press, 1995.

Smith, John Thomas, *Vagabondiana; or, Anecdotes of Mendicant Wanderers through the Streets of London.* London: 1817.

Snell, Hannah. *The Female Soldier; or, The Surprising Life and Adventures of Hannah Snell, Born in the City of Worcester.* London: 1750.

Speaight, George. *The History of the English Puppet Theatre.* 2nd ed. Carbondale: Southern Illinois University Press, 1990.

Spence, Joseph. *Anecdotes, Observations and Characters of Books and Men, Collected from the Conversation of Mr. Pope and Other Eminent Persons of His Time by the Reverend Joseph Spence.* Ed. Samuel Weller Singer. Carbondale: Southern Illinois University Press, 1964.

Steele, Richard. *The Tatler.* Ed. Donald F. Bond. 3 vols. Oxford: Clarendon Press, 1987.

——— and Joseph Addison. *The Spectator.* Ed. Donald F. Bond. 5 vols. Oxford: Clarendon Press, 1965.

Steele, Richard. *The Theatre.* Ed. John Loftis. Oxford: Clarendon Press, 1962.

Stone, George Winchester, Jr., and George M. Karhl. *David Garrick: A Critical Biography.* Carbondale: Southern Illinois University Press, 1979.

Stone, Lawrence. *The Family, Sex and Marriage in England 1500–1800.* New York: Harper & Row, 1977.

———. *The Road to Divorce: England 1530–1987.* Oxford: Oxford University Press, 1990.

Straub, Kristina. *Sexual Suspects: Eighteenth-Century Players and Sexual Ideology.* Princeton, N.J.: Princeton University Press, 1992.

Strype, John [Stowe, John]. *A Survey of the Cities of London and Westminster. Corrected, Improved and very much Enlarged. Brought to the present time by John Strype.* 6 Books. London: 1720.

Sulloway, Frank J. *Born to Rebel: Birth Order, Family Dynamics, and Creative Lives.* New York: Pantheon Books, 1996.

Templeton, William. *The Strolling Player; or, The Life and Adventures of William Templeton.* 3 vols. London: 1802.

The Theatre-Royal Turn'd into a Mountebank's Stage. In Some Remarks upon Mr. Cibber's Quack-Dramatical Performance, called the Non-Juror. London: 1718.

Thomas, David, and Arnold Hare. *Theatre in Europe: A Documentary History. Restoration and Georgian England.* Ed. David Thomas. Cambridge, Eng.: Cambridge University Press, 1989.

Tierney, James E. *The Correspondence of Robert Dodsley 1733–1764.* Cambridge, Eng.: Cambridge University Press, 1988.

Traub, Valerie. *The Renaissance of Lesbianism in Early Modern England.* Cambridge, Eng.: Cambridge University Press, 2002.

Trumbach, Randolph. "London's Sapphists." In *Body Guards: The Cultural Politics of Gender Ambiguity.* Ed. Julia Epstein and Kristina Straub. London: Routledge, 1991: 112–41.

The Tryal for a Cause For Criminal Conversation, Between Theophilus Cibber, Gent. Plaintiff, and William Sloper, Esq., Defendant. London: Printed for T. Trott, 1739.

The Tryal of Colley Cibber, Comedian, &c. For Writing a Book intitled An Apology for his Life, &c. Being a thorough Examination thereof; wherein he is proved guilty of High Crimes and Misdemeanors against the English Language, and in characterizing many Persons of Distinction. London: 1740.

The Tryals of Two Causes, between Theophilus Cibber, Gent. Plaintiff, and William Sloper, Esq., Defendant. The First for Criminal Conversation. The Second, for Detaining the Plaintiff's Wife. London: 1740.

Tupper, Fred S. "Colley and Caius Cibber." *Modern Language Notes,* May 1940: 393–96.

Turberville, A. S., ed. *Johnson's England: An Account of the Life and Manners of His Age.* 2 vols. Rev. ed. Oxford: Clarendon Press, 1952.

Turner, Cheryl. *Living by the Pen: Women Writers in the Eighteenth Century.* London: Routledge, 1992.

Uffenbach, Zacharias Conrad von. *London in 1710. From the Travels of Zacharias Conrad Von Uffenbach.* Trans and ed. W. H. Quarrell and Margaret Mare. London: Faber & Faber, 1934.

Uglow, Jenny. *Hogarth: A Life and a World.* London: Faber and Faber, 1997.

The Usefulness of the Stage to Religion and to Government: shewing the Advantage of the Drama in all Nations, since its first Institution. 2nd ed. London, 1738.

Van Der Kiste, John. *King George II and Queen Caroline.* Stroud, Gloucestershire: Sutton Publishing, 1997.

Vaughan, Anthony. *Born to Please: Hannah Pritchard, Actress, 1711–1768.* London: Society for Theatre Research, 1979.

Vertue, George. *Notebooks.* 6 vols. Oxford: Walpole Society, 1930.

Vicinus, Martha. " 'They Wonder to Which Sex I Belong': The Historical Roots of the Modern Lesbian Identity." In *Lesbian Subjects: A Feminist Studies Reader.* Ed. Martha Vicinus. Bloomington: Indiana University Press, 1996: 233–59.

Victor, Benjamin. *The History of the Theatres of London and Dublin from the Year 1730 to the Present Time.* 3 vols. London: 1761. Rpt. New York: Benjamin Bloom, 1969.

Vincent, Howard P. "Two Letters of Colley Cibber." *Notes and Queries,* January 5, 1935: 3–4.

Walford, Edward. *Village London: The Story of Greater London.* 2 vols. 1883–84. Rpt. London: Alderman Press, 1984.

Walpole, Horace. *Horace Walpole's Correspondence.* Ed. W. S. Lewis, George L. Lam, and Charles H. Bennett. Vol. I. New Haven, Conn.: Yale University Press, 1948.

Wanko, Cheryl. *Roles of Authority: Thespian Biography and Celebrity in Eighteenth-Century Britain.* Lubbock: Texas Tech University Press, 2003.

Weinreb, Ben, and Christopher Hibbert, eds. *The London Encyclopedia.* Bethesda, Md.: Adler & Adler, 1986.

Whyte, Samuel. "The Theatre, A Didactic Essay." In *Poems on Various Subjects, Ornamented with Plates, and illustrated with Notes, Original Letters and Curious Incidental Anecdotes.* Ed. Edward Athenry Whyte. Dublin: 1792 [actual publication date 1794].

Wiles, R. M. *Serial Publication in England before 1750.* Cambridge, Eng.: Cambridge University Press, 1957.

Wilkinson, Tate. *Memoirs of His Own Life.* 4 vols. York: 1790.

———. *The Wandering Patentee; or, A History of the Yorkshire Theatres from 1770 to the Present Time.* York: 1795.

Wilson, John Harold. *All the King's Ladies: Actresses of the Restoration.* Chicago: University of Chicago Press, 1958.

Winton, Calhoun. *John Gay and the London Theatre.* Lexington: University Press of Kentucky, 1993.

Wright, Richardson. *Revels in Jamaica 1682–1838.* New York: Dodd, Mead & Co.: 1937.

ACKNOWLEDGMENTS

My first, deeply heartfelt thanks go to my husband, Edward Lee, who turned his attention from Plato to Charlotte and eighteenth-century London. His involvement in this project was profound: he was the best sounding board and highest-powered research assistant any writer could wish for, and he made invaluable contributions to this book.

Among my treasured London friends, Dana Kubick and Mark Leffler both read sections of the manuscript, and I benefited enormously from their advice, their love for their city, and the gifts of their hospitality and architectural sight-seeing. Thanks to Mark for advice based upon his extensive knowledge of London history and to Dana for her author photo. Avril and John Marcus have warmly welcomed me into their home for more than twenty-five years, and have often generously driven me around England, most recently to Winchester and Canterbury, both important to Charlotte's story. These trips have been among the best parts of my visits.

Thanks also to Joss Bennathan, who first told me about the Theatre Museum Study Room, and to Sudha Berry, who offered to conduct research on my behalf despite her onerous lawyer's schedule—and to both for their hospitality.

Fortune must have been responsible for introducing me to my newest London friend, Nicki Faircloth of Strawberry Hill, who happened to be our guide there one afternoon—and who, wonderfully, turns out to be Charlotte's third cousin five times removed. I never dreamt that I would discover anyone who possesses a bit of Charlotte's DNA, and I am grateful for Nicki's help with and enthusiasm about this book.

Thanks also to Pastor Thomas Reventlow Bruun of the Danish Church of London, Regent's Park, and to Patricia Allderidge of the Bethlem Hospital Museum, Eden Park, Kent, for information about Caius Gabriel Cibber and his sculptures; and to Colin Thom of the *Survey of London* for information about Clerkenwell hovels.

I am greatly indebted to my writing partner here in San Diego, Karen Hollis, who has played a critical role in helping me think about, shape, and revise this book, and whose own writing is an enviable model of elegance and wit. Many

thanks also go to the members of my writing group in the Department of Literature at the University of California, San Diego, who gave me unwavering support
as I was beginning this project: Stephanie Jed, Susan Larsen, Marta Sánchez, and
Nicole Tonkovich. Among other friends and colleagues, Andrew Wright read the
early part of the book and offered encouragement I value greatly; Milane Chris-
tiansen, proprietor of Book Works bookstore, has given me particularly useful
advice. Thanks, too, to Louise Kollenbaum, Olaf Simons, Judith Halberstam, Shel-
ley Streeby, Curtis Marez, Page duBois, Todd Kontje, Liberty Smith, Rosemary
George, and Don Wayne. Thanks also to my students in one undergraduate class
and two graduate seminars, whose insightful responses to Charlotte's autobiography enhanced my own thinking about her. Elizabeth Sánchez gave generously of
her time and Internet expertise to track down sources. Thanks to Robert Folkenflick for assistance and advice, and to Laraine Mestman for giving me a home in
Los Angeles when I conducted research there. My stepdaughter, Susanna Lee, who
was writing her own book as I was writing mine, has lent a sympathetic ear to my
groaning, and unwaveringly cheered me on.

Thanks are due to the knowledgeable staff of the British Library Rare Books and
Manuscripts reading rooms, always my home base in London, and to the lovely
people who run the Theatre Museum Study Room and the City of Westminster
Archives Center (both favourites of mine). Thanks also to the staffs at the National
Archives, the London Metropolitan Archives, the Guildhall Library, the British
Museum Department of Prints and Drawings, and the National Portrait Gallery. I
am grateful to Joanne Ichimura and Paul Stebbing, of the Derbyshire Record Office,
for their assistance with Charlotte's last two letters. Thanks, too, to Daryl Morrison
and John Skarstad at the Department of Special Collections, University of California, Davis, and to Annette Fern and Thomas Ford of the Harvard University
Libraries; also to Aaron Greenlee and the staff at the Huntington Library, and to the
New York Public Library's Theatre Collection. Lynda Claassen and others at the
Department of Special Collections, and the inter-library loan, microfilm, and circulation staffs, all at UCSD's Geisel Library were of continual assistance over the past
several years. Grants from UCSD's Academic Senate Committee on Research helped
to support my research trips to Britain.

Among the many scholars who have paved the way with their own work on Charlotte, Fidelis Morgan deserves gratitude and praise for being among the first to find
Charlotte's life worth investigation, and for defending Charlotte against two centuries of calumny; all subsequent work on Charlotte's life is indebted to hers.
Robert Rehder's more recent edition of the *Narrative* is a useful source, and Robert
Folkenflick's article on portraits of Charlotte has been invaluable. I would also like
to acknowledge the scholarly work of Robert D. Hume on London theatre and the
late Helene Koon on Colley Cibber, which I returned to again and again.

One unsung scholar deserves particular praise: the late John D. Holland, who
wrote an unpublished biography of Charlotte in the 1980s. On more than one
occasion, as I was tracking down evidence, I found signs that he had been there
before me. Holland's admiration of Charlotte and his affection for her come
through strongly in his manuscript, now in the collection of London's Theatre
Museum Study Room. In many instances, his work has helped to guide my own. I
regret that I never met Mr. Holland, but I wish to honour his memory here.

In this, my first foray out of the realm of academic publishing, I have been
greatly blessed—in fact, unbelievably lucky—to have landed George Hodgman as
my editor. I cannot imagine a better one. George believed in Charlotte from the

beginning, providing me with unceasing support and encouragement, offering invaluable counsel throughout the entire process of drafting the book, and teaching me how to think and write anew. He has made me a better writer, and I have loved every minute of working with him. Thanks, too, go to others at Henry Holt, particularly Supurna Banerjee, Kenn Russell, and Raquel Jaramillo for her jacket design: Charlotte would have loved it, and so do I. And thanks to my UK editor, Rosemary Davidson at Bloomsbury, for her assistance.

Final thanks go to two very important people. To my agent, Amy Rennert, for her amazing energy, savvy, enthusiasm for this book, and friendship. And to the late Liza Nelligan, my former student who became my teacher as I ventured for the first time into the realm of commercial publication, whose excitement about this project, professional advice, and keen editorial eye made this book possible. Her death at much too young an age, before she could see the fruition of her early labours on this book, saddens me profoundly.

INDEX

Entries in *italics* refer to illustrations.

A NOTE THE AUTHOR

A specialist in eighteenth-century British literature and culture, Kathryn Shevelow is an award-winning professor at the University of California San Diego, and has regularly taught classes in Restoration and eighteenth-century drama. She has published articles on eighteenth-century topics and is the author of *Women and Print Culture: The Construction of Femininity in the Early Periodical.* She lives in Solana Beach, California